MANHATTAN GMAT

The Official Guide Companion

13th Edition

GMAT Strategy Supplement

This book provides detailed, step-by-step approaches to every Problem Solving and Data Sufficiency question in *The Official Guide for GMAT Review, 13th Edition*.

Official Guide Companion, 13th Edition

10-digit International Standard Book Number: 1-937707-33-4
13-digit International Standard Book Number: 978-1-937707-33-0
eISBN: 978-1-937707-34-7

Copyright © 2013 MG Prep, Inc.

ALL RIGHTS RESERVED. No part of this work may be reproduced or used in any form or by any means—graphic, electronic, or mechanical, including photocopying, recording, taping, web distribution—without the prior written permission of the publisher, MG Prep, Inc.

Note: *GMAT, Graduate Management Admission Test, Graduate Management Admission Council,* and *GMAC* are all registered trademarks of the Graduate Management Admission Council, which neither sponsors nor is affiliated in any way with this product.

Layout Design: Dan McNaney and Cathy Huang
Cover Design: Evyn Williams and Dan McNaney
Cover Photography: Sam Edla

INSTRUCTIONAL GUIDE SERIES

0 GMAT Roadmap
(ISBN: 978-1-935707-69-1)

1 Fractions, Decimals, & Percents
(ISBN: 978-1-935707-63-9)

2 Algebra
(ISBN: 978-1-935707-62-2)

3 Word Problems
(ISBN: 978-1-935707-68-4)

4 Geometry
(ISBN: 978-1-935707-64-6)

5 Number Properties
(ISBN: 978-1-935707-65-3)

6 Critical Reasoning
(ISBN: 978-1-935707-61-5)

7 Reading Comprehension
(ISBN: 978-1-935707-66-0)

8 Sentence Correction
(ISBN: 978-1-935707-67-7)

9 Integrated Reasoning & Essay
(ISBN: 978-1-935707-83-7)

SUPPLEMENTAL GUIDE SERIES

Math GMAT Supplement Guides

Foundations of GMAT Math
(ISBN: 978-1-935707-59-2)

Advanced GMAT Quant
(ISBN: 978-1-935707-15-8)

Official Guide Companion
(ISBN: 978-1-937707-33-0)

Verbal GMAT Supplement Guides

Foundations of GMAT Verbal
(ISBN: 978-1-935707-01-9)

March 26th, 2013

Dear Student,

Thank you for picking up *The Official Guide Companion* ("OGC" for short). This book is designed to accompany the *Official Guide for GMAT Review 13th Edition*, an important resource for those studying for the GMAT. Through the OGC, we strive to provide clear, insightful explanations for every math problem in the Official Guide.

As with most accomplishments, there were many people involved in the creation of the book you are holding. First and foremost is Zeke Vanderhoek, the founder of Manhattan Prep. Zeke was a lone tutor in New York when he started the company in 2000. Now, 13 years later, Manhattan Prep has instructors and offices nationwide and contributes to the studies and successes of thousands of students each year.

Our GMAT Strategy Guides are based on the continuing experiences of our instructors and students. For this volume, we are indebted to our instructors Josh Braslow, Faruk Bursal, Jen Dziura, Liz Ghini-Moliski, Steven Jupiter, Stacey Koprince, Ben Ku, Dave Mahler, Ron Purewal, Jon Schneider, Emily Sledge, and Hemanth Venkataraman for their hard work drafting and editing the explanations. Dan McNaney and Cathy Huang provided design expertise to make the books as user-friendly as possible, and Liz Krisher made sure all the moving pieces came together at just the right time. Special thanks to Chris Ryan and Noah Teitelbaum, the driving forces behind all of our curriculum efforts. Finally, thank you to all of the Manhattan Prep students who have provided input and feedback over the years. This book wouldn't be half of what it is without your voice.

At Manhattan Prep, we continually aspire to provide the best instructors and resources possible. We hope that you will find our commitment manifest in this book. If you have any questions or comments, please email me at dgonzalez@manhattanprep.com. I'll look forward to reading your comments, and I'll be sure to pass them along to our curriculum team.

Thanks again, and best of luck preparing for the GMAT!

Sincerely,

Dan

Dan Gonzalez
President
Manhattan GMAT

www.manhattanprep.com/gmat 138 West 25th St., 7th Floor, NY, NY 10001 Tel: 212-721-7400 Fax: 646-514-7425

HOW TO ACCESS YOUR ONLINE RESOURCES

If you...

are a registered Manhattan GMAT student

and have received this book as part of your course materials, you have AUTOMATIC access to ALL of our online resources. This includes all practice exams, question banks, and online updates to this book. To access these resources, follow the instructions in the Welcome Guide provided to you at the start of your program. Do NOT follow the instructions below.

purchased this book from the Manhattan GMAT online store or at one of our centers

1. Go to: www.manhattanprep.com/gmat/studentcenter.
2. Log in using the username and password used when your account was set up.

purchased this book at a retail location

1. Create an account with Manhattan GMAT at the website: www.manhattanprep.com/gmat/register.
2. Go to: www.manhattanprep.com/gmat/access.
3. Follow the instructions on the screen.

Your one year of online access begins on the day that you register your book at the above URL.

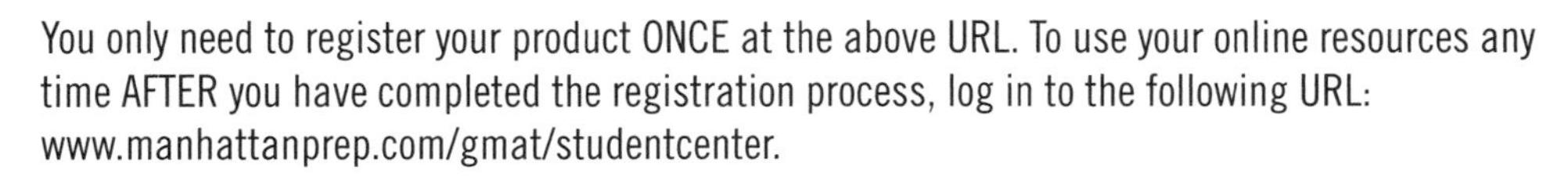

You only need to register your product ONCE at the above URL. To use your online resources any time AFTER you have completed the registration process, log in to the following URL: www.manhattanprep.com/gmat/studentcenter.

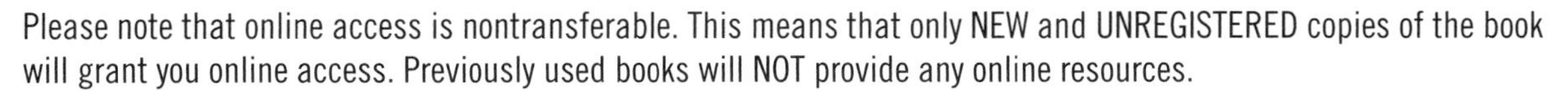

Please note that online access is nontransferable. This means that only NEW and UNREGISTERED copies of the book will grant you online access. Previously used books will NOT provide any online resources.

purchased an eBook version of this book

1. Create an account with Manhattan GMAT at the website: www.manhattanprep.com/gmat/register.
2. Email a copy of your purchase receipt to gmat@manhattanprep.com to activate your resources. Please be sure to use the same email address to create an account that you used to purchase the eBook.

For any technical issues, email techsupport@manhattanprep.com or call 800-576-4628.

Please refer to the following page for a description of the online resources that come with this book.

YOUR ONLINE RESOURCES

Your purchase includes ONLINE ACCESS to the following:

6 Computer-Adaptive Online Practice Exams

The 6 full-length computer-adaptive practice exams included with the purchase of this book are delivered online using Manhattan GMAT's proprietary computer-adaptive test engine. The exams adapt to your ability level by drawing from a bank of more than 1,200 unique questions of varying difficulty levels written by Manhattan GMAT's expert instructors, all of whom have scored in the 99th percentile on the Official GMAT. At the end of each exam you will receive a score, an analysis of your results, and the opportunity to review detailed explanations for each question. You may choose to take the exams timed or untimed.

The content presented in this book is updated periodically to ensure that it reflects the GMAT's most current trends and is as accurate as possible. You may view any known errors or minor changes upon registering for online access.

Important Note: The 6 computer adaptive online exams included with the purchase of this book are the SAME exams that you receive upon purchasing ANY book in the Manhattan GMAT Complete Strategy Guide Set.

OG Archer Official Guide Tracker

The OG Archer is an online interface for answering OG problems and measuring your performance. Time yourself on individual questions, mark the problems you guessed on, and note those you'd like to do again later. Then, view performance statistics and review answer explanations written by Manhattan GMAT Instructors (OG 13 quant questions only).

Online Updates to the Contents in this Book

The content presented in this book is updated periodically to ensure that it reflects the GMAT's most current trends. You may view all updates, including any known errors or changes, upon registering for online access.

TABLE *of* CONTENTS

Chapter 1

of The Official Guide Companion

Introduction

In This Chapter...

Why This Book

Have you ever ***wanted more from the explanations*** in the Official Guide?

So have we.

Don't get us wrong—we love the Official Guide! As one of the few legit sources of retired GMAT problems, the "OG" should play a central role in your preparation for the exam. It forms a pillar of our curriculum as well.

The problems in the OG are fantastic, by and large. The *explanations,* on the other hand… well, some are just fine. But others can be inadequate, according to both our students and our instructors.

That's why we wrote this book.

Inside, you'll find ***over 450 detailed explanations***—one for every quant problem in the 13th Edition of the Official Guide.

How To Use This Book

1. Do some OG problems.

Here is where to find all the quant problems in *The Official Guide for GMAT Review, 13th Edition*:

Section	Format	Numbers	# of Problems	Pages
Diagnostic Test	Problem Solving	D 1 – D 24	24	20–23
Diagnostic Test	Data Sufficiency	D 25 – D 48	24	25–26
Sample Questions	Problem Solving	PS 1 – PS 230	230	152–185
Sample Questions	Data Sufficiency	DS 1 – DS 174	174	275–291

Notation: a number with just a "D" in front of it, such as D 24, refers to problem 24 in the Diagnostic Test. Among the Sample Questions, "PS" refers to Problem Solving, and "DS" refers to Data Sufficiency.

When you do a set of OG problems, ***should they all be the same topic?*** At first, yes. This is a great way to learn a topic and build skills in a particular area. Later, you should start to mix topics, just as the GMAT itself does.

How many at once? Early on in your preparation, do just a few at once. Later, as the GMAT gets closer, you can lengthen out the sets.

Should you time yourself or not? At first, probably not. Give yourself space to struggle and learn. However, you also need to train yourself to "take a shot" under time pressure. To strike a balance, what some instructors recommend for your first time is that you write down an answer at the 2-minute mark, but keep going until you finish the problem. Record your total time, and if you took over 2 minutes & 30 seconds, put the problem on a list to redo for speed.

Later, as you do longer mixed sets, you should put yourself under exam-like time pressure. Do those sets as if they were "mini-GMAT's," averaging no more than 2 minutes per problem.

2. Go through our explanations.

Each problem is ***Categorized*** with a broad topic and a narrower subtopic.

There are five broad topics, corresponding to our five quantitative Strategy Guides (published separately):

1. **FDPs** stand for Fractions, Decimals, & Percents.
2. **Algebra** includes Linear Equations, Quadratic Equations, Inequalities, and more.
3. **Word Problems** include various kinds of word problems, such as Rates & Work and Overlapping Sets.
4. **Geometry** includes subtopics such as Triangles and Circles.
5. **Number Properties** include subtopics such as Divisibility & Primes and Odds & Evens.

There are numerous subtopics, most of which are self-explanatory.

OG Page: We cannot legally reprint the full questions and answer choices, so you should turn to the OG Page in the 13th Edition to see the question itself as you review our explanation.

Within the text of each explanation, you'll find ***Bolded Tools*** or concepts in bold italics. These highlighted terms will help you keep track of major techniques, topics, and themes. For students using this book in conjunction with our Strategy Guides, these tools and concepts are explained in more detail in the Guides.

For some problems, we've included an ***Alternative Approach*** or a second explanation. We have been selective about these inclusions. Theoretically, many problems can be tackled in a variety of ways, but one of those ways is often better than the others. We like to emphasize the *best* way to solve a problem—and it's not always the classic textbook approach, either. We prefer methods grounded in solid conceptual foundations, but we also know that the best solution can be quick and dirty.

As a result, your toolkit will contain many different tools. So that you don't get confused on game day, you need to ***know what your first-choice tool will be for any problem***. That's why we've often included just one thorough explanation and process per question.

However, many problems lend themselves to more than one approach. Also, having more than one way to look at certain problems can deepen your understanding of a whole topic. When we've included a second or even third approach, we've done so for a good reason. ***Be sure to study Alternative Approaches thoroughly.***

Difficulty level: The problems in the *Official Guide* (outside of the Diagnostic Test) are numbered in order of difficulty, according to the GMAT folks.

Our experience largely confirms that the problems, ***on average***, get more difficult as the numbers get higher. But some lower numbered problems seem quite difficult, and some higher numbered problems are fairly easy for students.

The GMAT measures difficulty by the percent of people who get a problem right during the experimental stage. The ***OG Archer*** tool, available on our online student center, has given us our own record of the percent of students who get a question right, collected from thousands of students of different ability levels.

We've divided every OG problem into 4 difficulty ratings, based on the percent of students who answer the question correctly: Easy, Medium, Hard, and Devilish.

Difficulty Rating	*Minimum % answered correctly*	*Maximum % answered correctly*	*% of Problems in OG*
Easy	85	100	40
Medium	65	85	35
Hard	50	65	15
Devilish	0	50	10

3. Redo the problem right away—or very soon.

Don't stop after you've read the explanation. To cement your learning, ***put pen to paper one more time***. Force yourself to solve the problem all over again—maybe even right away. Or put it on a list for the weekend. But try to get two "touches on the ball" before you forget.

The goal is not exposure, but mastery. You're far better off doing fewer OG problems overall, if you can truly *own* those problems by doing them more than once. Here's the test: are you absolutely *certain* that you could do that problem again quickly, easily, and accurately, if you were to see it on the GMAT in a month? If not, you haven't mastered it. Put it on a list to redo.

4. Track your progress.

OG Archer: Purchase of the *Official Guide Companion* comes with access to OG Archer, an online tool that allows you to track your progress, read written explanations, and watch video explanations for both Quant and Verbal OG problems.

Simply enter your answers and times, and OG Archer will automatically crunch the numbers. You can easily analyze your accuracy and speed by topic and subtopic.

The Hot List

As anyone who has taken the GMAT knows, the test writers are good at writing tricky questions. Sometimes, they go above and beyond and write questions that consistently tie students in knots. The hot list contains ***51 extra-tricky problems that deserve your attention***:

Hot List Problem	*Beginning of Stem*	*Page in OG*	*Page in This Book*
D 10 (Diagnostic)	In the figure shown...	21	25
D 11	Of the three-digit integers...	22	26
D 13	If s and t are positive integers...	22	27
D 15	The product of all the...	22	29
D 16	If $\sqrt{3-2x}$...	22	29
D 24	Aaron will jog home...	23	33
D 30	The only gift certificates...	25	37

PS 9	Which of the following...	153	54
PS 35	$\sqrt{(16)(20)}$...	156	66
PS 51	If y is an integer...	159	73
PS 87	In n is an integer...	164	90
PS 100	On a scale that measures...	166	97
PS 115	A pharmaceutical company...	168	105
PS 136	In Town X, 64%...	171	116
PS 143	Which of the following inequalities...	172	120
PS 162	During a trip, Francine traveled	175	129
PS 163	If $n = ...$	175	130
PS 166	A border of uniform width...	175	131
PS 170	If $d = ...$	176	133
PS 172	For any positive integer n...	176	134
PS 177	Last year the price per share...	177	136
PS 178	Of the 300 subjects who participated...	177	137
PS 181	If $m > 0$...	177	139
PS 182	A photography dealer...	178	139
PS 198	Last Sunday a certain store...	180	147
PS 199	(0.99999999)/(1.0001)	180	149
PS 200	The ratio, by volume...	180	149
PS 204	If $n = 4p$ ...	181	153
PS 205	John and Mary were each paid...	181	153
PS 218	List T consists of 30 positive decimals...	183	160
PS 229	How many of the integers...	185	167
DS 58	What is the tens digit...	280	195
DS 69	Of the four numbers represented...	281	201
DS 72	If m is an integer...	281	203
DS 77	A total of $60,000 was invested...	281	205
DS 90	Is the number of seconds required....	283	212
DS 93	Is the number of members...	283	214
DS 96	If [x] denotes...	283	215
DS 105	Material A costs $3 per kilogram...	284	219
DS 106	While on a straight road...	284	220
DS 109	List M (not shown)...	284	221
DS 114	A department manager distributed...	285	224
DS 118	For any integers, x and y...	285	226
DS 128	The hypotenuse of a right triangle...	286	232
DS 129	In the xy-plane...	286	232
DS 131	Six shipments of machine parts...	287	235
DS 132	Joanna bought only...	287	235
DS 135	A school administrator...	287	238
DS 141	Last year, a certain company...	288	242
DS 160	If n is a positive integer	290	253
DS 162	Is 5^k less...	290	254

In the explanations that follow, we've marked these 51 problems with a ***Hot Tamale*** (🌶) and given additional care to our explanations on those problems.

We've also included a special appendix to provide further comments about each problem:

- How students typically go wrong
- What you should focus on in the problem
- What we think of the explanation printed in the OG (which occasionally creates more confusion than it clears up)

Look at the Hot List appendix only after you've tried the problems.

Official Guide Problem Lists by Category

The last chapter of this book lists all the OG math problems by topical category. If you want a list of all the problems about Triangles, for instance, you can find it there. We have classified problems only by their major topic. For problems that involve more than one topic, this classification is a judgment call. For the sake of simplicity, each problem only appears once in these lists.

As we mentioned earlier, you should do topic-focused sets of problems while you are still learning the basic concepts and skills related to each topic. Over time, you should start to mix up the sets, so that you get used to seeing problems out of context. After all, the GMAT itself is a big mixed set.

Practice Tests

As a bonus for buying this book, you get free access to our 6 Computer Adaptive Tests, which contain over 1,200 GMAT-like problems written by our instructors. Be sure to ***log onto our website*** and take advantage of these exams as part of your overall GMAT preparation. See pages 7–8 for details.

Chapter 2

of

The Official Guide Companion

Diagnostic Test Explanations

In This Chapter...

Diagnostic Test Explanations

D 1. <u>FDPs</u>: Digits & Decimals
Difficulty: Hard **OG Page:** 20

This problem asks us to figure out what the total price of six compact discs was if the first one cost \$15.95 and the other five cost \$3.99 each.

We can write out the math as:

total price = 15.95 + 5(3.99)

The tricky part about this question is that none of the answers match this simple form of the expression. Rather than calculate the price and then calculate the values of all of the answers, a faster approach is to compare the expression to each answer choice and look for a match.

Start with answer choice (A). Is 15.95 + 5(3.99) equal to 5(4.00) + 15.90 ?

Notice that answer choice (A) contains the term 5(4.00). This is close to the term 5(3.99). If we can rewrite 5(4.00) to make it look more like 5(3.99) we can make a more direct comparison. 4.00 is equal to 3.99 + 0.01:

$$\begin{aligned} 5(4.00) + 15.90 &= 5(3.99 + 0.01) + 15.90 \\ &= 5(3.99) + 5(0.01) + 15.90 \\ &= 5(3.99) + 0.05 + 15.90 \\ &= 5(3.99) + 15.95 \end{aligned}$$

We have a match, and (A) is the correct answer.

The correct answer is (A).

D 2. <u>Word Problems</u>: Consecutive Integers
Difficulty: Easy **OG Page:** 20

This problem asks us to determine the difference between the ***Averages*** (arithmetic means) of two different sequences of ***Consecutive Integers***: 200 through 400, and 50 through 100. The ***Average Formula*** tells us that in general, the average of a set of numbers is found by dividing the sum of the numbers by the number of terms:

$$A = \frac{S}{n}$$

However, when the number of terms is large, finding the sum through simple addition would take far too long. Instead, we may use a shortcut: the average of an evenly spaced set of numbers is simply the middle term. Any set of consecutive integers is evenly spaced, so this shortcut is legal in this situation.

If the middle term is not particularly easy to find, we can use an alternative method for computing the average of an evenly spaced set: find the average of the first and the last term.

For the two given sequences, the means of each sequence can be found as follows:

$$A_1 = \frac{(200+400)}{2} = 300$$

and

$$A_2 = \frac{(50+100)}{2} = 75$$

The desired difference is therefore:

$$A_1 - A_2 = 300 - 75 = 225$$

The correct answer is (D).

D 3. <u>Algebra</u>: Formulas
Difficulty: Medium **OG Page:** 20

The problem gives us this ***Sequence*** for all $n \geq 3$:

$$A_n = \frac{A_{n-1} + A_{n-2}}{2}$$

This recursive formula for the sequence can be translated into words this way: Any term beyond the first two is equal to half the sum of the previous two terms.

We are given the third and fifth terms. Create a diagram to keep track of terms, leaving blanks for unknown terms (the question asks for the sixth term, so a circle is placed around the sixth slot):

____ ____ 4 ____ 20 (____)

We can use the values of the third and fifth terms to find the fourth term. If $n = 5$:

$$A_5 = \frac{A_4 + A_3}{2}$$
$$20 = \frac{A_4 + 4}{2}$$
$$40 = A_4 + 4$$
$$36 = A_4$$

___ ___ 4 36 20 ⊖

Now that we know the fourth and fifth terms, we can use them to get the sixth term:

$$A_6 = \frac{A_5 + A_4}{2}$$
$$A_6 = \frac{20 + 36}{2}$$
$$A_6 = 28$$

The correct answer is (E).

D 4. Word Problems: Overlapping Sets
Difficulty: Medium **OG Page:** 20

In this ***Overlapping Sets*** problem, people in the group invest or do not invest in municipal bonds. They also invest or do not invest in oil stocks. Some people invest in both bonds and stocks, and some in neither.

To avoid unnecessary computation, we can fill in a ***Double-Set Matrix*** with the given percents.

Oil Stocks?		Municipal Bonds?		
		Yes	**No**	**Total**
	Yes			
	No			
	Total			

Because we are using percents, the total population will be 100(%). 35 percent of the people invest in mutual bonds, so 35 goes in the bottom left box. 18 percent invest in oil stocks, so we put an 18 in the top right box. 7 percent invest in oil stocks AND municipal bonds, so we put a 7 in the top left box.

Finally, the question asks for the probability that someone invests in municipal bonds but NOT in oil stocks, so we shade the middle left box, because that is the value that we want.

Oil Stocks?		Municipal Bonds?		
		Yes	**No**	**Total**
	Yes	7		18
	No	?		
	Total	35		100

In a Double-Set Matrix, the first two entries in any row or column will add up to the third entry. In the left column, 7 plus the value of the shaded box will equal 35. Therefore, 28 percent of the people invest in municipal bonds, but NOT in oil stocks. Thus, the ***Probability***, which equals

$\frac{\textit{desired outcomes}}{\textit{total outcomes}}$, is $\frac{28}{100} = \frac{7}{25}$. This is the **answer.**

It turns out that the given total number of people (2,500) is irrelevant. However, we could use this piece of information to calculate the actual number of people in each category and fill in the matrix with the results:

(0.35)(2,500) = 875 people invested in municipal bonds,
(0.18)(2,500) = 450 people invested in oil stocks,
(0.07)(2,500) = 175 people invested in both.

Oil Stocks?		Municipal Bonds?		
		Yes	**No**	**Total**
	Yes	175		450
	No	?		
	Total	875		2,500

Of the 875 people who invested in municipal bonds, 175 of them also invested in oil stocks, so 875 – 175 = 700 people invested in municipal bonds but NOT in oil stocks.

$$\frac{\textit{Investors of muncipal bonds but NOT oil stocks}}{\textit{Total People in the group}}$$

$$= \frac{700}{2,500} = \frac{7}{25}.$$

The correct answer is (B).

D 5. Geometry: Circles & Cylinders
Difficulty: Hard **OG Page:** 20

Note: there is an error in the text of this problem in the OG. The problem should say that the height of the water in the tank is 4 feet, not 2 feet. The OG solution (and the correct answer!) make a lot more sense if this is corrected.

This ***Cylinders*** problem specifies that a closed cylindrical tank contains 36π cubic feet of water, which represents half of the tank's total capacity. We also know that, when the cylinder is upright, the height of the water is 4 feet. A diagram is not given, so our first task is to ***Draw a Picture***. Be sure to label the cylinder:

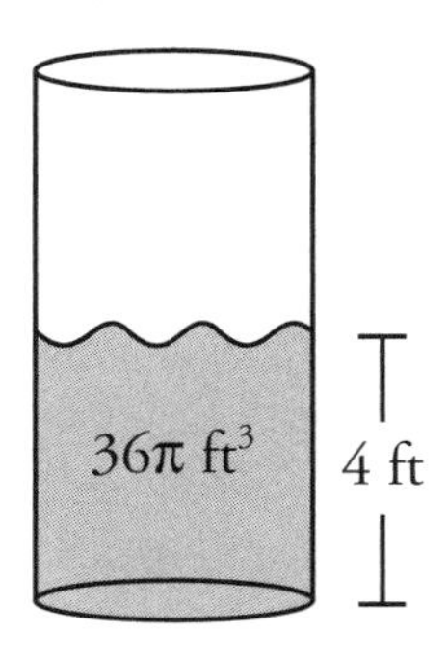

The problem asks us to turn the tank on its side and calculate the new height of the water above the ground.

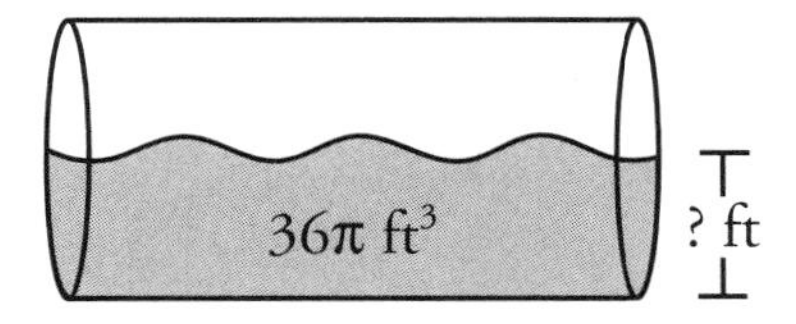

The water still represents half of the total volume of the cylinder regardless of whether the cylinder is upright or on its side. The new height, therefore, reaches halfway up the circular face of the cylinder. This height is equivalent to the circle's radius.

If we find the radius, we will also have found the new height. We can calculate the radius using the formula for the ***Volume of a Cylinder***. When the cylinder is upright, the water has a volume of 36π cubic feet and a height of 4 feet.

$$\begin{aligned} \textit{Volume} &= \pi r^2 h \\ 36\pi &= \pi r^2 (4) \\ 36 &= 4r^2 \\ 9 &= r^2 \\ 3 &= r \end{aligned}$$

The radius is 3 feet. Therefore, the new height of the water is also 3 feet.

The correct answer is (B).

D 6. Word Problems: Overlapping Sets
Difficulty: Medium **OG Page:** 21

In this ***Overlapping Sets*** problem, households can be classified in two ways: whether they use Brand A soap and whether they use Brand B soap. Some households use both brands, and some use neither.

This information can be best represented using a ***Double-Set Matrix*** to show which brands of soap are used. Begin by filling in the numbers given in the question.

	A	**Not A**	**Total**
B	?		
Not B	60	80	
Total			200

Summing the row that contains the "Not B" information, we find that the total number of households not using Brand B is 140, and thus the total number of households using Brand B is 60. We are told that, for every household that used both brands of soap, 3 used only Brand B soap, which means that 3 times as many people used only Brand B as used both A and B. We can place an x in the box for "Both A and B," and a $3x$ in the box for "B but Not A."

	A	Not A	Total
B	x	$3x$	**60**
Not B	60	80	**140**
Total			200

We can now make an equation using the top row of our matrix:

$$x + 3x = 60$$
$$4x = 60$$
$$x = 15$$ 15 is the **answer.**

Notice that if we solved for $3x$, we would get 45, which is one of the wrong answers. Be sure to answer the question that is asked.

The correct answer is (A).

D 7. <u>Number Properties</u>: Probability
Difficulty: Hard **OG Page:** 21

If we select according to the order given in the problem statement (president, then secretary, then treasurer), then this ***Probability*** problem can be solved using the ***Domino Effect*** (multiplying consecutive probabilities). Remember that "AND" implies multiplication and that "OR" implies addition.

The probability that Harry is chosen as secretary incorporates two consecutive events: someone *other* than Harry must be chosen as president, AND then Harry must be chosen from the *remaining* candidates as secretary. These probabilities are 9/10 and 1/9, respectively, so the probability that Harry is chosen as secretary is $\left(\frac{9}{10}\right)\left(\frac{1}{9}\right)=\frac{1}{10}$.

For Harry to be chosen as treasurer, other candidates must first be chosen as president and secretary, with probabilities 9/10 and 8/9. Harry's subsequent probability of being chosen as treasurer is 1/8. As before, all three events must happen: someone else must be chosen as president, AND someone else must be chosen as secretary, AND finally Harry must be chosen as treasurer. The overall probability of Harry's being chosen as treasurer, then, is $\left(\frac{9}{10}\right)\left(\frac{8}{9}\right)\left(\frac{1}{8}\right)=\frac{1}{10}$.

Since Harry cannot be both secretary and treasurer, these outcomes are completely separate. So the probability that Harry is chosen as secretary OR treasurer is $\frac{1}{10}+\frac{1}{10}=\frac{2}{10}$ or $\frac{1}{5}$. This is the **answer.**

We can solve this problem more efficiently using ***Symmetry***. There is nothing special about Harry or about any of the other members. Everyone has exactly the same likelihood of being chosen for any of the three positions. It does not matter that we are choosing these positions sequentially. Therefore, Harry has a 1/10 chance of being chosen as secretary, and he also a 1/10 chance of being chosen as treasurer. He cannot be chosen as both. Thus, the chance that he is chosen as secretary OR as treasurer is $\frac{1}{10}+\frac{1}{10}=\frac{2}{10}$, or $\frac{1}{5}$.

The correct answer is (E).

D 8. <u>FDPs</u>: Fractions
Difficulty: Medium **OG Page:** 21

A toy store's revenue in January was a ***Fraction*** of its revenue in November, which was a fraction of its revenue in December. Since no specific amounts are given in the problem, we should choose ***Smart Numbers*** to solve this problem. The revenues in November and January are based directly or indirectly on the revenue in December, so we should pick a Smart Number for the December revenue and then calculate the November and January revenue.

In questions involving fractions, we can choose a Smart Number by multiplying all the denominators given in the question. If we use this number to perform calculations, it is likely that we will be dealing with integers all the way through the problem. In this case, we should choose (5)(4) = 20 as the revenue in December.

The revenue in November is 2/5 the revenue in December, so:

$$\frac{2}{5}(20) = 8$$

The revenue in January was 1/4 the revenue in November, which was 8, so:

$$\frac{1}{4}(8) = 2$$

The average (arithmetic mean) of the store's revenues in November and January is $\frac{8+2}{2} = 5$. Since 20 is 4 times 5, the store's revenue in December is 4 times the average of its revenues in November and January. This is the **answer**.

This problem can be solved algebraically (that is, by representing the quantities with letters and the relationships with equations). However, doing so would be more cumbersome.

The correct answer is (E).

D 9. Word Translations: Statistics
Difficulty: Medium **OG Page:** 21

This ***Statistics*** problem refers to a set of performance scores with a specific ***Mean***, ***Median***, and ***Standard Deviation*** (the specific values are not given) and asks which of those will be affected by adding 5 to each of the scores.

Mean (average) is calculated by dividing the sum of the scores by the number of scores. If each score is increased by 5, the sum of the terms will increase by 5 × *(the number of terms)*, and thus the mean will increase by 5 as well.

The median is the middle score in the set if there is an odd number of scores or the average of the two middle scores if there is an even number of scores. If each score is increased by 5, the median will also increase by 5.

Standard deviation is a measure of how far away the scores are from the mean. If each of the scores increases by 5 and the mean also increases by 5, the spread of scores (i.e., their distances from the mean) will remain unchanged. Thus, the standard deviation will remain unchanged.

Putting it all together, we can see that only the mean and the median would change. This is the **answer**.

In theory, we could choose sample numbers to derive or verify these results. However, the transformation we are asked to consider (adding 5 to each term) is not very complex. Thus, we should try to reason out this problem using the properties of mean, median, and standard deviation.

The correct answer is (D).

D 10. Geometry: Lines & Angles
Difficulty: Devilish **OG Page:** 21

We can simplify this problem by relating the labeled angles to something with which we are more familiar: the pentagon at the center of the star. Label these five interior angles *a, b, c, d,* and *e*.

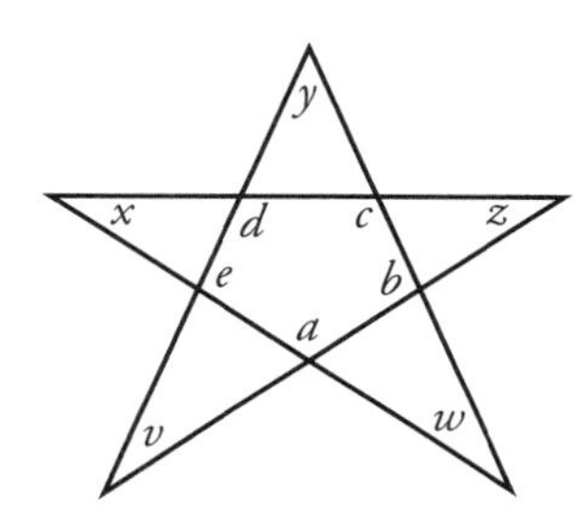

Use the formula for the ***Sum of Interior Angles of a Polygon:***

$$a + b + c + d + e = 180(n - 2) = 180(5 - 2) = 540$$

Now that we know what the 5 interior angles add up to, we can save ourselves a lot of time and energy by replacing *a, b, c, d,* and *e* with numbers. As long as the numbers we choose add up to 540, we will arrive at the correct answer. The easiest numbers to choose will make every angle the same. We are taking advantage of ***Symmetry*** to make the problem simpler. The right answer must be the same for all cases, including the symmetrical one, so we know that we can find the answer this way—with less work.

$540/5 = 108$, so we can make a, b, c, d, and e each equal to 108.

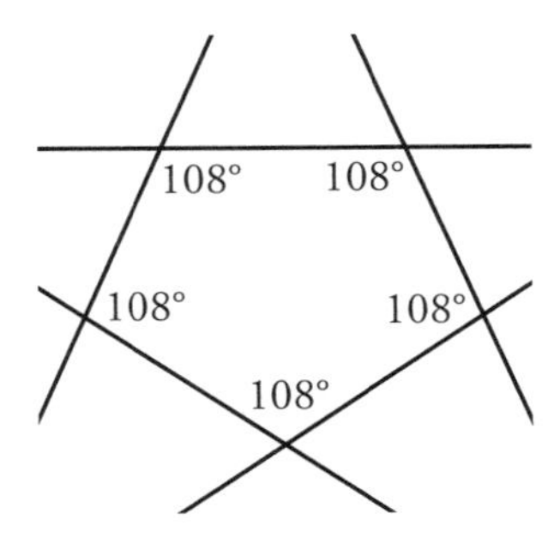

Now that we have values for the internal angles of the pentagon, we can also find values for their supplements. Each interior angle is supplementary to two angles in the small triangles surrounding the pentagon. Because we made every interior angle the same, every supplementary angle will be the same. Every angle will be $180 - 108 = 72$.

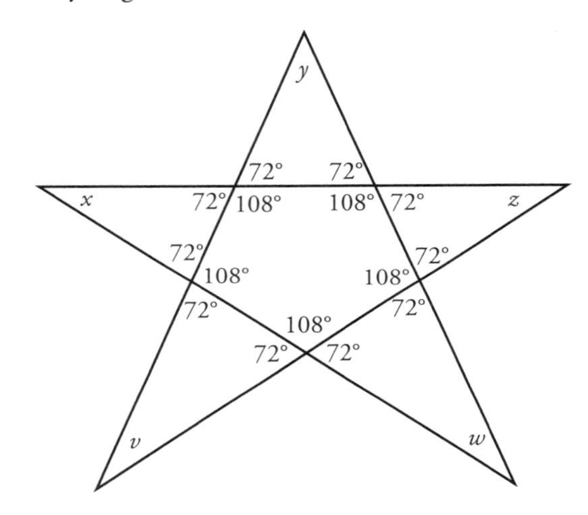

Now that we have the values of all the supplementary angles, we can find the values of v, w, x, y, and z. Let's find the value of v. We know that $72 + 72 + v = 180$. That means that $v = 36$. But all five angles will be the same, because they are all the third angle in a triangle with two angles of 72. All five angles have a degree measure of 36. The sum is therefore $5 \times 36 = 180$. This is the **answer.**

If we get stuck, we can also ***Estimate*** the answer, as long as we draw a careful picture that is essentially symmetrical. With such a picture, we might estimate v to be somewhere between 30 and 40, which would put our answer between 150 and 225. Only one answer (180) fits that range. It turns out that estimation works rather well for this problem. However, we should still be sure to understand the first approach, which is based on useful geometrical principles.

The correct answer is (C).

D 11. FDPs: Digits & Decimals
Difficulty: Devilish **OG Page:** 22

This problem asks us to figure out the number of three digit integers between 701 (the smallest integer greater than 700) and 999 (the largest three digit integer) that have exactly two digits that are the same.

We could calculate this by listing all of the three digit integers between 701 and 999, but that would take longer than two minutes, so there must be an easier way. We could also try to count the number of these numbers directly, using something like ***the Slot Method***, but the problem is that the two duplicated digits could be in any two of the three (hundreds, tens, or ones) places, which will be time consuming to calculate.

Whenever ***Combinatorics*** or ***Probability*** problems involve a large number of combinations, we should think about whether it would be easier to count the number of cases that meet the criteria or use the ***1 – x Principle*** and count the number of cases that do NOT meet the criteria and subtract them from the total number of cases.

If we think about three digit numbers, they either have no digits that are the same (ex. 789), or they have two digits that are the same (ex. 799 or 808), or they have three digits that are the same (ex. 999).

In this case, it will be much easier to figure out the number of three-digit numbers that have no digits in common and that have all three digits in common, and subtract from the total number of numbers in the range.

First, calculate the total number of three digit integers between 701 and 999:

$$999 - 701 + 1 = 299$$

Now figure out the number of integers that have all three digits in common. They are 777, 888, and 999. So there are 3 numbers that have all three digits in common.

The more challenging calculation we need to make is to figure out the number of integers between 701 and 999 that have no digits in common. To figure out how many numbers have no digits in common, we have to decide how many possible values there are for the hundreds digit, the tens digit, and the ones digit.

The hundreds digit has 3 possible values (7, 8, and 9).

The tens digit normally has 10 possible values (the digits from 0 to 9). However, the tens digit has to be different from the hundreds digit. Therefore, there are only 9 possible values for the tens digit.

The ones digit normally has 10 possible values (the digits from 0 to 9). However, the ones digit has to be different from the hundreds digit and the tens digit. Therefore there are only 8 possible values for the ones digit.

Because we are selecting a hundreds digit AND a tens digit AND a ones digit, we multiply the possible values for each to determine the total number of three-digit numbers with no digits in common.

3	×	9	×	8	= 216
hundreds		tens		ones	

There must be 216 three digit integers greater than 700 that have no duplicate digits. We can now subtract to find the number of integers with exactly 2 duplicate digits:

$$299 - 3 - 216 = 299 - 219 = 80$$

299	−	3	−	216	=	80
(Total)		(three digits in common)		(no digits in common)		(two digits in common)

The correct answer is (C).

D 12. <u>FDPs</u>: Percents
Difficulty: Medium **OG Page:** 22

We can solve this ***Successive Percents*** problem by ***Translating*** the given statements into equations. Noting that "percent" is equivalent to division by 100 and that the word "of" implies multiplication, we get:

$$y = \left(\frac{50}{100}\right)\left(\frac{50}{100}\right)x = \left(\frac{2{,}500}{10{,}000}\right)x = 0.25x$$

and

$$\left(\frac{y}{100}\right)x = 100$$

Substituting $0.25x$ for y into the second equation yields:

$$\left(\frac{0.25x}{100}\right)x = 100$$

$$\left(\frac{0.25x^2}{100}\right) = 100$$

$$0.25x^2 = 10{,}000$$

$$x^2 = 40{,}000$$

Because we are told that x is a positive integer, the only solution is:

$x = 200$ This is the **answer.**

Alternatively, we can ***Work Backwards from the Answers***. Plug in values for x, solve for y using the first relationship, and then test the second relationship. However, this approach is time-consuming. If we learn to write "y percent" as $\frac{y}{100}$, then the algebraic approach is faster and easier.

The correct answer is (C).

D 13. <u>Number Properties</u>: Divisibility & Primes
Difficulty: Devilish **OG Page:** 22

The problem states that when s is divided by t, the quotient is 64.12. We are asked which of the answer choices could be the ***Remainder.***

Let's use a simple example to clarify the relationship between integer remainders and decimals in a quotient. If, for instance, 7 is divided by 5, the quotient is 1 (since 5 goes into 7 one complete time), and the remainder is 2.

However, when we do long division to find 7 divided by 5, we get 1.4. The 0.4 left over is *0.4 of 5—which equals 2, the remainder.* That is, the decimal part of the quotient (0.4) can be multiplied by the divisor (5) to get the integer remainder (2).

Thus, for the OG problem, the remainder is actually 0.12 *of the divisor t.* That is, $0.12t$ equals the remainder.

Now we are ready to ***Work Backwards from the Answers***. Since a remainder must be an integer, see whether it is possible for 0.12 times an integer to equal each answer choice. Don't waste time actually doing the math if it is obvious that we are not going to get an integer.

(A) If $0.12t = 2$, then t will not be an integer

(B) If $0.12t = 4$, then t will not be an integer

(C) If $0.12t = 8$, then t will not be an integer

(D) If $0.12t = 20$, then t will not be an integer

(E) If $0.12t = 45$, then $t = 375$ **CORRECT**

Alternatively, we can use ***Divisibility Theory*** to predict which answer choice will produce an integer. Again, split the original equation into a sum:

$$s = (64.12)t = 64t + 0.12t$$

$64t$ is the multiple of t and $0.12t$, as we've seen, is the remainder. This remainder must be an integer.

$$\frac{12}{100}t = \text{integer}$$

$$\frac{3}{25}t = \text{integer}$$

$$3t = 25 \times \text{integer}$$

Since 25 has no 3's in it, the integer on the right must contain a 3. (The ***Prime Factors*** on each side must match, because each variable is an integer.) So the remainder, which is that integer, must be a multiple of 3. Of the answer choices, only 45 is a multiple of 3.

The correct answer is (E).

D 14. Word Problems: Overlapping Sets
Difficulty: Hard **OG Page:** 22

In this ***Overlapping Sets*** problem, parents either volunteered to supervise children or did not volunteer. They also either volunteered to bring refreshments or did not volunteer. Some did both; some did neither.

First, we can ***Name Variables***. Let x equal the number of parents who neither volunteered to supervise children nor volunteered to bring refreshments. Therefore, $1.5x$ equals the number of parents who volunteered to bring refreshments.

Now set up a ***Double-Set Matrix***, using the numbers given in the question. Notice that we are looking to find a value for $1.5x$.

Supervise?		Bring Refreshments?		
		Yes	**No**	**Total**
	Yes	11		35
	No		x	
	Total	$1.5x$		84

Given that 11 of the 35 parents who volunteered to supervise the children also volunteered to bring refreshments, 35 – 11 = 24 of the parents who volunteered to supervise the children did NOT volunteer to bring refreshments.

We can continue to fill in our Double-Set Matrix, noting that the number of parents who did NOT volunteer to bring refreshments is $24 + x$.

Supervise?		Bring Refreshments?		
		Yes	**No**	**Total**
	Yes	11	24	35
	No		x	
	Total	$1.5x$	$24 + x$	84

We can now set up an algebraic equation for the bottom row of the matrix. We are adding together the "refreshment" parents and the "non-refreshment" parents to get the total:

$$(1.5x) + (24 + x) = 84$$
$$1.5x + 24 + x = 84$$
$$2.5x = 60$$
$$x = 24$$

We are looking for the number of parents who volunteered to bring refreshments.

$$1.5x = (1.5)(24) = 36$$

The correct answer is (B).

D 15. Number Properties: Divisibility & Primes
Difficulty: Devilish **OG Page:** 22

The problem first requires us to identify all of the ***Prime Numbers*** less than 20. They are 2, 3, 5, 7, 11, 13, 17, and 19.

The problem next asks us to find the answer choice "closest to" the product of these prime numbers. As a result, we know that we can use ***Estimation*** on this problem. Our decision to estimate is further reinforced by the fact that the answer choices are very far apart. (If you have difficulty visualizing this, try writing out the numbers with all of the zeroes. For instance, $10^5 = 100{,}000$ and $10^6 = 1{,}000{,}000$.)

Since the answer choices are in ***Powers of Ten***, the key is to *group the numbers* so that the products are close to powers, or multiples, of ten.

Given 2, 3, 5, 7, 11, 13, 17, and 19:

$$2 \times 5 = 10$$
$$3 \times 7 = 21 \approx 20$$
$$11 \times 19 \approx 10 \times 20 = 200$$
$$13 \times 17 \approx 10 \times 20 = 200$$

Notice that we have rounded in both directions to get more accurate estimates. For instance, we have rounded 11 down and 19 up. The true product of 11 and 19 is 209, which is very close to (10)(20) = 200. There is less than a 5% difference.

Multiply the rounded numbers together:

$$10 \times 20 \times 200 \times 200 = 8 \times 10^6$$

Round this result once again:

$$8 \times 10^6 \approx 10 \times 10^6 \approx 1 \times 10^7$$

This is the **answer**.

Notice that we have to round 8 *up* to 10. The 8 came from the three 2's, which we should *not* have simply dropped or rounded down to 1.

Depending upon how we chose to group the numbers, we may have arrived at this answer differently. However, grouping and rounding is a far more efficient approach than multiplying all of the individual numbers.

The correct answer is (C).

D 16. Algebra: Quadratic Equations
Difficulty: Devilish **OG Page:** 22

This ***Quadratic Equations*** problem asks us to solve for the value of $4x^2$. Therefore, instead of attempting to solve the equation for x, we can manipulate the equation until the term $4x^2$ appears in the equation. Since there are square roots on both sides of the equation, we must first square both sides of the equation:

$$(\sqrt{3-2x})^2 = (\sqrt{2x}+1)^2$$

Squaring the left side is straightforward. Taking the square of a square root cancels out the square root, leaving behind what was inside. In this case, that leaves $3 - 2x$ on the left side of the equation.

To compute $(\sqrt{2x}+1)^2$, remember one of the ***Special Products:*** $(x + y)^2 = x^2 + 2xy + y^2$

$$(\sqrt{2x}+1)^2 = (\sqrt{2x})^2 + 2(\sqrt{2x})(1) + (1)^2$$
$$= 2x + 2\sqrt{2x} + 1$$

After squaring both sides, the equation becomes:

$$3 - 2x = 2x + 2\sqrt{2x} + 1$$

Since we do not yet know the value of $4x^2$, we must continue manipulating. None of the answer choices has a square root in it, so we should isolate $\sqrt{2x}$ and square both sides once more:

Combine terms: $2 - 4x = 2\sqrt{2x}$

Divide both sides by 2: $1 - 2x = \sqrt{2x}$

Square both sides: $(1 - 2x)^2 = \left(\sqrt{2x}\right)^2$

FOIL: $1 - 4x + 4x^2 = 2x$

Finally, we isolate the $4x^2$ term:

$4x^2 = 6x - 1$ This is the **answer.**

Common errors are represented among the wrong answer choices. For instance, if we misread the right side of the original equation as $\sqrt{2x+1}$ and then solve correctly for x, we will mistakenly choose (A).

The correct answer is (E).

D 17. Algebra: Exponents & Roots
Difficulty: Easy **OG Page:** 22

The best way to begin solving this ***Roots*** problem is to simplify the expression.

Roots can be distributed over division. That is, the square root of a fraction is the square root of the numerator over the square root of the denominator. Therefore, $\sqrt{\frac{16}{81}} = \frac{\sqrt{16}}{\sqrt{81}}$, or $\frac{4}{9}$, so n is equal to $\frac{4}{9}$.

Be careful, though! The problem asks not for the value of n, but for the value of $\sqrt{n}$. Therefore, we must take the square root of this expression *again.*

As before, we can distribute the root: $\sqrt{\frac{4}{9}} = \frac{\sqrt{4}}{\sqrt{9}}$, or $\frac{2}{3}$.

This is the **answer**.

Notice that one of the wrong choices is indeed $\frac{4}{9}$. Always be sure to answer the actual question.

The correct answer is (D).

D 18. Number Properties: Divisibility & Primes
Difficulty: Easy **OG Page:** 22

$n = (1)(2)(3)(4)(5)(6)(7)(8)$. Thus, n has the following ***Prime Factors***: 2, 3, 5, and 7. But are there any other prime numbers that are factors of n?

For the non-prime factors of n (4, 6, and 8), we can take a prime factorization:

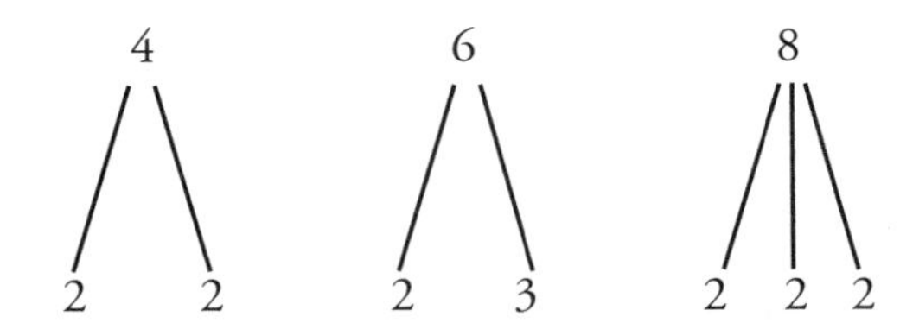

Thus 4, 6, and 8 are constructed of 2's and 3's only, which are already on our list.

Additionally, any products of the various factors of n are also factors of n. For example, the primes 2 and 5 combine to create a factor of $(2)(5) = 10$. However, all such products of prime numbers are non-prime. Indeed, they are all composed of the same prime factors we have already listed.

The prime factors of n are therefore 2, 3, 5, and 7. There are exactly four different prime factors of n. This is the **answer.**

A common misconception is that 1 is a prime number. This is not the case. By definition, primes have exactly two distinct factors: 1 and the prime itself. Since the integer 1 has exactly one factor, it is considered non-prime. By asking about "different prime factors greater than 1," the GMAT writers gave us free help by eliminating 1 from consideration.

The correct answer is (A).

D 19. Geometry: Triangles & Diagonals
Difficulty: Hard **OG Page:** 22

We are given that two of the three sides of the triangle have lengths of 2 and 7. We are also told that the third side k is greater than 2 and less than 7. By the ***Triangle Inequality*** law, the length of the third side of a triangle must lie between the difference and the sum of the two given sides, so $(7 - 2) < k < (7 + 2)$ or $5 < k < 9$.

To gain concrete understanding of this rule, ***Draw a Picture*** or two. Try drawing a triangle with side lengths 2, 3, and 7, or a triangle with side lengths 3, 7, and 10. In both cases, even if we put the two smaller sides end to end, we cannot span the largest side and form a triangle.

Now we can ***Test Scenarios***. There are only 3 integer values of k that fulfill the criterion that $5 < k < 9$. These values are 6, 7, and 8. However, only 6 is between 2 and 7 (the condition we are given). Thus, there is only one possible value for k. This is the **answer**.

Note that there is logic (even if it's incorrect logic) behind the wrong answers. For instance, "five" (E) is the difference between 7 and 2. Understanding the Triangle Inequality law is critical to solving this problem correctly.

The correct answer is (A).

D 20. Geometry: Circles & Cylinders
Difficulty: Hard **OG Page:** 23

Although this ***Circles*** problem might seem complex at the outset, it is straightforward if we follow a standard process. First, ***Draw a Picture***. Because the cone is inscribed in a hemisphere, draw the hemisphere first.

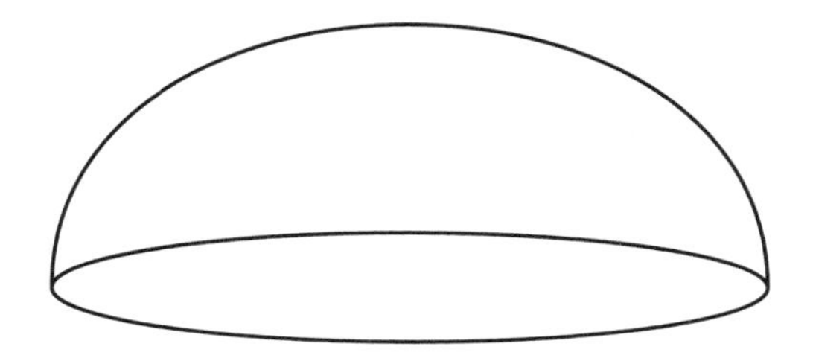

Next, draw the cone so that the base of the cone is the same as the base of the hemisphere.

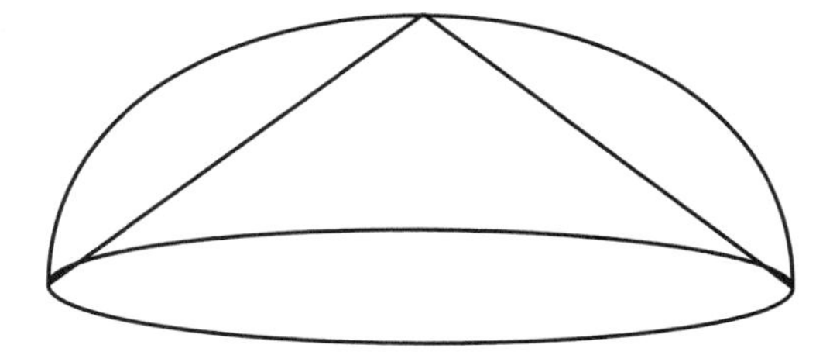

Finally, place a dot at the center of the circular base, and extend a line up to the top of the cone, representing the height.

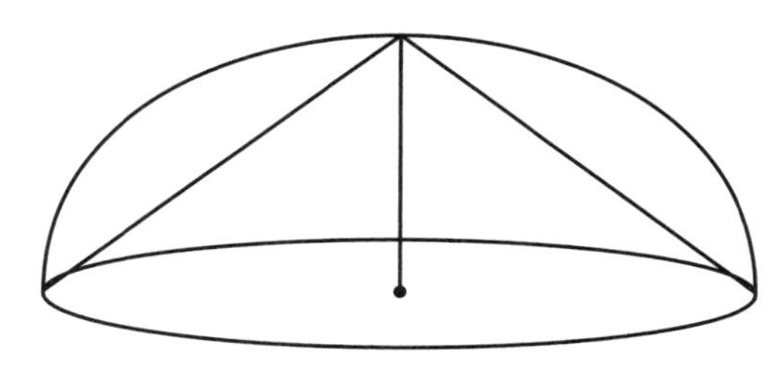

At this point, note that the height of the cone is the same as the radius of the hemisphere. After all, the height extends from the center of the sphere to the surface, just like any other radius. Thus, the ratio of the height to the radius is 1 : 1. This is the **answer**.

Because of perspective, a 3-dimensional diagram could appear distorted, as ours is. Don't try to get exact numbers out of a 3-D drawing. Instead, use it to visualize the situation conceptually.

The correct answer is (B).

D 21. FDPs: Percents
Difficulty: Medium **OG Page:** 23

When an annual ***Interest Rate*** is compounded quarterly, one-fourth of the annual rate (as a percent) is applied to the account every three months. The interest accrued every quarter then gets added to the principal. For instance, in the second quarter, John earns interest on both the original principal and the interest earned in the first quarter. This concept is critical in ***Compound Interest*** problems.

If John deposited \$10,000 at 4% annual interest, compounded quarterly, his account will be paid 1%

of its balance every three months (1% is one-fourth of 4%). In the first three-month period, John will receive 10,000 × (0.01) or $100 in interest. That means that after three months, there will be $10,100 in the account. In the second three-month period, John will receive 10,100 × (0.01) or $101 in interest. Altogether, there will be $10,201 in John's account at the end of 6 months.

Note that adding 1% interest to the principal makes the new amount 101% of the principal. Another way to do the calculations in this problem is to multiply $10,000 by 1.01, which will give us the amount in the account after three months, and to multiply that value by 1.01 to give us the amount in the account after six months. Either method will give us the same answer.

$10,000 × 1.01 = $10,100
$10,100 × 1.01 = $10,201

The correct answer is (D).

D 22. <u>Geometry</u>: Circles & Cylinders
Difficulty: Medium **OG Page:** 23

In this ***Cylinders*** problem, we are told that a right circular cylinder of height 9 inches contains 36 cubic inches of water when it is half full. To begin the solution, we note that the cylinder would contain 72 cubic inches of water if it were completely full. In other words, the volume of the cylinder is 72 cubic inches.

The formula for the ***Volume of a Cylinder*** with base radius r and height h is:

$$V = \pi r^2 h$$

Of course, we should ***Draw a Picture***.

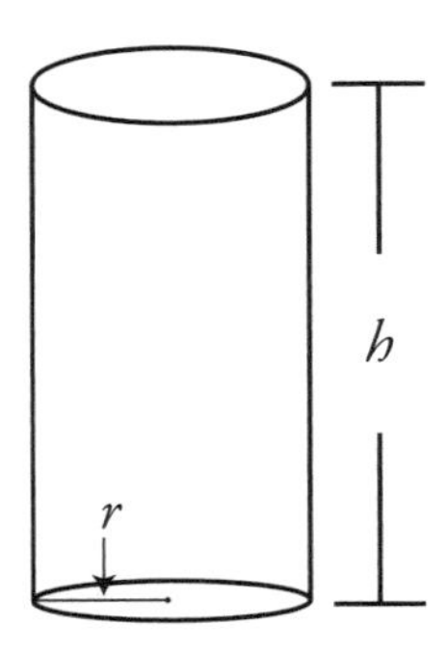

If the radius and height are given in inches, this formula yields a volume in cubic inches. Substituting for $V = 72$, $h = 9$ and leaving out the units, we obtain:

$$72 = \pi r^2 \times 9$$
$$8 = \pi r^2$$
$$\frac{8}{\pi} = r^2$$
$$\sqrt{\frac{8}{\pi}} = r$$

The ***Square Root*** of 8 can be simplified by factoring out a 4, which is a perfect square:

$$\sqrt{\frac{8}{\pi}} = \sqrt{\frac{4 \times 2}{\pi}} = \sqrt{4} \times \sqrt{\frac{2}{\pi}} = 2\sqrt{\frac{2}{\pi}}$$

Therefore, the base diameter, which is twice the base radius, is given by:

$$d = 2r = 4\sqrt{\frac{2}{\pi}}$$

The correct answer is (E).

D 23. <u>Number Properties</u>: Divisibility & Primes
Difficulty: Medium **OG Page:** 23

We can use our knowledge of ***Factors and Multiples*** to solve this problem.

If x is a multiple of 4 and y is a multiple of 6, then xy must be a multiple of 24. Any multiple of 24 is also a multiple of all of the factors of 24 (1, 2, 3, 4, 6, 8, 12, 24). Test each option individually:

I. 8 is a factor of 24. If xy is a multiple of 24, it is also a multiple of 8.

II. 12 is a factor of 24. If xy is a multiple of 24, it is also a multiple of 12.

III. 18 is not a factor of 24. If xy is a multiple of 24, it COULD also be a multiple of 18, but it certainly need not be.

Only I and II *must* be true.

The correct answer is (B).

D 24. Word Problems: Rates & Work
Difficulty: Hard **OG Page:** 23

Although the question asks for a distance, it will be easiest to first rearrange the ***Rate–Time–Distance Formula*** ($RT = D$) to get $\text{Time} = \frac{\text{Distance}}{\text{Rate}}$.

Next, ***Name a Variable*** to represent distance. Letting d equal the one-way distance from home, we can find the times for each part of Aaron's trip:

$$\text{Hours to jog from home } = \frac{d \text{ miles}}{x \text{ miles per hour}}$$

$$\text{Hours to walk back home } = \frac{d \text{ miles}}{y \text{ miles per hour}}$$

The total time Aaron spends jogging and walking is t hours, so we can add the two one-way times and solve for d, the value the question is asking for:

$$\frac{d}{x} + \frac{d}{y} = t$$

$$\frac{dy}{xy} + \frac{dx}{xy} = t$$

$$\frac{dy + dx}{xy} = t$$

$$dy + dx = xyt$$

$$d(y + x) = xyt$$

$$d = \frac{xyt}{x + y}$$

The problem asks for the one-way distance, which is d. Thus, we have the **answer**.

Alternatively, we could ***Choose Smart Numbers***. Because we have two different rates, we need to start backward and determine the total distance first. Suppose Aaron travels 12 miles away from home.

If he jogs $x = 4$ miles per hour, then he will jog for $\frac{12 \text{ miles}}{4 \text{ miles per hour}} = 3 \text{ hours}$. If he walks at $y = 2$ miles per hour, then he will walk for $\frac{12 \text{ miles}}{2 \text{ miles pre hour}} = 6 \text{ hours}$. His total traveling time is $t = 3 + 6 = 9$ hours. Plug in these values into the answer choices to see which one results in 12 miles, our ***Target Value***.

(A) $\frac{xt}{y} = \frac{(4)(9)}{(2)} = 18$
INCORRECT

(B) $\frac{x+t}{xy} = \frac{(4)+(9)}{(4)(2)} = 1\frac{5}{8}$
INCORRECT

(C) $\frac{xyt}{x+y} = \frac{(4)(2)(9)}{(4)+(2)} = 12$
CORRECT

(D) $\frac{x+y+t}{xy} = \frac{(4)+(2)+(9)}{(4)(2)} = 1\frac{7}{8}$
INCORRECT

(E) $\frac{y+t}{x} - \frac{t}{y} = \frac{(2)+(9)}{(4)} - \frac{(9)}{(2)} = \frac{11}{4} - \frac{18}{4} = -1\frac{3}{4}$
INCORRECT

The correct answer is (C).

D 25. FDPs: Digits & Decimals
Difficulty: Medium **OG Page:** 25

The problem asks us to determine the value of the ***Units Digit*** of some integer n. Since we are told that this units digit is greater than 2, it must be 3, 4, 5, 6, 7, 8, or 9. Now we must ***Test Scenarios*** in each statement.

(1): INSUFFICIENT. If the units digit of n is the same as the units digit of n^2, we can narrow the possible values of the units digit by testing potential values for n. Use a ***Table*** to stay organized.

Possible n	n^2	Same units digit?
3	9	No, so n can't be 3
4	16	No, so n can't be 4
5	25	**Yes**, so n can be 5
6	36	**Yes**, so n can be 6 (stop)

As soon as we determine that there are at least two possible values for the units digit of n (5 or 6), we know that the statement is insufficient to determine n.

(2): INSUFFICIENT. If the units digit of n is the same as the units digit of n^3, we can narrow the possible values of the units digit by testing potential values for n. Remember to test each possible units digit in a table.

Possible n	n^3	Same units digit?
3	27	No, so n can't be 3
4	64	**Yes**, so n can be 4
5	125	**Yes**, so n can be 5
6	216	**Yes**, so n can be 6 (stop)

As soon as we determine that there are at least two possible values for the units digit of n (5 and 6), we know that the statement is insufficient to determine n.

By the way, to avoid computing the cubes fully, we can take a little shortcut. If x and y are integers, we can find the units digit of xy by multiplying the units digit of x by the units digit of y.

In this case, after we know that $6 \times 6 = 36$, we can find the units digit of 6^3 by multiplying the units digit of 36 by 6. In other words, we don't need to multiply 36 by 6 all the way. The units digit of 36 is 6, so we can find the units digit of 6^3 by multiplying 6 by 6.

Without knowing the full value of 6^3, we know it ends in a 6. In this case, we don't save tons of time, but the shortcut is still worth knowing.

(1) AND (2) INSUFFICIENT. Statements (1) and (2) each permit the units digit to be either 5 or 6. Thus, when we combine the statements, both 5 and 6 are still possible units digits for n. As a result, we do not know the actual value of the units digit of n.

The correct answer is (E): Statements (1) and (2) TOGETHER are not sufficient.

D 26. Number Properties: Divisibility & Primes
Difficulty: Easy **OG Page:** 25

The problem asks for the value of p, an unknown integer. There is no need to rephrase the question.

(1): INSUFFICIENT. Given that the prime numbers 2, 3, and 5 are ***Factors*** of p, we can create the following ***Prime Box*** for p:

p

2, 3, 5, ... ?

We do not know anything else about the possible prime factors in p, so we cannot determine a value for p.

(2): INSUFFICIENT. Similarly, we can create a prime box containing the integers 2, 5, and 7, but we have no information about other possible prime factors of p. Therefore, we cannot determine a value for p.

(1) AND (2): INSUFFICIENT. Combining the statements, we know more about the prime factors of p, but we have no way of knowing whether we have been given *all* the prime factors of p. If we were sure that we had the complete set of prime factors of p, we could determine the value of p by multiplying these prime factors together, but we cannot do so without that assurance.

Incidentally, the prime box we get by combining the two statements does not double-count prime factors mentioned in both statements:

p

2, 3, 5, 7, ... ?

We can be certain that p contains the prime factors 2, 3, 5, and 7, but again, we have no information about other possible prime factors of p. Thus, we cannot determine a single value for p.

The correct answer is (E): Statements (1) and (2) TOGETHER are not sufficient.

D 27. Word Problems: Algebraic Translations
Difficulty: Medium **OG Page:** 25

This ***Algebraic Translations*** problem involves a typical situation: a telephone pricing plan.

In order to know how many minutes Wanda was charged for, we would have to know details about the pricing scheme. We would also need to know the total cost (or simply the number of minutes she talked).

(1): INSUFFICIENT. This statement gives only the cost of the call. To find the length of the call, we need information about the company's pricing structure.

(2): INSUFFICIENT. This statement gives some information about the phone company's pricing structure, but no information about the amount Wanda was actually charged. Therefore, it is impossible to determine the cost or length of the call.

(1) AND (2): INSUFFICIENT. Even together, we do not have information regarding pricing and length of call. Thus, an answer cannot be reached. We can prove this through either of the following methods.

Algebra: First, ***Name Variables***. Let n stand for the length of the call, in minutes, and c the cost, in cents, of each minute *after* the first. In this case, Wanda was billed for 1 minute at $(c + 50)$ cents and for $(n - 1)$ minutes at c cents per minute. Thus, the total amount charged for the call was $(1)(c + 50) + (n - 1)(c)$, or $50 + nc$. Since the total charge was \$6.50, which equals 650 cents, $50 + nc = 650$, or $nc = 600$. Many pairs of positive integers n and c satisfy this condition (for instance, 2 and 300, or 3 and 200). Thus, the two statements together are still insufficient to determine the value of n.

Smart Numbers: As is usual with Data Sufficiency number picking, the goal is to *try* to prove "insufficiency"—i.e., to look for two different values that fit the conditions but give different answers to the question.

First, ***Simplify the Problem*** by realizing that the extra \$0.50 added to the first minute may be regarded as an extra charge. If this charge is considered separate, then the whole call is charged at the same rate per minute. Therefore, we can solve the problem as if the call were charged at a constant rate per minute, and as if the call cost \$6.50 – \$0.50 = \$6.00 in total.

Let's ***Test Scenarios***.

Try $n = 2$ minutes; the charge is \$3.00 per minute.
Try $n = 3$ minutes; the charge is \$2.00 per minute.

With two plausible values for n, this information is insufficient.

The correct answer is (E): Statements (1) and (2) TOGETHER are not sufficient.

D 28. Geometry: Triangles & Diagonals
Difficulty: Hard **OG Page:** 25

By definition, an ***Isosceles Triangle*** is one in which two sides are equal. Even though we know that triangle *MNP* is isosceles, we do not know which two sides are equal. We need to ***Test Scenarios***, and for this problem, the best way to do so is by ***Drawing Pictures***. Draw 3 isosceles triangles with exaggerated sides, so that we can easily see which sides are equal and which are not.

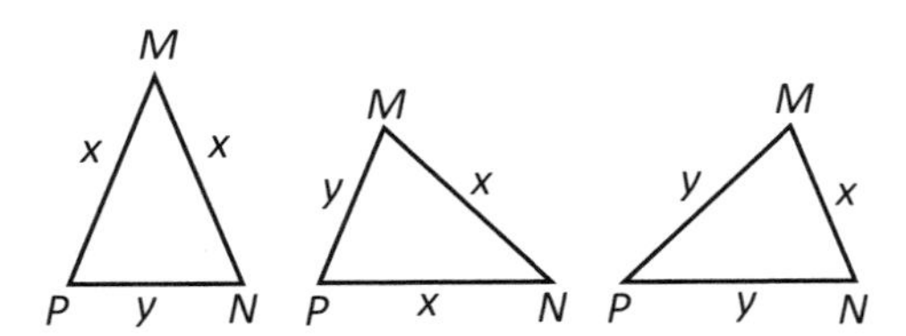

In all of the triangles above, we have labeled $MN = x$. The perimeter of the triangle is either $2x + y$ or $2y + x$. To answer the question, we need not only x and y, but also the scenario (i.e., are the equal sides x or y?).

(1): INSUFFICIENT. $MN = x = 16$, so let's label the pictures accordingly.

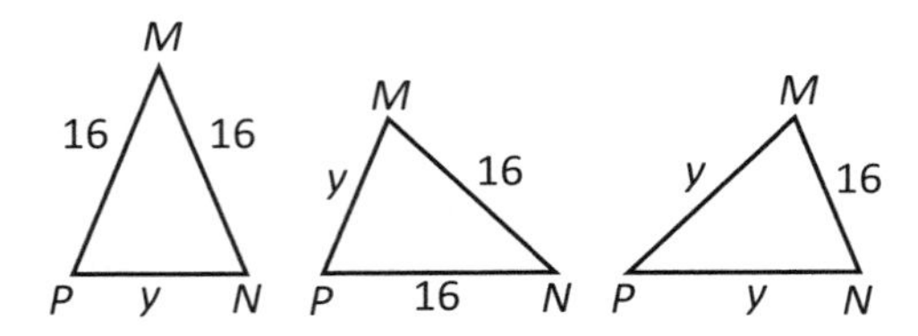

The perimeter is either $(32 + y)$ or $(2y + 16)$. We have uncertainty not only about the value of y, but also about which expression applies.

(2): INSUFFICIENT. $NP = 20$, so let's label the pictures accordingly.

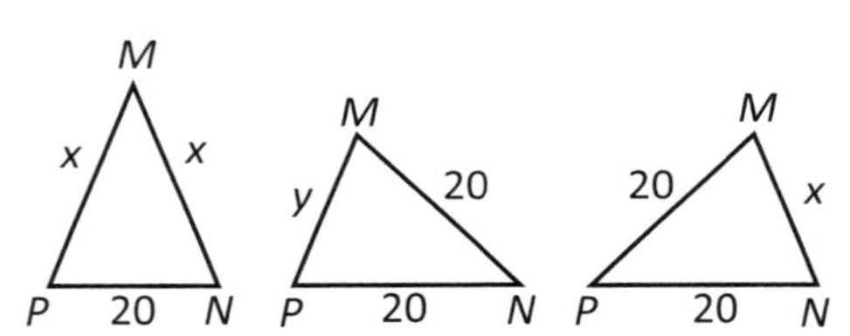

The perimeter is $(20 + 2x)$ or $(40 + y)$ or $(40 + x)$. We have uncertainty not only about the values of x and y, but also about which expression applies.

(1) AND (2): INSUFFICIENT. If $MN = 16$ and $NP = 20$, we can again label all three sides in each picture:

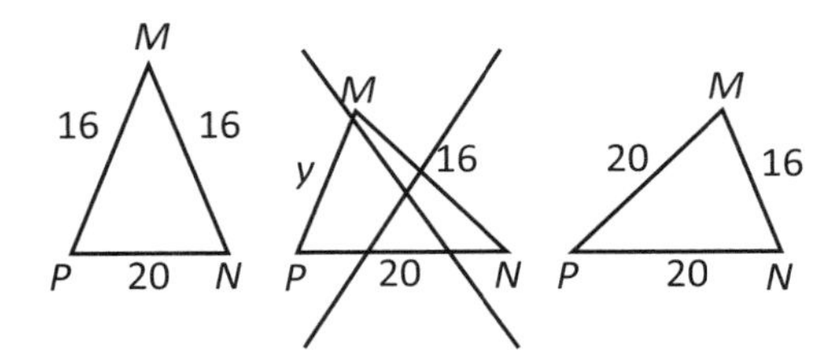

One scenario can be eliminated, as $MN \neq NP$. Although we know both x and y, we still do not know which two sides of the triangle are equal (i.e., are the equal sides 20 or 16?)

The perimeter could be either $16 + 16 + 20 = 52$ or $20 + 20 + 16 = 56$.

The correct answer is (E): Statements (1) and (2) TOGETHER are not sufficient.

D 29. Word Problems: Overlapping Sets
Difficulty: Medium **OG Page:** 25

This ***Overlapping Sets*** problem describes retailers surveyed who either owned their own stores or did not and who either purchased computers for business purposes or did not. The question asks whether we can determine what percent of retailers had purchased computers for business purposes. Using a ***Double-Set Matrix***, we can identify what cell we are trying to fill. Since this is also a percent question with an unspecified amount, we can choose a ***Smart Number*** of 100 for the total number of retailers.

Purchased for Business? (columns); **Own Store?** (rows)

	Yes	No	Total
Yes			
No			
Total	?		100

(1): INSUFFICIENT. Let's ***Name a Variable.*** If x is the number of retailers who owned their own store, 85% of those retailers (or $0.85x$) owned their own stores *and* purchased computers for business purposes. This also implies that $0.15x$ owned their own stores but did *not* purchase computers for business purposes. However, we cannot calculate what percent of retailers surveyed had purchased computers for business purposes.

Purchased for Business?

Own Store?	Yes	No	Total
Yes	$0.85x$	$0.15x$	x
No			
Total	?		100

(2): INSUFFICIENT. Knowing that 40% of the retailers surveyed owned their own store tells us that 40 of the 100 owned their own store and 60 did not. Again, however, we cannot calculate what percent of retailers purchased computers for business purposes.

Purchased for Business?

Own Store?	Yes	No	Total
Yes			40
No			60
Total	?		100

(1) AND (2): INSUFFICIENT. With these combined pieces of information, we know that 85% of 40 (or 34) retailers owned their own store and purchased computers for business purposes. This also tells us that 6 retailers owned their own store but did *not* purchase computers for business purposes. (Note that these numbers actually refer to percents of the total number of retailers surveyed, since we used 100 as a Smart Number.) However, we have no information about the percent of retailers who did *not* own their own store but *did* purchase computers for business purposes. Thus we are unable to calculate the total percent of retailers who purchased computers for business purposes.

Purchased for Business?

Own Store?	Yes	No	Total
Yes	34	6	40
No			60
Total	?		100

The correct answer is (E): Statements (1) and (2) TOGETHER are not sufficient.

D 30. Algebra: Inequalities
Difficulty: Devilish **OG Page:** 25

This ***Inequalities*** problem also involves ***Algebraic Translation***.

Let's begin by ***Naming Variables*** for the two unknowns. Let h represent the number of hundred-dollar certificates sold, and let t represent the number of ten-dollar certificates sold. (Notice that there is an ***Integer Constraint*** here: h and t must be integers, since we use them to count physical objects.) We can create two equations:

$h + t = 20$ (The store sold 20 certificates.)

$100h + 10t =$ Total Value

Notice that for the second equation, we have multiplied the monetary value of each type of certificate by the number of such certificates sold. (Some people confuse this step by thinking of the variables as *equal* to 100 and 10. This is incorrect, since our variables represent the *number* of such certificates, not their monetary value.)

The question asks us for the value of t.

(1): SUFFICIENT. This statement seems insufficient at first glance. After all, it does not give us an exact amount for the Total Value but only a range: the Total Value is between 1,650 and 1,800. Thus:

$$1{,}650 \leq 100h + 10t \leq 1{,}800$$

For this information to be sufficient, we must be left with only one solution for t. So let's ***Test Scenarios*** to see whether we can find two or more solutions. Given the lower boundary, we can start by testing $h = 16$ and $t = 4$. (We have to try values that sum to 20.) This set of test numbers yields $100(16) + 10(4) = 1{,}640$, which is too low.

Next, try $h = 17$ and $t = 3$. This yields $100(17) + 10(3) = 1{,}730$, which works. But is 1,730 the only value that works?

Let's also try $h = 18$ and $t = 2$. This yields $100(18) + 10(2) = 1{,}820$, which is too high.

Thus, 1,730 is the only possible Total Value between 1,650 and 1,800. As a result, we can say with certainty that $t = 3$ and that this information is sufficient. Notice that the integer constraint on h and t is crucial. Otherwise, there would be more than one possible Total Value in the given range.

(2): INSUFFICIENT. This statement tells us that $h > 15$.

This leaves multiple possible values for h (16, 17, 18, 19, or 20), and thus multiple corresponding values for t (4, 3, 2, 1, or 0).

The correct answer is (A): Statement (1) ALONE is sufficient, but statement (2) alone is not sufficient.

D 31. <u>Word Problems</u>: Statistics
Difficulty: Medium **OG Page:** 25

Standard Deviation measures the tendency of the terms in a set to cluster around the mean (average) of the set. To calculate standard deviation, we need to find the distance of every term from the average, square these differences, take the average of these squares (this is called the ***Variance***) and then take the square root of the variance. While this sounds like a rather complicated formula, do not be scared off by it. Our job is to know whether we can arrive at an answer—not to perform calculations.

We are asked whether a certain standard deviation is less than 3. This question cannot easily be rephrased.

(1) SUFFICIENT: If we know the variance of the set, we know the standard deviation, since the standard deviation is simply the square root of the variance. So if the variance is 4, the standard deviation is 2. Thus, we know whether the standard deviation is less than 3.

(2) SUFFICIENT: If we know that the difference between each term of the set and the average of the set is 2, we can calculate the standard deviation of the set.

First, square all the differences. This yields 4 for each term. Average the squares:

$$\frac{(4 \times 20)}{20} = \frac{80}{20} = 4$$

Take the square root of the average:

$$\sqrt{4} = 2$$

Thus, the standard deviation of the set is 2, and we know whether the standard deviation is less than 3.

Bear in mind, however, that we did not need to actually calculate the standard deviation in either statement. We needed only to determine whether it was less than 3. If we recognize that knowing the variance or the difference of each term from the average allows us to find the standard deviation, we don't need to do any calculations.

The correct answer is (D): EACH statement ALONE is sufficient.

D 32. <u>Word Problems</u>: Statistics
Difficulty: Hard **OG Page:** 25

This ***Statistics*** problem concerns the ***Range*** of a set, which is the difference between the largest and smallest numbers of the set. We cannot know the range of the set of numbers in this problem without knowing something about the two missing integers, x and y. Therefore, a natural rephrasing might be to ask what x and y are. However, notice that this question is a Yes/No question. Most such questions can actually be answered without precise knowledge of every quantity involved.

Therefore, in this case it is best to move on to the numbered statements without rephrasing the question, knowing that we are trying to figure out whether the difference between the largest and smallest numbers is more than 9. We will ***Test Scenarios*** as we go.

(1): INSUFFICIENT. To begin, consider a simple concrete case. If $x = 0$, then y must be greater than $3 \times 0 = 0$. Now let's ***Test Extreme Values*** of y, to see whether we can find cases yielding different results. Suppose that y is the smallest it can be: $y = 1$. In that case, 6 remains the largest number in the set, and the range is $6 - 0 = 0$, which is less than

9. Thus, if $x = 0$ and $y = 1$, the answer to the given question is *No*.

Now try a large value of y, with x still equal to zero. If $y = 10$, then the range is $10 - 0 = 10$, which is greater than 9. Thus, we can also answer the given question *Yes* while satisfying this statement. As a result, we cannot determine the answer to the question.

(2): INSUFFICIENT. We can proceed in a similar manner by testing numbers. This statement is satisfied as long as x is greater than 3 and y is greater than x. Again, start with the smallest possible case. If $x = 4$ and $y = 5$, the range is $6 - 3 = 3$, which is less than 9. Thus, the answer to the given question would be *No* in this case.

Now try a large value of y. If $x = 4$ and $y = 14$, then the range is $14 - 4 = 10$, which is greater than 9. Thus, we can also answer the given question *Yes* while satisfying this statement, and again, we cannot determine the answer to the question.

(1) AND (2): SUFFICIENT. Combining the two statements, we know that x is an integer greater than 3, and y is an integer greater than $3x$. We start with the smallest possible case. The smallest that x can be is 4. Since y is greater than $3x$, we know that y has to be at least 13. Thus, the range in this case is at least $13 - 3 = 10$.

If x is 5, then y has to be greater than 15. That is, y is at least 16, yielding a range of at least $16 - 3 = 13$. As x increases, y increases even faster, so the range widens further. As a result, the range will always be greater than 9, and we can answer the given question with a definitive *Yes*.

The correct answer is (C): BOTH statements TOGETHER are sufficient, but NEITHER statement ALONE is sufficient.

D 33. Algebra: Inequalities
Difficulty: Medium **OG Page:** 25

Before looking at the statements, we should see whether we can ***Rephrase*** the question. Notice that we will need to make use of both ***Inequalities*** and ***Exponents*** knowledge.

$$\text{Is } \frac{5^{x+2}}{25} < 1?$$

Note that 25 is simply 5^2. Therefore:

$$\frac{5^{x+2}}{5^2} < 1?$$

Since the numerator and denominator each have a base of 5, we can divide and subtract the exponents:

$$5^{x+2-2} < 1?$$
$$5^x < 1?$$

The rephrased question is simply "Is $5^x < 1$?"

(1): SUFFICIENT. $5^x < 1$. This answers our rephrased question directly.

(2): SUFFICIENT. x is negative. Therefore, 5^x is a fraction less than 1. We can ***Test Numbers*** to verify our understanding. For instance, if $x = -1$, $5^x = 5^{-1} = 1/5$. If $x = -3$, $5^x = 5^{-3} = 1/(5^3) = 1/125$. The more negative x becomes, the smaller the fraction will become.

The correct answer is (D): EACH statement ALONE is sufficient.

D 34. Word Problems: Overlapping Sets
Difficulty: Medium **OG Page:** 25

This ***Overlapping Sets*** problem does not specify the number of companies surveyed, so we can choose 100 companies as a ***Smart Number*** to simplify the percentages given.

The companies surveyed either required or did not require computer skills. They also either required or did not require writing skills. The question asks for the companies that required *neither computer nor writing skills*. This quantity is shaded in our ***Double-Set Matrix***:

Writing?		Computer?		
		Yes	No	Total
	Yes	20		
	No		?	
	Total			100

(1): INSUFFICIENT. Note that half of the companies *that required computer skills* (not all companies surveyed) required writing skills too. Because 20 companies required both computer and writing skills, 20 companies required computer skills but not writing skills. This means that 40 companies required computer skills. However, the only other piece of information we can infer is that 60% of companies do not require computer skills. This is not enough information to answer the question.

Writing?		Computer?		
		Yes	No	Total
	Yes	20		
	No	20	?	
	Total	40	60	100

(2): INSUFFICIENT. We now know 65 companies required writing skills and 35 companies did not. We can input this information into the table, but we do not have enough information to answer the question.

Writing?		Computer?		
		Yes	No	Total
	Yes	20	45	65
	No		?	35
	Total			100

(1) AND (2): SUFFICIENT. With both statements, we know that 15 companies required neither skill, which means that 15% of all companies require neither computer skills nor writing skills.

Writing?		Computer?		
		Yes	No	Total
	Yes	20	45	65
	No	20	?	35
	Total	40		100

The correct answer is (C): BOTH statements TOGETHER are sufficient, but NEITHER statement ALONE is sufficient.

D 35. Algebra: Linear Equations
Difficulty: Easy **OG Page:** 25

The problem asks for the value of a ***Combined Expression,*** or Combo. The Combo is $w + q$. Note that we do not need the values of w and of q individually (although knowing those values would be sufficient).

(1): SUFFICIENT. The equation can be manipulated to determine the value of the Combo $w + q$:

$$3w = 3 - 3q$$
$$3w + 3q = 3$$
$$w + q = 1$$

Note that we cannot determine the values of w and of q individually, but we know the sum, and thus we can answer the question.

(2): SUFFICIENT. The equation can be manipulated to determine the value of the combined expression $w + q$:

$$5w + 5q = 5$$
$$w + q = 1$$

As above, we do not know the values of the variables separately. Nevertheless, we can answer the question.

The correct answer is (D): EACH statement ALONE is sufficient.

D 36. Geometry: Circles & Cylinders
Difficulty: Easy **OG Page:** 25

In this ***Circles*** problem, we must think about properties of the radius of a circle.

In order for point Y to lie inside circle C, the distance from the center of the circle to Y must be less than the radius of the circle. Since we are told that the radius is 2, we can ***Rephrase*** the question as "Is the length of line segment OY less than 2?"

(1): INSUFFICIENT. Given that point X lies inside the circle and that the length of line segment XY is 3, it is possible for point Y to lie inside or outside of the circle. To verify, we should ***Test Scenarios***. For instance, X and Y may be two points on the diameter of the circle, located 3 units apart.

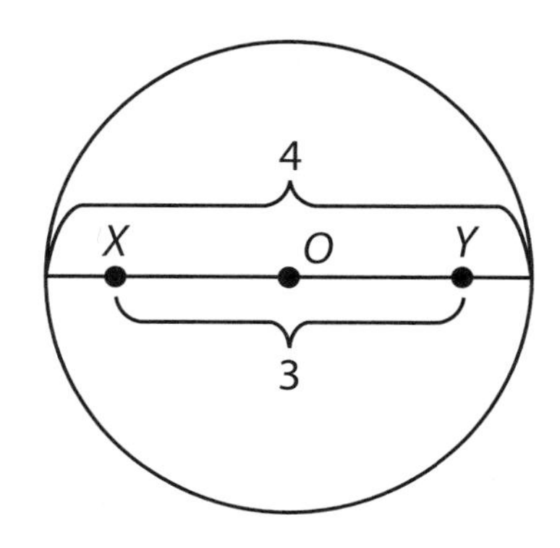

However, Y may be located outside the circle as well.

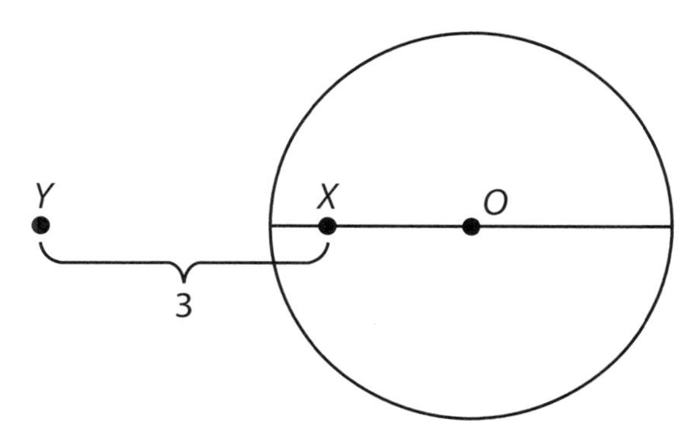

(2): SUFFICIENT. This statement directly answers our rephrased question. If the length of line segment OY is 1.5, Y must be inside the circle. The only possible locations for Y are shown on the dotted circle below.

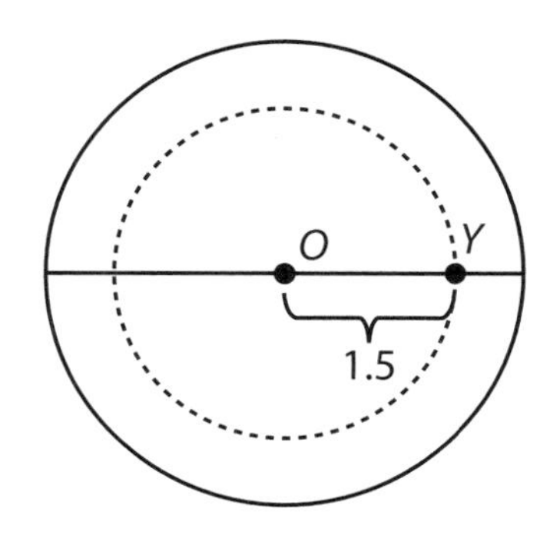

The correct answer is (B): Statement (2) ALONE is sufficient, but statement (1) alone is not sufficient.

D 37. Algebra: Linear Equations
Difficulty: Medium **OG Page:** 25

This ***Linear Equations*** question asks whether x is greater than y. The question involves ***Inequalities***.

(1): SUFFICIENT. This statement tells us that x is equal to $y + 2$. We can conclude that x is greater than y (by 2 units, in fact).

(2): INSUFFICIENT. We can see that x could be greater than y or less than y by either of the following methods.

Substitution: Multiply both sides of this equation by 2 to yield $x = 2y - 2$. We can now substitute into the prompt question, giving "Is $2y - 2 > y$?" Simplify this inequality by subtracting y and adding 2 to both sides, yielding "Is $y > 2$?" However, we do not know whether y is greater than 2 or not.

Smart Numbers: Multiply both sides of this equation by 2 to yield $x = 2y - 2$. Since x is stated in terms of y, pick a value for y and calculate the corresponding x value. ***Test Extreme Values*** for y. If $y = 100$, then $x = 200 - 2 = 198$, so $x > y$.

However, if $y = 0$, then $x = 0 - 2 = -2$, so x is not greater than y. Since these two answers are contradictory, it is unnecessary to attempt further plug-ins.

The correct answer is (A): Statement (1) ALONE is sufficient, but statement (2) alone is not sufficient.

D 38. Algebra: Inequalities
Difficulty: Medium **OG Page:** 26

This ***Inequalities*** problem also involves ***Rates***.

We are given Paula's average speed and asked about her time. Since the statements both provide information on the distance Paula drove, we should ***Rephrase*** the original question about time into an equivalent question about distance. We can use the

Rate-Time-Distance Formula: $RT = D$, which can be rearranged into $T = \frac{D}{R}$.

Is $T < 3$ hours?

Is $\frac{D}{R} < 3$ hours?

Now, we do not have an exact rate, but we know that Paula's speed was "greater than 70 kilometers per hour." We can actually insert this fact into the inequality:

$$\text{Is } \frac{D}{\text{a number over 70 km/hour}} < 3 \text{ hours?}$$

Now we can cross-multiply and simplify:

Is $D <$ (3 hours)(a number over 70 km/hour)?

Is $D >$ a number over 210 km?

Finally, asking whether D is less than a number over 210 km is equivalent to asking whether D is less than or equal to 210 km.

Is $D \leq 210$ km?

This question should make sense: if Paula drove home faster than 70 km per hour (but possibly only a little faster), then we can only guarantee she made the trip in less than 3 hours if her home is less than 210 km away.

(1): INSUFFICIENT. If $D > 200$ km, D might be either greater than or less than 210 km.

(2): SUFFICIENT. If $D < 205$ km, D is definitely less than 210 km.

The correct answer is (B): Statement (2) ALONE is sufficient, but statement (1) alone is not sufficient.

D 39. <u>Geometry</u>: Coordinate Plane
Difficulty: Hard **OG Page:** 26

In this ***Coordinate Plane*** problem, we know that line k passes through the point $(-5, r)$ and has a negative ***Slope*** (indicating that the line goes down to the right). Since we do not know the sign of r, the point $(-5, r)$ can be in quadrant II or III as pictured below. This yields many possible lines for k, three of which are shown below: k_1, k_2 and k_3. The question asks us whether the x-intercept of line k is positive. Note that k_1 has a positive x-intercept, whereas k_2 and k_3 both have a negative x-intercept. We will need to ***Test Scenarios*** by drawing several lines, whether we have specific numbers or not.

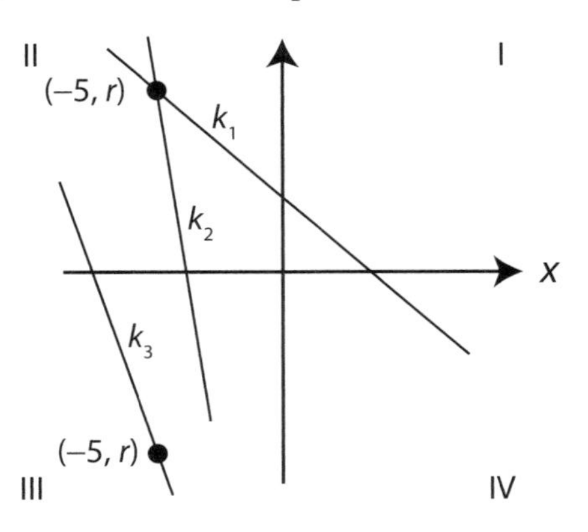

(1): INSUFFICIENT. A slope of −5 means that line k falls 5 units for every 1 unit of movement to the right. That means that if r were 25, the line would pass through the origin.

If $r < 25$, line k will have a negative x-intercept. Similarly, if $r > 25$, line k will have a positive x-intercept.

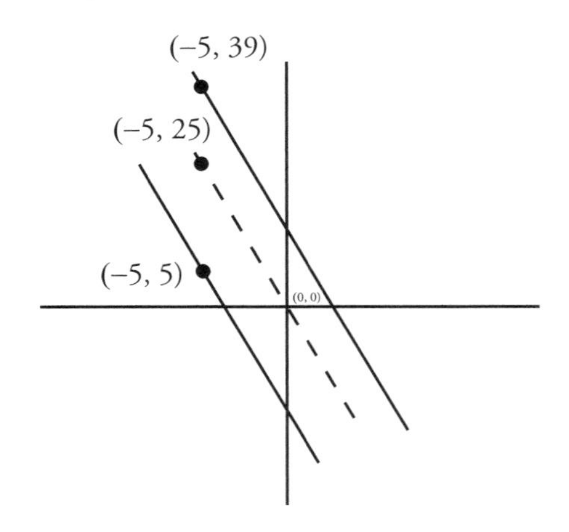

We don't know whether r is greater than or less than 25. Thus, we can't determine whether the x-intercept is positive.

(2): INSUFFICIENT. Just knowing that $r > 0$ is not enough to tell us whether the x-intercept of line k is positive. For both lines discussed in statement (1), $r > 0$, but one has a positive x-intercept, and one has a negative x-intercept.

(1) AND (2): INSUFFICIENT. Knowing that the slope is -5 and that $r > 0$ is not enough. As discussed in statement (1), it matters whether $r > 25$, not whether $r > 0$. Line k could still have a negative x-intercept or a positive x-intercept.

The correct answer is (E): Statements (1) and (2) TOGETHER are not sufficient.

D 40. FDPs: Percents
Difficulty: Easy **OG Page:** 26

Given the information in the question stem, we can set up a ***Simple Interest Formula*** to show the knowns and unknowns involved in this ***Percents*** problem:

(Principal) × (Interest rate) × (Time) = Yield ($)

With this formula and the information given about the first investment, we can find p. Since the interest rate is given as *p percent*, we should write that rate as $p/100$. (The word "percent" means "per hundred," or "divided by 100.")

$(\$5{,}000) \times (p/100) \times (1) = 500$
$p = 10$

The second situation described in the problem is an investment at k percent simple interest. We know the time (1 year), and we want the yield to be the same as above ($500). We are left with two unknowns:

(Principal)(k/100)(1) = $500

To find the principal, we must know k. Thus, we can ***Rephrase*** the question as "What is k?"

(1): SUFFICIENT. Here we are given the relationship between k and p: $k = 0.8p$

As we already know the value of p, this relationship allows us to solve for k, which equals 8.

(2): SUFFICIENT. This statement gives us the value of k directly.

The correct answer is (D): EACH statement ALONE is sufficient.

D 41. Number Properties: Positives & Negatives
Difficulty: Hard **OG Page:** 26

This ***Positives & Negatives*** problem requires us to handle ***Inequalities*** carefully. It is tempting to cross-multiply here and assume we will get $x + y > 0$, but since we don't know whether z is positive or negative, we don't know in which direction the inequality will point (remember that we have to flip an inequality if we multiply or divide it by a negative). We do know, however, that if $\frac{x+y}{z} > 0$, then $x + y$ and z are either both positive or both negative. That is, $x + y$ and z have the same sign.

(1) INSUFFICIENT: Knowing that x is less than y does not tell us whether x is positive or negative.

(2) INSUFFICIENT: Knowing that z is negative tells us that $x + y$ is negative, but we don't know whether x itself is positive or negative. We could have a positive x and a negative y and still get a negative sum ($x = 1$ and $y = -3$, for example, sum to -2).

(1) AND (2) SUFFICIENT: We know from statement (2) that $x + y$ is negative. We also know from statement (1) that x is less than y, so x must be negative. In order to get a negative sum, at least one of the variables x and y must be negative. If x were positive, y would have to be a larger positive, and their sum would therefore be positive ($x = 3$ and $y = 5$, for example). Therefore, x must be negative.

The correct answer is (C): BOTH statements TOGETHER are sufficient, but NEITHER statement ALONE is sufficient.

D 42. Number Properties: Divisibility & Primes
Difficulty: Medium **OG Page:** 26

This ***Divisibility*** question asks us to determine whether integer k has at least three different positive ***Prime Factors***.

Although it is not strictly necessary to do so, we can certainly answer the question if we can determine what the prime factors of k are, or at least a subset of three different prime factors.

(1): INSUFFICIENT. If $k/15$ is an integer, then k must be divisible by 15. Put differently, k must have the prime factors of 15 in its ***Prime Box***, and therefore, k has 3 and 5 as prime factors.

However, we cannot tell whether k has at least three positive prime factors, since k may or may not have other prime factors besides 3 and 5.

(2): INSUFFICIENT. If $k/10$ is an integer, then k must be divisible by 10. Put differently, k must have the prime factors of 10 in its Prime Box, and therefore, k has 2 and 5 as prime factors.

Again, however, we cannot tell whether k has at least three positive prime factors, since k may or may not have other prime factors besides 2 and 5.

(1) AND (2): SUFFICIENT. With these combined pieces of information, we know that k has 2, 3 and 5 as prime factors. Whether or not it has more prime factors, we are sure that k has a minimum of three different positive prime factors.

The correct answer is (C): BOTH statements TOGETHER are sufficient, but NEITHER statement ALONE is sufficient.

D 43. Word Problems: Statistics
Difficulty: Medium **OG Page:** 26

Was the ***Average*** (arithmetic mean) of a list of numbers greater than the ***Median***? To answer, we need information about the average and the median. If we know the sum and the number of items in the list, we can calculate the average.

(1): INSUFFICIENT. We are given the sum and the number of elements in the list. This is enough to determine the average, but we still have no information regarding the median.

(2): SUFFICIENT. 60% of the elements in the list are less than the average. Imagine arranging the items in the list in order from least to greatest. We do not know anything about the last 40%, but we do know that each of the first 60% of entries is less than the average. When a list is arranged in order from least to greatest (or greatest to least), the median is either the middle number or the average of the two middle numbers. Thus, the median must be contained within the 60% of entries that are less than the average. The median is therefore less than the average.

The correct answer is (B): Statement (2) ALONE is sufficient, but statement (1) alone is not sufficient.

D 44. Number Properties: Exponents & Roots
Difficulty: Medium **OG Page:** 26

Although the mathematical notation is intimidating, this ***Roots*** question is easier than it looks. We are told that m and n are both positive integers and asked whether $(\sqrt{m})^n$ is an integer.

(1): SUFFICIENT. This statement tells us that $\sqrt{m}$ is an integer. If we know that, then the question is just asking if the result of raising a positive integer to a positive integer power is an integer. From our rules of exponents, we can answer this with a definitive yes. If a and b are integers then a^b is just a times itself b times, which must be an integer, since an integer times an integer is always an integer.

(2): INSUFFICIENT. If $\sqrt{n}$ is an integer, then n must be a perfect square, such as 1, 4, 9, 16, etc. However, we know nothing about the value of $\sqrt{m}$. It could be an integer, which would make the answer to the question true, or it could be the square root of an integer that is not a perfect square, which would make the answer to the question false.

We could also prove insufficiency using a table to ***Test Numbers.***

If $\sqrt{n} = 1$ (an integer), then $n = 1$. Pick different values of m to show that $\left(\sqrt{m}\right)^n$ does not have to be an integer:

n	m	$\sqrt{m}$	$\left(\sqrt{m}\right)^n$	**Answer to question**
1	1	1	$1^1 = 1$	YES
1	2	$\sqrt{2}$	$\sqrt{2}^1 = \sqrt{2}$	NO

The correct answer is (A): Statement (1) ALONE is sufficient, but statement (2) alone is not sufficient.

D 45. Word Problems: Extra Problem Types
Difficulty: Hard **OG Page:** 26

This ***Grouping*** problem specifies that there are 66 people in an auditorium and that no more than 6 people have birthdays during the same month. The yes/no question asks whether at least one person has a birthday in January. The distinction, then, is whether we can tell that *nobody* has a birthday in January or that *one or more* people have a birthday in January. Because "one or more" opens up many possibilities, we should begin by determining what conditions would be necessary for *nobody* to have a birthday in January.

In order for nobody to have a January birthday, the 66 people need to be split among the other 11 months. As a result, the maximum allowed per month, 6 people, would have to be assigned to each of the other 11 months:

0	6	6	6	6	6	6	6	6	6	6	6
J	F	M	A	M	J	J	A	S	O	N	D

If any month falls below the maximum (that is, has fewer than 6 people), we know that at least one person must have a birthday in January, because the extra birthday(s) cannot push any of the other monthly totals above 6 birthdays. Thus, we can ***Rephrase*** the question as follows: "Does any month besides January contain fewer than 6 birthdays?"

(1): SUFFICIENT. If there are more February birthdays than March birthdays, then March cannot have the maximum allowed (6). At most, March can have 5 birthdays. Thus, we know that at least one month besides January has fewer than 6 birthdays, forcing at least one person to have a birthday in January.

(2): SUFFICIENT. If March has 5 birthdays, then we can answer the rephrased question directly. Note that even if each of the other 10 months from February through December has 6 birthdays, we have only accounted for $5 + 6 \times 10 = 65$ birthdays. There is still one more birthday, which must happen during the one leftover month: January.

The correct answer is (D): EACH statement ALONE is sufficient.

D 46. Word Problems: Statistics
Difficulty: Hard **OG Page:** 26

Using a rearrangement of the ***Average Formula***, (Average) × (# of terms) = (Sum), we can determine that the sum of the salaries of the employees last year was $42,800 × 10 = $428,000. Since the number of employees has not changed, in order to calculate this year's average we need only know how this sum has changed.

We should ***Rephrase*** the question as "What was the sum of the salaries for the 10 employees this year?" Indeed, we did not need to calculate the sum of last year's salaries, since we are concerned only with finding this year's sum.

(1): INSUFFICIENT. For 8 of the 10 employees, this year's salary went up by 15%. We know nothing about the other 2 employees, so it is impossible to know the sum of all 10 salaries this year.

(2): INSUFFICIENT. We know that the salaries of two of the employees stayed the same, but we know nothing about the other employees', so we cannot determine the sum of this year's salaries.

(1) AND (2): INSUFFICIENT. Even knowing that 2 salaries remained the same and 8 salaries increased by 15%, we cannot calculate a numerical value for the sum of the salaries this year. The result depends on the size of the 8 changing salaries. For example, imagine that last year 8 employees earned \$10,000 each and 2 employees earned \$174,000 each (producing a total of \$428,000). Increasing those \$10,000 salaries by 15% produces new salaries of \$11,500. The total sum of all the salaries would be:

$$2 \times \$174{,}000 + 8 \times \$11{,}500 = \$440{,}000$$

If, however, the 8 employees earned \$50,000 each last year, the 2 other employees earned \$14,000 each, and we increase the \$50,000 salaries by 15%, the new sum of all the salaries would be:

$$2 \times \$14{,}000 + 8 \times \$57{,}500 = \$488{,}000$$

If, in Statement (1), we were told that the salary of *each* employee was 15% greater this year than last year, even without knowing individual salaries we could compute this year's sum by multiplying \$428,000 by 1.15. However, that is not the information we have been given.

The correct answer is (E): Statements (1) and (2) TOGETHER are not sufficient.

D 47. **Word Problems:** Overlapping Sets
Difficulty: Easy **OG Page:** 26

In this ***Overlapping Sets*** problem, books can be classified in two different ways: (1) fiction and nonfiction, and (2) Spanish and not Spanish. We construct a ***Double-Set Matrix*** according to these criteria, inserting the information from the prompt and circling the desired quantity. Be sure to fill in as much of the table as you can. For instance, if we know that 24 of the 80 books are fiction, then we know that 56 are non-fiction.

	Spanish	**Not Spanish**	**Total**
Fiction	?		24
Non-Fiction			56
Total	23	57	80

(1): SUFFICIENT. ***Translate*** the specified relationship. Let's first ***Name a Variable***. If we write the smaller number of books (those written in Spanish) as x, then the larger number (those not written in Spanish) is $x + 6$. Fill the numbers into the chart:

	Spanish	**Not Spanish**	**Total**
Fiction	x	$x + 6$	24
Non-Fiction			56
Total	23	57	80

Since all the rows in the matrix add up, we can write the equation $x + (x + 6) = 24$. This is a ***Linear Equation*** that can be solved for a single value of x. Thus, we can answer the question. (Incidentally, the value of x is 9, but you should try to avoid unnecessary algebra on Data Sufficiency questions.)

(2): SUFFICIENT. Again, translate the specified relationship. If we write the smaller number of books (the fiction books) as x, then the larger number (the nonfiction books) is $x + 5$. Fill the numbers into the chart:

	Spanish	**Not Spanish**	**Total**
Fiction	x		24
Non-Fiction	$x + 5$		56
Total	23	57	80

Since all the columns in the matrix add up, we can write the equation $x + (x + 5) = 23$. This is another linear equation that can be solved for a single value of x. Again, we can answer the question.

The correct answer is (D): EACH statement ALONE is sufficient.

D 48. Geometry: Polygons
Difficulty: Hard **OG Page:** 26

To attack this ***Polygons*** problem, first ***Draw a Picture*** of rectangle Q. We should also ***Name Variables*** and label the sides, since the side lengths are used to determine the perimeter.

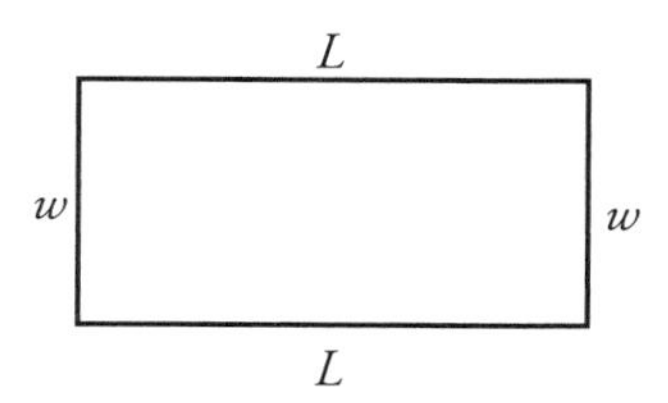

The perimeter is $2w + 2L = 2(w + L)$. Thus, we can ***Rephrase*** the question as "What is the value of $w + L$?"

(1): INSUFFICIENT. The diagonal of rectangle Q is given, so let's label the picture accordingly.

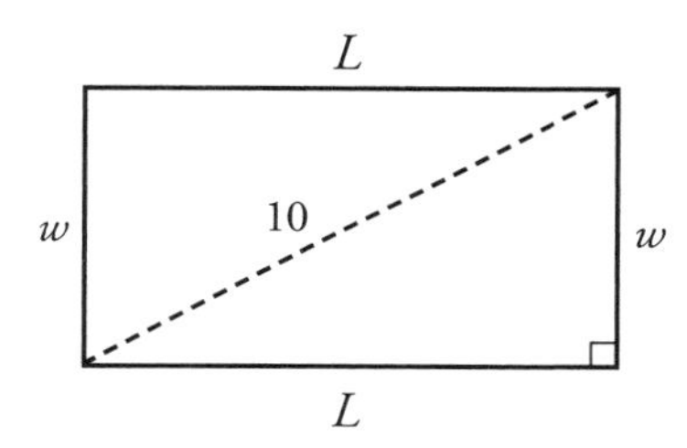

Cutting a rectangle in half diagonally creates two right triangles, so we can set up an equation for the diagonal using the ***Pythagorean Theorem***.

$$w^2 + L^2 = 10^2$$
$$w^2 + L^2 = 100$$

From this equation, we cannot determine the value of $(w + L)$, nor can we determine the values of w and L individually.

(2): INSUFFICIENT. The area of a rectangle is wL, so $wL = 48$. From this equation, we cannot determine the value of $(w + L)$, nor can we determine the values of w and L individually.

(1) AND (2): SUFFICIENT. We have two equations and two unknowns. At this point, we might think that because we have two equations and two unknowns, *of course* we can solve for the variables. However, this thinking is dangerous. Since neither equation is linear, we have no way of knowing whether the two equations are sufficient to solve for the variables or for an expression such as the one we are looking for (that is, $w + L$). As it turns out, we do not have enough information to find the variables themselves, but we can get a unique value for $w + L$.

There are several approaches at this point. The standard method is ***Substitution***: solve one equation for one variable and substitute into the other equation.

From (2), we have

$$wL = 48$$
$$w = \frac{48}{L}$$

Substituting into the equation from (1), we get

$$w^2 + L^2 = 100$$
$$\left(\frac{48}{L}\right)^2 + L^2 = 100$$
$$\frac{48^2}{L^2} + L^2 = 100$$
$$48^2 + L^4 = 100L^2$$
$$L^4 - 100L^2 + 48^2 = 0$$
$$(L^2 - 36)(L^2 - 64) = 0$$
$$L^2 = 36 \text{ or } 64$$
$$L = 6 \text{ or } 8$$

When $L = 6$, $w = 8$, so $(w + L) = 8 + 6 = 14$.

When $L = 8$, $w = 6$, so $(w + L) = 6 + 8 = 14$.

As it turns out, we have enough information to get a unique value for $w + L$.

The algebraic approach to this problem is not only messy, but also time-consuming, since factoring the quadratic is difficult.

A better approach is to ***Make an Educated Guess*** about the values of w and L, then check whether the values satisfy both constraints.

One very common triangle on the GMAT is the ***3–4–5*** right triangle and its multiples, such as 6–8–10. Since the diagonal of rectangle Q is 10, side lengths of 6 and 8 would satisfy the constraint from statement (1). Do these values satisfy the constraint from statement (2)?

area = $wL = (6)(8) = 48$ ✓

Thus, $w + L = 6 + 8 = 14$.

Finally, if we recognize that we are given the components of a common quadratic form, we can use ***Special Products***:

$$(w + L)^2 = w^2 + 2wL + L^2 = (w^2 + L^2) + 2(wL)$$

If $w^2 + L^2 = 100$ and $wL = 48$, then $(w + L)^2 = (w^2 + L^2) + 2(wL) = 100 + 2(48) = 196$.

Therefore, $(w + L) = \sqrt{196} = 14$. Notice that with this method, we do not try to solve or substitute for the individual variables w or L. Rather, we substitute for entire expressions, such as $w^2 + L^2$ and wL.

The correct answer is (C): BOTH statements TOGETHER are sufficient, but NEITHER statement ALONE is sufficient.

Chapter 3

of The Official Guide Companion

Problem Solving Explanations

In This Chapter...

Problem Solving Explanations

PS 1. <u>Word Problems</u>: Algebraic Translations
Difficulty: Easy **OG Page:** 152

To solve this ***Direct Computation*** problem, we should stay organized and go step by step.

If the budget is $12,600, spread out over 12 equal installments, then each installment should be 12 ÷ 12,600 = $1,050.

After 4 months, 4 × $1,050 = $4,200 should have been spent.

If $4,580 was spent instead, then the project went over budget by $4,580 – $4,200 = $380.

The correct answer is (A).

PS 2. <u>Number Properties</u>: Divisibility & Primes
Difficulty: Easy **OG Page:** 152

To determine which of the answer choices yields a non-integer value for the given expression, simply plug each answer choice into the expression. Using ***Divisibility Rules*** will speed up the process.

$$(A) = \frac{100+1}{1}$$

Any integer divided by 1 is an integer.

$$(B) = \frac{100+2}{2}$$

Any even integer divided by 2 is an integer. 100 + 2 is 102, an even integer.

$$(C) = \frac{100+3}{3}$$

NOT AN INTEGER. A quick way to determine that 103 is not divisible by 3 is to add the digits of 103 (1 + 0 + 3 = 4). If the sum is a multiple of 3, the number is a multiple of 3 (and if the sum is not a multiple of 3, neither is the number). **CORRECT**

$$(D) = \frac{100+4}{4}$$

104 divided by 4 is an integer. Since 100 is divisible by 4, we only have to consider the last two digits of any number over 100 to determine whether the number is a multiple of 4. Note that it is not necessary to calculate 104/4 = 26.

$$(E) = \frac{100+5}{5}$$

Any integer that ends in 5 is a multiple of 5, so 105 divided by 5 is an integer. Note that it is not necessary to calculate 105/5 = 21.

The correct answer is (C).

PS 3. <u>Geometry</u>: Polygons
Difficulty: Easy **OG Page:** 152

In a geometry problem, such as this ***Polygons*** question, it is often helpful to ***Draw a Picture.*** This way, we can visualize the information given in the problem.

Floor X has dimensions 12 feet by 18 feet. Floor Y is 9 feet wide, but we don't know how long it is. We can ***Name a Variable*** and let x represent the length of floor Y in feet.

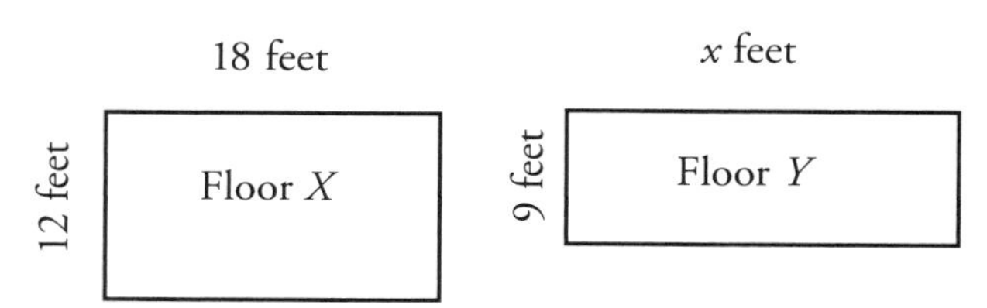

The formula for the ***Area of a Rectangle*** is

Area = Length × Width

Because Floor Y has the same area as Floor X, we can set the expression for their areas equal to each other.

Area of Floor X = Area of Floor Y
(12 feet)(18 feet) = (9 feet)(x feet)

$$x = \frac{(12)(18)}{(9)} = \frac{12 \times \cancel{18}2}{\cancel{9}} = 24 \text{ feet}$$

The correct answer is (E).

PS 4. Word Problems: Algebraic Translations
Difficulty: Easy **OG Page:** 152

This ***Algebraic Translations*** problem can be solved in several ways. The most straightforward method is ***Direct Algebra.*** Write each sentence or clause as an equation, replacing "contains" with "equals" (=).

First sentence: 1 case = c cartons
Second sentence: 1 carton = b boxes

Multiply both sides of the second equation by c:
c cartons = bc boxes

Thus, we know 1 case = bc boxes

We can also think of this process as substituting "b boxes" in for the "carton" unit in the first equation:
1 case = c (b boxes) = bc boxes

Now, translate the rest of the second sentence:
1 box = 100 paper clips

Substituting in for the "box" unit in the previous equation, we get
1 case = bc (100 paper clips)
= $100bc$ paper clips

Therefore, 2 cases contain double this number, or $200bc$ paper clips. This is the **answer**.

Alternatively, we could ***Choose Smart Numbers.*** Let $c = 3$ and $b = 2$. Thus each case contains 3 cartons and each carton contains 2 boxes.

Each case must contain $3 \times 2 = 6$ boxes. Since each box contains 100 paper clips, each case must contain $6 \times 100 = 600$ paper clips. We are asked for the number of paper clips in 2 cases, so doubling the number for one case, we ***Calculate The Target Value*** of 1,200 paper clips. We can now plug $c = 3$ and $b = 2$ in to each answer choice to see which yields a value of 1,200:

(A) $100bc = 100(2)(3) = 600$
INCORRECT

(B) $\frac{100b}{c} = \frac{100(2)}{3} = \frac{200}{3}$
INCORRECT

(C) $200bc = 200(2)(3) = 1{,}200$
CORRECT

(D) $\frac{200b}{c} = \frac{200(2)}{3} = \frac{400}{3}$
INCORRECT

(E) $\frac{200}{bc} = \frac{200}{(2)(3)} = \frac{200}{6}$
INCORRECT

Only answer choice (C) matches the target value of 1,200.

The correct answer is (C).

PS 5. Number Properties: Divisibility & Primes
Difficulty: Easy **OG Page:** 152

This problem has no shortcuts, unfortunately. We can only solve it by directly listing all the ***Prime Numbers*** greater than 60 and less than 70.

To determine whether a number is prime, try to find ***Prime Factors*** of the number (similar to the technique used in assembling a number's ***Prime Box***).

Try dividing by 2. The numbers 62, 64, 66, and 68 are divisible by 2, so none of them is prime. No even number larger than 2 is prime.

Next, try dividing by 3. Of the remaining numbers, 63 and 69 are divisible by 3, so neither is prime.

Next, try dividing by 5. Of the remaining numbers, 65 is divisible by 5, so it is not prime.

The remaining numbers, 61 and 67, are not divisible by any primes smaller than themselves, so they are prime. We only need to check up to the square root of the number in question. $\sqrt{61}$ are $\sqrt{67}$ around 8, so we only have to check that 7 does not go into either 61 or 67; it does not.

Since the only primes between 60 and 70 are 61 and 67, the desired sum is 61 + 67 = 128.

The correct answer is (B).

PS 6. <u>FDPs</u>: Percents
Difficulty: Easy **OG Page:** 152

For word problems that represent real situations, whether involving ***Percents*** or not, it is often helpful to ***Draw a Picture*** before diving into the math.

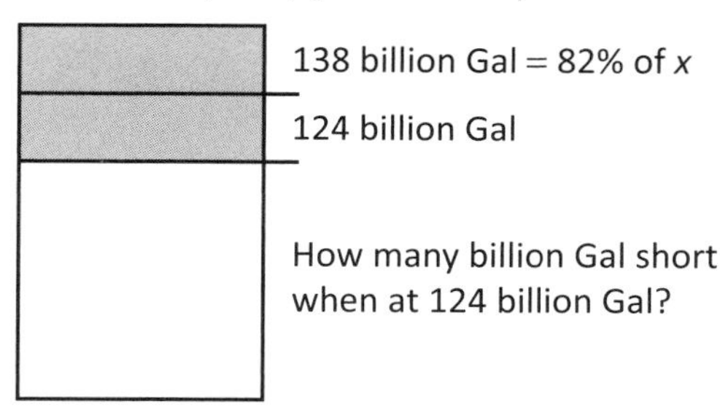

The reservoir was short by $x - 124$ billion gallons prior to the storm, so we need to determine x.

138 billion gallons is 82% of x, so 138 = (0.82)(x), which implies that $x = \frac{138}{0.82}$. We should not bother to compute the exact value of x, as the question specifically asks "approximately how many...." Instead, we ***Estimate*** the value of x. Note that we can reduce approximation error by rounding both numerator and denominator the same direction. As the numerator decreases, the fraction decreases. As the denominator decreases, the fraction increases. Therefore, by decreasing both the numerator and the denominator, we can offset the changes to the fraction.

$$x = \frac{138}{0.82} \approx \frac{136}{0.8} = \frac{136}{4/5} = \frac{136}{4} \times 5 = 34 \times 5 = 170$$

The reason to round to 136 is that we want a number divisible by 4, since we have 4/5 in the denominator of the fraction. This makes it easier to ***Cancel Factors***.

The answer is approximately 170 − 124 = 46. The closest answer choice is 44.

The correct answer is (E).

PS 7. <u>Geometry</u>: Coordinate Plane
Difficulty: Easy **OG Page:** 153

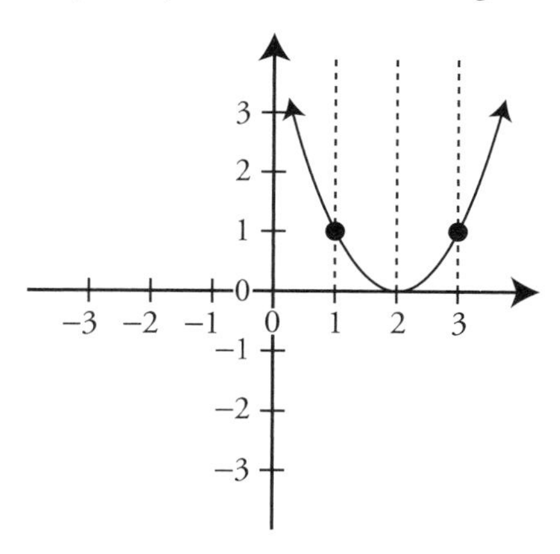

We know from the stem of this ***Coordinate Plane*** question that the graph (of what appears to be a parabola) is symmetric with respect to the vertical line at $x = 2$. This means that any two points on the graph with x-coordinates that are equally distant from $x = 2$ (i.e., one a certain distance *to the right* of 2, the other the same distance *to the left* of 2) will have the same y-coordinate. In other words, the left half of the graph is a mirror image of the right half of the graph, and we can apply ***Symmetry*** arguments.

The question asks us for the y-coordinate of the point at $x = 3$. This point has an x-coordinate that is 1 unit to the right of 2, so we must look at a point on the graph with an x-coordinate that is 1 unit to the left of 2 to get our answer (i.e., $x = 1$). The question tells us that when $x = 1$, $y = 1$. Therefore when $x = 3$, y must also equal 1. This is the **answer**.

Although the graph is not necessarily drawn precisely to scale, we should also be able to read off the graph that when $x = 3$, y is approximately 1. We might not be sure about 1/2 as a possibility, but we can certainly rule out 0, −1/2, and −1, since the graph is clearly above the x-axis at $x = 3$.

The correct answer is (E).

PS 8. FDPs: FDP Connections
Difficulty: 300–500 **OG Page:** 153

For this problem, which draws ***Connections Between Fractions, Decimals, and Percents***, we need to translate each of the pieces carefully. First, we must find 1/10 *percent* of 5,000. Note that "percent" literally means "per one hundred," signaling us to divide by 100:

$$\frac{1/10}{100}(5,000)$$

Next, simplify this term:

$$\frac{1/10}{100}(5,000) = \frac{1}{1,000}(5,000) = 5$$

Thus, 1/10 percent of 5,000 equals 5.

Next, we must simplify the second term:

$$\frac{1}{10}(5,000) = 500$$

At this point, we can deal with the surrounding language, which instructs us to subtract the first term from the second. Thus, we can solve:

$500 - 5 = 495$ This is the **answer**.

Alternatively, we could have set up the entire equation before simplifying any of the terms:

$$[\frac{1}{10}(5,000)] - [\frac{1/10}{100}(5,000)] = 500 - 5 = 495$$

In either case, be careful with the phrasing of the problem. Note that the passive voice phrasing "is subtracted from" requires us to place the term that is first described at the end of the equation.

The correct answer is (D).

PS 9. Algebra: Exponents & Roots
Difficulty: Medium **OG Page:** 153

To solve this ***Roots*** problem, first find the cube root of 0.000064 and then find the square root of that value.

Step 1: The cube root of 0.000064 is 0.04. To find this value, first realize that 64 is the cube of 4. In other words, $4^3 = 64$. Therefore, 4 is the cube root of 64. Next, deal with the ***Decimal Places***. Since 0.000064 has six decimal places, its cube root will have one-third as many, or two decimal places:

$$\sqrt[3]{0.000064} = 0.04$$

We can also check this result by cubing 0.04 to get the original number: $(0.04)^3 = 0.000064$

Step 2: The square root of 0.04 is 0.2. Again, we can start with the fact that the square root of 4 is 2. Since 0.04 has two decimal places, the square root of 0.04 will have half as many, or one decimal place:

$$\sqrt{0.04} = 0.2$$

If necessary, perform a check: $(0.2)^2 = 0.04$

Thus, 0.2 is the **answer.**

Alternatively, we can look at the problem in terms of ***Powers of Ten***. 0.000064 is equivalent to 64×10^{-6}. Therefore we can rewrite the problem and apply rules of exponents and roots:

$$\sqrt{\sqrt[3]{64 \times 10^{-6}}}$$
$$= \sqrt{(\sqrt[3]{64})(\sqrt[3]{10^{-6}})}$$
$$= \sqrt{(4)(10^{-2})}$$
$$= (\sqrt{4})(\sqrt{10^{-2}})$$
$$= 2 \times 10^{-1}$$
$$= 2 \times 0.1$$
$$= 0.2$$

The correct answer is (E).

PS 10. Number Properties: Probability
Difficulty: Medium **OG Page:** 153

In this ***Probability*** problem, we have a pool of tickets numbered 101 through 350, inclusive. We want to find the probability of selecting out of that pool a ticket that displays a hundreds digit of 2.

We need to apply the ***Basic Probability Formula***. The general method for calculating the probability of success is to divide the number of successful outcomes by the total number of possible outcomes. Thus, we need to count the tickets whose hundreds digit equals 2, and we also need to count all the tickets.

In this case, the total number of tickets is given by $350 - 101 + 1 = 250$. Always remember when counting integers, ***Add One Before You Are Done***.

Next, we need to count the tickets with 2 as the hundreds digit. This group of tickets includes numbers 200 through 299. Therefore, the total number of desired outcomes is $299 - 200 + 1 = 100$.

Finally, the probability of success is given by the following ratio:

$P = \frac{100}{250}$, which reduces to $\frac{2}{5}$.

The correct answer is (A).

PS 11. <u>FDPs</u>: Percents
Difficulty: Easy **OG Page:** 153

In this ***Percents*** problem, we first need to ***Name a Variable***. Let's label the total value of the item t. Then we can express the portion of the total value that is in excess of \$1,000 as $(t - 1{,}000)$. Finally, a 7% tax on this excess portion of the total value can be ***Translated*** as

$0.07 \times (t - 1{,}000)$, or simply $0.07\ (t - 1{,}000)$

Since the tax paid is \$87.50, set up an equation as follows:

$0.07\ (t - 1{,}000) = 87.5$
$0.07t - 70 = 87.5$ Distribute the 0.07
$0.07t = 157.5$ Add 70 to both sides

We can multiply both sides of the equation by 100 to eliminate the ***Decimals:***

$7t = 15{,}750$

Finally, perform long division:

$$7\overline{)15{,}750} = 2{,}250$$

$t = 2{,}250$

The correct answer is (C).

PS 12. <u>Word Problems</u>: Statistics
Difficulty: Easy **OG Page:** 153

The number of cars sold by a dealership on six of the last seven days was 4, 7, 2, 8, 3, and 6 respectively. On the seventh day, either 2, 4, or 5 cars were sold.

We can recognize that this is a ***Statistics*** problem because it asks us to determine whether the ***Average*** (arithmetic mean) is equal to the ***Median*** for each possible number of cars sold on the seventh day.

We need to find the averages and the medians for the three different possibilities and compare them.

To find the average of a set of numbers (A), sum the numbers in the set (S), and divide the sum by the number of numbers (N):

$A = S/N$

To find the median of a list of seven numbers, put the numbers in order from least to greatest and look up the value of the middle number, which is the 4th number. It is going to be faster to do this than to calculate the averages, so we do this first:

Ordered list of terms

2, 3, 4, 6, 7, 8

If the number of cars sold on the seventh day is 2 or 4, the median number of cars sold will be 4. If it is 5, the median number of cars sold will be 5.

Now we need to figure out how to efficiently compute the averages. Rather than summing the number of cars three times, sum them once for the six days and then add the three different values for the seventh day to get the three different seventh day sums.

Sum the number of cars sold on the six days:

$$4 + 7 + 2 + 8 + 3 + 6 = 30$$

Now compute the averages:

#cars sold on 7th day	median	Average	
2	4	32/7	← not 4
4	4	34/7	← also not 4
5	5	35/7 = 5	← aha!

Only 5 works as the possible number of cars sold on the seventh day.

The correct answer is (B)

PS 13. Geometry: Polygons
Difficulty: Easy **OG Page:** 154

We are given a ***Rectangle*** that is twice as long as it is wide and told that 360 yards of fencing will completely enclose the rectangle.

This is a ***Polygons*** problem that has to do with the ***Perimeter*** of a rectangle. Fencing goes around the edge of a shape, so the total amount of fencing used will be equal to the perimeter of the rectangle. We are asked to find the length of this garden.

Draw a picture of a rectangle:

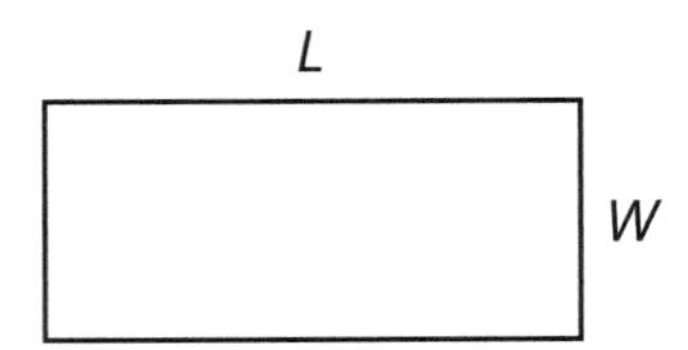

The perimeter is equal to twice the length plus twice the width.

$$P = 2 \times L + 2 \times W$$

Since we know the perimeter is 360, we can reduce the number of variables in the equation by plugging 360 in for the perimeter. Reducing the number of variables is a good thing because it is a step along the path to solving for L.

$$360 = 2L + 2W$$

To solve for L, we need another equation that relates L and W. The question states that the rectangle is twice as long as it is wide. In other words:

$$L = 2W$$

(You can check for a translation error by plugging in some numbers to be sure that the equation matches the words, i.e. if the length is 100, the width should be 50, and $100 = 2 \times 50$.)

We can solve by ***Substitution***, because we have two different ***Linear Equations*** using the same two variables.

$$360 = 2L + 2W$$
$$L = 2W$$

Substitute $(2W)$ for L in the first equation:

$$180 = 2W + W$$
$$180 = 3W$$
$$60 = W$$

Use the value of W to solve for L:

$$L = 2W$$
$$L = 2(60)$$
$$L = 120$$

The correct answer is (A).

PS 14. Algebra: Linear Equations
Difficulty: Easy **OG Page:** 154

We are given an ***Inequality*** with an absolute value and asked for the answer choice that *could be* a value of y.

This is an algebra problem that has to do with inequalities. The "could be" in the question means that there is more than one number that could work for y, but that four of the five answer choices are numbers that would make the inequality not be true.

Because of the "could be," the easiest way to solve this problem is just to ***Work Backwards from the Answer Choices*** and stop when we get to one that makes the inequality true, rather than manipulating the inequality algebraically.

(A) $\left|-11-\frac{1}{2}\right|=\left|\frac{-22}{2}-\frac{1}{2}\right|=\left|\frac{-23}{2}\right|=\frac{23}{2}\leftarrow$ this is $>\frac{11}{2}$,

so -11 cannot be y

(B) $\left|\frac{-11}{2}-\frac{1}{2}\right|=\left|\frac{-12}{2}\right|=\frac{12}{2}\leftarrow$ this is $>\frac{11}{2}$,

so $\frac{-11}{2}$ cannot be y

(C) $\left|\frac{11}{2}-\frac{1}{2}\right|=\left|\frac{10}{2}\right|=\frac{10}{2}\leftarrow$ this is $<\frac{11}{2}$,

so $\frac{11}{2}$ could be y

(D) $\left|11-\frac{1}{2}\right|=\left|\frac{22}{2}-\frac{1}{2}\right|=\left|\frac{21}{2}\right|=\frac{21}{2}\leftarrow$ this is $>\frac{11}{2}$,

so 11 cannot be y

(E) $\left|22-\frac{1}{2}\right|=\left|\frac{44}{2}-\frac{1}{2}\right|=\left|\frac{43}{2}\right|=\frac{43}{2}\leftarrow$ this is $>\frac{11}{2}$,

so 22 cannot be y

Note that we could have stopped once we got to an answer that worked because there must be one and only one answer choice that makes the inequality true.

Alternatively, we could have solved this problem algebraically. The tricky part is the absolute value, which means that we have to consider two possibilities.

if $y-\frac{1}{2}>0$ then

$$y-\frac{1}{2}<\frac{11}{2}$$
$$y<\frac{11}{2}+\frac{1}{2}$$
$$y<\frac{12}{2}$$
$$y<6$$

or

if $y-\frac{1}{2}<0$ then

$$-\left(y-\frac{1}{2}\right)<\frac{11}{2}$$
$$-y+\frac{1}{2}<\frac{11}{2}$$
$$-y<\frac{11}{2}-\frac{1}{2}$$
$$-y<\frac{10}{2}$$
$$-y<5$$
$$y>-5$$

The only answer given that fits either case is 11/2.

The correct answer is (C).

PS 15. <u>FDPs</u>: Fractions
Difficulty: Easy **OG Page:** 154

We are told that John spent 1/2 of his money on fruits and vegetables, 1/3 on meat, 1/10 on bakery products, and $6 on candy.

We know that this is a ***Fractions*** problem because we are given fractions instead of amounts for the money spent on several items. However, we are given the actual amount of money that was spent on candy, and asked to figure out the total actual amount spent, so we *cannot* solve this problem by ***Choosing Smart Numbers***.

We need to figure out the fraction of the money that was spent on candy so that we can set up an equation setting that fraction of the total spent equal to the $6 spent on candy and solve.

We can figure out the fraction that was NOT spent on candy by adding up the other fractions:

$$\frac{1}{2}+\frac{1}{3}+\frac{1}{10}=\frac{15}{30}+\frac{10}{30}+\frac{3}{30}=\frac{28}{30}=\frac{14}{15}$$

The remaining 1/15 of the total amount of money was spent on candy. We can say that $6 is equal to 1/15 of the total amount of money spent. Let t stand for the total amount spent:

$$\frac{1}{15}t=6$$
$$t=15\times 6$$
$$t=90$$

The correct answer is (C).

PS 16. <u>Word Problems</u>: Statistics
Difficulty: Medium **OG Page:** 154

In this ***Weighted Average*** problem, we need to find the average weight of all the packages mailed on the two days. We can express the ***Average Formula*** in either of these ways:

$$\left(\begin{array}{c}\text{Average}\\ \text{weight}\end{array}\right)=\frac{\text{Sum of weights of the packages}}{\text{Number of packages}}$$

or

(Sum of weights) =
(Average weight) × (Number of packages)

We'll need both of these versions as we go.

On Monday, 8 packages weighing an average of 12⅜ pounds were mailed. Although we do not have the exact weight of each package, we can find the sum of the weights using the second formula above:

$$\begin{pmatrix}\text{Sum of}\\ \text{weights}\end{pmatrix} = \left(12\frac{3}{8}\right)(8) = \left(\frac{99}{8}\right)(8) = 99\,\text{pounds}$$

On Tuesday, 4 packages weighing an average of 15 1/4 pounds were mailed. We can find the sum of the weights of these in the same way:

$$\begin{pmatrix}\text{Sum of}\\ \text{weights}\end{pmatrix} = \left(15\frac{1}{4}\right)(4) = \left(\frac{61}{4}\right)(4) = 61\,\text{pounds}$$

Over the two days, the person mailed a total of 12 packages that weighed 99 + 61 = 160 pounds. We can use the first formula above to find the average weight for all the packages over the two days:

$$\begin{pmatrix}\text{Average}\\ \text{weight}\end{pmatrix} = \frac{160\,\text{pounds}}{12\text{ packages}} = \frac{40\,\text{pounds}}{3\text{ packages}}$$

$$\begin{pmatrix}\text{Average}\\ \text{weight}\end{pmatrix} = 13\frac{1}{3}\text{ pounds per packages}$$

This is the **answer**.

In this problem, we can quickly eliminate unrealistic answer choices. We know the average of all the packages over the two days will fall between each day's average weights. If we examine the answer choices to see which ones fall between 12⅜ and 15¼, we can immediately eliminate answer choices (C), (D), and (E).

The correct answer is (A).

PS 17. <u>FDPs</u>: Digits & Decimals
Difficulty: Easy **OG Page:** 154

This ***Decimals*** problem asks us to add three quantities. In order to perform the calculation correctly, we need to follow the ***Order of Operations***, which we can remember using the acronym ***PEMDAS***. In the context of this problem, PEMDAS means that we have to apply the ***Exponents*** first and then perform the Addition.

Begin with the second term: $(0.1)^2 = (0.1) \times (0.1)$

When multiplying decimals, first ignore the decimals and multiply the numbers: 1 × 1 = 1. Then count the number of ignored decimal places to the right of the decimal point. In this case, we ignored two decimal places to the right of the decimal. Insert the missing decimals back into the solution:

1. → 0.01 Therefore, $(0.1)^2 = 0.01$

Then, compute the third term using the same method:

$(0.1)^3 = (0.1) \times (0.1) \times (0.1)$.

Ignoring the decimals, we have 1 × 1 × 1 = 1. We ignored three decimal places, so add those back in:

1. → 0.001 Therefore, $(0.1)^3 = 0.001$

Finally, sum the three terms. Line up the decimal points, so that you don't accidentally add the digits incorrectly.

$$\begin{array}{r} 0.1 \\ +0.01 \\ +0.001 \\ \hline 0.111 \end{array}$$

The correct answer is (B).

PS 18. <u>Geometry</u>: Polygons
Difficulty: Medium **OG Page:** 154

This ***3-Dimensional Geometry*** problem requires us to understand how the capacity, or ***Volume***, of a rectangular solid changes if we double its length, width, and height. Note that "capacity" is a code word for volume. Another clue is the unit "cubic feet": all units of volume are cubic lengths, such as cubic feet or cubic centimeters. The applicable geometric formula is

Volume = length × width × height, or $V = lwh$.

In order to see what happens to the volume after doubling each dimension, we can substitute $2l$, $2w$, and $2h$ into the formula:

$New\ V = (2l) \times (2w) \times (2h)$

Rearranging the factors, we see that $New\ V = 2 \times 2 \times 2 \times lwh = 8 \times lwh$. The original volume was equal to lwh, so we can see that the new volume is equal to 8 times the original volume. This will always be true for a rectangular solid—if the length, width, and height are doubled, the volume will increase by a factor of 8.

In this problem, the original capacity is 10 cubic feet. Therefore, after doubling the length, width, and height of the sandbox, the new capacity will be $8 \times 10 = 80$ cubic feet. This is the **answer**.

Alternatively, we could ***Choose Smart Numbers*** for the length, width, and height of the original sandbox. Let $l = 5$ feet, $w = 2$ feet, and $h = 1$ foot. (Choose any numbers that multiply together to 10 cubic feet and that are easy to deal with.) Then the new sandbox will have a length of 10 feet, a width of 4 feet, and a height of 2 feet. This new sandbox will have a volume of $10 \times 4 \times 2 = 80$ cubic feet.

The correct answer is (D).

PS 19. FDPs: Percents
Difficulty: Easy **OG Page:** 154

This ***Percent Change*** problem calls for ***Direct Computation*** according to the figures given. Note that there is no reason to convert from dozens to individual rolls, as both the given information and the requested answer are in units of dozens.

The bakery opened with 40 dozen rolls. Half of these, or 20 dozen, were sold by noon, leaving $40 - 20 = 20$ dozen rolls. Of these 20 dozen *remaining* rolls, 80 percent, or $(0.80)(20) = 16$ dozen, were sold by closing time. Therefore, $20 - 16 = 4$ dozen rolls remained.

The correct answer is (D).

PS 20. FDPs: Digits & Decimals
Difficulty: Medium **OG Page:** 154

In this ***Digits & Decimals*** problem, we are asked for the 25th digit to the right of the decimal point when 6 is divided by 11. The GMAT does not require more calculation than is reasonable in two minutes (the approximate amount of time available per problem on the exam). In this case, we should expect to find a ***Pattern*** that we can easily extend to the 25th decimal place *without* calculating every digit in between.

Thus, we can begin ***Long Division,*** preparing to stop when the pattern becomes apparent:

$$0.54\overline{54}$$

```
   0.5454
11)6.0000
  -55
    50
   -44
     60
    -55
      50
```

The pattern we notice is an alternating cycle of 5's and 4's.

We want to know the 25th digit after the decimal. Note that odd places (1st, 3rd, 5th…) after the decimal are the digit 5, and even places after the decimal (2nd, 4th, 6th…) are the digit 4.

$$0.54\overline{54}$$

odd places ↑ (5) even places ↑ (4)

Thus, we can infer that the 25th place is the digit 5.

The correct answer is (C).

PS 21. FDPs: Percents
Difficulty: Easy **OG Page:** 154

We can do a literal ***Algebraic Translation*** to obtain an equation for this ***Percents*** problem. First, we should ***Name a Variable*** to represent the question word "what." Let's use x. Represent "percent" by putting x over 100. Finally, represent "of" with multiplication, and solve for x using ***Direct Algebra***.

150 is what percent of 30?

$$150 = x\% \text{ of } 30$$
$$150 = \left(\frac{x}{100}\right)30$$
$$150 = \frac{30x}{100}$$
$$150 = \frac{3}{10}x$$
$$\frac{10}{3}(150) = x$$
$$x = 500$$

Thus, $x\%$ is 500%.

The correct answer is (E).

PS 22. FDPs Ratios
Difficulty: Easy **OG Page:** 155

Begin by writing down the given ***Ratio***:

$$2 : \frac{1}{3}$$

Next, quickly scan the answer choices. Notice that all of the answer choices express the ratio in integers. Thus, we need to eliminate the ***Fraction*** from the right-hand side of our ratio without changing the ratio itself.

To eliminate the fraction from the right-hand side of the ratio, we should multiply by 3. To maintain the proper ratio, however, we must multiply the left-hand side by 3 as well. Multiplying both sides by 3 gives us the ratio 6 : 1. This is the **answer**.

Alternatively, we could have chosen to express 2 and $\frac{1}{3}$ in terms of a ***Common Denominator*** of 3. Thus:

$$\frac{6}{3} : \frac{1}{3}$$

This quickly simplifies to a ratio of 6 to 1.

Finally, since ratios are equivalent to fractions, we could have written the original ratio as follows:

$$\frac{2}{1/3}$$

Since dividing by a fraction is the same as multiplying by the ***Reciprocal***, we get the following:

$$\frac{2}{1/3} = 2 \times \frac{3}{1} = \frac{6}{1}$$

The fraction $\frac{6}{1}$ is equivalent to a ratio of 6 to 1.

The correct answer is (A).

PS 23. Word Problems: Rates & Work
Difficulty: Easy **OG Page:** 155

This ***Rates & Work*** problem does not require a chart. Rather, if we figure out the working rate of each machine, then we can find the effective rate of 10 machines.

When equal machines are ***Working Together***, each machine's rate is an equal fraction of the overall rate. So, if six identical machines produce a total of 270 bottles per minute, then each machine produces 1/6 of that amount every minute, or 270/6 = 45 bottles per minute.

Ten such machines, working together, could produce (10)(45) = 450 bottles per minute.

We now apply the ***Work Formula***, which is simply Rate × Time = Work. In four minutes, the ten machines could produce (450)(4) = 1,800 bottles.

The correct answer is (B).

PS 24. <u>Number Properties:</u> Positives & Negatives
Difficulty: Easy **OG Page:** 155

In this problem, we are asked to determine which of five points on a number line has the greatest ***Absolute Value*** of its coordinate. A coordinate is a number that represents a position. On a number line, we need just one coordinate. For instance, the coordinate of point A is –2.

The absolute value of a number is the distance between that number and 0, when the number is plotted on a number line. By definition, absolute values are positive, since there is no such thing as a negative distance. In other words, the farther a number is from zero, the greater its absolute value.

In this case, point A has a coordinate of –2, so the absolute value of its coordinate is $|-2| = 2$.

None of the other points is as far from the origin as point A is. Thus, the absolute values of the other coordinates are all less than 2. Point A's coordinate has the greatest absolute value.

The correct answer is (A).

PS 25. <u>Word Problems:</u> Overlapping Sets
Difficulty: Medium **OG Page:** 155

This ***Overlapping Sets*** problem is best solved with a ***Double-Set Matrix***. In this case, the total group is the 50 researchers. The first categorization is "Assigned to A" vs. "Assigned to B." The second categorization is "Prefer A" vs. "Prefer B."

Begin by filling in the known information.:

	Assigned to A	Assigned to B	Total
Prefer A			35
Prefer B			15
Total	20	30	50

We are looking for the lowest possible number of researchers who will NOT be assigned to the team they prefer. In other words, this is an ***Optimization*** problem as well. We want the lowest possible sum of the "Prefer A but in B" and "Prefer B but in A" boxes:

	Assigned to A	Assigned to B	Total
Prefer A			35
Prefer B			15
Total	20	30	50

In order to minimize the numbers in each of these boxes, we must maximize the numbers in each of the other two unfilled boxes. This method of maximizing one value to minimize another is characteristic of optimization problems.

	Assigned to A	Assigned to B	Total
Prefer A	20		35
Prefer B		15	15
Total	20	30	50

Note that, although we want to maximize the number of people in the top-left and middle boxes, we are constrained by the totals. Because only 15 people prefer B, the maximum number of people who can be assigned to the middle box is 15. A ***Hidden Constraint*** is at work here: the number of people in any box cannot be negative. Similarly, only 20 people are assigned to A, so 20 is the maximum number of people who can be in the top-left box. We now have enough information to fill in the two cells we need to know.

	Assigned to A	Assigned to B	Total
Prefer A	20	15	35
Prefer B	0	15	15
Total	20	30	50

$0 + 15 = 15$ represents the minimum number of people assigned to a team other than the one they prefer. This is the **answer**.

Notice that one box contains zero people—the minimum possible. If negative values were allowed in some boxes, we could increase the desired maximum further, so we should expect the non-negative constraint to come into play.

The correct answer is (A).

PS 26. <u>Number Properties</u>: Divisibility & Primes
Difficulty: Easy **OG Page:** 155

The simplest and fastest way to solve this problem involving ***Primes*** and ***Remainders*** is simply to ***Choose a Smart Number*** for n. Given the constraints of the problem, we need to choose a prime number greater than 3.

If $n = 5$, then n^2 is 25. The remainder when 25 is divided by 12 is 1. This is the **answer.**

No more work is needed! The question requires that the remainder be the same, no matter which prime number greater than 3 is selected for n. Otherwise, there would be more than one right answer. As a result, we can be certain of our answer.

Of course, if we really want to check, we can pick other primes larger than 3. If $n = 7$, then n^2 is 49, and the remainder when 49 is divided by 12 is also 1. If $n = 11$, then $n^2 = 121$, and 121 divided by 12 also yields remainder 1.

While this problem is best solved by simply picking a number, as above, a useful point about ***Number Properties*** may be made here. Several of the answer choices are impossible, according to what we know about n^2.

A remainder of 0 would mean that n^2 is divisible by 12, which cannot be true. For a number to be divisible by 12, it must contain 12's prime factors (2, 2, and 3). However, n^2 contains no primes other than n, which cannot be 2 or 3.

2 can also be easily eliminated: since n must be a prime greater than 3, it is necessarily odd. An odd times an odd is an odd, so n^2 must also be odd. It is not possible for an odd n^2 to yield an even remainder when divided by an even.

Finally, n^2 could only yield a remainder of 3 after being divided by 12 if n^2 were a multiple of 3. This is not possible, since n^2 is the square of a prime greater than 3.

The theoretical approach to this problem is in fact very difficult and should be avoided.

The correct answer is (B).

PS 27. <u>FDPs</u>: Fractions
Difficulty: Easy **OG Page:** 155

This problem involves ***Double-Decker Fractions***, which are fractions embedded within larger fractions. The best strategy is to "unravel" the fraction by simplifying the embedded parts first and working outward.

$$\frac{1}{1+\frac{1}{3}} - \frac{1}{1+\frac{1}{2}}$$

$$= \frac{1}{\frac{3}{3}+\frac{1}{3}} - \frac{1}{\frac{2}{2}+\frac{1}{2}}$$

Combine terms in the denominator by using a ***Common Denominator.***

$$= \frac{1}{\frac{4}{3}} - \frac{1}{\frac{3}{2}}$$

Use the reciprocal rule to "flip" the fractions in the denominators.

$$= \frac{3}{4} - \frac{2}{3}$$

Subtract the fraction by using a common denominator.

$$= \frac{9}{12} - \frac{8}{12} = \frac{1}{12}$$

The correct answer is (D).

PS 28. <u>Geometry</u>: Coordinate Plane
Difficulty: Easy **OG Page:** 155

This problem asks us to find the coordinates of a particular point, V, on the given ***Coordinate Plane.***

The coordinates of a point are always written in the form (x, y). The first number, x, refers to the horizontal position of the point along the x-axis. The second number, y, refers to the vertical position of the point along the y-axis.

The origin, where the axes cross, always has coordinates (0, 0). Not all the tick marks are labeled, but the 5 and the −5 on the diagram tell us that the scale is 1. That is, the distance between successive tick marks is 1.

First, find the value of the x-coordinate. Point V is to the right of the origin (0, 0), so the x-value is positive. The point corresponds to the 7th horizontal tick mark, so the x-coordinate is 7.

Next, find the value of the y-coordinate. Point V is below the origin (0, 0), so the y-value is negative. The point corresponds to the 5th vertical tick mark, so the y-coordinate is –5.

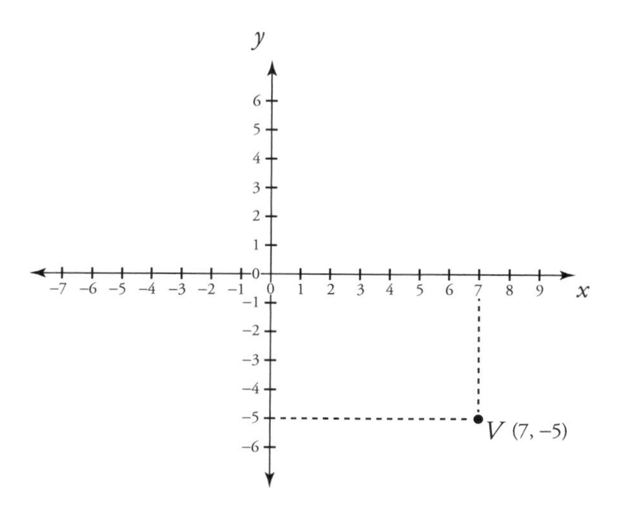

Putting these coordinates together in the proper order, we write the coordinates of point V as (7,–5).

The correct answer is (E).

PS 29. Word Problems: Algebraic Translations
Difficulty: Easy **OG Page:** 156

This ***Algebraic Translations*** word problem mentions that a piece of rope is cut into 2 pieces. It then gives us a relationship between the lengths of the two pieces. We can use this relationship to establish expressions for each piece of rope. First, we ought to ***Name a Variable***:

Piece 1 (the shorter piece) = x
Piece 2 (the longer piece) = $x + 18$

Naming just one variable (x) will save us time later. Now, we can use these two definitions to create a single equation, since we know that the two pieces together sum to a length of 40.

$$x + (x + 18) = 40$$
$$2x + 18 = 40$$
$$2x = 22$$
$$x = 11$$

That means that the length of the shorter piece (x) is 11 and the length of the longer piece ($x + 18$) is 29. We are asked for the shorter length, 11 feet. This is the **answer**.

In this problem, it's worth taking a look at the wrong answer choices. Notice that there are two pairs of answers that sum to 40: 11 + 29 = 40 and 18 + 22 = 40. In such a scenario, answer choice (A), which does not have a partner, is unlikely to be the correct answer. Also, since we are looking for the length of the shorter piece, the higher number in each pair is also unlikely to be correct, eliminating 22 and 29 as possibilities. 18 is also somewhat unlikely, since it is a number given in the problem (one piece of rope is 18 feet longer than the other).

Finally, note that 29 is a trap answer that results from solving the right equation but reporting the length of the *longer* piece instead of the shorter piece.

The correct answer is (B).

PS 30. Word Problems: Statistics
Difficulty: Easy **OG Page:** 156

Like other problems involving the average (arithmetic mean), this problem calls for the ***Average Formula***, often written as:

$$\frac{\text{Sum}}{\text{Number of Data Points}} = \text{Average}$$

We rearrange this formula as follows:

(Average) × (Number of Data Points) = Sum.

Using this formula, we first find the sum of the first four test scores, then write an equation including the 5th test score.

Since the first four test scores average to 78, we can find the sum of these scores:

Average	×	Number of Data Points	=	Sum
78	×	4	=	312

We are looking for the 5th score. Let's call it x. Now, we can express the sum of all five scores as

$312 + x$. Since we want the average of all five scores to be 80, use the Average Formula again:

Average	×	Number of Data Points	=	Sum
80	×	5	=	$312 + x$

Thus, we have the following:

$400 = 312 + x$
$88 = x$ This is the **answer**.

We can also visualize these steps in the following ***Chart***:

	Average	× Number	= Sum
First 4 Exams	78	4	312
New Exam	x	1	x
All Exams	80	5	400

The sums add up, since they are total numbers of points. Therefore, $312 + x = 400$ and $x = 88$.

Finally, we could take an intuitive route. Assume that each of the first 4 exam scores is actually 78. Then each score is 2 points short of the average we want (80), leading to a total deficit of 8 points. The fifth score has to make up that 8-point deficit completely, so it must be 80 + 8 = 88. This method of ***Residuals*** (overages and deficits) can be fast and effective.

The correct answer is (E).

PS 31. FDPs: Percents
Difficulty: Medium **OG Page:** 156

We can approach this ***Successive Percents*** problem by calculating the change in value each year to find the new balance.

Original Investment:	$10,000
At the end of Year One: 10% increase = (0.10)($10,000) = $1,000 New balance = $10,000 + $1,000 = $11,000	
At the end of Year Two: 5% increase = (0.05)($11,000) = $550 New balance = $11,000 + $550 = $11,550	
At the end of Year Three: 10% decrease = (0.10)($11,550) = $1,155 New balance = $11,500 – $1,155 = $10,395	

We can also approach this problem by using the following ***Formulas for Percent Increase/ Decrease***:

To find the amount after an x% increase,

$$\text{Original Amount} \times \left(1 + \frac{x}{100}\right) = \text{New Amount}$$

To find the amount after an x% decrease,

$$\text{Original Amount} \times \left(1 - \frac{x}{100}\right) = \text{New Amount}$$

We can multiply these changes to the original amount to find the final value after three years:

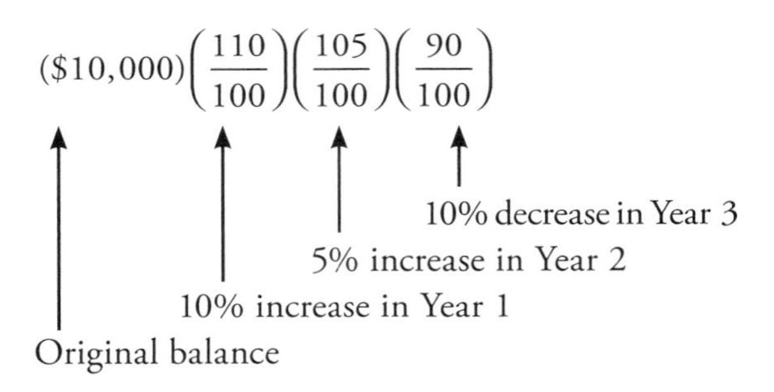

We can now simplify this product:

$$(\$\cancel{10{,}000})\left(\frac{110}{\cancel{100}}\right)\left(\frac{105}{\cancel{100}}\right)\left(\frac{90}{100}\right)$$

$$\$(11\cancel{0})(105)\left(\frac{9\cancel{0}}{\cancel{100}}\right)$$

$$\$(11)(105)(9)$$

= $10,395 This is the **answer**.

By the way, never simply add or subtract successive percents. In other words, a 10% increase, followed by a 5% increase and then a 10% decrease, is *never* equivalent to a simple 5% increase. Answer choice (C), which represents this simple 5% increase, is a trap.

The correct answer is (B).

PS 32. Number Properties: Positives & Negatives
Difficulty: Easy **OG Page:** 156

If the quotient of $\frac{a}{b}$ is positive, a and b must have the same sign (i.e., they are either both positive or both negative). This ***Positives & Negatives*** question asks us what else *must* be true.

(A) $a > 0$ *only* if b is also positive. Note that a could be negative, as long as b is negative. INCORRECT

(B) $b > 0$ *only* if a is also positive. As above, both variables could be negative. INCORRECT

(C) $ab > 0$ This *must* be true, as we know that a and b both have the same sign. The product of two variables with the same sign is always positive. **CORRECT**

(D) $a - b > 0$ This does not have to be true, as $a = 3$ and $b = 5$ would demonstrate. The variables just need to have the same sign. We know nothing about their relative size. INCORRECT

(E) $a + b > 0$ Both a and b could be negative, resulting in a negative sum. INCORRECT

We now have the **answer**.

If we only think of positive possibilities, then several of the wrong answers work. Be sure to consider negative possibilities in questions such as this one. Any variable (such as a or b) can take on negative values unless the variable itself is specifically restricted to positive values. If a variable is labeled as "positive" or "> 0," or if it represents a number of physical objects, then we know that the variable cannot take on negative values. In this problem, however, no such restrictions apply to a or to b.

The correct answer is (C).

PS 33. Word Problems: Extra Problem Types
Difficulty: Easy **OG Page:** 156

The problem asks us to read a ***Chart*** and determine the number of cars that meet two criteria: a weight of more than 2,500 pounds and a miles-per-gallon rating above 22. So we must count the dots on the chart that fit *both* criteria at once. We should not simply add up the dots that fit each of the criteria independently.

The weight is listed in hundreds of pounds, so any dot that appears to the right of the line at "25" will meet the first criterion. There are ten dots to the right of the line. We should leave out the dots that lie on the line for "25" itself, as we wish to include only cars weighing "more than" 2,500 pounds.

Now that we have satisfied the first condition, let's consider the second one. The line representing 22 miles-per-gallon appears directly between the lines marking "20" and "24." Five of the dots that met the first criterion fail this test. Thus, of the 10 dots that we counted at first, only 5 remain. This is the **answer.**

Alternatively, we could simply examine both criteria at once and then carefully count the dots that appear in the correct portion of the graph (to the right of 25 hundred pounds and above 22 miles-per-gallon). This would yield a total of 5 dots.

The correct answer is (B).

PS 34. Word Problems: Rates & Work
Difficulty: Easy **OG Page:** 156

If John types at the rate of x words per minute, then in m minutes, he can type xm words. This step applies the ***Work Formula***, which is simply Rate × Time = Work. Here, work is measured in words.

Since John types a total of y words, it must be true that $xm = y$. The question asks for the number of minutes, so to isolate m, we divide both sides by x, yielding $m = y/x$. This is the **answer.**

Alternatively, we can ***Choose Smart Numbers*** for x and y.

Let $x = 2$ (words per minute) and $y = 6$ (words). To type 6 words at the rate of 2 words per minute, John would therefore need 3 minutes, since (6)/(2) = 3. Therefore 3 is our ***Target Value.*** If we plug in 2 for x and 6 for y in all of the choices, the choice that yields a value of 3 will be our answer:

(A) 2/6 = 1/3	INCORRECT
(B) 6/2 = 3	**CORRECT**
(C) (2)(6) = 12	INCORRECT
(D) ((60)(2))/6 = 120/6 = 20	INCORRECT
(E) 6/((60)(2)) = 6/120 = 1/20	INCORRECT

The correct answer is (B).

PS 35. Algebra: Exponents & Roots
Difficulty: Medium **OG Page:** 156

This ***Roots*** problem makes us wish we had a calculator. First, recognize that we cannot break up the given radical into two radicals, because of the plus sign. When we add under a radical sign, we cannot separate the two parts.

The fastest way to simplify this radical expression is to ***Factor*** out the largest square you can from the sum. We have the following sum under the radical:

(16)(20) + (8)(32)

An initial candidate for a common square factor is 4, but we can do better. Notice that 16 is a factor of the first product *and* of the second product (since 16 is a factor of 32, and the order of multiplication does not matter). So we can rewrite the sum as follows:

$$\begin{aligned}(16)(20)+(8)(32) &= (16)(20)+(8)(2)(16)\\ &= (16)[20+(8)(2)]\\ &= (16)[20+16]\\ &= (16)(36)\end{aligned}$$

Now, we can put the result under the radical sign:

$$\sqrt{(16)(20)+(8)(32)} = \sqrt{(16)(36)}$$

Because the only operation under the radical is multiplication, we can finally ***Split the Radical*** and solve:

$$\sqrt{(16)(36)} = \sqrt{16} \times \sqrt{36} = 4 \times 6 = 24$$

This is the **answer**.

In theory we could perform the indicated calculation directly. First, we would compute (16)(20) + (8)(32) = 576, and then we would take the square root of 576. However, finding the square root of such a large number can be troublesome. Unless we have memorized a long list of squares, we would need to factor $576(= 2^6 \times 3^2)$ and then construct the square root $(= 2^3 \times 3^1 = 8 \times 3 = 24)$. This ***Prime Factorization*** method will always work, but if we can pull out a large square factor right away, we can get to the right answer faster.

The correct answer is (B).

PS 36. Geometry: Circles & Cylinders
Difficulty: Easy **OG Page:** 157

This question, about the shaded ***Fraction*** of a ***Circle***, is technically asking us to compare areas (the shaded area versus the overall area of the circle). A simpler approach is to compare central angles. That is, we just need to figure out what fraction of 360° (a whole circle) is included as central angles in the two shaded sectors.

The given angle of 150° makes a straight line with either of the shaded regions. Since the two ***Angles*** that make up a straight line sum to 180°, each of the shaded regions has a central angle of 30°.

The two central angles of 30° add up to 60°. As a fraction, 60° out of an entire central angle of 360° may be expressed as:

$$\frac{60}{360} = \frac{1}{6}$$

The correct answer is (C).

PS 37. <u>Algebra</u>: Quadratic Equations
Difficulty: Easy **OG Page:** 157

The question asks us to find the equation that is NOT equivalent to the equation given in the question; this means that four of the five answer choices are equivalent to the given equation, but the correct answer is not.

Since there are variables in the answer choices, we could try to solve by plugging in a number for y and figuring out what x would have to be, but it looks like it would be very hard to get nice, easy to work with integers because the equation involves exponents.

Looking again at the problem and at the answer choices, notice that this problem almost certainly has to do with ***Quadratic Equations*** because of the $(x + 2)(x - 2)$ in the given equation. This is a clue that should help us solve.

Rewrite the original equation by FOILing the right side:

$$10y^2 = x^2 - 4$$

This form of the given equation now looks a lot more like most of the answer choices. This tells us that it shouldn't be too hard to solve this problem by transforming the given equation into each of the answers. If the given equation can be transformed to look like an answer choice, we know the two equations are equivalent, and can eliminate that answer choice and move on to the next one. If we get stuck, we can also move on to the next answer choice, but we can't eliminate the one we got stuck on.

(A) $30y^2 = 3x^2 - 12$ ← multiply both sides of the given equation by 3 to get this

(B) $20y^2 = (2x - 4)(x + 2)$ ← FOIL the right side to simplify

$20y^2 = 2x^2 - 4x + 4x - 8$ ← Notice the x terms cancel out

$20y^2 = 2x^2 - 8$ ← Multiply the original equation by 2 to get this

(C) $10y^2 + 4 = x^2$ ← add 4 to both sides of the given equation to get this

(D) $5y^2 = x^2 - 2$ ← If the original equation is divided by 2, we get

$$5y^2 = \frac{x^2}{2} - 4.$$

D cannot be the same. STOP!

(E) $y^2 = \dfrac{x^2 - 4}{10}$ ← divide both sides of the given equation by 10 to get this

The correct answer is (D).

PS 38. <u>Word Problems</u>: Rates & Work
Difficulty: Medium **OG Page:** 157

To solve this ***Rates & Work*** problem, we will use ***Direct Algebra***.

First, we need the ***Rate-Time-Distance Formula***, which can be written this way:

$$\text{Rate} = \frac{\text{Distance}}{\text{Time}}$$

Juan's rate for running y yards is:

$$\text{Rate} = \frac{y \text{ yards}}{11 \text{ seconds}}$$

Let's now ***Name a Variable***. Using t to represent the seconds it takes to run x yards, we can express the second rate this way:

$$\text{Rate} = \frac{x \text{ yards}}{t \text{ seconds}}$$

Because both rates are the same, we can set these two expressions equal to each other:

$$\text{Rate} = \frac{y}{11} = \frac{x}{t}$$

Finally, we can solve for time t by ***Cross-Multiplying*** the equation and then dividing by y:

$$yt = 11x$$

$$t = \frac{11x}{y}$$ This is the **answer**.

Alternatively, we can ***Choose Smart Numbers***. Let's pick $y = 22$ and $x = 44$. If Juan can run 22 yards in 11 seconds, then he can run 44 yards in 22 seconds. Our ***Target Value*** is 22. Note: normally we do not want to select multiples for the unknowns. However, these values make it easy to calculate the rates. Now ***Find a Match*** in the answer choices.

(A) $\frac{11x}{y} = \frac{(11)(44)}{(22)} = 22$ **CORRECT**

(B) $\frac{11y}{x} = \frac{(11)(22)}{(44)} = \frac{11}{2}$ INCORRECT

(C) $\frac{x}{11y} = \frac{(44)}{(11)(22)} = \frac{2}{11}$ INCORRECT

(D) $\frac{11}{xy} = \frac{11}{(44)(22)} = \frac{1}{88}$ INCORRECT

(E) $\frac{xy}{11} = \frac{(44)(22)}{11} = 88$ INCORRECT

The correct answer is (A).

PS 39. <u>Word Problems</u>: Extra Problem Types
Difficulty: Easy **OG Page:** 157

The problem specifies that John has 10 pairs of matched socks, or 20 individual socks. He loses 7 individual socks. Therefore, he keeps 13 socks. We are asked to determine the maximum number of matching pairs of socks he can still have.

Often, in ***Optimization*** problems, finding the *maximum* of one quantity entails finding the *minimum* of some other quantity. In this particular problem, if we want to maximize the number of matching pairs remaining, we need to minimize the number of different pairs from which he loses a sock.

In other words, we want John still to have the *most* matching pairs after he loses 7 socks from his 10 pairs. Therefore, we want him to lose the *fewest* matching pairs. Let's imagine that when John loses one sock, he also loses that sock's mate, until he has no socks left to lose.

Now list John's sock pairs in a quick ***Table***:

Pair #	Any lost?
1	2 lost
2	2 lost
3	2 lost
4	1 lost, 1 not lost
5	Neither lost
6	Neither lost
7	Neither lost
8	Neither lost
9	Neither lost
10	Neither lost

John lost 3 matching pairs and 1 sock from a 4th pair. Thus, the maximum number of matched pairs John can have left is 6.

The correct answer is (B).

PS 40. <u>Number Properties</u>: Divisibility & Primes
Difficulty: Medium **OG Page:** 157

The "lowest positive integer that is divisible" by several numbers is the ***Least Common Multiple***, or LCM, of those numbers.

One easy way to find the LCM of several small numbers is to construct the LCM one step at a time, starting with just two of the numbers.

The LCM of 1 and 2 is 2.
The LCM of 1, 2, and 3 is $2 \times 3 = 6$.
The LCM of 1, 2, 3, and 4 is *not* $2 \times 3 \times 4 = 24$.

Note that $4 = 2 \times 2$ and that we already have one factor of 2 in the previous product, which was 6. Thus, we only need to put in one more factor of 2.

Thus, the LCM of 1, 2, 3, and 4 is $2 \times 3 \times 2 = 12$.
The LCM of 1, 2, 3, 4, and 5 is $2 \times 3 \times 2 \times 5 = 60$.

The LCM of 1, 2, 3, 4, 5, and 6 is still 60, since 60 is divisible by 6. All the ***Prime Factors*** of 6 are already accounted for in $2 \times 3 \times 2 \times 5 = 60$.

Finally, the LCM of 1, 2, 3, 4, 5, 6, and 7 is $2 \times 3 \times 2 \times 5 \times 7 = 60 \times 7 = 420$. This is the **answer**.

Note that if we merely multiply all of the integers from 1 to 7 inclusive we obtain 7!, or 5040, given in choice (E). However, in doing so, we neglect to eliminate duplicate factors.

The correct answer is (A).

PS 41. FDPs: Fractions
Difficulty: Easy **OG Page:** 157

We can use ***Fraction-Decimal Equivalents*** to change this expression into one involving fractions. Specifically, 0.75 equals the fraction 3/4. Make a ***Common Denominator*** by converting 1 to 4/4, as shown below:

$$\frac{1}{\frac{3}{4}-1}=\frac{1}{\frac{3}{4}-\frac{4}{4}}$$

Proceed by subtracting the two fractions in the denominator of the larger fraction. Finally, multiply the numerator by the ***Reciprocal*** of the denominator.

$$\frac{1}{\frac{3}{4}-\frac{4}{4}}=\frac{1}{\frac{-1}{4}}=1\times\left(\frac{4}{-1}\right)=-4$$

This is the **answer.**

Alternatively, we can multiply the top and bottom of $\frac{1}{\frac{3}{4}-\frac{4}{4}}$ by the common denominator of the smaller fractions, which is 4. If we do so, we can get to the right answer as well:

$$\frac{1}{\frac{3}{4}-\frac{4}{4}}\times\frac{4}{4}=\frac{4}{3-4}=\frac{4}{-1}=-4$$

Starting with the original stem, $\frac{1}{0.75-1}$, we can perform a decimal computation to yield 1/(–0.25).

Using fraction-decimal equivalents (0.25 = 1/4) or by moving decimal points (1/0.25 = 100/25), we can reduce 1/(–0.25) to –4.

The correct answer is (A).

PS 42. Algebra: Linear Equations
Difficulty: Easy **OG Page:** 157

To solve this ***Linear Equations*** problem, we can use ***Direct Algebra.***

First, ***Cross-multiply.*** Then we can solve for x:

$$\frac{1.5}{0.2+x}=5$$

$$1.5=5(0.2+x)$$

$$1.5=1+5x$$ Don't forget to distribute the 5.

$$0.5=5x$$

$$0.1=x$$

This is the **answer.**

Alternatively, we could look at this problem intuitively. If the fraction on the left side of the given equation is equal to 5, the denominator must be 1/5 of the numerator, or 0.3. Therefore, x must be 0.1 to make the sum $(0.2 + x)$ equal to 1/5 of 1.5.

The correct answer is (B).

PS 43. Geometry: Coordinate Plane
Difficulty: Easy **OG Page:** 158

This ***Coordinate Plane*** question asks us to find the point on segment PQ that is twice as far from P as from Q. The ***Slope of a Line*** describes the relationship between any two points on the line (rise/run) and can be used to find one point from another on the line. By knowing two points on the line, we can calculate the slope of the line segment.

Point Q lies at (3, 2) and point P lies at (0, –1). The slope of $PQ=\frac{2-(-1)}{3-0}=1$. This means that we can travel up 1 and over to the right 1 to find points between P and Q. One iteration of the "slope-step" from P brings us to the point (1, 0), two iterations brings us to the point (2, 1), and three iterations brings us to the point Q (3, 2).

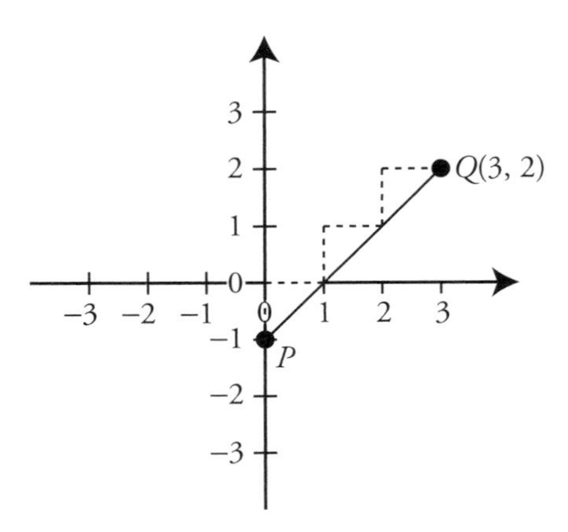

The point twice as far from P as from Q is two steps up from P and one step down from Q. The point we find is (2, 1). This is the **answer**.

Alternatively, since PQ is a straight line segment, we can solve the problem by looking at x and y separately. First, focus on the horizontal dimension (left-right position) and ask what x-coordinate is twice as far from P's x-coordinate (0) as from Q's x-coordinate (3). In other words, what number between 0 and 3 is twice as far from 0 as from 3? The answer is 2.

In a similar fashion, we now focus on the vertical dimension (up-down position) and ask what y-coordinate is twice as far from P's y-coordinate (−1) as from Q's y-coordinate (2). In other words, what number between −1 and 2 is twice as far from −1 as from 2? The answer is 1. Putting these two answers together, we get the point (2, 1).

The correct answer is (B).

PS 44. Number Properties: Odds & Evens
Difficulty: Easy **OG Page:** 158

We are told that n is an integer and then asked which of the given terms must be even. The key word in this ***Odds & Evens*** problem is "must." The correct choice will be an even integer in every possible case, whether or not n itself is even.

A quick scan might reveal the answer right away, if we recognize ***Algebraic Forms of Odds & Evens***. The expression $2n$ means 2 times n. Any integer, when multiplied by an even integer, will result in an even integer. Since 2 is even, $2n$ will be even in all cases. In fact, the general way to represent a random even integer is $2n$ (using n to represent any integer). So $2n$ is the **answer**.

Alternatively, we can use ***Arithmetic Rules of Odds and Evens.*** To test both n = odd and n = even, make a ***Table***:

Answer Choice	n = even	n = odd
$n + 1$	E + 1 = O	O + 1 = E
$n + 2$	E + 2 = E	O + 2 = O
$2n$	2(E) = E	2(O) = E
$2n + 1$	2(E) + 1 = O	2(O) + 1 = O
n^2	(E)(E) = E	(O)(O) = O

The only answer choice that always yields an even is the third choice, $2n$.

Finally, we can also ***Test Numbers***. We must be sure to test both an odd number and an even number for n. If we test both $n = 3$ and $n = 4$, we will see that only $2n$ yields an even number in both cases.

The correct answer is (C).

PS 45. Algebra: Quadratic Equations
Difficulty: Medium **OG Page:** 158

The most direct way to tackle this ***Quadratic Equations*** problem is to plug 4 into the equation (since 4 is given as a solution value for x) and solve for the variable k:

$$(4)^2 + (3)(4) + k = 10$$
$$16 + 12 + k = 10$$
$$28 + k = 10$$
$$k = -18$$

Since $k = -18$, the original equation can now be solved as follows:

$$x^2 + 3x - 18 = 10$$
$$x^2 + 3x - 28 = 0$$
$$(x - 4)(x + 7) = 0$$
$$x = 4 \text{ or } x = -7$$

We know that we can ***Factor the Quadratic*** into $(x - 4)(x + 7)$ because we need two numbers that add to 3 but multiply to -28. Since 4 was the solution given in the problem, the solution the question seeks is -7. This is the **answer**.

Alternatively, we might spot another path to the answer by applying ***Properties of Quadratics***. First, subtract 10 from both sides of the original equation: $x^2 + 3x + (k - 10) = 0$. Since the 4 is given as a solution to the equation, we know that this quadratic will factor into $(x - 4)(x \pm ?)$. Since the middle coefficient of the quadratic is 3, we know that the two numbers in the parentheses above, -4 and the question mark, must sum to 3. (The two numbers in the parentheses always sum to the middle coefficient of a quadratic, as we can show by ***FOIL***ing the product.)

We need a number which will yield 3 when added to -4: this number turns out to be 7. Therefore, we can factor the quadratic as $(x - 4)(x + 7)$, and the second value of x must be -7.

The correct answer is (A).

PS 46. FDPs: Fractions
Difficulty: Easy **OG Page:** 158

In this ***Fractions*** problem, it is not necessary to find a common denominator and add 7/8 and 1/9—instead, note that the answers are expressed in ranges. Thus, we can solve the problem with efficient ***Estimation***.

7/8 is close to 1. In fact, 7/8 would actually *be* 1 if it weren't missing precisely 1/8. If adding 1/8 to 7/8 would produce 1, then adding 1/9 (which is smaller than 1/8) to 7/8 will produce something slightly less than 1. At the same time, the result must be larger than 7/8, since we are adding a positive number to 7/8.

Only one answer choice offers a range that includes values between 7/8 and 1.

The correct answer is (B).

PS 47. Algebra: Linear Equations
Difficulty: Easy **OG Page:** 158

In this ***Linear Equations*** problem, we are trying to find the value of t for which $x = y$. Since we know x in terms of t, and we also know y in terms of t, we can set the two expressions equal to each other and solve for t.

$x = 1 - 3t \quad y = 2t - 1$

$1 - 3t = 2t - 1$	Set x equal to y.
$1 - 5t = -1$	Subtract $2t$ from both sides.
$-5t = -2$	Subtract 1 from both sides.
$t = \frac{-2}{-5} = \frac{2}{5}$	Divide both sides by -5.

2/5 is the **answer**.

Alternatively, ***Work Backwards from the Answers***, but in this case, the technique is slower and more prone to error.

The correct answer is (D).

PS 48. FDPs: Fractions
Difficulty: Easy **OG Page:** 158

This ***Fractions*** problem asks us to subtract several quantities. In order to perform the calculation correctly, we need to follow the ***Order of Operations***, which we can remember using the acronym ***PEMDAS***. In the context of this problem, PEMDAS means that we have to perform the operation inside the Parentheses (which happens to be a subtraction) before doing the first Subtraction.

Begin with the portion inside the parentheses. First, manipulate each fraction to get a ***Common Denominator***. Once that is done, subtract the numerators.

$$\frac{1}{2} - \frac{2}{3} = \frac{3}{6} - \frac{4}{6} = \frac{-1}{6} = -\frac{1}{6}$$

Next, insert the result from above into the full equation. Don't forget about the negative sign, and remember that subtracting a negative number is equivalent to adding a positive number.

$$1-\left(-\frac{1}{6}\right)=1+\frac{1}{6}=\frac{6}{6}+\frac{1}{6}=\frac{7}{6}$$

The correct answer is (B).

PS 49. Word Problems: Rates & Work
Difficulty: Medium **OG Page:** 158

We are given that Car X gets 25.0 miles per gallon of gas and Car Y gets 11.9 miles per gallon of gas. We are also given that both cars are driven 12,000 miles. The question asks *approximately* (this word is a hint to round the numbers) how many more gallons of gas Car Y will use than Car X.

This is a ***Rates & Work*** problem with a twist. Instead of miles per hour, we are given miles per gallon. The basic rate equation is still the key to solving this problem, but we need to change it to reflect the fact that our rate is expressed as miles per gallon, NOT miles per hour.

D	=	R	×	T
(miles)	=	$\left(\frac{\text{miles}}{\text{hour}}\right)$	×	(hours)

becomes

D	=	R	×	G
(miles)	=	$\left(\frac{\text{miles}}{\text{gallon}}\right)$	×	(gallons)

in order to take into account the fact that we need to calculate the number of gallons required by Car Y and by Car X. A ***Table*** will help keep everything organized, and we can introduce the variables x and y as placeholders for the number of gallons used by Cars X and Y.

	D	=	R	×	G
Car X	12,000	=	25	×	x
Car Y	12,000	=	11.9	×	y

Looking at the numbers in the table, we should round 11.9 to 12 (the problem did say *approximately*) to make the arithmetic easier.

$$y=\frac{12{,}000}{12}=1{,}000$$

and

$$x=\frac{12{,}000}{25}=\frac{120\times 100}{25}=120\times 4=480$$

Car Y used approximately 1,000 gallons of gas and Car X used approximately 480 gallons.

1,000 – 480 – 520.

The correct answer is (C).

PS 50. Algebra: Inequalities
Difficulty: Medium **OG Page:** 158

When manipulating ***Compound Inequalities,*** we must perform ***Direct Algebra*** on *every term* of the inequality. Begin by subtracting 5 from each term in the inequality to isolate $5n$:

$$1 < 5n + 5 < 25$$
$$-4 < 5n < 20$$

Divide all of the terms by 5 to isolate n:

$$-\frac{4}{5}<\frac{5n}{5}<\frac{20}{5}$$
$$-\frac{4}{5}<n<4$$

Since n must be an integer, n can be 0, 1, 2 or 3, so there are four possible integers. This is the **answer**.

The method above is the surest and quickest path to the goal. Alternatively, we can ***Test Scenarios,*** plugging various integer values into the original inequality to see how many integers satisfy the inequality. If we start with $n = 0$, the center expression becomes 5(0) + 5 = 5, which is both greater than 1 and less than 25. Since this value is greater than 1, we should try $n = -1$ to make sure that zero is the smallest value of n that works. –1 turns the center expression to 0, which is NOT greater than 1.

In this way we can continue testing increasingly larger values for n until the value of the center expression is no longer less than 25. We find that n values of 0, 1, 2 and 3 all work. However, this method takes more time, and we also run the risk of missing values or over-including values at either end of the defined range.

The correct answer is (B).

PS 51. Number Properties: Positives & Negatives
Difficulty: Medium **OG Page:** 159

At first, we might be tempted to say that the least possible value for the given ***Absolute Value*** is 3. This seems sensible enough because when $y = 4$, then $5y = 20$, and $23 - 5y = 23 - 20 = 3$. Certainly, if y is anything less than 4, then $5y$ will be less than 20, and the absolute value will be larger than 3.

However, what happens when y is an integer larger than 4? When $y = 5$, then $5y = 25$, and $23 - 5y = 23 - 25 = -2$. Now, -2 has an absolute value of 2, which is *less* than 3. We can test larger values for y, but the absolute value of the outcome will grow. For instance, if $y = 6$, then $|23 - 5y| = |23 - 5(6)| = |23 - 30| = |-7| = 7$, which is larger than 2.

As a result, when y is 5, we minimize the absolute value of $23 - 5y$. This minimum value, 2, is the **answer**.

We should expect tricks with absolute values. After all, absolute value converts negatives to positives. When we see absolute values, we need to be aware of ***Negative Possibilities.*** At the very least, we should examine the first y value that makes the term inside the absolute value negative, just to see what happens. This y value, 5, leads us to the answer, which is 2.

We could also look at this problem from the perspective of ***Divisibility.*** "$5y$," where y is an integer, just means "some multiple of 5." We are looking for the multiple of 5 that, when subtracted from 23, leaves the lowest possible absolute value.

Absolute value expresses distance on a number line. So we are looking for the multiple of 5 that is closest to 23. This turns out to be the fifth multiple of 5, or 25. When $y = 5$, the distance between 23 and $5y$ will be as small as possible: 2.

Finally, remember to answer the right question. The question is not which value of y leads to the smallest absolute value, *but what that smallest absolute value is.*

The correct answer is (B).

PS 52. Algebra: Exponents & Roots
Difficulty: Easy **OG Page:** 159

This problem asks us to find the ***Sum of Roots.***

Because $\sqrt{80}$ and $\sqrt{125}$ do not have the same number underneath the root symbol, we cannot directly add them together. However, we can ***Simplify Each Root,*** decreasing the number that remains under the radical.

First, express the number under the radical as the product of ***Prime Factors.*** Because pairs of factors under the radical form a perfect square, we can take that factor outside the radical.

$$\sqrt{80} = \sqrt{\underline{2\times 2}\times \underline{2\times 2}\times 5} = 2\times 2\times \sqrt{5} = 4\sqrt{5}$$
$$\sqrt{125} = \sqrt{\underline{5\times 5}\times 5} = 5\times \sqrt{5} = 5\sqrt{5}$$

We can now add the two terms together because they contain the same root:

$4\sqrt{5} + 5\sqrt{5} = 9\sqrt{5}$ This is the **answer**.

As an alternative, we can ***Estimate*** the answer. $\sqrt{80}$ is just under $9(=\sqrt{81})$, and $\sqrt{125}$ is just over $11\ (=\sqrt{121})$. Thus, the sum we are looking for is approximately 20.

Among the answer choices, we see $\sqrt{5}$, which is a little more than $2(=\sqrt{4})$, and $\sqrt{205}$, which is between $14(=\sqrt{196})$ and $15(=\sqrt{225})$.

Only answer choice (A) is close to 20, since $9\sqrt{5} \approx 9(2) = 18$, rounding down.

The correct answer is (A).

PS 53. Word Problems: Statistics
Difficulty: Easy **OG Page:** 159

The most straightforward way to solve this problem is to use the ***Average Formula:***

$$\text{Average} = \frac{\text{Sum}}{\text{Number of Data Points}}$$

We are seeking an unknown quantity. Let's ***Name a Variable*** and call that unknown quantity x.

Translate to turn the question into the following equation:

$$\frac{10+30+50}{3} = \frac{20+40+x}{3} + 5$$

Multiply both sides by 3:

$10 + 30 + 50 = 20 + 40 + x + 15$
$90 = 75 + x$.

Hence $x = 15$. This is the **answer.**

Notice that the first average is 5 more than the other average. This is not the same as saying that the *sum* of the first set of numbers is 5 more than the other sum. If we had made this mistake, we would have picked 25 as the answer.

The correct answer is (A).

PS 54. Algebra: Linear Equations
Difficulty: Easy **OG Page:** 159

In this ***Linear Equations*** problem, we are told that $y = kx + 3$, where k is a constant. In other words, x and y can vary, but k is always the same. Although we do not know the value of k, in this circumstance k is *not* a variable. Rather, k is an ***Unknown Constant.***

We know from the question that when $x = 2$, $y = 17$. Having a set of values for x and y allows us to determine the unknown constant k. Plug these values into the given equation and solve for k:

$y = kx + 3$
$(17) = (2)k + 3$
$14 = 2k$
$7 = k$

Now we know that $y = 7x + 3$.

Thus, when $x = 4$, $y = 7(4) + 3 = 28 + 3 = 31$.

The correct answer is (B).

PS 55. Algebra: Linear Equations
Difficulty: Easy **OG Page:** 159

This difficult ***Linear Equations*** problem asks for the number of green marbles in Jar R. We are therefore looking for the value of z. We can use the information in each row to create an equation corresponding to each jar:

Jar P: $x + y = 180$ [1]
Jar Q: $y + z = 120$ [2]
Jar R: $x + z = 160$ [3]

In general, systems of three equations and three unknows are painful to solve, but the GMAT tends to keep the work under control. We should look for shortcuts or ***Symmetries*** in the form of the equations to reduce the number of steps needed to solve.

In the given table of equations, we can see that x, y, and z each appear two times. Therefore, we can save time by ***Combining Equations.***

If we add our original three equations, we obtain $2x + 2y + 2z = 360$. Divide both sides by 2 and obtain $x + y + z = 180$. Now, since Equation [1] tells us that $x + y = 80$, we can substitute 80 for the ***Combined Expression*** $x + y$ in our equation:

$(x + y) + z = 180$
$80 + z = 180$
$z = 100$ This is the **answer.**

Alternatively, we can always utilize ***Substitution and Combination.*** Ultimately we need the value of z, so let's first isolate one of the variables in Equation [1] and substitute it into another equation. For example, we can solve for y in Equation [1]: $y = 80 - x$.

Now replace y in Equation [2] with $80 - x$: $(80 - x) + z = 120$. Subtract 80 from both sides, obtaining $-x + z = 40$. We'll call this equation [4].

Now we can see that combining Equations [3] and [4] using addition would cause the x terms to cancel, leaving an equation with only z:

$$\begin{array}{rll} x + z = 160 & [3] & \\ + \quad (-x + z) = 40 & [4] & \\ \hline 2z = 200 & & \text{Divide by 2} \\ z = 100 & & \end{array}$$

The correct answer is (D).

PS 56. <u>FDPs</u>: Ratios
Difficulty: Medium **OG Page:** 159

We know that this is a ***Ratios*** problem because the time worked by the different staffers is given as a ratio. The "CANNOT be" tells us that four of the answers could be the total number of hours worked by the four staffers, so we need to figure out the four answers that could be the total number of hours and eliminate them.

Since there are four different staffers, there are four possibilities for the staffer who worked 30 hours. A straightforward way to solve is just to try each possibility for the staffer who worked 30 hours and see what the total number of hours worked would be. This is not too difficult because we have just one giant ratio, 2 : 3 : 5 : 6, and all of the times in the ratio divide evenly into 30 hours.

Assume the first staffer worked 30 hours. Since $30/2 = 15$, multiply each number in the ratio by 15 in order to keep the ratio the same. To save time, just multiply $(2 + 3 + 5 + 6)$ by 15 rather than multiplying each staffer's hours by 15 separately (correct but slow) because we know that:

$$15 \times 2 + 15 \times 3 + 15 \times 5 + 15 \times 6 =$$
$$15 \times (2 + 3 + 5 + 6) = 15 \times 16$$

We can use this trick for the entire problem in order to reduce the tedious (and error prone) computation.

staffer who worked 30 hours	multiplier	total hours worked
1st	$30/2 = 15$	$15 \times 16 = 240$
2nd	$30/3 = 10$	$10 \times 16 = 160$
3rd	$30/5 = 6$	$6 \times 16 = 96$
4th	$30/6 = 5$	$5 \times 16 = 80$

The correct answer cannot be 240, 160, 96, or 180 because those are possible numbers of hours. The only remaining answer is 192 hours.

The correct answer is (D).

PS 57. <u>FDPs</u>: Percent
Difficulty: Medium **OG Page:** 159

We are given that Company P had 15 percent more employees in December than it had in January and that it had 460 employees in December. We are asked how many employees it had in January.

To solve this ***Percents*** problem, ***Translate*** the information and solve. If Company P had 15 percent more employees in December than in January, then the number of employees in December is 115% of the number of employees in January.

$$(\text{December}) = 1.15 \times (\text{January})$$

The number of employees in December was 460. Let x represent the number of employees in January:

$$460 = 1.15x$$

Divide both sides by 1.15 and perform long division. Remember that 460/1.15 is the same as 46,000/115:

$$\begin{array}{r} 400 \\ 115\overline{)46{,}000} \\ \underline{460} \\ 0 \end{array}$$

There were 400 employees in January.

The correct answer is (B).

PS 58. FDPs: Percents
Difficulty: Medium **OG Page:** 160

We begin with 10 ounces of water. However, we lose 0.01 ounces per day for 20 days, for a total loss of $0.01 \times 20 = 0.2$ ounces. We must now determine a ***Percent Change:*** what percent of the original amount was lost in total. In other words, 0.2 is what percent of 10?

Translate the question into an equation and solve for what (x):

$$0.2 = \frac{x}{100} \times 10$$
$$20 = 10x$$
$$2 = x$$

The correct answer is (D).

PS 59. FDPs: Percents
Difficulty: Medium **OG Page:** 160

If the solution contains 15 grams of glucose per 100 cubic centimeters of solution, then the ***Ratio*** of glucose to solution is $\frac{15}{100} = \frac{3}{20}$.
We can ***Name a Variable*** to represent the grams of glucose in 45 cubic centimeters of solution. Let's call this amount x.

To determine x, we can now set up a ***Proportion*** and ***Cross-Multiply***:

$$\frac{3}{20} = \frac{x}{45}$$
$$135 = 20x$$
$$\frac{135}{20} = x$$
$$\frac{27}{4} = x$$
$x = 6.75$ This is the **answer.**

Alternatively, we could express the concentration of glucose as a ***Percent***. The algebra works essentially the same way as above.

The correct answer is (E).

PS 60. Word Problems: Algebraic Translations
Difficulty: Hard **OG Page:** 160

This is a very wordy problem, which makes it challenging to extract the given information. Use a ***Chart*** to help translate this ***Algebraic Translations*** problem.

The first sentence tells us that there are two days, and that an equal amount of orange juice and water are mixed to make orangeade on the first day and that the same amount of juice is mixed with twice as much water on the second day. The next sentence tells us that all of the orangeade made on both days was sold, so we need to track the total amount of orangeade. ***Name a Variable***, j, to represent the amount of orange juice used.

Day	amount of orange juice	+	amount of water	=	amount of orangeade
1	j	+	j	=	$2j$
2	j	+	$2j$	=	$3j$

The next piece of information that we are given is that the revenue from selling the orangeade was the same for both days and that the price per glass on day 1 was $0.60. The question asks for the price per glass on the second day.

Although we don't know the number of glasses of orangeade made, we do know the formula for total revenue:

Total Revenue = Price per Item × Number of Items

We can use this relationship to create two equations: one for day 1 and one for day 2. Remember that the revenue was the same for both days, so let x represent total revenue. We don't know the exact number of glasses sold on day 1 or the exact number of glasses sold on day 2, but we do know the total amount of orangeade sold on both days. We can use $2j$ to represent the number of items sold on day 1, and $3j$ to represent the number of items sold on day 2. Finally, let p represent the price per glass on day 2:

$x = 0.60 \times 2j$ Day 1

$x = p \times 3j$ Day 2

Because the revenues are the same, we can set $0.60 \times 2j$ equal to $p \times 3j$:

$$0.60 \times 2j = p \times 3j$$
$$1.2j = 3pj \quad \text{Divide both sides by } j$$
$$1.2 = 3p$$
$$0.4 = p$$

On day 2, each glass of orangeade sold for \$0.40. This is the **answer.**

Another way to solve this problem would have been to use ***Ratios***. The ratio of the amount of orangeade sold on Day 1 to the amount of orangeade sold on day 2 is $2j : 3j$, or 2 : 3. Since the revenues were the same, and the ratio of the number of glasses of orangeade sold was 2 : 3, the ratio of the prices per glass of orangeade had to be the inverse of 2 : 3, or 3 : 2.

$$\frac{3}{2} = \frac{0.60}{p}$$
$$3p = 1.2$$
$$p = 0.4$$

The correct answer is (D).

PS 61. Geometry: Coordinate Plane
Difficulty: Easy **OG Page:** 160

We are given a line and asked for the ***Slope***.

This is a ***Coordinate Plane*** problem. The best way to solve this problem is to put the equation into ***Slope-Intercept form***, which we can use to find the slope.

Slope-intercept form:

$$y = mx + b$$

In this form of the equation, m is the slope and b is the ***y-intercept***. Put the original equation into slope-intercept form by isolating y on one side of the equation.

$$3x + 7y = 9$$
$$7y = -3x + 9$$
$$y = -\frac{3}{7}x + \frac{9}{7}$$

x is multiplied by −3/7, which means that the slope of the line is −3/7.

The correct answer is (B).

PS 62. Geometry: Lines & Angles
Difficulty: Easy **OG Page:** 160

We can look at a parallelogram as a pair of ***Parallel Lines*** intersected by another pair of parallel lines. Redraw the diagram, extending the lines past the corners of the parallelogram.

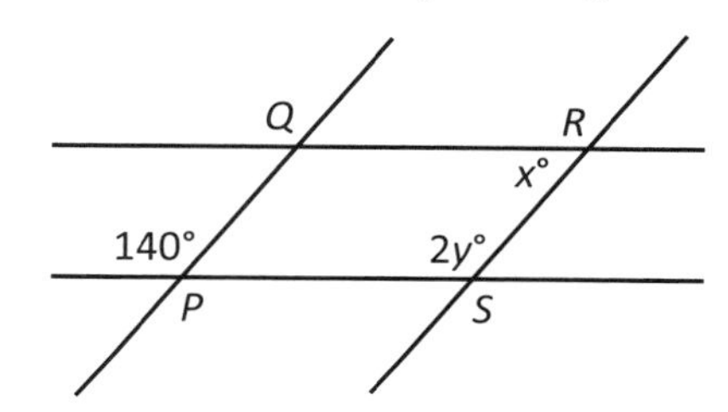

Remember that if we cross two parallel lines with another line (called a *transversal*), then we create equal angles. The acute angles (smaller than 90 degrees) will all be the same, and the obtuse angles (larger than 90 degrees) will all be the same as well. As a result, the corresponding acute angles inside or bordering a parallelogram will all be equal. The same is true for corresponding obtuse angles inside or bordering a parallelogram.

In this case, the angle labeled $2y°$ corresponds to the angle labeled 140°. Because corresponding angles are equal, $2y = 140$. Thus, $y = 70$.

Moreover, in the diagram above, any acute angle plus any obtuse angle equals 180°. This is because we can always put one of the acute angles next to one of the obtuse angles and form a ***Straight Line:***

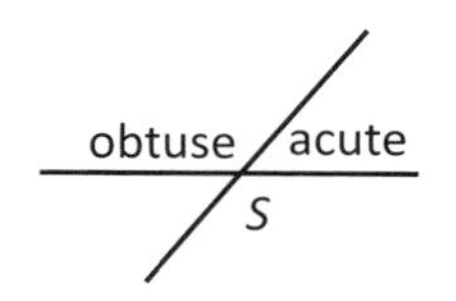

Thus, we know that x and $2y$ sum to 180:

$$x + 2y = 180$$
$$x + 2(70) = 180$$
$$x + 140 = 180$$
$$x = 40$$

Alternatively, we could have used the fact that ***Adjacent Angles of a Parallelogram*** add up to 180°, if we remembered that fact.

Either way, the desired answer is given by

$$y - x = 70 - 40 = 30$$

The correct answer is (A).

PS 63. FDPs: Ratios
Difficulty: Medium **OG Page:** 160

A ***Proportion*** will solve this ***Ratios*** problem most efficiently:

$$\frac{1\,\text{km}}{0.6\,\text{miles}} = \frac{x\,\text{km}}{2\,\text{miles}}$$

Note that it is helpful to label units when setting up a proportion to insure that the proportion is correct. However, once we have set up the proportion, it is often easier to drop the units.

Cross-multiply: $2 = 0.6x$

Since the answer choices are given in fraction form, multiply both sides of the equation by 10 to eliminate the decimal:

$$20 = 6x$$

Divide by 6: $\frac{20}{6} = x$

Simplify the fraction: $\frac{10}{3} = x$

The correct answer is (A).

PS 64. Word Problems: Algebraic Translations
Difficulty: Medium **OG Page:** 161

The first sentence tells us that apples cost \$0.70 each and bananas cost \$0.50 each. The second sentence tells us that a customer purchased both apples and bananas and spent a total of \$6.30. The question then asks us for the total number of apples and bananas purchased.

This ***Algebraic Translation*** problem is tricky because we have two variables, call them a and b, for the number of apples and bananas respectively, but we are only given enough information to write one equation:

$$0.70a + 0.50b = 6.30$$

We can multiply both sides by 10 and re-write that equation in order to simplify the numbers, but we still have only one equation:

$$7a + 5b = 63$$

The key to getting around this impasse is realizing that the question contains an ***Integer Constraint***. We know that the values of a and b must be integers. Although this might seem like a minor detail, it actually greatly restricts the possible values of a and b. This constraint will allow us to solve for a unique number of pieces of fruit.

The way to solve this problem is to start listing out the possibilities and stop as soon as we find one that works because only one answer can be the correct one. We'll have fewer possibilities to consider if we start with the higher priced item, apples in this case, and then figure out if an integer number of bananas could be bought with the money remaining after that many apples were bought.

Remember that the problem also explicitly tells us that the customer purchased apples and bananas, which means that neither a nor b can be 0. Thus, we can eliminate the possibility that the customer bought 9 apples and 0 bananas.

# apples	Cost of apples	Amount remaining to purchase bananas	# bananas
1	7	63 – 7 = 56	56 is NOT divisible by 5
2	14	56 – 7 = 49	49 is NOT divisible by 5

3	21	$49 - 7 = 42$	42 is NOT divisible by 5
4	28	$42 - 7 = 35$	35 IS divisible by 5, so 7 bananas

So 4 apples for $2.80 and 7 bananas for $3.50 works out to 11 pieces of fruit for $6.30.

The correct answer is (B).

PS 65. <u>FDPs</u>: Digits & Decimals
Difficulty: Hard **OG Page:** 161

A distance is given in inches. This ***Digits & Decimals*** problem asks us for the equivalent distance in kilometers.

To avoid changing the value, we must multiply the given distance by 1. If 1 kilometer is approximately 3.9×10^4 inches, then $\frac{1 \text{ kilometer}}{3.9 \times 10^4 \text{ inches}} = 1$. This fraction is called a ***Conversion Factor***.

Now, multiply the given distance by the conversion factor. Be sure to set up the conversion factor correctly. Since we are given a quantity in inches, put inches in the denominator and cancel:

$$2.3 \times 10^{14} \text{ in} \times \left(\frac{1 \text{km}}{3.9 \times 10^4 \text{ in}}\right) = \frac{2.3 \times 10^{14}}{3.9 \times 10^4} \text{km}$$

Cancel *Powers of Ten* $= \left(\frac{2.3}{3.9}\right)\left(\frac{10^{14}}{10^4}\right) \text{km}$

$$= \left(\frac{2.3}{3.9}\right) \times 10^{10} \text{ km}$$

$$= \left(\frac{23}{39}\right) \times 10^{10} \text{ km}$$

Use *Estimation* $\approx \left(\frac{24}{40}\right) \times 10^{10} \text{ km}$

$$= \left(\frac{6}{10}\right) \times 10^{10} \text{km}$$

$$= 6 \times 10^9 \text{ km}$$

The closest answer choice is 5.9×10^9. This is the **answer**.

Approximating is effective on this problem because the values given in the answer choices are spread out.

Alternatively, we could set up ***Proportions***:

$$\frac{x \text{ km}}{2.3 \times 10^{14} \text{ in}} = \frac{1 \text{km}}{3.9 \times 10^4 \text{ in}}$$

Then ***Cross-Multiply*** and solve as above.

The correct answer is (B).

PS 66. <u>FDPs</u>: Ratios
Difficulty: Medium **OG Page:** 161

The first sentence of this rather wordy problem tells us that the Ratio of 2nd graders to 4th graders is 8 to 5, and the ratio of 1st graders to 2nd graders is 3 to 4. The second sentence tells us that the ratio of 3rd graders to 4th graders is 3 to 2. We are then asked what the ratio of 1st graders to 3rd graders is.

We need an easy way to combine these ratios. If the ratio only involved two different grades, we might use variables to help answer the question. Because the ratio involves 4 different grades, using variables will generally just make this kind of problem harder. Instead, we can put all of the information into a ***Table*** and then use that table to merge the ratios by finding common terms.

1st	:	2nd	:	3rd	:	4th
		8			:	5
3	:	4				
				3	:	2

The next step is to start "merging" the rows, by multiplying the ratios in order to get the numbers in each column to match up. This works because ratios can be thought of as fractions, and it does not change the value of the fraction to multiply both the numerator and the denominator by the same number. For instance, the ratio of 8 to 5 is exactly the same as the ratio of 16 to 10.

1st	:	2nd	:	3rd	:	4th
		$8 \times 2 = 16$			:	$5 \times 2 = 10$
$3 \times 4 = 12$	:	$4 \times 4 = 16$				
				$3 \times 5 = 15$	:	$2 \times 5 = 10$

We can now write the entire ratio as:

1st	:	2nd	:	3rd	:	4th
12	:	16	:	15	:	10

The ratio of 1st graders to 3rd graders is 12 : 15, which reduces to 4 : 5.

The correct answer is (E).

PS 67. Word Problems: Consecutive Integers
Difficulty: Easy **OG Page:** 161

In an ***Evenly-Spaced Set,*** the ***Mean*** and the ***Median*** will always be the same. Since the multiples of any integer are evenly spaced (in this case, by 5), it must be true that $m = M$. Thus, $M - m$ must equal 0. This is the **answer**.

Alternatively, we can handle this question by ***Direct Computation.*** List out the first 10 positive multiples of 5: 5, 10, 15, 20, 25, 30, 35, 40, 45, 50.

Since these numbers are evenly spaced, the average of the whole set will be the average of the smallest and largest terms in the set. Use the ***Average Formula.*** $(5 + 50)/2 = 55/2 = 27.5$. Therefore, $m = 27.5$.

Since we have an even number of terms in the set, the median of the set will be the average of the two middle terms: $(25 + 30)/2 = 55/2 = 27.5$. Therefore, $M = 27.5$.

$M - m = 27.5 - 27.5 = 0$.

The correct answer is (B).

PS 68. Number Properties: Probability
Difficulty: Medium **OG Page:** 161

We can solve this problem by either of the two fundamental approaches to probability: by the basic formula or by combining probabilities of component events.

We can use the ***Basic Probability Formula***, $\text{Probability} = \frac{\text{\# of successful outcomes}}{\text{total \# of outcomes}}$, as long as we are careful to define "outcomes" so that they are equally likely. In this case, an "outcome" consists of a choice of exactly one number from each set. Since set A has four elements and set B has five, the total number of outcomes is $4 \times 5 = 20$.

Of these outcomes, exactly four are successful:

Outcome	Set A		Set B
Choose	2	and	7
Choose	3	and	6
Choose	4	and	5
OR Choose	5	and	4

The probability in question is therefore 4/20, or 0.2. This is the **answer**.

We can also use the ***Domino Effect***, which tells us to multiply successive independent probabilities. First, we calculate, separately, the probability of *each* of the four events listed above (2 and 7, 3 and 6, 4 and 5, 5 and 4). For each of these cases, the chance of picking the "correct" first number (from set A) is 1/4, and the chance of picking the "correct" second number (from set B) is 1/5. Therefore, the probability of *each* of these outcomes is $\frac{1}{4} \times \frac{1}{5}$, or 1/20.

Since the four outcomes are mutually exclusive (that is, no two of them can happen at the same time), we add together the four probabilities to get $4/20 = 0.2$.

The correct answer is (B).

PS 69. Geometry: Circles & Cylinders
Difficulty: Medium **OG Page:** 161

We are given that a ***Circle*** in the ***Coordinate Plane*** has center (2,–3) and that (5,0) is a point on the circle. We are asked to solve for the area of the circle.

In order to compute the area of this circle, we need to figure out its radius, because the formula for the area of a circle is:

area of a circle = πr^2

Drawing a Picture can help us figure out a way to determine the radius:

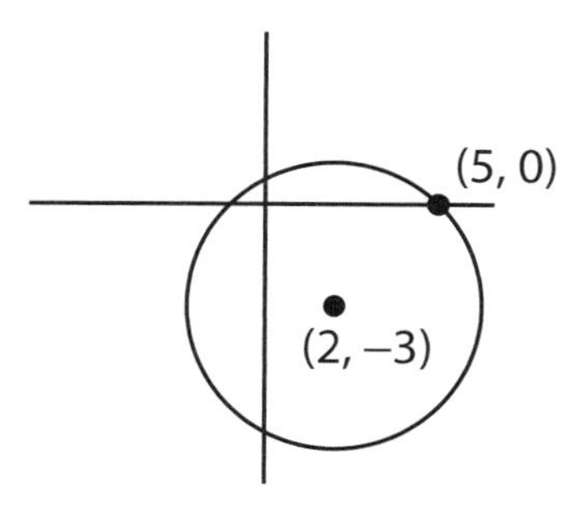

The distance between two points on a coordinate plane can always be thought of as the hypotenuse of a ***Right Triangle***. Notice that the x-axis can act as one of the legs of the right triangle. We can also draw a line that connects the point (2, –3) to the x-axis. That point is at (2, 0).

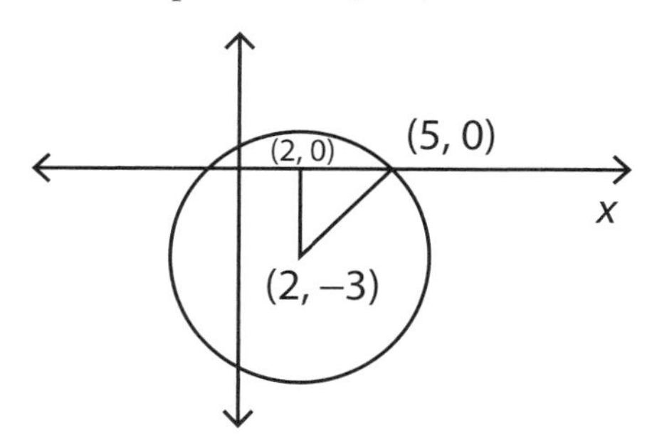

The horizontal leg of the right triangle goes from point (2, 0) to point (5, 0), which means the length of the leg is 3. The vertical leg of the right triangle goes from point (2, –3) to point (2, 0), which means the length of the leg is also 3.

If both the legs are equal then we have a ***45–45–90 Right Triangle*** with a side length of 3 and thus a hypotenuse length of $3\sqrt{2}$, which is the circle's radius.

Alternatively, we could have plugged the side lengths into the Pythagorean theorem:

$a^2 + b^2 = c^2$

We could use this formula to figure out the radius.

Either way, the next step is to just plug the radius into the area formula for a circle:

$$\text{Area} = \pi r^2 = \pi\left(3\sqrt{2}\right)^2 = 18\pi$$

The correct answer is (E).

PS 70. Algebra: Formulas
Difficulty: Medium **OG Page:** 161

The question asks for N. We are given this complicated formula: $N = \dfrac{20Ld}{600 + s^2}$, where

L = # of lanes in the same direction = 2
d = length of highway in feet (we are given 1/2 mile, which seems rather short for a highway!)
s = average speed in mph = 40

We need to convert d to the correct units (feet) before plugging into the formula for N. If 1 mile is 5,280 feet, then 1/2 a mile is 1/2 of 5,280 feet, or 2,640 feet. So d = 2,640 feet.

Now we plug the values of L, d, and s into the function for N and simplify. We should avoid computing products before ***Canceling*** as many ***Factors*** as possible.

$$\begin{aligned} N &= \frac{20Ld}{600+s^2} \\ &= \frac{20(2)(2{,}640)}{600+(40)^2} \\ &= \frac{(40)(2{,}640)}{600+1{,}600} \\ &= \frac{(4)(264)(100)}{2{,}200} \\ &= \frac{(4)(264)}{22} \\ &= \frac{(2)(264)}{11} = (2)(24) = 48 \end{aligned}$$

The correct answer is (D).

PS 71. FDPs: Percents
Difficulty: Hard **OG Page:** 162

This rather wordy problem tells us that yesterday's prices for 2,420 different stocks were all different from today's prices. We are also told that the number of stocks with higher prices today than yesterday was 20% greater than the number with lower prices.

We know that this is a ***Percent*** problem because of the phrase "20% greater than." We are asked to figure out how many stocks had a higher price today.

Use the information in the question to set up two equations. Let L be the number of stocks that closed at a lower price and let H be the number of stocks that closed at a higher price.

First, we know that the total number of stocks was 2,420:

$$L + H = 2{,}420$$

If a number is 20% greater than another number, it is 120% of the number, or 1.2 times the number. Therefore:

$$H = 1.2L$$

We now have two equations and two variables. Ultimately, we need to solve for the value of H, so isolate L in the first equation:

$$L + H = 2{,}420$$
$$L = 2{,}420 - H$$

Now substitute into the second equation and solve for H.

$$H = 1.2 \times (2{,}420 - H)$$

Either perform long multiplication to find the product of 2,420 and 1.2 or recognize that 0.2 is equivalent to 1/5:

$$H = 2{,}420 + 484 - 1.2H$$
$$2.2H = 2{,}904$$

Divide both sides by 2.2 and perform long division. Remember that 2904/2.2 is the same as 29,040/22:

$$\begin{array}{r} 1320 \\ 22\overline{)29{,}040} \\ \underline{22} \\ 70 \\ \underline{66} \\ 44 \\ \underline{44} \\ 00 \end{array}$$

The correct answer is (D).

PS 72. Algebra: Linear Equations
Difficulty: Easy **OG Page:** 162

This ***Linear Equations*** problem tells us that $y \neq 0$, so we know that it is "legal" to divide both sides by y. Remember, dividing by 0 leaves an undefined result, which is unacceptable. ***Dividing by a Variable*** is always a method to apply with care.

Since we know that y is *not* equal to 0, we can divide both sides of the equation by y right away. This leaves us with a much simpler equation with only one variable:

$$\frac{3x-5}{2} = 1$$

From here, we can solve for x:

$$3x - 5 = 2$$
$$3x = 7$$
$$x = 7/3$$

The correct answer is (C).

PS 73. Algebra: Inequalities
Difficulty: Easy **OG Page:** 162

In order to solve this ***Inequalities*** problem, we need to isolate x in each inequality:

$$x + 5 > 2$$
$$x > 2 - 5$$
$$x > -3$$

$$x - 3 < 7$$
$$x < 7 + 3$$
$$x < 10$$

Combining these two inequalities into a ***Compound Inequality*** yields:

$-3 < x < 10$

Thus, x must be between -3 and 10.

The correct answer is (A).

PS 74. Number Properties: Divisibility & Primes
Difficulty: Easy **OG Page:** 162

This ***Divisibility*** problem specifies that the people in a gym class can be evenly divided into either 8 or 12 teams. This implies that the number of people is a ***Multiple*** of both 8 and 12. Because we are asked to find the lowest possible number of people satisfying this condition, we must determine the ***Least Common Multiple*** (LCM) of 8 and 12.

For two relatively simple numbers such as 8 and 12, we can just ***List Multiples*** of each number, looking for the smallest number on both lists.

8: 8, 16, 24, 32...
12: 12, 24, 36...

Since 24 is the first number on both lists, 24 is the LCM. This is the **answer**.

We can also find the LCM using the ***Venn Diagram Method for LCM***. The prime factorizations of the two numbers in question are $8 = 2 \times 2 \times 2$ and $12 = 2 \times 2 \times 3$ As shown below, write the common factors of two 2's into the shared area and the remaining factors into the non-shared areas.

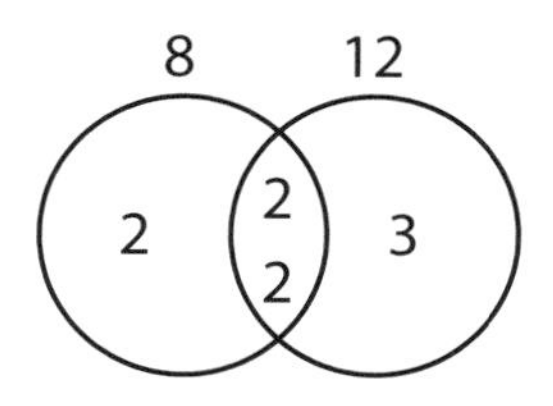

The LCM is the product of all primes in the diagram:

$\text{LCM} = 2 \times 2 \times 2 \times 3 = 24$

The smallest possible number of people in the gym class is 24.

The correct answer is (B).

PS 75. Geometry: Triangles & Diagonals
Difficulty: Hard **OG Page:** 162

We are told that ***Triangle*** *ABC* is ***Equilateral*** and that P is equidistant from the vertices A, B, and C.

Since ABC is equilateral, we know that all of its sides have the same length and that all of its angles are 60 degrees. Since P is the same distance from A as it is from B and C, P must be at the center of Triangle ABC.

The problem asks us how many degrees we need to rotate the triangle in a clockwise direction (rotate to the right, so that B goes through where C is now) in order to have B end up where A is now. It is helpful to draw the triangle inside of a circular clock face and imagine the vertical arm rotating from its position pointing at B, past C, all of the way to A.

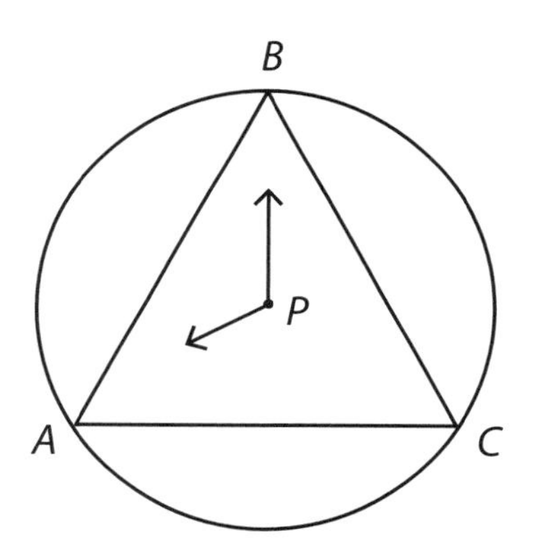

Intuitively, the vertical clock arm has to rotate more than 180 degrees clockwise, because a 180-degree turn would leave it pointing straight down, which is not far enough. If it rotated clockwise by 270 degrees, it would be pointing straight to the left. So, we know that it needs to rotate more than 180 degrees but less than 270 degrees, and the only answer choice in that range is 240 degrees.

More mathematically, you might notice that the equilateral triangle's vertices cut the circumference of the circle into three equal pieces. Since the circle has a total of 360 degrees, that means arc BC, arc CA, and arc AB are each 1/3 of the circle, so triangle ABC would have to be rotated 2/3 of a circle in the clockwise direction for B to end up where A is now. 2/3 of 360 is 240.

The correct answer is (D).

PS 76. Word Problems: Algebraic Translations
Difficulty: Easy **OG Page:** 162

This ***Optimization*** problem specifies that there are 40 members on a committee and that, in order for a resolution to pass, at least 2/3 of those 40 members have to vote "yes."

$$40 \times \left(\frac{2}{3}\right) = \frac{80}{3} = 26\frac{2}{3}$$

We cannot, of course, have a fraction of a person, and at least $26\frac{2}{3}$ must have voted "yes," so at least 27 people must vote in favor of the resolution in order for it to pass. That is, Minimum Yes's = 27. We need to be careful when ***Rounding*** to meet a ***Hidden Constraint,*** such as the condition that the number of people must be an integer.

The question asks us to determine the maximum number of members who could vote against the resolution and still have the resolution pass. We already know that Minimum Yes's = 27 and Minimum Yes's plus Maximum No's equals the total 40. So we have at most 40 − 27 = 13 members who could vote against the resolution and still have it pass. This is the **answer**.

Alternatively, if at least 2/3 must vote yes for the resolution to pass, then no more than 1/3 can vote against it.

$$40 \times \left(\frac{1}{3}\right) = \frac{40}{3} = 13\frac{1}{3}$$

Again, we cannot have a fraction of a person, and since no more than $13\frac{1}{3}$ can vote against the resolution, a maximum of 13 people can vote against it. Be sure not to round $13\frac{1}{3}$ up to 14, which is a trap answer.

The correct answer is (E).

PS 77. Number Properties: Divisibility & Primes
Difficulty: Medium **OG Page:** 163

We are given that $n = 20! + 17$ and asked whether n is divisible by each of 15, 17, and 19.

This is an intimidating ***Divisibility*** problem because 20! + 17 is a very large number. We couldn't possibly compute it in less than two minutes. The fact that we couldn't reasonably compute it is a clue, though, that we need another approach.

The key to this problem is two closely related divisibility rules that involve addition:

> **A multiple of *N* plus a multiple of *N* is a multiple of *N*.**
>
> **A multiple of *N* plus a *non-multiple* of *N* is NOT a multiple of *N*.**

For instance, 14 (a multiple of 7) plus 35 (a multiple of 7) equals 49 (a multiple of 7).

On the other hand, 14 (a multiple of 7) plus 30 (a non-multiple of 7) equals 44 (a non-multiple of 7).

These rules are relevant because the number 20! is a multiple of 15, 17, and 19 (because 20! = 20 × **19** × 18 × **17** × 16 × **15**...).

If 20! is a multiple of 17, then 20! + 17 must also be a multiple of 17. (II) must be included in the correct answer, so we can eliminate choices (A) and (B).

Similarly, we can guarantee that 20! + 17 is not divisible by either 15 or 19.

20! (a multiple of 15) + 17 (a non-multiple of 15) equals a non-multiple of 15.

20! (a multiple of 19) + 17 (a non-multiple of 19) equals a non-multiple of 19.

n is only divisible by (II) 17.

The correct answer is (C).

PS 78. Geometry: Polygons
Difficulty: Medium **OG Page:** 163

We are told that the three sides of the rectangular solid have areas 12, 15, and 20 respectively and we are asked to figure out the volume of the solid.

Solving this ***Polygons*** problem requires the formula for the volume of a rectangular solid, which is:

Volume = length × width × height = lwh

We now need to figure out what lwh is. We could also try to figure out l, w, h separately, but that is usually harder than figuring them out as a ***Combined Expression*** or ***Combo***.

We know the surface area of three of the sides. Fortunately, it is irrelevant which side is the length, which side is the width, and which side is the height. We can say that:

$12 = lw$

$15 = lh$

$20 = wh$

At this point, we may notice that 12 = 3 × 4, 15 = 3 × 5, and 20 = 4 × 5. In that case, the dimensions of the solid must be 3 × 4 × 5 = 60.

Fortunately, we can still get the answer even without this realization. First, multiply all of the equations together:

$lw \times lh \times wh = 12 \times 15 \times 20$

$l^2w^2h^2 = 12 \times 15 \times 20$

To solve for lwh, we can take the square root of both sides. l, w, and h are all positive, so there is no danger in taking the square root. Also, instead of multiplying 12 by 15 by 20, we can break each number into prime factors. This will make taking the square root easier.

$$\sqrt{l^2w^2h^2} = \sqrt{12 \times 15 \times 20}$$
$$lwh = \sqrt{(3 \times 2^2) \times (3 \times 5) \times (2^2 5)}$$
$$lwh = \sqrt{2^4 3^2 5^2}$$
$$lwh = 2^2 \times 3 \times 5$$
$$= 60$$

Alternatively, we could have multiplied the numbers. 12 × 15 × 20 = 3,600, which is 60^2.

The correct answer is (A).

PS 79. Word Problems: Rates & Work
Difficulty: Hard **OG Page:** 163

This is a very wordy problem, which makes it challenging to extract the given information without missing anything. We need to go through it carefully, line by line.

The first sentence tells us that Bob plans to start running south from a parking lot and then turn around and run north along the same path. That means that the distance he travels south is equal to the distance he travels north.

The next sentence tells us that he runs 3.25 miles south and then decides to only run for 50 more minutes. That means that he will run some additional number of miles south before turning around. Let's call this added distance x. Bob runs a total of $x + 3.25$ miles south. Then he will turn around and run $x + 3.25$ miles north to get back to where he started. A diagram makes it easier to understand what is happening in this ***Rates & Work*** problem:

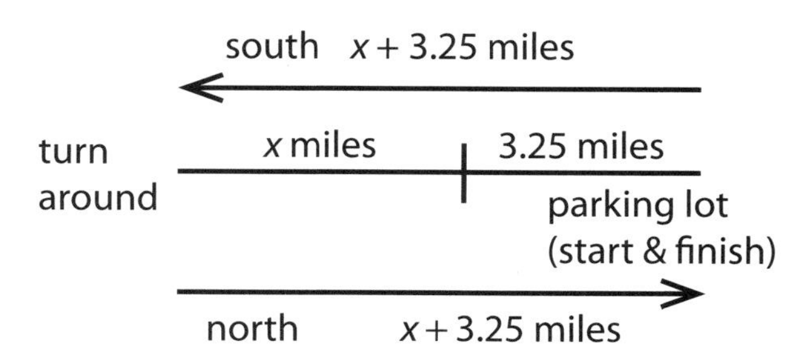

We are asked to figure out how far south he can run before he has to turn around and start running north. This distance is represented by x in our diagram.

According to the diagram, Bob will run $2x + 3.25$ miles in 50 minutes.

Use the rate equation to solve this problem.

D	=	R	×	T
(miles)	=	$\left(\frac{\text{miles}}{\text{minute}}\right)$	×	(minutes)

Although we are told that Bob runs at 8 miles per minute, we can't fill in 8 for the rate because the rate has to be in minutes per mile. Since Bob can run a mile in 8 minutes, his rate is 1/8 miles per minute, or 1 mile every 8 minutes.

	D (miles)	=	R $\left(\frac{\text{miles}}{\text{minute}}\right)$	×	T (minutes)
Bob	$2x + 3.25$	=	1/8	×	50

Now create an equation and solve for x:

$$2x + 3.25 = 50/8$$
$$8(2x + 3.25) = 50$$
$$16x + 26 = 50$$
$$16x = 24$$
$$x = 1.5$$

The correct answer is (A).

PS 80. FDPs: Fractions
Difficulty: Hard **OG Page:** 163

M is defined as the sum of the ***Reciprocals*** of the ***Consecutive Integers*** from 201 to 300, inclusive, which means that the endpoints, 201 and 300, are included.

Since there is no way to calculate M by hand in less than two minutes, there has to be a better way. A quick scan of the answers reveals that they all give ranges for M, so it looks like the best approach is to establish bounds for M and see if we can rule some answer choices out.

First, calculate the number of terms that we are asked to sum:

$$300 - 201 + 1 = 100$$

100 is a nice number, and a good clue that we are on the right track.

Let's make the numbers that we are summing a little more concrete to look for a pattern.

$$1/201 + 1/202 + 1/203 + \ldots + 1/300$$

We know that $1/201 > 1/202 > 1/203 > \ldots > 1/300$.

The smallest value of a term in the series is 1/300, and the largest value of a term is 1/201. We can multiply both values by 100 to get a range for M.

Since 1/300 is the smallest number in the sum of 100 numbers, we know that

$$M > 100 \times \frac{1}{300}$$
$$M > \frac{1}{3}$$

Only one answer has $M > 1/3$, so we could stop here.

If we had started by trying to compute an upper bound for M, we would have gotten

$$M < 100 \times \frac{1}{201} < 100 \times \frac{1}{200}$$
$$M < \frac{1}{2}$$

Although this would not have ruled out any of the answers, we can see that combined with the lower bound, it would have gotten us to the correct answer.

The correct answer is (A).

PS 81. Word Problems: Work & Rates
Difficulty: Hard **OG Page:** 163

We are given that Machines A and B work simultaneously at their respective rates to produce 800 nails in x hours. We are also told that when

Machine A works alone, it produces 800 nails in y hours. The question asks for the number of hours it would take Machine B, working alone, to produce 800 nails, in terms of x and y.

This is a ***Rates & Work*** problem and the word "simultaneously" is a clue that the solution will involve adding (or subtracting) rates. The phrase "in terms of x and y" and the variables in the answer choices tell us that we could pick numbers for x and y to make the question more concrete. Since ***Choosing Smart Numbers*** requires us to come up with numbers that both make sense in the problem and are easy to work with, we should set up the ***Rate Chart***, using the rate equation, before picking numbers.

W	=	R	×	T
(nails)	=	$\left(\frac{\text{nails}}{\text{hour}}\right)$	×	(hours)

Name a Variable, b, for the amount of time that it would take Machine B working alone to make 800 nails. For each scenario, we know the values of W and T, allowing us to solve for R:

	W	=	R	×	T
A	800	=	$\frac{800}{y}$	×	y
B	800	=	$\frac{800}{b}$	×	b
A & B together	800	=	$\frac{800}{x}$	×	x

We know that A & B's combined rate is the sum of A's and B's separate rates, so we can compute Machine B's rate by subtracting A's rate from A and B's combined rate. This algebra doesn't look too hard, so we could just do it and not worry about picking good numbers for x and y:

$$\frac{800}{b}=\frac{800}{x}-\frac{800}{y}$$
$$\frac{800}{b}=\frac{800y}{xy}-\frac{800x}{xy}$$
$$\frac{800}{b}=\frac{800(y-x)}{xy}$$

We are solving for b, so take the reciprocal of both sides:

$$\frac{b}{800}=\frac{xy}{800(y-x)}$$
$$b=\frac{xy}{y-x}$$

Alternatively, we could have picked smart numbers for x and y. Since the time that the two machines take working together must be less than the time that either one takes alone, x must be less than y. Also, in order to make it easy to compute the rates, both x and y should be factors of 800. 10 for y and 8 for x work with the logic of the problem and are easy to work with:

	W	=	R	×	T
A	800	=	$\frac{800}{y}=\frac{800}{10}=80$	×	10
B	800	=	$\frac{800}{b}$	×	b
A & B together	800	=	$\frac{800}{x}=\frac{800}{8}=100$	×	8

We know that A & B's combined rate is the sum of A's and B's separate rates, so we were able to compute Machine B's rate by subtracting A's rate from A and B's combined rate. Then all we need to do is solve for b and test the answer choices.

$$100-80=\frac{800}{b}$$
$$20=\frac{800}{b}$$
$$20b=800$$
$$b=40$$

40 is our ***Target Value***. Plug 8 for x and 10 for y into the answer choices and ***Find a Match***.

(A) $\frac{x}{x+y}=\frac{8}{8+10}=\frac{8}{18}$ NO! TOO SMALL!

(B) $\frac{y}{x+y}=\frac{10}{18}$ NO! TOO SMALL!

(C) $\frac{xy}{x+y}=\frac{8\times10}{18}$ NO! NOT AN INTEGER!

(D) $\frac{xy}{x-y}=\frac{80}{8-10}=\frac{80}{-2}$ NO! NEGATIVE!

(E) $\frac{xy}{y-x}=\frac{80}{10-8}=\frac{80}{2}=40$ YES!

The correct answer is (E).

PS 82. FDPs: Ratios
Difficulty: Easy **OG Page:** 163

We are told that the dollar amounts allocated to household expenses, food, and miscellaneous items are in the ratio 5 : 2 : 1, respectively. We are also told that the total amount allocated to these three categories is $1,800. When we are given a three-part ***Multiple Ratio*** and the total for all three quantities, it is often best to use an ***Unknown Multiplier***.

Make a quick ***Table:***

Household Expenses	Food	Misc. Items
$5x$	$2x$	$1x$

Now create an equation that shows that the total amount of money allocated is $1,800:

$$5x + 2x + 1x = 1{,}800$$
$$8x = 1{,}800$$
$$x = 225$$

Now that we know the value of the unknown multiplier, x, we can substitute to obtain the desired quantity: the amount allocated for food.

Food = $2x$
Food = $2(225) = 450$

The correct answer is (D).

PS 83. Word Problems: Algebraic Translations
Difficulty: Easy **OG Page:** 164

We can use ***Direct Algebra*** to solve this ***Algebraic Translations*** problem. First, to represent the numbers of men and women, we should ***Name a Variable*** and create expressions:

women = x
men = $x - 4$

The expression for the number of men incorporates the constraint that there are 4 more women than men. Thus, there are 4 fewer men than women.

(We could have chosen x to be the number of men, but the above choices are more convenient since the problem asks for the number of women.)

Since the total number of people on the board is 10, we know that $x + (x - 4) = 10$. Therefore, $2x - 4 = 10$, so $x = 7$. This is the **answer**.

Alternatively, if we name two variables (such as w and m), we will need to do just a little more algebra to solve the problem.

women = w
men = m

Then we have two equations:

$w = m + 4$ 4 more women than men
$w + m = 10$ Total of 10 people

Now solve for w, using ***Substitution:***

$w - 4 = m$ Write m in terms of w
$w + (w - 4) = 10$ Substitute
$2w - 4 = 10$ Simplify
$2w = 14$
$w = 7$

Be sure to choose the number of *women* as the answer. The correct number of *men* is an *incorrect* answer choice.

The correct answer is (D).

PS 84. FDPs: Percents
Difficulty: Medium **OG Page:** 164

To solve a ***Compound Interest*** problem such as this, treat it like a ***Successive Percents*** problem.

"An annual rate of 8 percent compounded semi-annually" means two payments in one year, each payment for half of the annual rate. Thus, Leona's certificate of deposit pays 4% interest at the end of the 6th month, which increases the principal in the certificate of deposit. Then another 4% interest will be paid on that new principal balance at the end of the 12th month. In other words, we have these transactions:

$ 10,000 Leona deposits $10,000 initially
\+ 400 4% of $10,000 = 1st semiannual payment

$ 10,400 Resulting principal
\+ 416 4% of $10,400 = 2nd semiannual payment
$ 10,816 Final value

Note that the second interest payment is calculated on $10,400, not $10,000. To compute 4% of $10,400, write (0.04)(10,400). In a product involving decimals, we can simplify the computation by ***Trading Decimal Places.*** That is, we can move the decimal place of 0.04 two places to the right, and to compensate, we move the decimal place of 10,400 two places to the left: (0.04)(10,400) = (4)(104) = 416. The extra $16 is the "interest on the interest": 4% of the first 4% of $10,000.

At the end of a year, Leona had $816 more than she originally deposited. The total interest paid was $816. This is the **answer.**

Note that $800 = 8% of $10,000 is a trap answer. We must not only know the definition of "compounded semiannually," but also remember to include in our computation the interest paid on the interest already earned.

The correct answer is (C).

PS 85. FDPs: Digits & Decimals
Difficulty: Hard **OG Page:** 164

When we see ***Fractions with Decimals*** in the numerator and the denominator, it's a good idea to ***Get Rid of Decimals.*** In order to convert these decimals into whole numbers, we should multiply by a ***Power of 10*** (the same power of 10 for both the top and the bottom of the fraction).

Multiplying by a power of 10 is the same as moving the decimal point. Thus, we can just move the decimal points—as long as we move the top and bottom decimals the same total number of places, and in the same direction.

To convert (0.0036)(2.8) to (36)(28), we have to move the decimal points a total of 5 places to the right. We need to move 4 places for 0.0036 and 1 place for 2.8. This is equivalent to multiplying by 100,000, or 10^5.

To convert (0.04)(0.1)(0.003) to (4)(1)(3), we have to move the decimal points a total of 6 places to the right. We need to move 2 places for 0.04, 1 place for 0.1, and 3 places for 0.003. This is equivalent to multiplying by 1,000,000, or 10^6.

To take care of all the decimals, we should choose to move the decimal points 6 places in both the numerator and the denominator. The extra place in the numerator becomes an extra zero on one number:

(0.0036)(2.8) becomes (36)(280) or (360)(28).

Again, this is equivalent to multiplying top and bottom by 1,000,000, or 10^6.

$$\frac{(0.0036)(2.8)}{(0.04)(0.1)(0.003)} \times \left(\frac{10^6}{10^6}\right)$$
$$= \frac{(36)(280)}{(4)(1)(3)}$$
$$= \frac{(^3\cancel{36})(280)}{(\cancel{4})(1)(\cancel{3})}$$
$$= (3)(280)$$
$$= 840$$ This is the **answer.**

Alternatively, we can eliminate the decimals in the original by expressing each term with powers of ten.

$$\frac{(36\times10^{-4})(28\times10^{-1})}{(4\times10^{-2})(1\times10^{-1})(3\times10^{-3})}$$
$$=\frac{(36)(28)}{(4)(3)}\times\frac{10^{-5}}{10^{-6}}$$
$$=84\times10^{1}$$
$$=840$$

The correct answer is (A).

PS 86. Word Problems: Rates & Work
Difficulty: Easy **OG Page:** 164

This is a ***Working Together*** problem. Let's begin by writing down the given rates for each machine. These rates are expressed in the first sentence. "120 bolts every 40 seconds" means 120 bolts per 40 seconds, or 120 bolts divided by 40 seconds. Thus, perform the divisions to simplify the rates.

$$r_a=\frac{120\text{ bolts}}{40\text{ sec}}=3\text{ bolts/sec}$$
$$r_b=\frac{100\text{ bolts}}{20\text{ sec}}=5\text{ bolts/sec}$$

Now, because the machines are working together, we ***Add the Rates.***

3 bolts/sec + 5 bolts/sec = 8 bolts/sec

This 8 bolts/sec represents the machines' combined rate. Working together, the two machines can make 8 bolts every second.

Now, we want to determine how long it will take for the machines to create 200 bolts. Having already determined the combined rate, we create an ***Rate-Time-Work Chart:***

Rate	×	Time	=	Work
8 bolts/sec		t sec		200 bolts

$8t = 200$
$t = 200/8 = 25$ This is the **answer.**

If necessary, include the units (in this problem "bolts" and "seconds") in the table. In the end, the units should cancel properly, leaving the correct unit for the answer.

The correct answer is (B).

PS 87. Number Properties: Divisibility & Primes
Difficulty: Hard **OG Page:** 164

This tricky ***Divisibility*** problem asks us which of the answers *must be* divisible by 3.

The "must be" language is a hint about how to solve this problem. It tells us that four of the answers aren't always divisible by 3. That means that we should be able to ***Choose Smart Numbers*** and rule out four of the five possible answer choices.

Randomly testing numbers could take a very long time, so we need to think carefully about the numbers we test. There is no need to pick a multiple of 3 for n because then every answer would be divisible by 3 (since every answer includes an n term in the product).

A good place to start then is with the smallest possible n that is not divisible by 3. That number is 7.

Since any answer choice that is a ***Multiple*** of 3 will be the product of at least one multiple of 3, we don't have to multiple out the answer choices. We simply eliminate any answer choice that does not contain a term that is a multiple of 3.

(A) $n(n+1)(n-4)=7\times8\times3$
(B) $n(n+2)(n-1)=7\times9\times6$
(C) $n(n+3)(n-5)=7\times10\times2$ ← ELIMINATE, NO MULTIPLE OF 3
(D) $n(n+4)(n-2)=7\times11\times5$ ← ELIMINATE, NO MULTIPLE OF 3
(E) $n(n+5)(n-6)=7\times12\times1$

Choices (C) and (D) are out, but we still need to test another number to get rid of the remaining wrong answers. The next non-multiple of 3 is 8:

(A) $n(n + 1)(n - 4) = 8 \times 9 \times 4$

(B) $n(n + 2)(n - 1) = 8 \times 10 \times 7$ ⟵ ELIMINATE, NO MULTIPLE OF 3

(C)

(D)

(E) $n(n + 5)(n - 6) = 8 \times 13 \times 4$ ⟵ ELIMINATE, NO MULTIPLE OF 3

There is only one answer choice remaining: (A).

Although using smart numbers is an effective approach to this problem, there is a principle of divisibility being tested:

The product of *k* consecutive integers is always divisible by *k*.

For instance, the product of 3 consecutive integers will always be divisible by 3 (test it out for yourself).

Another way to express this rule is to say that, out of every group of 3 consecutive numbers, one of them is a multiple of 3. So for any n greater than 6, either n, $n + 1$, or $n + 2$ must be a multiple of 3. So we know that $n(n + 1)(n + 2)$ must be a multiple of 3.

We can extend this basic rule to other cases though if we think some more about it. If n is a multiple of 3, so are $n - 6$, $n - 3$, $n + 3$, and $n + 6$. Similarly, if $n + 1$ is a multiple of 3, so are $n - 5$, $n - 2$, and $n + 4$. And if $n + 2$ is a multiple of 3, so are $n - 4$, $n - 1$, and $n + 5$.

So we could substitute any of $n - 5$, $n - 2$, or $n + 4$ for $n + 1$ in one of the answers and not change whether the product was divisible by 3. Similarly, we could substitute any of $n - 4$, $n - 1$, or $n + 5$ for $n + 2$ in one of the answers and not change whether the product was divisible by 3.

So $n(n + 1)(n - 4)$ has to be a multiple of 3 because $n - 4$ will be a multiple of 3 whenever $n + 2$ is a multiple of 3, and either n, $n + 1$, or $n + 2$ must be a multiple of 3.

The correct answer is (A).

PS 88. Word Problems: Algebraic Translations
Difficulty: Easy **OG Page:** 164

This ***Algebraic Translations*** problem involves a typical ***Cost Relationship.***

The cost to produce a batch of tools is \$10,000 plus \$3 per tool. While the natural next step seems to be to construct an equation such as $C = 10{,}000 + 3t$, a glance at the answers shows very small numbers. The question asks for the profit *per tool,* so we can save time if we avoid calculating large numbers when they are not needed. Instead, let's move forward by figuring out costs and revenues on a per-tool basis.

20,000 tools are produced. The cost of each tool is \$3 plus each tool's "share" of the fixed \$10,000 cost.

\$10,000 divided by 20,000 tools yields \$0.50 per tool, for a total cost per tool of \$3.50.

The tools are sold for \$8 each, so the profit per tool is:

$$\$8 - \$3.50 = \$4.50$$

The correct answer is (C).

PS 89. Word Problems: Algebraic Translations
Difficulty: Hard **OG Page:** 164

This ***Algebraic Translations*** problem involving a ***Profit Relationship*** asks for the price at which each battery was sold. We can first approach this problem using the ***Direct Algebra*** method.

If 100 batteries were purchased for a total cost of q dollars, each battery costs $q/100$ dollars.

The selling price for each battery is 50% above the cost of purchasing the battery. We can use the following ***Formula for Percent Increase***:

To find the amount after an x% increase, Original Amount $\times \left(1 + \frac{x}{100}\right)$ = New Amount

The selling price for the battery is therefore

$$\left(\frac{q}{100}\right)\left(1+\frac{50}{100}\right)=\left(\frac{q}{100}\right)\left(\frac{150}{100}\right)=\left(\frac{q}{100}\right)\left(\frac{3}{2}\right)=\frac{3q}{200}$$

This is the **answer**.

Alternatively, we could ***Choose Smart Numbers***. If we let $q = 400$, then each battery costs \$4.00. To calculate the selling price of the battery, we need to find the amount of markup.

Cost of Battery:	\$4.00
50% Markup: (0.50)(4) =	\$2.00
Selling price: \$4.00 + \$2.00=	\$6.00

We want to see which answer choice will result in our ***Target Value*** of 6 when we plug in $q = 400$.

(A) $\frac{3q}{200}=\frac{(3)(400)}{(200)}=6$
CORRECT

(B) $\frac{3q}{2}=\frac{(3)(400)}{(2)}=600$
INCORRECT

(C) $150q = (150)(400) = 60{,}000$
INCORRECT

(D) $\frac{q}{100}+50=\frac{(400)}{(100)}+50=54$
INCORRECT

(E) $\frac{150}{q}=\frac{(150)}{(400)}=\frac{3}{8}$
INCORRECT

The correct answer is (A).

PS 90. <u>Word Problems</u>: Consecutive Integers
Difficulty: Easy **OG Page:** 164

The problem indicates that there is a sequence of 10 ***Consecutive Integers.*** However, we do not know any of the specific numbers in the sequence. The problem then tells us that the sum of the first 5 integers in the sequence is 560, and asks us to calculate the sum of the last 5 integers in the sequence.

We can answer the question efficiently if we ***Recognize the Pattern*** between the first five elements of the set and the next five. If we label the first number in the set x, then the second number is $(x + 1)$, the third number is $(x + 2)$, etc. The tenth and final number is $(x + 9)$.

x	$x + 1$	$x + 2$	$x + 3$	$x + 4$
$x + 5$	$x + 6$	$x + 7$	$x + 8$	$x + 9$

To go from the 1st number in the top row to the 1st number in the bottom row, we add 5. To go from the 2nd number in the top row to the 2nd number in the bottom row, we add 5, and so on. There are five numbers in the top row, and each counterpart in the bottom row is 5 greater, so the sum of the entire bottom row is 25 greater than the sum of the entire top row:

x	$x + 1$	$x + 2$	$x + 3$	$x + 4$	= 560
↓ (+5)	↓ (+5)	↓ (+5)	↓ (+5)	↓ (+5)	
$x + 5$	$x + 6$	$x + 7$	$x + 8$	$x + 9$	= 585

585 is the **answer.**

Alternatively, we can apply ***Properties of Consecutive Integer Sets.*** Specifically, the median and the average of any such set will be equivalent.

If the first 5 numbers sum to 560, then their average is $A=\frac{560}{5}=112$.

That means the median of the 5 numbers is 112, so the first 5 numbers in the overall set are 110, 111, 112, 113 and 114.

That means that the next 5 numbers in the list are 115, 116, 117, 118 and 119. We can use the same shortcut to quickly find the sum of these 5 numbers. The median of this list is 117, so the average is also 117. Since 117 = Sum/5, the sum of these 5 numbers is $5 \times 117 = 585$.

The correct answer is (A).

PS 91. <u>Word Problems</u>: Statistics
Difficulty: Medium **OG Page:** 165

The problem states that Q is an odd number and that the ***Median*** of Q ***Consecutive Integers*** is 120.

The question asks what the largest of these consecutive integers is.

This is an interesting ***Consecutive Integers/ Statistics*** problem because there are variables in the answer choices.

Since we know from the language of the problem that this formula has to work for every possible Q, we can pick a small, easy to work with ***Smart Number*** for Q, such as 3.

The median value of an odd number of consecutive integers is just the middle number. So the set of 3 consecutive integers with a median of 120 is 119, 120, 121. The largest of these integers is 121, and we can now test the answer choices by plugging in 3 for Q.

(A) $\frac{3-1}{2}+120=1+120=121 \Leftarrow$ YES!

(B) $\frac{Q}{2}+119=\frac{3}{2}+119 \Leftarrow$ NO! NOT AN INTEGER

(C) $\frac{Q}{2}+120=\frac{3}{2}+120 \Leftarrow$ NO! NOT AN INTEGER

(D) $\frac{Q+119}{2}=\frac{122}{2} \Leftarrow$ NO! TOO SMALL

(E) $\frac{Q+120}{2}=\frac{123}{2} \Leftarrow$ NO! TOO SMALL

Theoretically, this formula works because $\frac{Q-1}{2}$ of the consecutive integers are greater than the median, and each one of those integers is one greater than the previous integer, so the last integer is $\frac{Q-1}{2}$ greater than the median integer.

The correct answer is (A).

PS 92. Geometry: Triangles & Diagonals
Difficulty: Medium **OG Page:** 165

This problem talks about the ladder of a fire truck, but this problem has nothing to do with ladders; it is about ***Triangles & Diagonals***.

The question asks us how many feet above the ground the top tip of the 70 ft long ladder is.

A picture will make this problem much easier to visualize and understand:

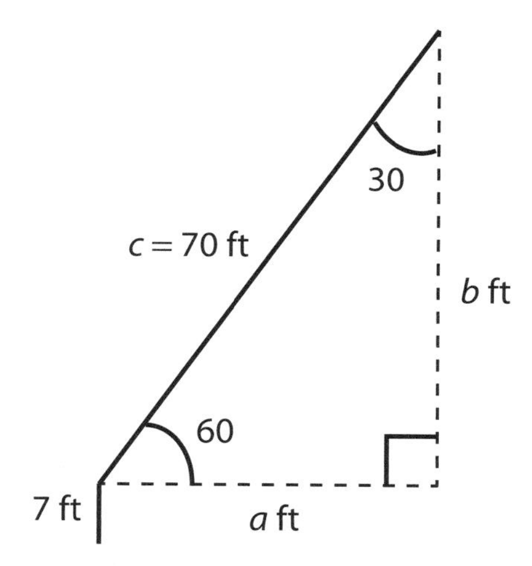

The fact that the ladder is at 60 degrees is an important clue. Using the information provided, we can create a ***30–60–90 Special Right Triangle*** as shown by the dotted lines in the above diagram.

The total height the ladder reaches above the ground is equal to 7 + b. Once we find b we can answer this question.

30–60–90 triangles are a favorite of the test writers because the side ratios of a 30–60–90 triangle are known to be in the ratio $x : x\sqrt{3} : 2x$. The longest side ($2x$) is the hypotenuse of the right triangle, or c, which we are told is 70 feet long. The shortest side (x) is opposite the shortest angle (30°) and is represented by a. The middle side ($\sqrt{3}x$) is opposite the middle angle (60°) and is represented by b:

$$c = 2x = 70$$

$$a = x = 35$$

$$b = x\sqrt{3} = 35\sqrt{3}$$

The height of the ladder is $7 + b$, or $7 + 35\sqrt{3}$.

The correct answer is (D).

PS 93. Word Problems: Algebraic Translations
Difficulty: Easy **OG Page:** 165

This is a standard ***Algebraic Translations*** problem that we can solve by ***Direct Algebra.*** These problems reward neat work and an organized approach.

Start by ***Naming Variables*** to represent Jake's weight and his sister's weight. Let's use j and s. Note that these variables represent the individuals' *current* weights.

Next, we need to create equations. In this case, our first equation should read as follows:

$j - 8$	=	$2s$
"If Jake loses 8 pounds	*he will weigh*	*twice as much as his sister."*

The second equation is a simple sum and should read:

$$j + s = 278$$

We must solve for j. While we would normally manipulate the equations to get rid of s, doing so in this case will force us to work with fractions. For sake of ease, we begin by putting j in terms of s in the first equation:

$$j - 8 = 2s$$
$$j = 2s + 8$$

We can then insert $2s + 8$ in the second equation, in place of j:

$$(2s + 8) + s = 278$$
$$3s + 8 = 278$$
$$3s = 270$$
$$s = 90$$

From here, we can solve for j in the first equation:

$$j - 8 = 2(90)$$
$$j - 8 = 180$$
$$j = 188$$ This is the **answer.**

We can easily double-check by using the second equation:

$$188 + 90 = 278$$

The correct answer is (E).

PS 94. FDPs: Percents
Difficulty: Medium **OG Page:** 165

This ***Percent Change*** problem asks us to express a year-to-year increase in sales from \$320 million to \$385 million in terms of an approximate percentage. In order to evaluate the answer, we must first calculate the dollar increase, and then relate it to the original figure. This yields the following:

$$\frac{\text{Percent Increase}}{100} = \frac{\$385M - \$320M}{\$320M}$$
$$\frac{\text{Percent Increase}}{100} = \frac{385-320}{320}$$
$$\frac{\text{Percent Increase}}{100} = \frac{65}{320}$$

Then we solve for the percent increase:

$$\text{Percent Increase} = \frac{65}{320} \times 100 = \frac{65 \times 100}{320} = \frac{650}{32}$$

We could do long division at this point but, because the question asks us for an approximate value, we can simply ***Estimate.*** Specifically, look for multiples of the denominator that are close in value to the numerator. Since 64 is 2 times 32, we can see that 640 is 20 times 32. Thus, our increase is just over 20%. Looking at the answer choices, we know that 20% is the **answer.**

An alternative approach is to use the ***Benchmarking*** technique. We can see that a 50% year-to-year increase from an original value of \$320 million would correspond to an increase of \$160 million (half of \$320 million), resulting in a final sales figure of \$320 million + \$160 million = \$480 million. This figure is clearly too high, so we can tell that the answer cannot be (D) or (E). Likewise, 10% year-to-year increase would correspond to an increase of \$32 million, resulting in a final sales figure of \$320 million + \$32 million = \$352 million. As this is figure is too small, we can eliminate choice (A). Of the remaining two choices, 20% is the easier to calculate, resulting in a final sales figure of \$320 million + \$64 million = \$384 million. This value is very nearly equal to the actual sales figure of \$385 million.

The correct answer is (C).

PS 95. Number Properties: Divisibility & Primes
Difficulty: Hard **OG Page:** 165

In this ***Divisibility*** problem, we need to recognize that, in an expression such as $x/y = 96.12$, the ***Remainder*** is equal to $0.12y$. In other words, the remainder must be equal to the decimal part of the quotient times the divisor, which in this case is y.

For example, $32/5 = 6.4$ as a ***Decimal.*** In remainder notation, $32/5 = 6$, with remainder 2. Notice that the remainder (2) must be equal to the decimal portion (0.4) times the divisor (5). In other words, $2 = 0.4 \times 5$.

Since our remainder must be equal to $0.12y$ and we are also told that the remainder is 9, set $0.12y$ equal to 9 and solve for y. To reduce the fraction quickly, move decimal points.

$$0.12y = 9$$

$$y = \frac{9}{0.12} = \frac{900}{12} = \frac{300}{4} = \frac{150}{2} = 75$$

The correct answer is (B).

PS 96. FDPs: Percents
Difficulty: Easy **OG Page:** 165

In this problem, all registered voters are either Democrats or Republicans. Moreover, all registered voters are expected either to vote for or not to vote for Candidate A. Because the problem gives us ***Percents,*** we can use 100 as a ***Smart Number*** to be the number of registered voters.

If we take an ***Overlapping Sets*** approach, we can fill out a ***Double-Set Matrix*** to organize the information in the problem. The shaded box answers the question.

	Vote for Candidate A?		
	Yes	**No**	**Total**
Republican			40
Democrat			60
Total	?		100

The problem states that 75% of the Democrats are expected to vote for Candidate A. If there are 60 Democrats, the number of Democrats expected to vote for Candidate A is:

$$(0.75)(60) = 45$$

The problem also states that 20% of the Republicans are expected to vote for Candidate A. If there are 40 Republicans, the number of Republicans expected to vote for Candidate A is:

$$(0.20)(40) = 8$$

We can fill in our Double-Set Matrix with the number of people from each party expected to vote for Candidate A.

	Vote for Candidate A?		
	Yes	**No**	**Total**
Republican	8		40
Democrat	45		60
Total	?		100

The total number of registered voters expected to vote for Candidate A is $8 + 45 = 53$. Since the number of all registered voters is 100, 53 also corresponds to the percent we are looking for. 53% is the **answer**.

Notice that we did not need the No column, so the full machinery of the Double-Set Matrix was not used. Several other approaches can work. However, the computations all wind up looking much the same.

The correct answer is (B).

PS 97. FDPs: Fractions
Difficulty: Easy **OG Page:** 165

This ***Fractions*** problem asks us to add, subtract, multiply, or divide various quantities. In order to do so correctly, we need to follow the ***Order of Operations,*** which we can remember using the acronym ***PEMDAS:***

Parentheses
Exponents
Multiplication
Division

Addition
Subtraction

$$\frac{1}{2}+\left[\left(\frac{2}{3}\times\frac{3}{8}\right)\div 4\right]-\frac{9}{2}=?$$

Begin with the multiplication inside the round parentheses. Look to ***Cancel Common Factors:***

$$\frac{2}{3}\times\frac{3}{8}=\frac{\cancel{2}^{1}}{{}_{1}\cancel{3}}\times\frac{\cancel{3}^{1}}{\cancel{8}_{4}}=\frac{1}{4}$$

and then divide inside the square brackets:

$$\frac{1}{4}\div 4=\frac{1}{4}\times\frac{1}{4}=\frac{1}{16}$$

The problem now reads:

$$\frac{1}{2}+\frac{1}{16}-\frac{9}{16}$$

When given only addition and subtraction with no parentheses, we can work from left to right. Start by converting $\frac{1}{2}$ to $\frac{8}{16}$ so that we can work with ***Common Denominators***:

$$\frac{8}{16}+\frac{1}{16}-\frac{9}{16}=\frac{9}{16}-\frac{9}{16}=0$$

The correct answer is (E).

PS 98. FDPs: Ratios
Difficulty: Easy **OG Page:** 165

We are told that the ***Ratio,*** by mass, of hydrogen to oxygen is 2 : 16. We are then asked to determine the number of grams of oxygen in 144 grams of water. Since 144 grams is the total mass of hydrogen and oxygen combined, it is best to use the ***Unknown Multiplier*** strategy.

First, we can make a ***Table:***

Hydrogen	Oxygen
$2x$	$16x$

Create an equation that shows that the total combined mass of hydrogen and oxygen is 144 grams:

$$2x + 16x = 144$$
$$18x = 144$$
$$x = 8$$

Now that we know the value of the unknown multiplier, x, we can substitute to determine the number of grams of oxygen:

Oxygen = $16x$
Oxygen = $16(8) = 128$

The correct answer is (D).

PS 99. Algebra: Quadratic Equations
Difficulty: Easy **OG Page:** 166

This problem presents two ***Quadratic Equations,*** both of which are already set to zero and factored. The solutions to these quadratics will be the numbers that cause one of the two factored parts to equal zero.

In the first equation, $x(2x + 1) = 0$, the factors are x and $2x + 1$. If the former is equal to zero, then $x = 0$. If the latter is equal to zero, then $x = -1/2$.

In the second equation, $(x + 1/2)(2x - 3) = 0$, the factors are $x + 1/2$ and $2x - 3$. If the former is equal to zero, then $x = -1/2$. If the latter is equal to zero, then $x = 3/2$.

Since both of the equations are true, x can only be equal to $-1/2$. This is the **answer.**

This problem can also be solved by ***Working Backwards***. We simply try the answer choices one by one, and stop when we find the number that solves both equations.

(A) is incorrect because $(-3)(2(-3) + 1)$ is not equal to zero. There's no need to try the second equation if the first doesn't work.

If we try (B), we find that $(-1/2)(2(-1/2) + 1) = 0$ in the first equation. We also find that $(-1/2 + 1/2)(2(-1/2) - 3) = 0$ in the second equation.

The correct answer is (B).

PS 100. <u>Algebra</u>: Formulas
Difficulty: Hard **OG Page:** 166

The wording of the given information in this problem is tricky. It says that a reading of $n + 1$ corresponds to an intensity that is 10 times the intensity that corresponds to a reading of n. Each term is defined in terms of the value of the previous term, which means this is a ***Sequence*** problem. In order to answer this question, we need to figure out a way to express each reading in terms of other readings.

There are really two variables to keep track of: reading and intensity. A reading of $n + 1$ is 10 times as intense as a reading of n. So, for instance, if a reading of 1 has an intensity of 5, a reading of 2 will have an intensity of 50.

The question asks about the relationship between a reading of 3 and a reading of 8.

A good way to solve this ***Formulas*** problem is to write out the sequence in a chart. We don't know what the intensity is for a reading of 3, so we can use a constant, k, to stand in for the real value. Every time the reading goes up by 1, the intensity is multiplied by 10.

Reading	Intensity
3	k
4	$k \times 10$
5	$k \times 10^2$
6	$k \times 10^3$
7	$k \times 10^4$
8	$k \times 10^5$

If a reading of 3 has an intensity of k, then a reading of 8 has an intensity of $k \times 10^5$. The question asks how many times greater $k \times 10^5$ is than k. In other words, what times k equals $k \times 10^5$? The answer is 10^5.

The correct answer is (C).

PS 101. <u>Word Problems</u>: Statistics
Difficulty: Easy **OG Page:** 166

We are given a set of 5 positive integers listed in increasing order:

$$n,\ n + 1,\ n + 2,\ n + 4,\ n + 8$$

In a set containing an *odd* number of values, the ***Median*** is the value that appears in the middle when the data is arranged in increasing order. In this case, $n + 2$ is the middle term and is therefore the median.

The ***Mean*** (average) can be calculated using the ***Average Formula:***

$$\begin{aligned}\text{Average} &= \frac{\text{Sum}}{\#\text{ of terms}}\\ &= \frac{n+(n+1)+(n+2)+(n+4)+(n+8)}{5}\\ &= \frac{5n+15}{5}\\ &= n+3\end{aligned}$$

The question asks how much greater the mean is than the median:

$$\text{mean} - \text{median} = (n + 3) - (n + 2) = 1$$

This is the **answer.**

Alternatively, we could have opted to ***Choose a Smart Number*** for n. If $n = 2$, the 5 numbers in the set would be 2, 3, 4, 6 and 10.

The median would be 4, the middle number.

The mean would be $\frac{2+3+4+6+10}{5} = \frac{25}{5} = 5.$

The mean would be $5 - 4 = 1$ greater than the median, so our ***Target Value*** would be 1.

Testing each answer choice, we can see that only (B) gives the target value.

(A) 0 INCORRECT
(B) 1 **CORRECT**
(C) 2 + 1 INCORRECT

(D) $2 + 2$ INCORRECT
(E) $2 + 3$ INCORRECT

The correct answer is (B).

PS 102. Algebra: Linear Equations
Difficulty: Medium **OG Page:** 166

This ***Linear Equations*** problem involves standard ***Algebraic Translations.*** In this case, we are given an actual value for one of our variables. As a result, we can use ***Direct Algebra.*** Insert the known value in place of the variable in the first equation:

$$290 = \frac{5}{9}(K - 32)$$

Next, multiply the whole equation by $\frac{9}{5}$ to remove the fraction from the right-hand side:

$$\frac{5}{9}(290) = K - 32$$

It may help to break 290 into two separate factors, 29 and 10, so that we can cancel more easily:

$$\frac{9}{5}(29)(10) = K - 32$$
$$(9)(29)(2) = K - 32$$
$$(18)(29) = K - 32$$
$$522 = K - 32$$
$$554 = K$$

The correct answer is (D).

PS 103. Word Problems: Rates & Work
Difficulty: Easy **OG Page:** 166

In this ***Rates & Work*** problem, we can ***Choose a Smart Number*** for the size of the pool to simplify the computations. Since we are given times of 9 hours and 5 hours, we should choose a size that is divisible by both 9 and 5. Let's pick 45 gallons. Using the relationship Rate × Time = Work, we can create a ***Rate–Time–Work Chart*** and solve for each outlet's rate of work.

	Rate (gal/hr)	×	Time (hours)	=	Work (gallons)
First Outlet	5	×	9	=	45
Second Outlet	9	×	5	=	45
Together					

The first outlet pumps 5 gallons per hour (= 1/9 of the pool), and the second outlet pumps 9 gallons per hour (= 1/5 of the pool). Together, then, they pump 5 + 9 = 14 gallons per hour. We are ultimately looking for t, the time it takes both outlets to fill the pool.

	Rate (gal/hr)	×	Time (hours)	=	Work (gallons)
First Outlet	5	×	9	=	45
Second Outlet	9	×	5	=	45
Together	5 + 9 = 14	×	t	=	45

Now, write an equation to represent the last row of the table:

$$14t = 45$$
$$t = 45 \div 14 = \frac{45}{14}$$

At this point, we can either perform long division or estimate, noting that the answer choices are relatively far apart. If the calculation were 45 ÷ 15, we would get exactly 3. The real answer is slightly bigger than 3, because the real denominator is slightly smaller than 15. Of the answer choices, only 3.21 fits. This is the **answer.**

There is a shortcut for straightforward ***Working Together*** problems, in which the task is the same for each machine and for the machines working together:

$$\frac{1}{9\text{ hours}} + \frac{1}{5\text{ hours}} = \frac{1}{\text{Time working together}}$$

This formula gets us to $\frac{45}{14\text{ hours}}$ quickly.

However, we should understand the formula as a special case of adding rates.

The correct answer is (D).

PS 104. **Geometry:** Polygons
Difficulty: Medium **OG Page:** 166

In this ***Polygons*** problem, we are asked to determine approximately the perimeter of a ***Square*** that has a diagonal of length 20. We should ***Name a Variable*** now to represent the key metric for any square: the length of any side. If we let x stand for the length of a side of the square, then the perimeter equals $4x$.

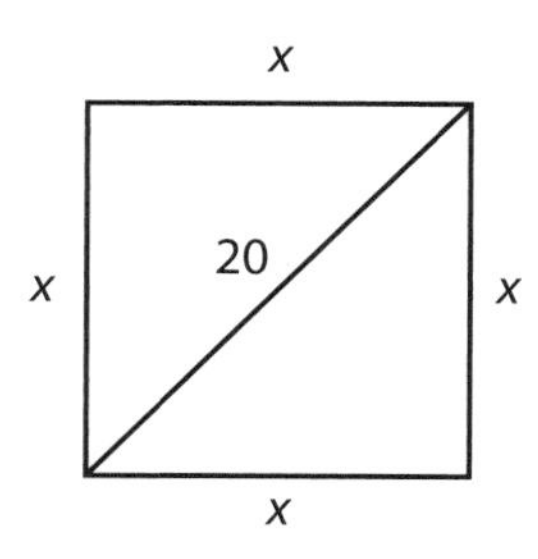

From the right triangle formed by the diagonal and two sides of the square, we can use the ***Pythagorean Theorem*** to write the following:

$$x^2 + x^2 = 20^2$$
$$2x^2 = 400$$
$$x^2 = 200$$
$$x = \sqrt{200} = \sqrt{100 \times 2} = \sqrt{100} \times \sqrt{2} = 10\sqrt{2}$$

Alternatively, we can observe that the triangle in question is a ***45–45–90*** triangle. We can solve for x using the side ratios of this special triangle:

$$x\sqrt{2} = 20$$
$$x = \frac{20}{\sqrt{2}} = \frac{20\sqrt{2}}{2} = 10\sqrt{2}$$

The square root of 2 is approximately equal to 1.4. Now we can ***Estimate:*** $x \approx 14$ and $4x \approx 56$. The closest answer choice is 60. This is the **answer.**

We may also note that in this case, with the choices so far apart, we can find the right answer by ***Working Backwards from the Answers*** and applying reasonable geometric constraints. If the perimeter were equal to 40, as in answer choice (A), then each side of the square would have to equal 10. However, in that case, the sum of the lengths of two sides would equal the length of the diagonal, which is not possible. Likewise, if the perimeter were equal to 80, as in answer choice (C), then each side of the square would have to equal 20, making the length of the diagonal equal to the length of a side. This is also unreasonable. The diagonal of a square would be longer than any of its sides. The only sensible answer available to us is 60.

The correct answer is (B).

PS 105. **FDPs:** Ratios
Difficulty: Medium **OG Page:** 166

The ***Ratio*** of students to teachers is 30 to 1, while adding 50 students and 5 teachers changes the ratio to 25 to 1. To solve this problem, we can use the ***Unknown Multiplier*** strategy.

The present student/teacher ratio of 30 to 1 can be written as this ***Proportion:***

$$\frac{30x}{(1)x}$$

where the real number of students is the 30th multiple of some number x (the Unknown Multiplier) and the real number of teachers is simply x. Adding 50 students and 5 teachers to create a new 25 to 1 ratio can therefore be written as:

$$\frac{30x + 50}{x + 5} = \frac{25}{1}$$

Now we can do ***Direct Algebra*** and solve for x:

$$30x + 50 = 25x + 125$$
$$5x = 75$$
$$x = 15$$

This value for x is not only the Unknown Multiplier but the actual number of teachers right now. x teachers = 15 teachers. This is the **answer.**

Note that in this case x is equal to our final answer, but this is only because a 1 happens to be part of the first ratio (30 to 1). Generally speaking, the Unknown Multiplier is not itself the final answer to the question.

The correct answer is (E).

PS 106. Algebra: Exponents & Roots
Difficulty: Easy **OG Page:** 166

Because the problem involves an ***Inequality*** between ***Exponents*** with different bases, we cannot compare the numbers directly.

$25^n > 5^{12}$

To simplify the problem, replace 25 with 5^2, so both sides have a ***Common Base.***

$(5^2)^n > 5^{12}$

$5^{2n} > 5^{12}$

Because the bases are the same, we can compare the exponents:

$2n > 12$
$n > 6$

The smallest integer for which $n > 6$ is 7. This is the **answer**.

Technically, by the way, we cannot compare exponents when the base is 0, 1, or –1, but those special cases do not apply here.

The correct answer is (B).

PS 107. Number Properties: Probability
Difficulty: Easy **OG Page:** 167

This ***Probability*** problem discusses a group but specifies only ***Percents*** when describing characteristics of the group. No real numbers are used. Use a ***Smart Number*** to make the work easier. Because this is a percentage problem, 100 is a Smart Number. Assume that there are 100 people in the study group.

The problem specifies that 60% of the members are women, so 60 out of the 100 people are women. The problem further specifies that 45% *of the (60) women* are lawyers.

So the number of female lawyers is 0.45 × 60. An easy way to do this calculation is to first convert 0.45 to a fraction, and then to cancel common factors.

$$\frac{45}{100}\times 60 = \frac{45}{_5\cancel{100}}\times \cancel{60}^3 = 9\times 3 = 27$$

27 of the women are lawyers.

The problem asks us to determine the probability that the random member selected will be a female lawyer. We can calculate this probability with the ***Basic Probability Formula:*** taking the number of desired outcomes and dividing by the total possible outcomes.

The desired outcome is a female lawyer. Because there are 27 female lawyers, there are 27 ways to select one female lawyer. There are 100 people total, so there are 100 ways to select one person from the group. The probability is 27/100 = 0.27.

The correct answer is (C).

PS 108. FDPs: Fractions
Difficulty: Hard **OG Page:** 167

This problem tells us that for 4 years, the number of trees in the orchard has been increased by 1/4 the number of trees in the orchard the previous year. So each year, the number of trees is 5/4, or 1.25, times the number of trees that were in the orchard the previous year.

We are told that the orchard had 6,250 trees at the end of the 4th year and asked to figure out how many it had at the beginning of the 1st year.

Any time a question involves a change that is made multiple times, it is a good idea to use a ***Chart***. The original number of trees at the beginning of year 1 is unknown, so we can use the variable k. Make sure you label the original number of trees in the chart as the number of trees at the end of year 0, so we don't get it confused with the number of trees as the end of year 1, after the first change has been made. Every year, the number of trees in the orchard the previous year is multiplied by 5/4.

Year	Number of trees at the end of the year
0	k
1	$k\times\frac{5}{4}$
2	$\left(k\times\frac{5}{4}\right)\times\frac{5}{4}=k\times\left(\frac{5}{4}\right)^2$
3	$\left(k\times\left(\frac{5}{4}\right)^2\right)\times\frac{5}{4}=k\times\left(\frac{5}{4}\right)^3$
4	$\left(k\times\left(\frac{5}{4}\right)^3\right)\times\frac{5}{4}=k\times\left(\frac{5}{4}\right)^4$

We know that the number of trees in year 4 is equal to 6,250. We can now set up an equation to solve for k.

At this point, a disclaimer is necessary. Even once you are able to set up the equation, this is still not an easy equation to simplify. One thing that can make it easier is to keep 5/4 a fraction, as opposed to changing it to 1.25. There are two reasons. First, $(5/4)^4$ is easier to calculate than 1.25^4. The second reason will become clear in a moment:

$$k\times\left(\frac{5}{4}\right)^4=6{,}250$$
$$k\times\frac{625}{256}=6{,}250$$

The GMAT has included a clever shortcut here. We can first divide both sides of the equation by 625, which is easy to divide into 6,250 on the right side of the equation. Solving for k is much more straightforward after that.

$$\frac{1}{625}\times\left(k\times\frac{625}{256}\right)=(6{,}250)\times\frac{1}{625}$$
$$k\times\frac{1}{256}=10$$
$$k=2{,}560$$

Although fractions can always be expressed as decimals and vice versa, leaving numbers as fractions is more likely to help you see patterns hidden in the question. Additionally, multiplication involving fractions is often faster, and less prone to error.

The correct answer is (D).

PS 109. Word Problems: Statistics
Difficulty: Hard **OG Page:** 167

This ***Statistics*** question asks for the ***Median*** annual number of shipments of manufactured homes in the United States for the years 1990–2000. The graph of this 10 year period shows the annual number of shipments for manufactured homes for each of the 11 years in this period (1990 and 2000 are both included in the set, so the number of years is 2000 − 1990 + 1 = 11).

To answer the question, we need to ***Read the Graph*** correctly. The median of a set with an odd number of terms is the middle term when the set is arranged in increasing order. For a set of 11 terms arranged in ascending order, the 6th term will be the median. It might be tempting to identify 1995 as the median term, since 1995 is the middle year for the sequence of 11 years starting with 1990. However, it is the *values* of the statistics themselves that must be placed in ascending order, not the years in which they occurred.

As we figure out the order of the values, we should avoid copying down the graph on our paper or estimating every value. One way to save time and avoid mistakes is to make a quick ***Left-to-Right Graph:***

90 1 2 3 4 5 6 7 8 9 00

Now, working *vertically* from smallest to largest, we mark the heights in order, using the gridlines as demarcations. Start at the shortest column. Our marks should mimic the vertical positions of the columns on the original graph. In this way, we can easily spot errors. Once we reach the 6th smallest column, we can stop.

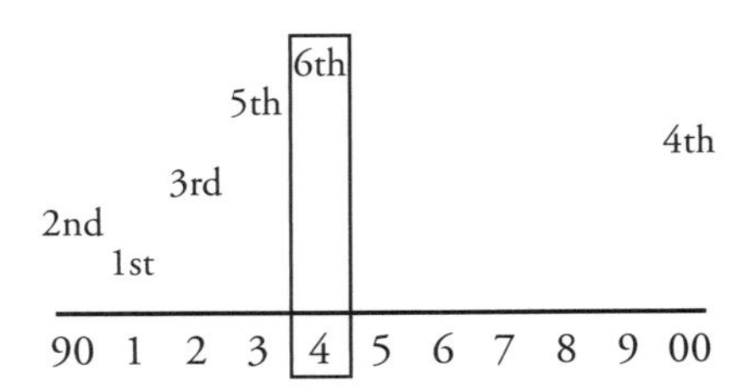

It may be difficult to distinguish the 4th smallest column (year 2000) and the 5th smallest column (year 1993). Notice, however, that distinction doesn't matter, because they are both clearly smaller than the 6th smallest column (year 1994), which is just slightly above the 300,000 gridline.

Likewise, some of the larger columns may be difficult to tell apart, but we can clearly tell that the 1994 column is smaller than all of them. Moreover, we do not need to mark these larger columns at all.

Using the answer choices, we see that the closest approximation of the number of shipments in 1994 is 310,000.

The correct answer is (C).

PS 110. <u>Number Properties</u>: Divisibility & Primes
Difficulty: Medium **OG Page:** 167

This ***Divisibility*** problem tells us that 2^k divides 72, but that 2^{k+1} does not. We are asked to figure out what the value of k is.

The language of this problem is unusual because it uses a strange symbol, "||", to relate a, b, and k. According to the definition of the function, $2^k \,||\, 72$ means that 2^k is a factor of 72, but 2^{k+1} is not. This is a sneaky way of saying that 2 is a factor of 72 exactly k times. To answer this question, we need to figure out how many times 72 is divisible by 2.

In order to figure out how may 2's there are among 72's ***Prime Factors***, use a factor tree to find the prime factorization of 72:

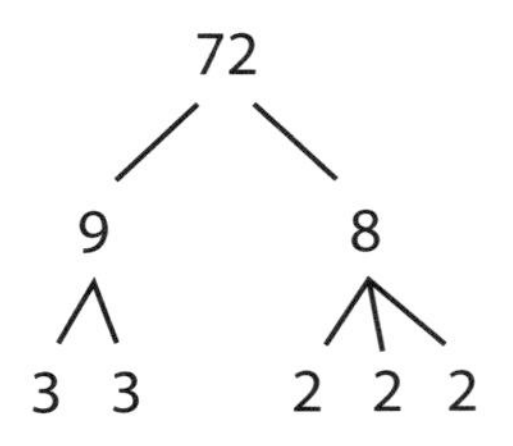

There are three 2's. That means that 72 is divisible by 2 three times. Therefore, k must equal 3.

The correct answer is (B).

PS 111. <u>FDPs</u>: Digits & Decimals
Difficulty: Devilish **OG Page:** 167

One straightforward approach to this ***Digits & Decimals*** question is to convert t to simple fractional form as follows.

$$t = \frac{1}{2^9 \times 5^3} = \frac{1}{512 \times 125} = \frac{1}{64{,}000}$$

Multiplying 512 by 125 directly is cumbersome. A more elegant approach is to group 2's and 5's to make ***Powers of 10:***

$$t = \frac{1}{2^9 \times 5^3} = \frac{1}{(2^6 \times 2^3) \times 5^3} = \frac{1}{2^6 \times (2^3 \times 5^3)}$$
$$= \frac{1}{2^6 \times 10^3} = \frac{1}{64 \times 10^3} = \frac{1}{64{,}000}$$

At this point, we have a few options.

(1) We can simply do ***Long Division*** of 64,000 into 1, counting the zeros after the decimal place and stopping once we get to a non-zero digit:

$$64{,}000\overline{)1.00000000...}\quad = 0.0000156...$$

Therefore, t has 4 zeros between the decimal point and the first nonzero digit to the right of the decimal point. This is the **answer**.

(2) Alternatively, we can compare t in this fractional form to some ***Benchmark*** fractions:

$$\frac{1}{100,000} < \frac{1}{64,000} < \frac{1}{10,000}$$

$$0.00001 < \frac{1}{64,000} < 0.0001$$

All numbers greater than 0.00001 and less than 0.0001 (such as 0.000011, 0.00002, 0.000078) all have 4 zeroes between the decimal point and the first nonzero digit.

(3) Finally, we can notice the following partial ***Power of Ten:***

$$\frac{1}{64,000} = \frac{1}{64} \times 10^{-3}$$

Using either long division or benchmarks as above, we can determine that 1/64 in decimal form has one zero between the decimal point and the first nonzero digit. The factor of 10^{-3} moves the decimal to the left, increasing the number of zeros by 3. Thus, t has $1 + 3 = 4$ zeros between the decimal point and the first nonzero digit after the decimal point.

The correct answer is (B).

PS 112. Word Problems: Statistics
Difficulty: Hard **OG Page:** 167

This ***Statistics*** problem is all about definitions. We are told that the population distribution is symmetric about the mean, m. So the shape of the distribution below the mean is the mirror image of the shape of the distribution above the mean.

We are also told that 68% of the distribution lies within one standard deviation, d, of the mean. Since the distribution is symmetric about the mean, that means that 34% of the population lies between $m - d$ and m and 34% lies between m and $m + d$.

A picture makes this much easier to understand:

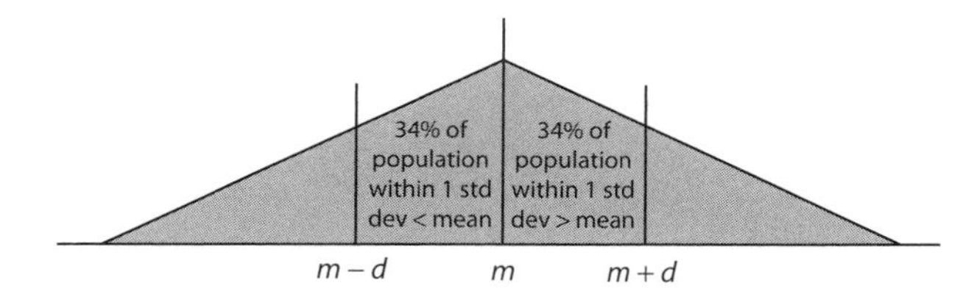

The question asks for the percent of the distribution that is less than $m + d$.

Note that although a Bell curve distribution has this characteristic, other distributions do as well, so we can't assume anything about the shape of the distribution other than its symmetry, but that is enough to allow us to solve this problem.

Since the distribution is symmetric, we know that 50% of it lies below the mean and 50% of it lies above. So the percent of the distribution that lies below $m + d$, aka below one standard deviation above the mean, is 50% + 34% = 84%.

The correct answer is (D).

PS 113. FDPs: Ratios
Difficulty: Medium **OG Page:** 167

This ***Ratios*** problem tells us that the ratio of Republicans to Democrats is 3/5 and that after 600 Republicans and 500 Democrats are added, the ratio becomes 4/5.

The question asks how many more Democrats there were than Republicans after the registration.

The ***Unknown Multiplier*** can be used to efficiently solve this type of problem. If the original ratio of Republicans to Democrats is 3/5, then we can represent the original number of Republicans as $3x$ and the original number of Democrats as $5x$. Using the unknown multiplier allows us to use only 1 variable to set up and answer this question (as opposed to using r and d to represent the original numbers).

First, set up a chart capturing the given information and showing the number of Republicans and Democrats before and after registration.

	Before	After
Republicans	$3x$	$3x + 600$
Democrats	$5x$	$5x + 500$

We know that the new ratio of Republican to Democrats is 4/5. In other words:

$$\frac{3x+600}{5x+500}=\frac{4}{5}$$

Use this equation to solve for x. Once we know x, we can use it to find the new numbers of Republicans and Democrats.

$5(3x + 600) = 4(5x + 500)$

$15x + 3{,}000 = 20x + 2{,}000$

$1{,}000 = 5x$

$200 = x$

Now plug x in and compute the number of Democrats and Republicans *after* the registration:

$5x + 500 = 1{,}000 + 500 = 1{,}500$ Democrats

$3x + 600 = 600 + 600 = 1{,}200$ Republicans

That means there were 300 more Democrats than Republicans after the voter registration.

Alternatively, this problem can be solved by setting up two equations with two variables, r for the number of Republicans and d for the number of Democrats, and doing substitution, as shown below.

Equation (1) before new voters were registered:

$$\frac{r}{d}=\frac{3}{5}$$

$5r = 3d$

Equation (2) after new voters were registered:

$$\frac{r+600}{d+500}=\frac{4}{5}$$

$5(r + 600) = 4(d + 500)$

$5r + 3{,}000 = 4d + 2{,}000$

Substitute (1) into (2):

$3d + 3{,}000 = 4d + 2{,}000$

$1{,}000 = d$

Plug the value of d back into equation (1):

$5r = 3{,}000$

$r = 600$

Then we can compute the number of Democrats and Republicans after the registration and solve the problem.

Note that answer (C) is a clever trap. It is the difference between the number of Democrats and Republicans *before* registration instead of *after*. Avoid this kind of trap by rereading the question before choosing an answer.

The correct answer is (B).

PS 114. FDPs: Percents
Difficulty: Medium **OG Page:** 168

This rather wordy ***Percents*** problem gives us dates for various percent changes and talks about unemployment rates. The key things to focus on though are the percent changes. This problem tells us that the unemployment rate among the workers dropped from 16% to 9% at the same time that the number of workers increased by 20%.

The question then asks for approximate percent change in the number of unemployed workers.

Since there are only percents and no quantities in the problem, one option is to ***Choose Smart Numbers***. Since the problem says "approximately," try to save time by rounding. At the same time, it is worth finding numbers that will make calculation easier.

A good number to use for the total number of workers is 100. In general, 100 is a good number to use in questions that involve percents.

A ***Chart*** is a useful tool to keep track of all the unknowns:

	Before	After
# Workers	100	$1.2 \times 100 = 120$
# Unemployed workers	$0.16 \times 100 = 16$	$0.09 \times 120 \approx$ $0.1 \times 120 \approx 12$

The number of unemployed workers decreased substantially, from 16 to 12, ruling out answers (C), (D), and (E).

We can calculate the approximate percent decrease by plugging the number of unemployed workers into the ***Percent Change Formula***.

$$\frac{\text{old}-\text{new}}{\text{old}}=\frac{16-12}{16}$$
$$=\frac{4}{16}$$
$$=25\%$$

25% is close to 30%. If there is any doubt, remember that rounding 0.09 to 0.1 made the percent change smaller, so it makes sense that the correct answer should be greater than 25%.

Alternatively, this problem could have been solved algebraically. The chart would look similar. Instead of using 100 for the original number of workers, use x:

	Before	After
# Workers	x	$1.2x$
# Unemployed workers	$0.16x$	$0.09 \times 1.2x \approx 0.1 \times 1.2x = 0.12x$

So the number of unemployed workers decreased from $0.16x$ to $0.12x$

We can still plug into the percent decrease formula:

$$\frac{\text{old}-\text{new}}{\text{old}}=\frac{0.16x-0.12x}{0.16x}$$
$$=\frac{0.04x}{0.16x}$$
$$=25\%$$

The correct answer is (B).

PS 115. FDPs: Percents
Difficulty: Devilish **OG Page:** 168

This ***Percent Change*** question breaks the pharmaceutical company's sales into two parts, giving the corresponding royalties for each part: the first \$20 million with \$3 million in royalties and the next \$108 million with \$9 million in royalties. List the parts in a ***Chart.***

	First	Second
Royalties	\$3 million	\$9 million
Sales	\$20 million	\$108 million
Royalties/Sales	3/20	9/108 = 1/12

The question then asks for the approximate percent decrease in the ratio of royalties to sales from the first part to the second part.

$$\text{Percent change}=\frac{\text{New}-\text{Original}}{\text{Original}}\times 100\%$$

The Original here is the ***Ratio*** of royalties to sales for the first part, and the New is the ratio of royalties to sales for the second part. The result is a ***Double-Decker Fraction*** that needs to be simplified:

$$\frac{\text{New}-\text{Original}}{\text{Original}}=\frac{\text{Second}-\text{First}}{\text{First}}$$
$$=\frac{\frac{1}{12}-\frac{3}{20}}{\frac{3}{20}}=\frac{\frac{5}{60}-\frac{9}{60}}{\frac{9}{60}}=\frac{-\frac{4}{60}}{\frac{9}{60}}$$
$$-\frac{4}{60}\times\frac{60}{9}=\frac{-4}{9}=-0.\overline{44}$$

To convert to a percent, multiply this value by 100%, so the percent change is approximately 45% (and the negative sign simply means that the value went down, not up).

The correct answer is (C).

PS 116. Number Properties: Divisibility & Primes
Difficulty: Hard **OG Page:** 168

p is the product of all of the integers from 1 to 30, or 30! (30 factorial). We are asked for the greatest integer k for which 3^k is a factor of p. In other words, in this ***Divisibility*** problem, we need to find how many 3's are factors of p.

The ***Factor Foundation Rule*** tells us that each multiple of 3 from 1 to 30 will contribute factors of 3 to the overall product. The non-multiples of 3 will not contribute factors of 3 and can thus be ignored.

$3 = \underline{3} \times 1$
$6 = \underline{3} \times 2$
$9 = \underline{3} \times \underline{3}$
$12 = \underline{3} \times 2 \times 2$
$15 = \underline{3} \times 5$
$18 = \underline{3} \times \underline{3} \times 2$
$21 = \underline{3} \times 7$
$24 = \underline{3} \times 2 \times 2 \times 2$
$27 = \underline{3} \times \underline{3} \times \underline{3}$
$30 = \underline{3} \times 5 \times 2$

We can see that, collectively, the multiples of 3 between 1 and 30, inclusive, contribute 14 factors of 3 to p. Therefore, 14 is the **answer**.

A different way to add up the 3's is to count by powers of 3. First, count all the multiples of 3 just once. There are 10 multiples of 3 between 3 and 30, inclusive. Now, add 1 for each multiple of 9, since each multiple of 9 contains at least one more 3. We have 3 multiples of 9 (9, 18, and 27) in the range. Finally, add 1 more for 27, since 27 contains three 3's, as shown above.

$10 + 3 + 1 = 14$ factors of 3.

The correct answer is (C).

PS 117. <u>Algebra</u>: Quadratic Equations
Difficulty: Devilish **OG Page:** 168

The question asks for the answer choice that is NOT a factor of n. The "is NOT a" language tells us that 4 of the 5 choices must be factors of n, because only one choice can be correct. If we can find the factors of n, then we can eliminate the 4 wrong answer choices.

In general, the best way to find the factors of a number is to break it down into its prime factors. Calculating $3^8 - 2^8$ in less than two minutes without a calculator will be very difficult, and finding the factors of a large number is typically difficult. Both of these factors point to there being a shortcut built into the problem.

The shortcut is built into the equation for n. $3^8 - 2^8$ is a ***Difference of Squares***. This special quadratic is easy to factor: $x^2 - y^2 = (x + y)(x - y)$

$3^8 - 2^8 = (3^4 - 2^4)(3^4 + 2^4)$
$= (81 - 16)(81 + 16)$
$= 65 \times 97$

We can now eliminate answer choices (A) and (B), but there are still two answer choices to go. That is because, although 97 is a prime number, 65 can be broken down even further:

$65 = 5 \times 13$

Answer choices (D) and (E) can also be eliminated.

The correct answer is (C).

PS 118. <u>Number Properties</u>: Divisibility & Primes
Difficulty: Hard **OG Page:** 168

This confusingly worded problem takes a fair amount of effort to understand. The first sentence tells us that a club has more than 10 but fewer than 40 members, so $10 < m < 40$ (m is the number of members).

Then we are told that the members can sit at tables with 3 at one table and 4 at each of the other tables. This means that if all m members were arranged in groups of 4, there would be one group left over with only 3 members in it. Translated into math, that means that when m is divided by 4, the remainder is 3.

Similarly, we are told that members can sit at tables with 3 at one table and 5 at each of the other tables. Translated into math, this means that when m is divided by 5, the remainder is 3.

The question tells us that the members can be seated at tables in groups of 6, with one table left over with fewer than six members, and asks us how many members would be sitting at the table with less than 6 members. Translated into math, this is asking what the remainder will be when m is divided by 6.

This is an interesting ***Remainders*** problem. Since there can only be one correct answer to this problem, a good way to solve it is to construct a number that could be m and then see what that number's remainder is when it is divided by 6.

Since we know that m divided by either 4 or 5 results in a remainder of 3, $m - 3$ must be divisible by both 4 and 5.

The first number greater than 10 that is divisible by both 4 and 5 is 20, so $m - 3$ could be 20, making 23 a possible value of m.

23 divided by 6 is 3 with a remainder of 5. In other words, there will be 3 tables with 6 people each, and the last table will have 5 people.

It is worth noting that the constraint that m is between 10 and 40 actually forces m to be 23, because the next possibility for $m - 3$ is the next multiple of 4×5 after 20, which is 40. That would make $m = 43$, which is too big, given that we were told that $m < 40$.

The correct answer is (E).

PS 119. Word Problems: Statistics
Difficulty: Hard **OG Page:** 168

The problem tells us that Terry originally planned to read 90 pages per day for some number of days, which we will call d, in order to finish an assignment on time. We also know that Terry fell behind and only read 75 pages per day for the first several days and now has to read 690 pages in 6 days.

The question asks us to figure out how many days in all Terry had to finish the assignment.

A good plan for solving this problem is to use the average formula to figure out an equation for the number of pages, which we will call p.

First, we know that Terry read 690 pages in the last 6 days.

Second we know that he read 75 pages per day for $d - 6$ days, where d is the total number of days.

The number of pages he read in that period of time was $75(d - 6)$.

Taken together, we know the total number of pages read:

$$p = 690 + 75(d - 6)$$

We know that the average number of pages read per day must be equal to p divided by d. We can manipulate this equation to get the number of pages in terms of the number of days:

$$90 \text{ pages/day} = \frac{p \text{ pages}}{d \text{ days}}$$

Replace p with $690 + 75(d - 6)$ and solve for d:

$$90 = \frac{690 + 75(d - 6)}{d}$$

$$90d = 690 + 75d - 450$$

$$15d = 240$$

$$d = 16$$

16 is the **answer.**

Another clever way to solve this problem is to think about the ***residual*** amount left over after subtracting the total number of pages that Terry had planned to read in the last 6 days from the higher amount that she actually has to read.

If Terry were on schedule, she would have had to read $90 \times 6 = 540$ pages in the last 6 days, but instead she had to read 690 pages, so the total amount that she is behind is

$$690 - 540 = 150 \text{ pages}$$

An extra 150 pages should have been read during the time Terry was reading 75 pages per day. We also know that every day Terry read 75 pages, she fell behind 15 pages. That mean it took her 150/15 = 10 days to fall 150 pages per day behind, and then she had 6 days to catch up, for a total of

$$10 + 6 = 16 \text{ days}$$

The correct answer is (B).

PS 120. Algebra: Exponents & Roots
Difficulty: Easy **OG Page:** 168

In this ***Roots*** problem, we are asked to solve for r in terms of s. This means that we need to manipulate the equation to get r by itself on one side of the equals sign. On the other side of the equation, there should be an expression involving s. In other words, we want this equation:

r = something involving s

One potential complication to the problem might have involved the sign of s, but we are told that s is, in fact, positive. This makes the algebra straightforward, and we can solve this problem using algebraically.

First, ***Square Both Sides*** to eliminate the square root:

$$\left(\sqrt{\frac{r}{s}}\right)^2 = s^2$$

$$\frac{r}{s} = s^2$$

Next, multiply both sides by the denominator of the left side, in order to eliminate the fraction and isolate r:

$r = s \times s^2 = s^3$ This is the **answer.**

An alternative approach is to ***Choose Smart Numbers***. First, pick a simple number for s. Say $s = 2$. Then we solve for r as follows:

$$\sqrt{\frac{r}{s}} = s$$

$$\sqrt{\frac{r}{2}} = 2$$

$$\left(\sqrt{\frac{r}{2}}\right)^2 = 2^2 = 4$$

$$\frac{r}{2} = 4$$

$$r = 8$$

Note that we still have to perform the algebraic steps to isolate r (such as squaring both sides). Now, we match the ***Target Value*** of 8 to the answer choices.

(A) $\frac{1}{s} = \frac{1}{2} \neq 8$
INCORRECT

(B) $\sqrt{s} = \sqrt{2} \neq 8$
INCORRECT

(C) $s\sqrt{s} = 2\sqrt{2} \neq 8$
INCORRECT

(D) $s^3 = 2^3 = 8$
CORRECT

(E) $s^2 - s = 2^2 - 2 = 2 \neq 8$
INCORRECT

The correct answer is (D).

PS 121. Geometry: Polygons
Difficulty: Medium **OG Page:** 169

In this ***Polygons*** problem, we are asked what ***Fraction*** of the door's surface is covered by the trim. To rephrase, we are looking for this ***Ratio*** of ***Areas:***

$$\frac{\text{Area of Trim}}{\text{Total Area of Door}}$$

It is clear that the total area of the door is simply $6 \times 8 = 48$ square feet. Therefore, the desired quantity is now:

$$\frac{\text{Area of Trim}}{48}$$

Because the trim is irregularly shaped, it may be easier to find the area of the two rectangles that are NOT covered by trim and subtract that area from the total area of the door in order to find the area of the trim. This is an application of the ***1* – x *Principle:***

What we want = Everything – What we don't want

If the trim is one foot wide, then the three strips of trim running horizontally take up 3 vertical feet. Since the height of the door is 8 feet, 5 feet of vertical distance is taken up by the non-trim areas.

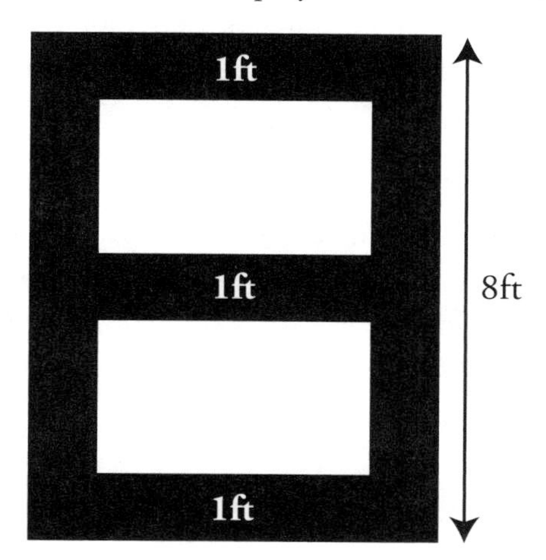

Since the width of the door is six feet and two strips of trim running vertically are each 1 foot wide, 4 feet of horizontal distance is taken up by the non-trim areas.

Therefore, the area of the door that is NOT covered by trim is $5 \times 4 = 20$ square feet. Note that it does not matter that the two non-trim areas are not touching—we have simply calculated their area as though they were sitting on top of one another, forming a single rectangle.

If the area of the non-trim portion of the door is 20 square feet, the area covered by trim is $48 - 20 = 28$ square feet. Finally, we compute the fraction of the door covered by the trim:

$$\frac{28}{48} = \frac{7}{12}$$

The correct answer is (D).

PS 122. **<u>FDPs</u>:** Digits & Decimals
Difficulty: Hard **OG Page:** 169

This ***Decimals*** problem asks us to compare a, a^2, and a^3, if we know that $a = -0.3$.

The particular value of a is not important. What we need is ***Number Line Awareness***. Specifically, we need to recognize that -0.3 is a negative proper fraction (a decimal between -1 and 0).

Without performing any computations, we can observe ***Positive & Negative Rules*** for ***Exponents*** to eliminate answer choices.

A negative number taken to an even power results in a positive number.

A negative number taken to an odd power results in a negative number.

From this observation, a^2 will be positive. On the other hand, both a and a^3 will be negative. Thus, a^2 is larger than both a and a^3. Any positive number is larger than any negative number (that is, any positive number is to the right of any negative number on a number line), since 0 is greater than any negative but less than any positive.

We can eliminate (A), (C), and (D) because a^2 is not the largest value in those answer choices.

Now we can apply additional knowledge about negative proper fractions. Specifically, when we raise a number such as -0.3 to an *odd* power, it gets closer to zero. In other words, it gets *larger*.

$$a^3 = (-0.3)^3 = -0.027, \text{ and } -0.027 > -0.3$$

Remember that the larger of two negative numbers is closer to zero. For instance, $-8 < -2 < 0$. So we know that $a < a^3 < 0$, and we also know that $0 < a^2$.

Putting the inequalities together, we have $a < a^3 < a^2$.

The correct answer is (B).

PS 123. FDPs: Percents
Difficulty: Medium **OG Page:** 169

This ***Successive Percents*** problem discusses a group but specifies only percentages when describing characteristics of the group. No real numbers are used. ***Choose a Smart Number*** to make the work easier.

Pick a real number for one of the three people (Mary, Tim, or Juan) and then calculate the appropriate value for the other two. We can start with any person, but because the question asks for a percentage of Juan's income, it's a good idea to pick a number for Juan. Let's pick 100, an easy number to deal with in terms of percentages.

The problem specifies that Tim's income is 40% less than Juan's income. We can ***Name Variables*** and use ***Direct Algebra*** to write $T = J - 0.4J$. If Juan's income is 100, then Tim's income is $100 - 40 = 60$.

The problem specifies that Mary's income is 60% more than Tim's income. That is, $M = T + 0.6T = 60 + (0.6)60 = 60 + 36 = 96$.

So, if Juan's income is 100, then Tim's income is 60, and Mary's income is 96.

Since Mary's income is 96 and Juan's income is 100, Mary's income is 96% of Juan's.

The correct answer is (C).

PS 124. Word Problems: Consecutive Integers
Difficulty: Hard **OG Page:** 169

We are asked to figure out how many entries there would be in the table if it were extended from 5 cities to 30. This would be very hard to do by drawing out 25 more rows and columns.

However, the problem shows us a picture of the table for a reason. Notice that there is a pattern in the entries. The number of dots is 1 for the first two cities, 1 + 2 for the first three cities, 1 + 2 + 3 for the first 4 cities, and 1 + 2 + 3 + 4 for all five cities. If a 6th city were added, there would need to be 5 additional dots, one for the distance from it to each of the existing cities. Similarly, if a 7th city were added after that, there would need to be 6 additional dots beyond the 5 already added.

So for 30 cities, there would need to be 1 + 2 + 3 + 4 + … + 29 dots. We can compute this sum using the formula for the ***Sum of a Series of Consecutive Integers:***

$$\begin{aligned}\text{Sum} &= \text{Average} \times \text{Number of Terms}\\ &= \frac{(\text{last} + \text{first})}{2} \times (\text{last} - \text{first} + 1)\\ &= \frac{(29+1)}{2} \times (29 - 1 + 1)\\ &= 15 \times 29\\ &= 435\end{aligned}$$

Another clever way to solve this problem is to notice that all of the entries above the diagonal of the table have dots and none of the entries either on the diagonal or below it have dots. So the number of dots in the table is just the total number of squares (5 × 5) minus the number in the diagonal (5), and then divided by 2, which equals (25 – 5)/2 = 10.

With 30 cities, there would be 30 × 30 = 900 squares, with 30 on the diagonal, so 870, and if we divide that by 2, we get 435.

The correct answer is (B).

PS 125. FDPs: Ratios
Difficulty: Easy **OG Page:** 169

For questions that ask for the "approximate length," we do not need to solve the problem completely. In fact, we probably should not bother to solve, since ***Estimation*** is likely to be faster.

Drawing a Picture of the rectangular display may be helpful:

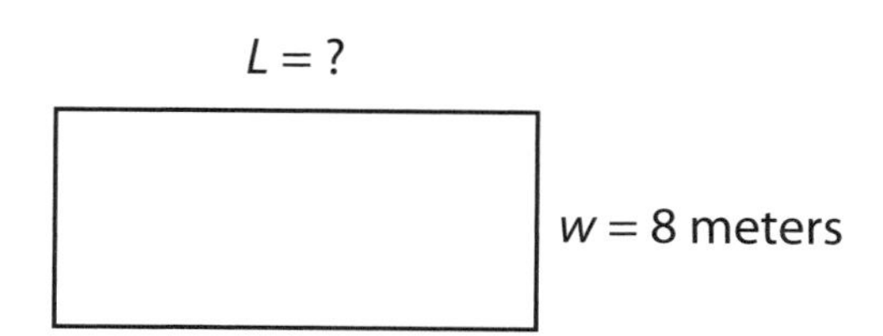

We have drawn the rectangle to make L a little more than 50% longer than w, since we are told that the ratio of length to width is 3.3 to 2. (If the ratio were exactly 3 to 2, the length would be exactly 50% longer, since $3/2 = 1.5 = 1 + 50/100$.) This observation alone allows us to eliminate answer choice (A) (7 is shorter than 8) and answer choice (B) (11 is not quite 50% longer than 8).

If 3.3 is a little more than 50% greater than 2, the length will be a little more than 50% greater than 8. That is, $L \approx 8 +$ (a little more than 4) $\approx$ a little longer than 12. The closest value among the answer choices is 13. This is the **answer**.

To actually solve, set up an ***Proportion*** for the ***Ratio*** and substitute $w = 8$:

$$\frac{L}{w} = \frac{3.3}{2}$$
$$L = \frac{3.3w}{2}$$
$$L = \frac{3.3(8)}{2}$$
$$L = 3.3(4) = 13.2$$

Note that even though we solved precisely, we are still required to estimate, since the exact length of L is not listed among the choices.

The correct answer is (C).

PS 126. Algebra: Formulas
Difficulty: Medium **OG Page:** 170

As stated in the problem, an ***Arithmetic Sequence*** is one in which each term after the first is equal to the sum of the preceding term and a constant. Since we can relate each term to its preceding term, ultimately we can relate each term to the first term by ***Direct Algebra.***

For the arithmetic sequence p, r, s, t, u, we can ***Name a Variable*** to express the constant difference between terms. Let's call this difference k.

$$r = p + k$$
$$s = r + k = (p + k) + k = p + 2k$$
$$t = s + k = (p + 2k) + k = p + 3k$$
$$u = t + k = (p + 3k) + k = p + 4k$$

Thus, the initial sequence in terms of p and k is:

$$p, r, s, t, u = p, p + k, p + 2k, p + 3k, p + 4k$$

Now we can plug in these terms to test the given sequences. Keep in mind that, for an arithmetic sequence, the difference between successive terms must be constant. This difference does not have to equal k, however.

I. $2p, 2r, 2s, 2t, 2u$
$= 2p, 2(p + k), 2(p + 2k), 2(p + 3k), 2(p + 4k)$
$= 2p, 2p + 2k, 2p + 4k, 2p + 6k, 2p + 8k$

The difference between successive terms is constant. Each time, we add $2k$.

YES: this is an arithmetic sequence.

II. $p - 3, r - 3, s - 3, t - 3, u - 3$
$= p - 3, (p + k) - 3, (p + 2k) - 3,$
$(p + 3k) - 3, (p + 4k) - 3$
$= p - 3, p - 3 + k, p - 3 + 2k,$
$p - 3 + 3k, p - 3 + 4k$

The difference between successive terms is constant. Each time we add k.

YES: this is an arithmetic sequence.

III. p^2, r^2, s^2, t^2, u^2
$p^2, (p + k)^2, (p + 2k)^2, (p + 3k)^2, (p + 4k)^2$
$= p^2, (p^2 + 2pk + k^2), (p^2 + 4pk + 4k^2)$, etc.

The difference between the first and second terms is $(p^2 + 2pk + k^2) - p^2 = 2pk + k^2$. The difference between the second and third terms is $(p^2 + 4pk + 4k^2) - (p^2 + 2pk + k^2) = 3k^2 + 2pk$. This is only an arithmetic sequence if $2pk + k^2 = 3k^2 + 2pk$. If $k \neq 0$, then $2pk + k^2 \neq 3k^2 + 2pk$.

NO: This is not an arithmetic sequence, unless $k = 0$ (in which case all the numbers in the sequence are the same).

We can also surmise that this last group is not a sequence by knowing something about exponents. Exponents increase larger bases faster than they do smaller bases. They do not operate with consistent rates. Thus, it would be impossible for the squares of evenly spaced nonzero terms to be evenly spaced themselves.

Thus, the only two sequences that must be arithmetic are I and II. This is the **answer**.

Alternatively, we can solve this problem by ***Choosing Smart Numbers.*** We must be sure that the numbers we pick create an arithmetic sequence:

$p = 3$
$r = 5$
$s = 7$
$t = 9$
$u = 11$

Using these terms, the three sequences would look like this:

I. 6, 10, 14, 18, 22
II. 0, 2, 4, 6, 8
III. 9, 25, 49, 81, 121

The first two sequences have a constant difference between the terms, and are therefore arithmetic. The third sequence is not spaced evenly, however, and is therefore not arithmetic.

The correct answer is (D).

PS 127. <u>Number Properties</u>: Divisibility & Primes
Difficulty: Hard **OG Page:** 170

The question asks us to figure out how many values of x that are greater than 3 and less than 100 are 3 times the square of a ***Prime Number***.

A good way to solve this problem is just to construct and list out the possible values of x. We shouldn't have too many numbers to list because the largest answer choice is nine.

Prime	Square of that prime	$x = 3 \times$ square of prime
2	4	12
3	9	27
5	25	75
7	49	147 ← TOO BIG!

Only 3 primes match the description: 2, 3, and 5.

The correct answer is (B).

PS 128. <u>Number Properties</u>: Combinatorics
Difficulty: Hard **OG Page:** 170

The question asks us to figure out the least number of letters that can be used to generate a unique 1 or 2 letter code to identify 12 different participants in an experiment. Notice that it says that the code has to be written out in alphabetical order, which means that *AB* is legal but *BA* is not.

This is a ***Combinatorics*** problem. The constraint that specifies "alphabetical order" is a sneaky way of saying that order does not matter, because *AB* is the same as *BA* after you put them in alphabetical order.

A good way to solve this problem is just to test the answer choices and stop at the first one that would result in 12 or more codes. The number of unique single letter codes will be the same as the number of letters, and it will be easy to list out all the possibilities for two-letter codes.

We start with 4 because that is the smallest possibility. Use the letters *A*, *B*, *C*, and *D*. With 4 letters, we can create 4 unique single letter codes. We can also create all the following two-letter codes:

AB *AC* *AD*
BC *BD*
CD

4 one-letter codes plus 6 two-letter codes is a total of 10 codes. We need more than 4 letters.

At this stage, it is reasonable to assume that the answer must be 5. It would make sense to select answer choice (B). However, we will also show that 5 letters will be enough. Add the letter E, and see how many additional codes we have.

There is 1 additional one-letter code (E). The additional two-letter codes are:

AE *BE* *CE* *DE*

Adding a fifth letter adds 5 more codes, for a total of 15 unique codes.

The correct answer is (B).

PS 129. Algebra: Formulas
Difficulty: Hard **OG Page:** 170

The question asks us to figure out the height of the object 2 seconds after it reaches its maximum height.

The key to this ***Formulas*** problem is finding the maximum height. Once we know the time at which the object reaches its maximum height, we can add 2 to that time to calculate the height the question asks for.

Take another look at the function:

$$h = -16(t-3)^2 + 150$$

How can we maximize the value of h?

The second term (150) does not contain a variable, and so does not change as t changes. The first term, however, does contain t.

The first term is the product of -16 and $(t-3)^2$. To maximize the height, we need to maximize this product. -16 is negative, and $(t-3)^2$ cannot be negative, which means this product cannot be positive. The largest number that is not positive is 0. We can maximize the height by making the value of $-16(t-3)^2$ equal to 0. This occurs when $t = 3$:

$$h = -16(t-3)^2 + 150$$
$$h = -16(3-3)^2 + 150$$
$$h = -16(0) + 150$$
$$h = 150$$

If the maximum height occurs at $t = 3$, 2 seconds after the maximum height is $t = 5$. Plug in 5 for t to get the height that the question asks us for.

$$h = -16(t-3)^2 + 150$$
$$h = -16(5-3)^2 + 150$$
$$h = -16(2)^2 + 150$$
$$h = -16(4) + 150$$
$$h = -64 + 150$$
$$h = 86$$

The correct answer is (B).

PS 130. Algebra: Inequalities
Difficulty: Easy **OG Page:** 170

Each of the given ***Inequalities*** can be simplified with ***Direct Algebra:***

$$x+6>10 \qquad x-3\leq 5$$
$$x>4 \qquad x\leq 8$$

We can combine these two inequalities into one ***Compound Inequality*** by turning the inequality signs in the same direction and merging the x's.

$$4<x \qquad x\leq 8$$

$$4<x\leq 8$$

The correct answer is (D).

PS 131. Word Problems: Algebraic Translations
Difficulty: Easy **OG Page:** 170

Begin this ***Algebraic Translations*** problem by setting up equations. Translating directly from the text, we find:

$$d = 3j = \frac{1}{2}p$$

We are asked for the total number of books, in terms of d. So let's simply put j and p each in terms of d:

Since $d = 3j$, we know that $j = \frac{1}{3}d$.

Since $d = \frac{1}{2}p$, we also know that $p = 2d$.

Finally, we add the three sets of books together:

$$d + j + p$$
$$= d + \frac{1}{3}d + 2d = \left(3\frac{1}{3}\right)d = \frac{10}{3}d$$

This is the **answer.**

Alternatively, we can ***Choose Smart Numbers.*** for d, j, and p. Since these variables are bound by certain ratios, the numbers that we pick must agree with these ratios. It would also be wise to pick a number for d that is a multiple of 3, because $d = 3j$. Let's pick numbers:

$d = 6$
$j = 2$
$p = 12$

According to our Smart Numbers, the total number of books is 20. Thus, 20 is our ***Target Value.***

Next, plug in 6 for d in each of the answer choices, in order to find one that matches the target value of 20.

(A) $\frac{5}{6}(6) = 5$ INCORRECT

(B) $\frac{7}{3}(6) = 14$ INCORRECT

(C) $\frac{10}{3}(6) = 20$ **CORRECT**

(D) $\frac{7}{2}(6) = 21$ INCORRECT

(E) $\frac{9}{2}(6) = 27$ INCORRECT

The correct answer is (C).

PS 132. Word Problems: Statistics
Difficulty: Easy **OG Page:** 170

For an ordered list with an even number of elements, the ***Median*** is the average (arithmetic mean) of the middle two terms. Thus, the list 3, 6, 8, 19 has a median of 7, the average of 6 and 8. Notice that the median of this set is not actually in the set.

Since the medians of both lists are equal, the list x, 3, 6, 8, 9 must also have a median of 7.

For an ordered list with an odd number of terms, the median is simply the middle term—that is, the median is always one of the elements of the list.

Since no 7 appears in List II, x itself must be 7.

The correct answer is (B).

PS 133. Number Properties: Combinatorics
Difficulty: Medium **OG Page:** 171

We need to know how many pairs of teams we can select from a pool of 8. We can solve this ***Combinatorics*** problem using the ***Anagram Method.*** In essence, whenever we select two teams to play each other, we are saying "yes" to 2 and "no" to the remaining 6. For example,

A	B	C	D	E	F	G	H
Y	Y	N	N	N	N	N	N

In the above scenario, we say "yes" to teams A and B and "no" to the remaining 6. Every time we rearrange these 2 Y's and 6 N's, we are saying "yes" to a different pair and "no" to a different group of 6 teams. So if we knew the number of ways we could arrange 2 Y's and 6 N's, we would know the number of ways we can select 2 teams out of 8.

To count the ways, divide the factorial of the total number of teams by the factorial of the number of teams we are choosing and by the factorial of the number of teams we are excluding. Divide by 2! and 6! to take into account that the 2 Y's and 6 N's are identical.

$$\frac{8!}{2!6!} = \frac{{}^{4}\cancel{8} \times 7 \times \cancel{6 \times 5 \times 4 \times 3 \times 2 \times 1}}{\cancel{2} \times 1 \times \cancel{6 \times 5 \times 4 \times 3 \times 2 \times 1}} = \frac{4 \times 7}{1} = 28$$

Thus, there are 28 different pairs of teams that could play each other. This is the **answer.**

Alternatively, using a ***Geometric*** argument, imagine an 8 × 8 ***Table*** that lists all the possible pairs of teams. Study the pattern of entries in this table.

	A	B	C	D	E	F	G	H
A	X	same						
B	same	X						
C			X					
D				X				
E					X			
F						X		
G							X	
H								X

There are $8 \times 8 = 64$ boxes in the table. Subtract 8 for the 8 "X" boxes in the diagonal, which would represent a team playing itself. We are left with $64 - 8 = 56$ boxes. Finally, every possible game is double-counted by the remaining boxes. For instance, the game between A and B corresponds to either box labeled "same." Thus, divide 56 by 2 to get 28 unique games.

Finally, we could do a summation. Team A plays 7 other teams. Team B plays 7 other teams as well, but we have already counted the A–B match, so we just count 6 new games. Likewise, Team C plays 5 games that we have not counted yet, and so on to Team H. The sum $7 + 6 + 5 + 4 + 3 + 2 + 1$ equals 28.

The correct answer is (C).

PS 134. Algebra: Formulas
Difficulty: Medium **OG Page:** 171

This problem defines a ***Strange Symbol Formula*** and gives us a relation based on that formula. We are asked to determine the value of one of the variables in terms of the other.

We need to solve for c in terms of a, given that $a\theta c = 0$.

First, ***Substitute*** a and c into the formula for the function, which is defined in terms of a and b. The variable a is in the same position as before, but c takes the place of b. Thus, we can write the following:

$$a\theta c = \frac{a-c}{a+c} = 0$$

Note that a fraction equals zero if its numerator equals zero. For example, $0/5 = 0$. Therefore, we must have

$$a - c = 0$$

or

$c = a$ This is the **answer**.

It is important to note that a fraction *will not* equal zero when the denominator is equal to zero. Dividing by zero results in an undefined expression. Thus, it is not possible for c to equal $-a$. In fact, we are even told that a does *not* equal $-c$, to prevent division by zero, so answer choice (A) cannot be the right answer.

The correct answer is (E).

PS 135. FDPs: Percents
Difficulty: Hard **OG Page:** 171

In this ***Percents*** problem, the price of lunch for 15 people was \$207, including 15% gratuity. Since the question asks for a cost per person excluding gratuity, use the following equation to find the total price excluding gratuity, where x is that pre-tip price:

$$x(1.15) = 207$$
$$x = \frac{207}{1.15}$$

We can simplify this fraction by multiplying top and bottom by 100 to eliminate the decimal:

$$x = \frac{20{,}700}{115}$$

Now ***Cancel Factors.*** We start with 5, which obviously goes into both top and bottom:

$$x = \frac{20{,}700 \div 5}{115 \div 5} = \frac{4{,}140}{23}$$

Since 23 is a prime and we want a precise number, we now have to resort to long division:

$$\begin{array}{r} 180 \\ 23\overline{)4140} \\ \underline{23} \\ 184 \\ \underline{184} \end{array}$$

Thus, \$180 was the total pre-tip price. Dividing this amount equally across 15 people, we get \$180 ÷ 15 = \$12 exactly. This is the **answer**.

This final step is a specific application of the ***Average Formula***:

$$\frac{\text{Total Price}}{\text{Number of People}} = \text{Average Price per Person}$$

The correct answer is (B).

PS 136. Word Problems: Overlapping Sets
Difficulty: Devilish **OG Page:** 171

In this ***Overlapping Sets*** problem, people in Town X are either male or female, and they are either employed or not employed. Because the problem gives us percentages, we can use 100 as a ***Smart Number*** to represent the population of Town X.

Fill out a ***Double-Set Matrix*** to organize the information in the problem. The shaded box helps to answer the question.

	Employed?		
	Yes	No	Total
Male	48		
Female	?		
Total	64		100

From the Double-Set Matrix, we can determine the number of employed females in Town X:

64 – 48 = 16 employed females

To compute the percent of employed people who are female, we need to evaluate this expression:

$$\frac{\text{number of employed females}}{\text{total employed people}} \times 100\%$$

$$= \frac{16}{64} \times 100\% = 25\%$$ This is the **answer**.

Pay careful attention to the wording in problems such as this one. For instance, we want to calculate the percent of *employed* people who are females. Thus, we should divide the number of employed females (16) by the total number of *employed* people (64), not the overall total (100).

The correct answer is (B).

PS 137. Word Problems: Algebraic Translations
Difficulty: Devilish **OG Page:** 171

The problem tells us that Don was paid \$336 to complete a job that he thought would take him some number of hours, which we will call h at his regularly hourly rate, which we will call r. We are told that the job actually took 4 hours longer than planned, and that this resulted in Dan earning \$2 per hour less than his regular hourly rate. That means that the actual number of hours he worked was $(h + 4)$, and the hourly wage was actually $(r – 2)$.

The question asks us to determine how many hours Dan had estimated for the job. In other words, we need to solve for h.

First, translate the given information into equations. There are two unknowns in this question (h and r), so we should expect 2 equations.

The first equation represents what Dan thought would happen and the second one represents what actually happened.

$336 = hr$ AND $336 = (h + 4)(r – 2)$

We could solve this by ***Substitution***. First we would rearrange the first equation to isolate r. Then we would replace r with $336/h$ in the second equation. The danger is that this will create a very messy quadratic equation.

How do you know it will become a quadratic equation? If a system of equations involves equations that multiply two different variables (ex. $336 = hr$), the resulting substitution will create a quadratic equation. Read the full explanation below to see the algebra involved.

Fortunately, there is another approach. ***Work Backwards from the Answer Choices.*** Use the first equation to solve for r, then use the second equation to test the values of h and r. Where possible, look to estimate:

Estimated hours (h)	Actual hours ($h + 4$)	Estimated hourly rate (r)	Actual hourly rate ($r - 2$)
28	32	336/28 = 12	336/32 = a little more than 10
24	28	**336/24 = 14**	**336/28 = 12**
16	20	336/16 = 21	336/20 = not an int
14	18	336/14 = 24	336/18 < 20
12	16	336/12 = 28	336/16 = 21

On the actual GMAT, don't do more of the math than necessary, so we would stop after testing answer choice (B).

Alternatively, here is the algebraic solution:

$$336 = rh$$

$$r = \frac{336}{h}$$

so

$$336 = (h+4)\left(\frac{336}{h} - 2\right)$$

Now FOIL the right side of the equation:

$$336 = 336 - 2h + \frac{4 \times 336}{h} - 8$$

$$0 = -2h + \frac{4 \times 336}{h} - 8$$

Now multiply the equation by h to get rid of h in the denominator:

$$0 = -2h^2 + 4 \times 336 - 8h$$

$$0 = h^2 - 2 \times 336 - 4h$$

$$0 = h^2 - 4h - 2 \times 336$$

$$0 = h^2 - 4h - 672$$

$$0 = (h - 24)(h + 28)$$

Since the estimated number of hours cannot be negative, the answer must be 24.

The correct answer is (B).

PS 138. <u>Algebra</u>: Inequalities
Difficulty: Easy **OG Page:** 171

This ***Inequalities*** problem specifies that p and q are both positive integers. We also know that $p/q < 1$. We are asked to determine which expression in the answer choices *must* be greater than 1.

To solve, we can ***Choose Smart Numbers.*** In fact, because of the ***Exponents & Roots,*** we do not even need to set a specific target value. We simply need to figure out whether the result is larger or smaller than 1.

This is a good problem for picking numbers. There are only two variables, with well-defined constraints. If $p/q < 1$, and p and q are both positive, then $p < q$. We can try $p = 2$ and $q = 3$.

(A) $\sqrt{\frac{p}{q}} = \sqrt{\frac{2}{3}} =$ less than 1
INCORRECT

(B) $\frac{p}{q^2} = 2/9 =$ less than 1
INCORRECT

(C) $\frac{p}{2q} = 2/6 =$ less than 1
INCORRECT

(D) $\frac{q}{p^2} = 3/4 =$ less than 1
INCORRECT

(E) $\frac{q}{p} = 3/2 = 1.5 =$ greater than 1
CORRECT

The correct answer is (E).

PS 139. Word Problems: Rates & Work
Difficulty: Easy **OG Page:** 171

In this ***Working Together*** problem, we are told that one machine can complete a production order in 4 hours, working alone, and that another machine can complete the same job in 3 hours, working alone. We must now determine how many hours it would take both machines working simultaneously to complete the order. Remember, if two or more agents are performing simultaneous work, we can ***Add The Rates.***

The first machine's rate is 1 order every 4 hours, or 1/4 orders per hour. Similarly, the second machine's rate is 1/3 orders per hour. Add these rates to get the combined rate:

1/4 + 1/3 = 3/12 + 4/12 = 7/12 orders per hour.

To determine the time to complete 1 order working together, we can create an ***Rate–Time–Work Chart:***

R (orders/hour)	×	T (hours)	=	W (orders)
7/12	×	T	=	1

$$\left(\frac{7}{12}\right)T = 1$$

$$T = \frac{12}{7} \text{ hours, or } 1\frac{5}{7} \text{ hours.}$$

This is the **answer**.

There is a shortcut for straightforward ***Working Together*** problems, in which the task is the same for each machine and for the machines working together:

$$\frac{1}{4 \text{ hours}} + \frac{1}{3 \text{ hours}} = \frac{1}{\text{time working together}}.$$

This formula can get us to 12/7 hours quickly, However, we should understand the formula as a special case of adding rates.

The correct answer is (C).

PS 140. Word Problems: Algebraic Translations
Difficulty: Medium **OG Page:** 172

We should begin this question by determining whether it will be cheaper to ship the packages separately or combined. Since the *first* pound is *more* expensive, it must be *cheaper to ship the combined package* (since the more expensive "first pound" is only paid once, rather than twice). We can use this sort of ***Algebraic Reasoning*** to gut-check our answer.

If we continue down the ***Direct Algebra*** road, we need to determine the cost to mail each package separately and the cost to mail them together. We'll begin with the cost to mail the packages separately. The first package weighs 3 pounds. The cost to ship the first pound is x cents/pound, for a total of x cents. The cost to ship the remaining 2 pounds is y cents/pound, for a total of $2y$ cents. So the cost to ship the 3 pound package is $x + 2y$ cents. The second package weighs 5 pounds. The cost to mail the first pound is x cents, and the cost to mail the remaining 4 pounds at y cents per pound is $4y$ cents for a combined cost of $x + 4y$ cents. That means that to ship both packages separately costs $(x + 2y) + (x + 4y) = 2x + 6y$ cents.

If the packages are mailed together, the total weight will be 8 pounds. The cost to mail the first pound is x cents and the cost to mail the remaining 7 pounds is $7y$ cents, for a total of $x + 7y$ cents. The cost of shipping the packages separately is $2x + 6y$. The cost of shipping them together is $x + 7y$. Since the latter is cheaper, the savings is $(2x + 6y) - (x + 7y)$, which reduces to $x - y$. This is the **answer**.

Alternatively, we can ***Choose Smart Numbers***, choosing specific values for the per-pound rates x and y. Let $x = 3$ and $y = 2$, so that all the answer choices will be different.

First we have to figure out how much it will cost to mail the packages separately. The cost to ship the 3 pound package will be 3 cents to ship the first pound and 2 cents/pound for the remaining 2 pounds, for a total cost of 7 cents. The cost to ship the 5 pound package will be 3 cents to ship the first pound and 2 cents/pound to ship the remaining 4 pounds, for a total cost of 11 cents. The cost to ship the packages separately is $7 + 11 = 18$ cents.

If the packages are mailed together the total weight is 8 pounds. It will cost 3 cents to mail the first pound and 2 cents/pound to ship the remaining 7 pounds, for a total cost of 17 cents. Therefore, it is cheaper by 1 cent to ship them together. This is our ***Target Value.***

Testing each answer choice, we can see that only (A) gives the target value.

(A) $3 - 2 = 1$	**CORRECT**
(B) $2 - 3 = -1$	INCORRECT
(C) 3	INCORRECT
(D) Separately	INCORRECT
(E) Separately	INCORRECT

The correct answer is (A).

PS 141. FDPs: Percents
Difficulty: Medium **OG Page:** 172

We are told that an investment doubles approximately every $70/r$ years, where r is the percent interest, compounded annually. Do not worry about where this ***Special Formula*** comes from. We are simply asked to use it. In fact, although the problem involves compound interest, we should not use the typical compound interest formula, which is unnecessary.

For this particular investment, $r = 8$, so this investment doubles every $70/r = 70/8 = 8.75$ years.

Now, we can use a ***Chart*** to track the growth of the investment.

Time	Investment Amount
now	$5,000
8.75 years from now	$10,000
17.5 years from now	$20,000

Notice that we track two stages of doubling. In 18 years, the initial investment has time to double twice.

When Pat is ready for college 18 years from now, the amount of the investment will be a little more than $20,000. The greatest (and therefore, closest) value among the answer choices is exactly $20,000. This is the **answer**.

Alternatively, we could have rounded 8.75 years right away to 9 years. Of course, there would still be two rounds of doubling.

The correct answer is (A).

PS 142. FDPs: Digits & Decimals
Difficulty: Hard **OG Page:** 172

On this problem, which involves both ***Decimals*** and ***Rates,*** Cindy's distance of travel (d) was 290 miles when rounded to the nearest 10 miles. Thus, her actual distance could have been any value that satisfies the following ***Inequality:*** $285 \leq d < 295$.

Notice that the 285 is included in the range (285 rounds up to 290), whereas the 295 is NOT. 295 rounds up to 300.

If Cindy used 12 gallons of gasoline, rounded to the nearest gallon, then her gallon usage, g, must satisfy the following inequality:

$$11.5 \leq g < 12.5$$

To find the possible range of values for Cindy's miles per gallon (mpg) for the trip, we must take the distance (d) and divide by the gallon usage (g). Since we are looking for a range, we must find both the smallest and largest possible values for her mpg. To ***Optimize*** the value of mpg in both directions, we should consider ***Extreme Values*** of d and g.

Since $mpg = d/g$, the *smallest* value for mpg can be found by taking the *smallest* d and dividing by the *largest* g. 285/12.5.

Conversely, the *largest* value for mpg can be found by taking the *largest* d and dividing by the *smallest* g: 295/11.5.

If we combine these two findings, the *mpg* must satisfy the following inequality:

$$\frac{285}{12.5} < mpg < \frac{295}{11.5}$$ This is the **answer.**

Note that the endpoints are technically NOT included here because each contains either a value of $d(295)$ or of $g(12.5)$ that was not included in the original inequalities. This is consistent with the word *between* in the question. *Between* is used to express an inequality for which the endpoints are NOT included.

The correct answer is (D).

PS 143. Algebra: Inequalities
Difficulty: Medium **OG Page:** 172

The number line shows that x ranges from −5 to 3, inclusive. The problem asks us to choose the algebraic form of an absolute value inequality that defines this range.

Since the range is continuous, a straightforward way to solve this problem is to test the endpoints of the given range in each answer choice. Plug −5 and 3 into each answer choice. If either value makes the inequality untrue, we can eliminate that answer choice:

Answer choice	Test lower bound, $x = -5$	Test upper bound, $x = 3$
(A) $\lvert x\rvert \le 3$	$\lvert -5\rvert =$ 5 ← FAIL!	
(B) $\lvert x\rvert \le 5$	$\lvert -5\rvert =$ 5 ← OK!	$\lvert 3\rvert =$ 3 ← OK!
(C) $\lvert x - 2\rvert \le 3$	$\lvert -5 - 2\rvert =$ 7 ← FAIL!	
(D) $\lvert x - 1\rvert \le 4$	$\lvert -5 - 1\rvert =$ 6 ← FAIL!	
(C) $\lvert x + 1\rvert \le 4$	$\lvert -5 + 1\rvert =$ 4 ← OK!	$\lvert 3 + 1\rvert =$ 4 ← OK!

Answers (B) and (E) both are both correct inequalities when the endpoints of the range are plugged in. We still need to eliminate the final wrong answer.

Notice that answer choice (B) is $|x| \le 5$. 4 and 5 are both numbers that make that inequality true, but are not in the original range (from −5 to 3). Therefore, (B) includes values not in the range, and is incorrect.

The correct answer is (E).

PS 144. FDPs: Percents
Difficulty: Easy **OG Page:** 172

In this ***Percents*** problem, there are currently 500 employees, 15% of whom are women. Thus, there are (0.15)(500) = 75 women at the company. If 50 more workers are hired, there will be a total of 550 workers. The question asks how many of the 50 will have to be women in order to raise the percentage of women at the company to 20%.

Since we know that we will have 550 total workers, the goal percentage, 20%, is equivalent to (0.20)(550) = 110 women.

We already have 75 women, so we must hire 110 − 75 = 35 women. This is the **answer.**

Alternatively, we can ***Name a Variable*** and call the number of new women x. Then we can set up the following equation, using the fraction 1/5 as an ***Equivalent*** of 20%:

$$\frac{75 + x}{550} = 20\% = \frac{1}{5}$$

Now ***Cross-Multiply*** and solve for x:

$375 + 5x = 550$

$5x = 175$

$x = 35$

Thus, 35 of the 50 new workers will have to be women in order to increase the percentage of women to 20%.

The correct answer is (E).

PS 145. Word Problems: Statistics
Difficulty: Easy **OG Page:** 172

This ***Statistics*** problem asks us to determine the average value of a subset of numbers, given the averages of the full set and of the other subset of numbers. The best approach is to use the ***Average*** formula separately on each set and on each subset. The average of a set is given by the sum of the terms, divided by the number of terms:

$$A = \frac{S}{N}$$

Then, we can solve for the sum as *Sum* = *Average* × *Number*. Let S_{10} denote the sum of the revenues for all 10 days. Likewise, let S_6 denote the sum of the revenues for the first 6 days and S_4 denote the sum of the revenues for the last 4 days. Using the above relation, we can write:

$$S_{10} = 10 \times \$400 = \$4,000$$
$$S_6 = 6 \times \$360 = \$2,160$$

Now, note that $S_{10} = S_6 + S_4$. Therefore,

$$S_4 = S_{10} - S_6 = \$4,000 - \$2,160 = \$1,840.$$

The desired average of the last 4 days is

$$A = \frac{S_4}{4} = \frac{\$1,840}{4} = \$460.$$

An alternative approach is to use ***Weighted Averages***. The first 6 days represent 60% of the total of 10 days, while the last 4 days represent the remaining 40%. These percentages constitute the weights carried by the subset averages in terms of their contribution to the overall average. If we let A stand for the average of the last 4 days, then

$$\$400 = (60\%) \times \$360 + (40\%) \times A$$
$$\$400 = \$216 + 0.4A$$
$$0.4A = \$400 - \$216 = \$184$$
$$A = \frac{\$184}{0.4} = \$460$$

Finally, we can use the method of ***Residuals***. Imagine that on each of the first 6 days, the shop actually makes only \$360, but it needs to make \$400. Then the shop is short \$40 on each of those days. (Each \$40 shortfall is the residual.) The total shortfall in the first 6 days is then 6 days × \$40 = \$240. In the last 4 days, the shop must make \$400 every day, plus an extra \$240 over the 4 days to make up the shortfall. The extra \$240 over 4 days = \$240 ÷ 4 = \$60 per day, so the shop must make \$400 + \$60 = \$460 per day (on average) over the last 4 days.

The correct answer is (D).

PS 146. <u>FDPs</u>: Digits & Decimals
Difficulty: Easy **OG Page:** 172

In this **Digits & Decimals** problem, "Per capita" means "per person." To find the per capita expenditure, we need to divide the total expenditure by the total population. That is, we need to calculate 1.2×10^{12} dollars divided by 240 million people. One million is 10^6, so we can use ***Powers of Ten*** to write the following ***Fraction:***

$$\frac{1.2 \times 10^{12}}{240 \times 10^6}$$

Notice that the nonzero portions of the numerator and denominator, 12 and 24, have a special relationship: 24 is 2 × 12. Thus, 12/24 = 1/2. However, we can avoid fractions or decimals (and thereby reduce our potential for error) by noting that 120/24 = 5. Let's therefore manipulate the numerator and denominator using powers of ten to yield 120 and 24. Since $120 = 1.2 \times 10^2$, we take 2 powers of 10 from the 10^{12} part of the numerator to write 120. Likewise, since $240 = 24 \times 10^1$, we convert 240 to 24 by moving 1 power of 10 into the 10^6 part of the denominator.

$$\frac{1.2 \times 10^{12}}{240 \times 10^6} = \frac{1.2 \times 10^2 \times 10^{10}}{24 \times 10^1 \times 10^6} = \frac{120 \times 10^{10}}{24 \times 10^7}$$

Finally, simplify, using rules for ***Dividing Exponents:***

$$\frac{120 \times 10^{10}}{24 \times 10^7} = \frac{120}{24} \times \frac{10^{10}}{10^7} = 5 \times \frac{10^{10}}{10^7}$$
$$= 5 \times 10^3 = 5,000$$

Since the units of the original numbers were dollars and people, the unit of the answer is "dollars per person." In per capita calculations, the "per person" unit is often implied at the end. We simply say that the per capita expenditure is \$5,000.

The correct answer is (E).

PS 147. <u>Geometry</u>: Polygons
Difficulty: Easy **OG Page:** 173

This ***Polygons*** problem gives us information about a rectangular window. If the window's length is twice its width, we can ***Name a Variable*** as follows:

w = the window's width
$2w$ = the window's length

Draw a Picture to visualize the information.

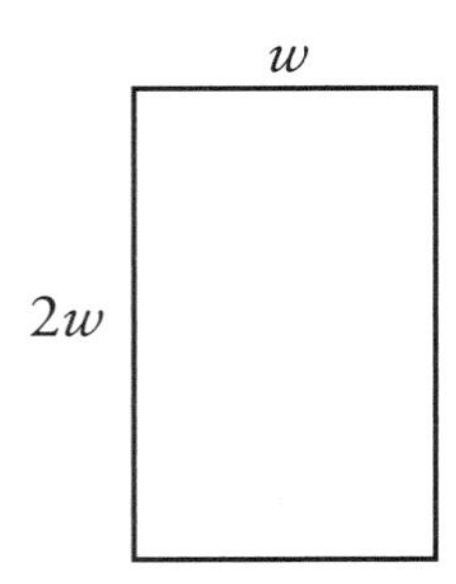

The ***Perimeter*** is the distance around the figure, so add the lengths of all four sides:

$$P = w + 2w + w + 2w = 10$$
$$6w = 10$$
$$w = \frac{10}{6} = \frac{5}{3}$$
$$2w = (2)\left(\frac{5}{3}\right) = \frac{10}{3}$$

The window has dimensions by $\frac{5}{3}$ by $\frac{10}{3}$.

The correct answer is (B).

PS 148. <u>Number Properties</u>: Combinatorics
Difficulty: Easy **OG Page:** 173

This ***Combinatorics*** problem gives a complicated diagram and asks us to determine the total number of different paths from point X to point Y.

A fast approach makes use of the ***Fundamental Counting Principle*** of Combinatorics.

The total number of paths is equal to the *product* of the number of options at each decision point, or fork in the road.

Start along the path from X until we get to the first fork. There are 2 different paths to choose, so we have 2 options for our first decision.

At the second fork, we also have 2 different options, and at the third and final fork, we have 3 different options. Therefore, the total number of paths is $2 \times 2 \times 3 = 12$. This is the **answer**.

Alternatively, we can count paths by literally ***Drawing Pictures,*** laying out the different paths. One possible path is:

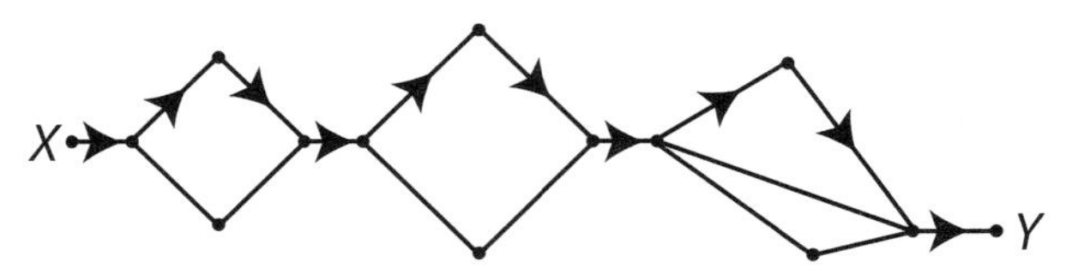

A second possible path is:

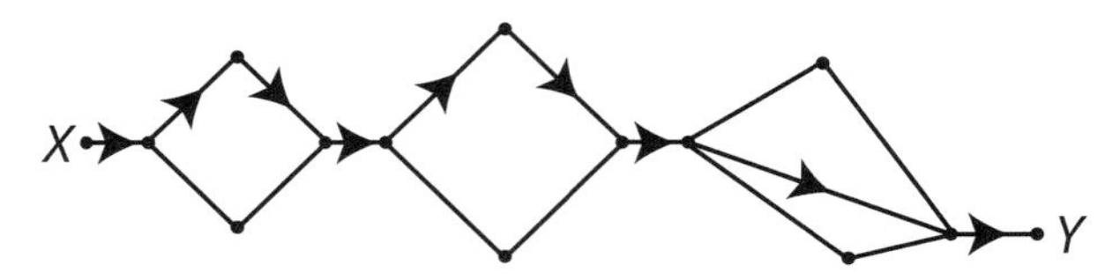

If we continued to draw out all the separate paths, we would find 12 unique paths. However, this approach is time-consuming and prone to error.

The correct answer is (C).

PS 149. <u>Algebra</u>: Formulas
Difficulty: Easy **OG Page:** 173

In this ***Strange Symbol*** problem, which also involves ***Roots,*** we must follow the procedure defined by the symbol while also paying attention to order of operations. First, simplify the expression in parentheses:

$$5 \odot 45 = \sqrt{5 \times 45} = \sqrt{(5) \times (5 \times 3 \times 3)}$$
$$= 5 \times 3 = 15$$

Now we can proceed from left to right and evaluate $15 \odot 60$:

$$15 \odot 60 = \sqrt{15 \times 60}$$
$$\sqrt{15 \times 60} = \sqrt{(3 \times 5) \times (2 \times 2 \times 3 \times 5)}$$
$$= 2 \times 3 \times 5 = 30$$

The correct answer is (A).

PS 150. Algebra: Exponents & Roots
Difficulty: Medium **OGs Page:** 173

In this tricky problem, which involves ***Repeating Decimals*** and ***Powers of Ten***, it is tempting to try to combine $10^4 - 10^2$ into 10^2. However, the only time that we can subtract exponents is when we are dividing exponential terms.

$10^4 - 10^2$ actually yields a rather unruly number:

$10{,}000 - 100 = 9{,}900$

In this case, the better approach is to ***Distribute*** the repeating decimal term:

$(10^4 - 10^2)(0.001212\ldots)$
$= (10^4)(0.001212\ldots) - (10^2)(0.001212\ldots)$

Multiplication by 10^4 moves the decimal point four places to the right, yielding 12.1212...

Multiplication by 10^2 moves the decimal point two places to the right, yielding 0.121212...

Now we can line up the two terms vertically

12.121212...
–.121212...

We can see that all the digits beyond the decimal point cancel upon subtraction, yielding a difference of 12. This is the **answer**.

Since the answer choices are generally far apart, ***Estimation*** is also a good way to solve this problem. Since $10^2 = 100$ is so small relative to $10^4 = 10{,}000$, the left-hand term can be estimated as 10,000. Also, the right-hand term can be estimated as 0.12. With these estimates, the product is 10,000 × 0.12, which is exactly 12.

The correct answer is (E).

PS 151. FDPs: Fractions
Difficulty: Medium **OG Page:** 173

In this ***Fractions*** problem, we are told about two work shifts: day and night. For each shift, we are also told about the number of workers and the number of boxes per worker. Since there is a lot of information, we need to keep it all organized. A great way to do so is with a ***Table,*** in which we calculate the number of boxes loaded by each shift.

	# of workers	Boxes per worker	Boxes Loaded
Day Crew			
Night Crew			
Total			

We can make the problem easier by ***Choosing Smart Numbers***. We are free to do so, since the question provides no actual numbers (such as the number of workers), but only relationships between variables (such as the ratio of one variable to another).

Each night worker loaded 3/4 as many boxes as each day worker. A Smart Number for the number of boxes per worker on the day crew is 4, the denominator of this ratio. In other words, if we simply say that each day worker loads 4 boxes, then each night worker loads (3/4) × 4 = 3 boxes.

The night crew has 4/5 as many workers as the day crew. A Smart Number for the number of day workers is 5, the denominator of this ratio. In other words, if we simply say that there are 5 day workers, then there are (4/5) × 5 = 4 night workers. Now, fill in the chart, multiplying across to get the number of boxes loaded on each shift. Notice that this problem is similar to a ***Rate*** problem. Here, the rate is boxes *per worker*, so we multiply by *workers* (not by time) to get total boxes.

	# of workers	Boxes per worker	Boxes Loaded
Day Crew	5	4	(5)(4) = 20
Night Crew	(4/5)5 = 4	(3/4)4 = 3	(4)(3) = 12
Total			20 + 12 = 32

The day crew loaded 20 of the 32 boxes, or 20/32 = 5/8 of all the boxes loaded.

The correct answer is (E).

PS 152. <u>FDPs</u>: Percents
Difficulty: Easy **OG Page:** 173

This ***Percents*** question provides us with a minimum and maximum tip percentage for a meal that costs \$35.50.

The minimum tip percentage is 10%, which would amount to a tip of $0.1 \times 35.50 = \$3.55$. (The easiest way to take 10% of any number is to move the decimal point to the left one place.)

The maximum tip percentage is 15%, which would amount to a tip of $0.15 \times 35.50 = \$5.33$, rounded to the nearest cent. (Another way to take 15% of a number is to take 1.5 times the 10% benchmark, which was found in the last step.)

The total amount paid for the meal must satisfy the following ***Inequality:***

$$\$35.50 + \$3.55 < \text{meal} < \$35.50 + \$5.33$$
$$\$39.05 < \text{meal} < \$40.83$$

Looking at the answer choices, we can see that the test writers decided to round this range "outward" to \$39 and \$41. This rounding is legitimate because a value between \$39.05 and \$40.84 *must* be between \$39 and \$41. The range \$39 to \$41 is the **answer**.

Note that there are limits to rounding an inequality's endpoints. We must round *outward* to ensure that we safely include the original inequality. For instance, if the actual maximum were \$40.40 and we rounded *down* to \$40, we would be cutting off part of the original inequality.

Alternatively, we could ***Estimate*** the range. \$35.50 plus 10%, or \$3.55, is \$39.05. An additional 5% on the tip is half of 10%, or half of \$3.55, which is less than \$2—let's say approximately \$1.75. Since the answer choices give \$2 ranges, we know that the top end will be \$39.05 + \$1.75, or just below \$41. Thus, \$39 to \$41 is the only safe range.

The correct answer is (B).

PS 153. <u>Word Problems</u>: Algebraic Translations
Difficulty: Easy **OG Page:** 173

This is a standard ***Algebraic Translations*** problem. We can begin by ***Naming Variables*** for the two unknown lifts. In this case, let's use f and s to represent the first and second lifts, respectively.

Next, translate the given information to create equations. We are told that the sum of the lifts equals 750 pounds. We can create our first equation as follows:

$$f + s = 750$$

The second equation comes from the second sentence, which states that "twice the weight of his first lift was 300 pounds more than his second lift."

$$2f = s + 300$$

By the way, the phrase "more than" technically places the "+ 300" *after* the s. For addition, this distinction doesn't matter, but if the problem read "300 pounds *less* than his second lift," we would write $s - 300$.

We are asked for f, so we want to make s disappear:

$$f + s = 750$$
$$s = 750 - f$$
$$2f = (750 - f) + 300$$ ***Substitute*** $(750 - f)$ for s in the second equation.

$$2f = 1{,}050 - f$$
$$3f = 1{,}050$$
$$f = 350$$

The correct answer is (D).

PS 154. <u>Word Problems</u>: Algebraic Translations
Difficulty: Easy **OG Page:** 173

This ***Optimization*** question asks us to determine the greatest number of members the club could have, given the fact that the club collected at least \$12 from each of its members and took in a total of \$599.

In order to *maximize the number* of members, we want to *minimize the amount* that each contributed. Since each contributed at least \$12, let's say that each member gave the minimum of \$12. We should find a number close to \$599 that is a multiple of 12. \$600 fits: $12 \times 50 = 600$. However, if the club really had 50 members and each member gave the minimum of \$12, then we cannot make the total any smaller than \$600. To make \$599 a possibility, there must be fewer than 50 members.

Let's try 49 members. If each contributes the minimum, then we have $\$12 \times 49 = 600 - 12 = \$588$. To reach \$599, one or more of the members contributes more than the minimum.

Alternatively, we can also simply divide 599 by 12, yielding $49\frac{11}{12}$. If partial members were allowed, then $49\frac{11}{12}$ members could contribute the minimum of \$12 for a total of \$599. The key is to know whether to round down or up. Because we cannot have a partial member, we round the fractional result down. The most memberships we can have is 49.

The correct answer is (C).

PS 155. <u>Number Properties</u>: Divisibility & Primes
Difficulty: Medium **OG Page:** 174

In this ***Divisibility*** problem, we are asked to find the smallest possible positive integer y such that $3{,}150y$ is the square of an integer, i.e., a perfect square.

The wrong way to do this problem is to test values of y, since that will take a very long time. The key is to focus on ***Prime Factors*** and to be aware that, in any perfect square, all of the prime factors will "pair up." That is, all prime factors will appear an even number of times. For instance, the perfect square 36 contains a pair of 2's and a pair of 3's in its prime factorization.

We must first find the prime factors of 3,150 to determine which ones are "single." Although 3,150 is a rather large number, it is clearly divisible by 10, making the factorization easier:

$$3{,}150 = 315 \times 10 = 63 \times 5 \times 10 = 7 \times 9 \times 5 \times 10$$

Breaking the numbers down further, and ordering the factors from smallest to largest, we finally obtain

$$3{,}150 = 2 \times 3 \times 3 \times 5 \times 5 \times 7$$

Therefore, the ***Prime Box*** of 3,150 contains two 3's and two 5's, but only one each of 2 and 7. We need the prime box of $3{,}150y$ to contain only pairs of primes if $3{,}150y$ is to be a perfect square. Single primes are not allowed. This means that y must provide at least one 2 and one 7. Also, because we are looking for the smallest possible y, those two factors should be all that y provides. This leads to $y = 2 \times 7 = 14$. This is the **answer.**

The figure below illustrates the prime box.

Prime box of $3{,}150y$

3	5	2	7
3	5	2	7

y provides the second 2 and the second 7.

The correct answer is (E).

PS 156. <u>FDPs</u>: Digits & Decimals
Difficulty: Medium **OG Page:** 174

This ***Decimals*** question tells us "[x] is the greatest integer less than or equal to x." A good way to rephrase this ***Strange Symbol*** is simply, "Round down." That is, if x is a positive integer, leave it alone. If it is positive but not an integer, delete the decimal portion.

So let's compute the function for the positive values first:

[3.4] = 3
[2.7] = 2

Be careful with the negative value. When we "round down" any number, we must move to the left on a number line. For negative numbers, this is *not* equivalent to just dropping the decimal portion. –1.6 rounds down to –2, not to –1.

$[-1.6] = -2$

Therefore,

$[-1.6] + [3.4] + [2.7] = -2 + 3 + 2 = 3$

This is the **answer**.

By the way, don't confuse the new bracket symbol $[x]$ with the absolute value $|x|$. We should NOT make the value of $[-1.6]$ positive.

The correct answer is (A).

PS 157. Algebra: Quadratic Equations
Difficulty: Medium **OG Page:** 174

In this ***Quadratic Equations*** problem, we are given the equation $\frac{4-x}{2+x} = x$ and are asked to find $x^2 + 3x - 4$.

We do not want to solve the equation for x. In fact, when we rearrange the equation with ***Direct Algebra*** into a standard quadratic, it looks like the expression we want to find.

Start by multiplying the entire equation by the denominator of the fraction. $(2+x)\left(\frac{4-x}{2+x}\right) = x(2+x)$

Distribute. $4 - x = 2x + x^2$

Add x to both sides. $4 = x^2 + 3x$

Subtract 4 from both sides. $0 = x^2 + 3x - 4$

The expression that the problem asks for, $x^2 + 3x - 4$ has a value of 0. This is the **answer**.

Remember, we are solving for the value of the expression $x^2 + 3x - 4$, *not* for x itself. Do not factor the quadratic! If we solve for x, we will run into a trap. Both valid solutions for x, -4 and 1, are given as answer choices.

The correct answer is (C).

PS 158. Word Problems: Consecutive Integers
Difficulty: Medium **OG Page:** 174

The problem tells us that Nancy saved $1 the first week and that in each subsequent week, she saved one dollar more than she saved the previous week, so in week 2 she saved $2, in week 3, she saved $3, etc.

We are asked to compute how much she saved over the course of 52 weeks.

The obvious way to solve this question is to start summing each week's savings, but this is not a practical approach given that we have no calculator and only 2 minutes to solve. So this must be one of those problems where there is a pattern to see and a trick to solving. A good way to look for such a pattern is to try to write out the mathematical expression:

$\text{Savings} = 1 + 2 + 3 + 4 + \ldots + 52$

The savings over 52 weeks is a sum of ***Consecutive Integers***. We can use the sum of consecutive integers formula to solve it. The sum of a series of consecutive numbers is equal to the average value of the numbers times the number of numbers in the set.

First, there are 52 numbers from 1 to 52. The average value is also straightforward to calculate. In a set of consecutive integers, the average is equal to the average of the first and last numbers in the set. The average of 1 and 52 is $(1 + 52)/2 = 26.5$.

The total sum is equal to the product of 52 and 26.5.

Do long multiplication:

$$\begin{array}{r} 26.5 \\ \times\ 52 \\ \hline 530 \\ 13250 \\ \hline 1378.0 \end{array}$$

The correct answer is (C).

PS 159. Geometry: Triangles & Diagonals
Difficulty: Easy **OG Page:** 174

This ***Triangles*** problem provides a diagram. Redraw this diagram and label it completely. We are given values for the two parallel sides: 2 and 5 feet, respectively. We are also told that line *AB* is 13 feet.

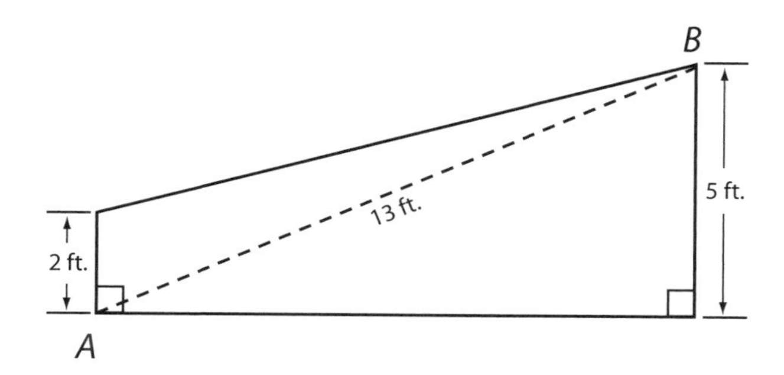

The formula for the ***Area of a Trapezoid*** is $A = \frac{(b_1 + b_2)h}{2}$.

The bases are the two parallel sides, so in this problem, $b_1 = 2$ and $b_2 = 5$. Note that a base is not necessarily the side that is on the ground. In this case, the bases are vertical. The height is the length of a perpendicular line drawn between the two bases. Thus, the bottom of the trapezoid is actually the height.

Line *AB*, which has length 13, represents the hypotenuse of a ***Right Triangle***. One leg of this triangle has length 5. The other leg is the unknown bottom of the trapezoid.

This is a common right triangle: the 5–12–13. Therefore, we know that the missing leg of the triangle is 12. (This length can also be found using the ***Pythagorean Theorem***.)

Since this length is also the height of the trapezoid, we now have all the numbers needed in the formula for the trapezoid's area:

$$A = \frac{(2+5)12}{2} = 7 \times 6 = 42 \text{ square feet}$$

This is the **answer**.

Alternatively, we can ***Split the Figure*** into a triangle and a rectangle and then add the two areas.

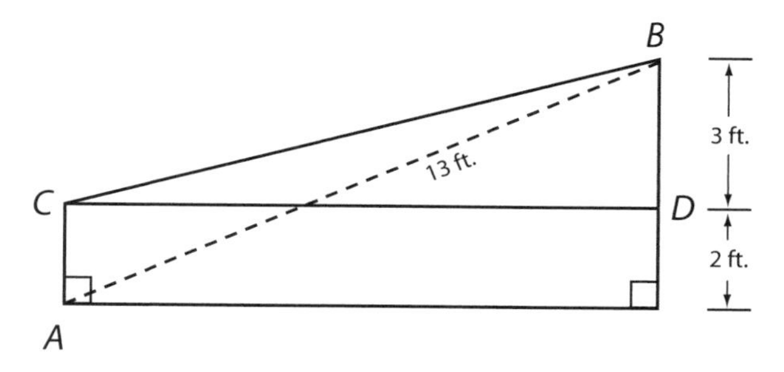

The base of the triangle, *CD*, is 12 (as calculated above) and its height is 3.

$$A = \frac{1}{2}bh = \frac{1}{2}(12)(3) = 18$$

For the rectangle, the length is 12 and the width is 2. $A = bw = 12 \times 2 = 24$.

Area of triangle + Area of rectangle = 18 + 24 = 42.

The correct answer is (C).

PS 160. Algebra: Formulas
Difficulty: Medium **OG Page:** 174

This problem involves a ***Recursive Sequence,*** in which each item of the sequence is defined in terms of the values of previous items in the sequence.

We are asked for the value of x_5, so substitute 3 for the value of n in the formula:

$$x_3 = 2x_2 - \frac{1}{2}x_1$$

The value of x_3 depends on the values of x_2 and x_1. We are told that $x_1 = 2$, but we do not yet know the value of x_2, so we will have to determine this value first.

$$x_2 = 2x_1 - \frac{1}{2}x_0 = 2(2) - \frac{1}{2}(3) = 4 - 1.5 = 2.5$$

We can now use the values of x_2 and x_1 to determine the value of x_3:

$$x_3 = 2x_2 - \frac{1}{2}x_1 = 2(2.5) - \frac{1}{2}(2) = 5 - 1 = 4$$

This is the **answer**.

A ***Sequence Diagram*** can keep us organized as we work. Draw blanks for each term, and fill in what we know. We are given two values, x_0 and x_1:

3 2 __ ◯

These two values give us $x_2 = 2.5$, so we can write:

3 2 2.5 ◯

Finally, we take the middle values (x_1 and x_2) and produce the target x_3:

3 2 2.5 (4).

The correct answer is (C).

PS 161. Geometry: Triangles & Diagonals
Difficulty: Easy **OG Page:** 175

This ***Triangles*** problem describes a distance *VR* but does not actually show this distance in the given diagram. Thus, we should ***Draw a Picture*** that shows *VR*. We should also name the point at the right angle. Let's call it *Q*:

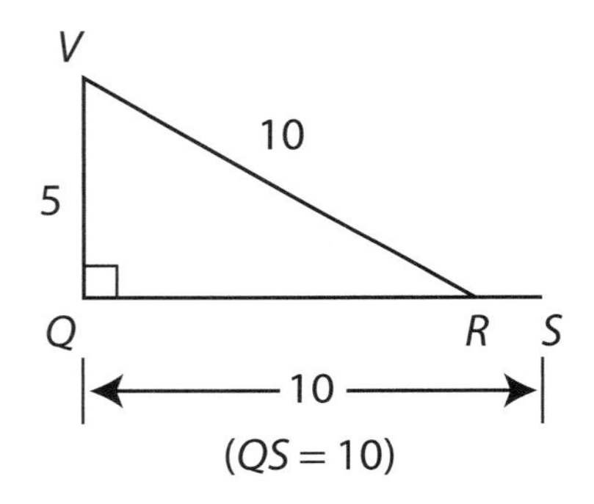

Knowing that $QS = 10$, we need to find *RS* to answer the question. We can use the triangle *VQR* to find *QR* and then subtract *QR* from the overall distance of 10.

VQR is a ***Right Triangle***. Since it contains a leg and hypotenuse in a 1: 2 ratio, it must be a 30–60–90 right triangle.

The sides of a 30–60–90 right triangle fit the following ratio:

Short side: x

Long side: $x\sqrt{3}$

Hypotenuse: $2x$

We know that the short side is 5, so $x = 5$. This means that the long side (*QR*) must be $5\sqrt{3}$.

Alternatively, we can use the ***Pythagorean Theorem*** to solve for *QR*:

$$QR^2 + 5^2 = 10^2$$
$$QR^2 + 25 = 100$$
$$QR^2 = 75$$
$$QR = \sqrt{75} = \sqrt{25}\sqrt{3} = 5\sqrt{3}$$

Now that we have found *QR*, we can subtract it from the total distance *QS*. We get $RS = QS - QR = 10 - 5\sqrt{3}$.

The correct answer is (A).

PS 162. Word Problems: Rates & Work
Difficulty: Devilish **OG Page:** 175

We can make this difficult ***Average Rates*** problem more approachable by ***Choosing Smart Numbers***. We can choose a smart number either for the total distance traveled or for x.

First, we can choose a Smart Number of 100 for the total distance traveled by Francine.

The ***Rate–Time–Distance Chart*** below represents the rates, times and distances for the two legs of Francine's trip. If we use a Smart Number of 100 for the total distance, the distance covered by the first leg equals x. The distance traveled in the second leg is $100 - x$. Here is the chart so far:

	Rate	Time	Distance
1st Leg	40		x
2nd Leg	60		$100 - x$
TOTAL	?		100

To calculate the times for each leg, divide the distance by the rate. The total time is the sum of the times of the two legs.

	Rate	Time	Distance
1st Leg	40	$x/40$	x
2nd Leg	60	$(100 - x)/60$	$100 - x$
TOTAL	?	$x/40 + (100 - x)/60$	100

Finally, compute the average rate by dividing the total distance by the total time. This is not the same as taking the simple average of the two rates (which is a mistake).

We can simplify the expression for the total time by finding a common denominator:

$$\frac{x}{40}+\frac{100-x}{60}=\frac{3x}{120}+\frac{200-2x}{120}=\frac{x+200}{120}$$

Now write the average speed for the trip:

$$\text{Avg speed}=\frac{\text{TOTAL distance}}{\text{TOTAL time}}=\frac{100}{\frac{x+200}{120}}$$

$$=\frac{12000}{x+200}$$

This is the **answer**.

We can also ***Choose a Smart Number*** for x. A value of 40 is a good pick since it can be nicely divided by the rate on the first leg (40 miles per hour).

If $x = 40$, then in the first leg of the trip, Francine traveled 40% of 100 miles, or 40 miles. In the second leg of the trip, she traveled the remaining 60 miles. The time for each leg works out to exactly 1 hour. Fill in the chart:

	Rate	Time	Distance
1st Leg	40	1	40
2nd Leg	60	1	60
TOTAL	?	2	100

The ***Target Value*** is the average speed = 100/2 = 50.

Only (E) gives the target value when we plug in 40 for the value of x.

(A) $\frac{180-40}{2}=70$ INCORRECT

(B) $\frac{40+60}{4}=25$ INCORRECT

(C) $\frac{300-40}{5}=52$ INCORRECT

(D) $\frac{600}{115-40}=8$ INCORRECT

(E) $\frac{12,000}{40+200}=50$ **CORRECT**

The correct answer is (E).

PS 163. FDPs: Digits& Decimals
Difficulty: Devilish **OG Page:** 175

The problem asks us to compute the units digit of n.

The obvious way to solve this question is to raise 33 and 43 to very high powers, but this is not a practical approach, even with a calculator; the numbers are too huge. There must be a shortcut.

Since the digit we are being asked about is the last digit, the ***Last Digit Shortcut*** can help us to simplify the problem. Because we only care about the units digits, we can ignore the tens digits. That simplifies the calculation from $(33)^{43} + (43)^{33}$ to $(3)^{43} + (3)^{33}$.

Now we need to think about patterns. It can't be necessary to compute these very high powers of 3 to solve this problem, so there must be a faster way. In other words, there must be a pattern we can see and use.

When dealing with an unknown pattern, start at the beginning and generate enough terms to figure out the pattern. In this case, to figure out the 43rd and 33rd powers of 3, start with the 1st power of 3 and work your way up.

$3^1 = 3$
$3^2 = 9$
$3^3 = 27$
$3^4 = 81$
$3^5 = 243$

$3^6 = \ldots.9$ because $3 \times 3 = 9$

$3^7 = \ldots.7$ because $9 \times 3 = 27$

$3^8 = \ldots.1$ because $7 \times 3 = 21$

Notice that there is a pattern to the last digits of the powers of 3 that repeats every four terms. The pattern is 3, 9, 7, 1.

(As a side note, every one of the digits (0–9) shows a units digit repeating pattern like this when you raise it to powers. Try this out with other digits to see it. You don't have to memorize the results for the GMAT, but it helps to know that these patterns exist.)

Now we need to use this pattern to find the units digits of 3^{43} and 3^{33}. Powers that are a multiple of 4 have a units digit of 1. Since 40 is divisible by 4, 3^{40} has 1 as its units digit. So 3^{41} has 3 as its units digit, 3^{42} has 9, and 3^{43} has 7.

Similarly, since 32 is divisible by 4, 3^{32} has 1 as its units digit. So 3^{33} has 3 as its units digit.

If you add a number with 7 as its units digit to a number with 3 as its units digit, the resulting number's unit's digit must be 0.

The correct answer is (A).

PS 164. Algebra: Exponents & Roots
Difficulty: Easy **OG Page:** 175

In this problem involving ***Equations with Exponents,*** we are given the value of x. Thus, simply plug this value into the equation and solve. Straight forward questions like this often carry a high risk for making arithmetic errors. We should first write down the equation as given, to make sure that our transcription is correct:

$$\frac{x^4 - x^3 + x^2}{x - 1}$$

Next, plug in (–1) for x in each case. Add parentheses around the –1 in order to deal with signs correctly. This extra precaution is especially important when we have ***Powers of Negative Numbers.*** Thus, we now have:

$$\frac{(-1)^4 - (-1)^3 + (-1)^2}{(-1) - 1}$$

Now simplify each component individually:

$$\frac{(1) - (-1) + (1)}{(-1) - 1}$$

$$\frac{1 + 1 + 1}{-1 - 1}$$

$$\frac{3}{-2} = -\frac{3}{2}$$

The correct answer is (A).

PS 165. Geometry: Triangles & Diagonals
Difficulty: Medium **OG Page:** 175

In this ***Triangles*** problem, the shaded portion of the figure is a ***Right Triangle*** with legs x and y and hypotenuse z. Given the area of this triangle and a further relation between the lengths of the legs, we are asked for the length of the hypotenuse. First, we should note that if we want to compute the ***Area of a Right Triangle,*** we can use the perpendicular legs of the triangle as a base and a altitude (or height). Therefore, we can write

$$A = \frac{1}{2}bh = \frac{1}{2}xy = 24$$

or

$$xy = 48$$

Furthermore, we are given the relation

$$x = y + 2$$

Substituting this expression for x into the equation above yields a ***Quadratic Equation:***

$$y(y + 2) = 48$$
$$y^2 + 2y - 48 = 0$$

Factor the quadratic expression:

$$(y + 8)(y - 6) = 0$$

The two roots of the quadratic equation are $y = -8$ and $y = 6$. However, the first of these is not a valid length for the side of a triangle. Lengths are not negative. Therefore, $y = 6$ and $x = 6 + 2 = 8$.

Notice that in factoring, we are asking "what two numbers multiply together to yield -48 and add up to 2?" In fact, we can directly solve $xy = 48$ and $x = y + 2$ by simply asking "what two numbers multiply together to 48 and differ by 2?" A quick check of the factors of 48 yields 6 and 8.

At this point, the easiest way to determine the value of z is to recognize that 6 and 8 are the legs of a ***3–4–5*** right triangle scaled up by a factor of 2. Therefore, z is also scaled up by the same factor. $z = 2 \times 5 = 10$. This is the **answer**.

Alternatively, we may solve for z using the ***Pythagorean Theorem:***

$$z^2 = x^2 + y^2 = 64 + 36 = 100$$
$$z = 10$$

The correct answer is (E).

PS 166. <u>Geometry</u>: Polygons

Difficulty: Devilish **OG Page:** 175

This problem talks about adding a border of uniform width to an 8 inch × 10 inch photo. It then tells us that the area of the border is 144 inches and asks for the width of the border. This is a geometry problem, so a clearly labeled picture will aid in comprehension.

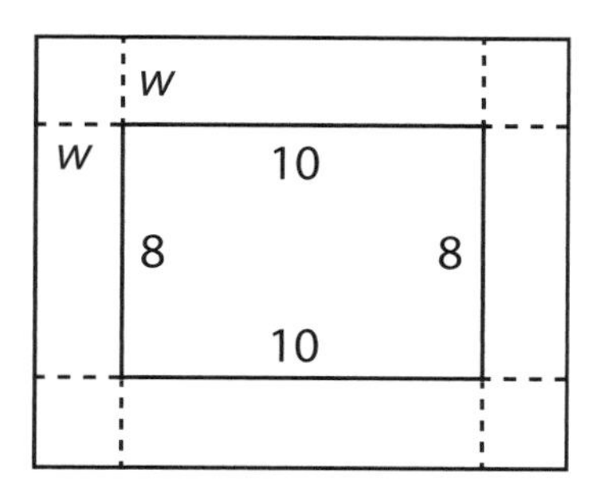

Use the picture to create an equation for the area of the border.

$$144 = 4 \times w^2 + 2 \times 8w + 2 \times 10w$$
$$144 = 4w^2 + 36w$$

This is a quadratic equation, so set it equal to 0 and factor to solve for w:

$$36 = w^2 + 9w$$
$$0 = w^2 + 9w - 36$$
$$0 = (w + 12)(w - 3)$$

Since w must be positive, it must be true that $w = 3$.

The correct answer is (A).

PS 167. <u>Word Problems</u>: Algebraic Translations

Difficulty: Medium **OG Page:** 176

This ***Algebraic Translations*** question asks us to solve a system of equations. If Jack is now 14 years older than Bill, then we can ***Name Variables*** and represent this relationship as follows:

$$J = B + 14 \quad \text{OR} \quad J - 14 = B$$

Note that J and B represent the current ages of Jack and Bill, respectively. The next equation states the relationship between the two ages "in ten years." Keep in mind that both people need to age ten years: thus, we need to write $J + 10$ and $B + 10$ to represent Jack's and Bill's future ages.

In 10 years, Jack will be twice as old as Bill:

$$(J + 10) = 2(B + 10)$$
$$(J + 10) = 2B + 20$$

Since we want Jack's age in 5 years, we can ***substitute*** for B. To save time on systems of equations, we substitute for the variable that is NOT the one we ultimately want.

$$J + 10 = 2(J - 14) + 20s$$
$$J + 10 = 2J - 28 + 20$$
$$J + 10 = 2J - 8$$
$$18 = J$$

Add 5 to get $18 + 5 = 23$. Jack's age in 5 years.

The correct answer is (D).

PS 168. <u>Word Problems</u>: Rates & Work

Difficulty: Medium **OG Page:** 176

We are told in this ***Rates & Work*** problem that it takes 8 hours to fill 3/5 of a pool. We are asked to find how long it takes to fill the remaining 2/5 of the pool at the same rate. In general, with Work problems, we use the ***Rate-Time-Work Formula***, which can be written this way:

$$\text{Rate} = \frac{\text{Work}}{\text{Time}}$$

However, this formula is unnecessary in this situation. The rate at which the pool is being filled is constant, so we can just set up a ***Ratio*** to solve for the remaining time. The time it took to fill 3/5 of the pool is ***Directly Proportional*** to the time it will take to fill the remaining 2/5 of the pool.

Naming a Variable, we can let t be the time it takes to fill 2/5 of the pool. Then we set up a ***Proportion:***

$$\frac{8}{t} = \frac{3/5}{2/5} \quad \text{Now solve for } t.$$

$$\frac{8}{t} = \frac{3}{5} \times \frac{5}{2}$$

$$\frac{8}{t} = \frac{3}{2}$$

$$16 = 3t$$

$$\frac{16}{3} = t$$

$$t = 5\frac{1}{3} \text{ hours.}$$

1/3 of an hour is 20 minutes. The time it takes to fill the remaining volume of the pool is 5 hours 20 minutes.

The correct answer is (B).

PS 169. Algebra: Quadratic Equations
Difficulty: Medium **OG Page:** 176

This ***Quadratic Equations*** problem specifies a series of mathematical operations to perform on the variable x. The words can be ***Translated*** into an equation containing the variable x.

The first sentence can be translated as: $2x/3$

The second sentence can be translated as: $\sqrt{\frac{2x}{3}} = x$

Notice the phrase "*positive* square root." This may seem redundant at first, since the GMAT almost never refers to negative square roots, and the square root symbol ($\sqrt{\ }$) always means the positive square root. However, the modifier is actually a subtle clue that zero is not an option.

Now we can solve the equation for x.

$$\sqrt{\frac{2x}{3}} = x$$

$$\frac{2x}{3} = x^2$$

$$2x = 3x^2$$

$$0 = 3x^2 - 2x$$

$$0 = x(3x - 2)$$

$$x = 0 \text{ or } x = \frac{2}{3}$$

Because the problem tells us that x is positive, and the square root is positive, x cannot be zero. Therefore, x equals 2/3. This is the **answer**.

Alternatively, we can use ***Algebraic Reasoning*** to solve the problem more quickly once we reached $\frac{2x}{3} = x^2$. Since $x \neq 0$, we can divide by x to get $\frac{2}{3} = x$.

The correct answer is (D).

PS 170. FDPs: Digits & Decimals
Difficulty: Devilish **OG Page:** 176

This ***Digits & Decimals*** problem asks us how many nonzero digits d, when expressed as a ***terminating decimal***, will have.

The phrase "terminating decimal" tells us that d has a finite number of nonzero digits.

Since it would be painful to calculate 5^7 without a calculator in under two minutes, much less multiply it by 2^3 and divide the result into 1, we know that there must be a faster way to solve this problem. Ugly computation problems generally allow for shortcuts. In this problem, notice that $2 \times 5 = 10$. This is helpful because powers of 10 are easy to work with.

$$\frac{1}{2^3 \times 5^7} = \frac{1}{(2^3 \times 5^3) \times 5^4}$$
$$= \frac{1}{10^3} \times \frac{1}{5^4}$$

Now we need a quick way to turn $1/5^4$ into a decimal. Fortunately, $1/5^4 = (1/5)^4$. That helps, because we can rewrite $1/5$ as 0.2. We can further simplify this operation by rewriting 0.2 as 2×10^{-1}:

$$\frac{1}{10^3} \times 0.2^4$$
$$= 10^{-3} \times (10^{-1} \times 2)^4$$
$$= 10^{-3} \times 10^{-4} \times 2^4$$
$$= 10^{-7} \times 16$$
$$= 0.00000016$$

The correct answer is (B).

PS 171. **FDPs:** Percents
Difficulty: Medium **OG Page:** 176

In this ***Percents*** problem, we are first told that a tank contains 10,000 gallons of a solution that is 5 percent sodium chloride. We can use the ***Percent Formula*** to determine how much sodium chloride is present in the tank. To fill in the formula, ***Name a Variable*** and call this unknown amount of sodium chloride x.

$$\frac{\text{PART}}{\text{WHOLE}} = \frac{\text{PERCENT}}{100}$$
$$\frac{x}{10{,}000} = \frac{5}{100}$$
$$100x = 50{,}000$$
$$x = 500$$

There are 500 gallons of sodium chloride in the tank.

2,500 gallons of water evaporate from the tank, leaving us with 7,500 gallons of total solution. Since only water evaporated, the amount of sodium chloride has not changed and is still 500 gallons. We are asked what percent of the remaining solution is sodium chloride, or "500 is what percent of 7,500?" Again, we can use the percent formula and name another variable, letting p equal the unknown percentage:

$$\frac{500}{7{,}500} = \frac{p}{100}$$
$$50{,}000 = 7{,}500p$$
$$\frac{50{,}000}{7{,}500} = p$$
$$\frac{500}{75} = p$$
$$\frac{20}{3} = p$$
$$p = 6\frac{2}{3} \text{ or } 6.67\%$$

The correct answer is (D).

PS 172. **Word Problems:** Consecutive Integers
Difficulty: Hard **OG Page:** 176

We are asked to figure out the sum of all of the even integers between 99 and 301. This is doable with the general form of the ***Sum of Consecutive Integers Formula***, but why does the GMAT give us another formula? Doesn't that mean that we have to use it? Well, actually, no.

The formula given is the same as the consecutive integer formula when all of the integers between 1 and n are being summed:

$$\text{Sum} = \text{average} \times \text{number of terms}$$
$$= \frac{(\text{first} + \text{last})}{2} \times (\text{last} - \text{first} + 1)$$
$$= \frac{(1+n)}{2} \times (n - 1 + 1)$$
$$= \frac{n+1}{2} \times n$$
$$= \frac{n(n+1)}{2}$$

Although we could solve this problem by using this formula, it would be more work than to use our more general version because using this one would require that we sum the consecutive integers from 1 to 301, then subtract out the sum of the consecutive integers from 1 to 98, and then finally figure out how to subtract out the sum of the odd integers from 99 to 301. This looks like a lot of work for two minutes!

Remember that GMAT test writers are not required to give us the easiest to use version of a formula any more than they are required to give us equations in simplest form. It is much easier to use the more general form of the formula for summing sequences of consecutive integers rather than it is to go through all of the steps required to use the given version.

Using the consecutive integers formula requires some thinking. The first even number between 99 and 301 is 100, so that is what we need to use for *first*, not 99. Similarly, the last even number between 99 and 301 is 300, so that is what we need to use for last, not 301.

The other tricky part of using the formula is that the number of terms is *not* 300 – 100 + 1 = 201. We are asked to sum only the *even* numbers in that range. How many even numbers are there between 100 and 300? Well, since 100 is the 50th even number and 300 is the 150th even number, we know that there are 150 – 50 + 1 = 101 even numbers between 100 and 300.

$$\begin{aligned}\text{Sum} &= \text{average} \times \text{number of terms} \\ &= \frac{(100+300)}{2} \times 101 \\ &= 200 \times 101 \\ &= 20,200\end{aligned}$$

The correct answer is (B).

PS 173. <u>Number Properties</u>: Probability
Difficulty: Easy **OG Page:** 176

We are given information about men and women on a committee, as well as changes to the membership of that committee. We can organize the variables in a ***Table***:

	Before	After ("enlarged committee")
Men	m	$m + 2$
Women	w	$w + 3$
Total	$m + w$	$m + w + 5$

If we randomly select one person from the committee *after members are added* (i.e., the right column of our chart), the ***Probability*** of selecting a woman is $\frac{\#\text{ of women}}{\text{total }\#\text{ of people}} = \frac{w+3}{m+w+5}$.

This is the **answer**.

EVERY other answer choice is a trap, in which the numerators and denominators appear somewhere in the chart or (in the case of $w + m + 3$) include the incorrect sum of expressions from the chart. As we set up the probability fraction, we have to use the expressions representing the "After" situation (after members are added), not the "Before" situation.

The correct answer is (E).

PS 174. <u>Number Properties</u>: Divisibility & Primes
Difficulty: Hard **OG Page:** 176

This ***Divisibility & Primes*** question asks how many unique prime factors between 1 and 100 the number 7,150 has. We can break 7,150 down into primes using ***Prime Factorization***. To expedite the process, start with the largest recognizable factor (in this case, start with 10). 7,150 = 715 × 10.

Continuing with the 715, we can see that 715 is divisible by 5. 715/5 = 143, so 7,150 = 143 × 5 × 10.

The final, tricky step in this prime factorization involves factoring 143. There is no prime factor less than or equal to 10 that is a factor of 143. 143 is, however, divisible by 11, which goes in 13 times. Be sure to check every prime up to the square root of the number 143, which is just under 12.

By the way, an abridged version of a divisibility rule for 11 holds that for all *three-digit integers*, if the units digit and the hundreds digit sum to the tens digit, the number is divisible by 11 (e.g., in the case of 143, 3 + 1 = 4, so 11 goes into 143).

We now have the full prime factor tree of 7,150:

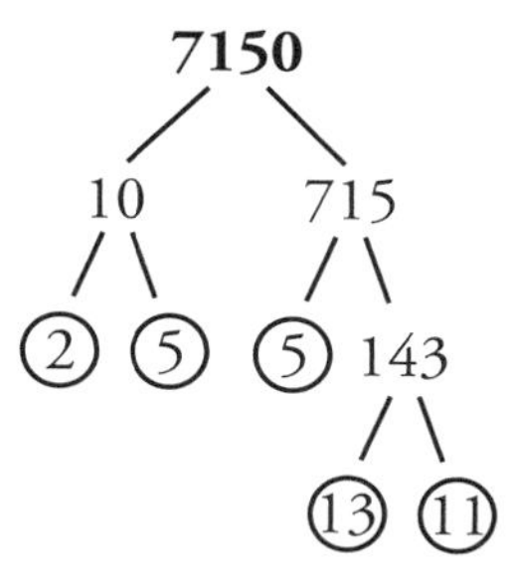

We can express 7,150 as the product of primes: $7{,}150 = 2 \times 5^2 \times 11 \times 13$.

Thus 7,150 has four unique prime factors—2, 5, 11 and 13—all of which are between 1 and 100. This is the **answer**.

Note that if we had mistakenly thought 143 was a prime, we would have identified only two unique primes between 1 and 100.

The correct answer is (D).

PS 175. <u>Geometry</u>: Circles & Cylinders
Difficulty: Easy **OG Page:** 177

In order to find the area of the ***Circular*** path, we must find the area of the flowerbed and subtract it from the area of the larger circle, which includes the flowerbed and the path. ***Subtract Areas*** to find the area of a figure, such as the circular path, that represents the difference between two simpler shapes (the two circles shown).

After re-creating the drawings, insert the information that the path is 3 feet wide:

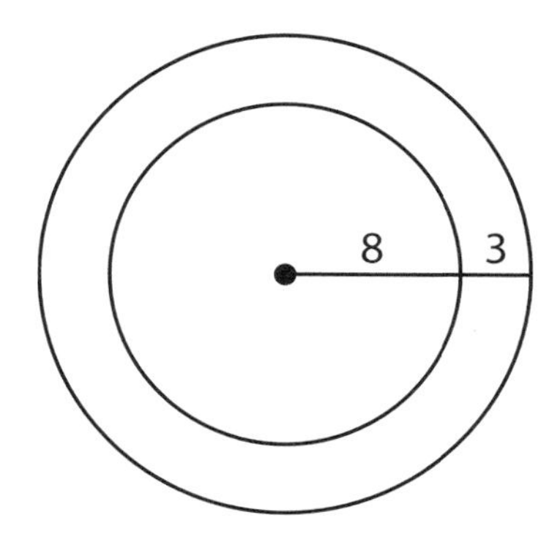

The ***Area of a Circle*** is simply πr^2. Note that the radius of the larger circle is 8 + 3, or 11. Thus, we can write out our equation as follows:

$$\text{Area}_{path} = \text{Area}_{large\ circle} - \text{Area}_{small\ circle}$$
$$\text{Area}_{path} = \pi(11)^2 - \pi(8)^2$$
$$\text{Area}_{path} = 121\pi - 64\pi$$
$$\text{Area}_{path} = 57\pi$$

The correct answer is (D).

PS 176. <u>Algebra</u>: Inequalities
Difficulty: Medium **OG Page:** 177

We can solve this ***Inequalities*** problem using ***Direct Algebra.*** First, we know that $\sqrt{n} > 25$. We want to find a possible value of $n/25$, so manipulate the given inequality to get $n/25$ on one side. To go from $\sqrt{n}$ to $n/25$, we should first square the inequality, then divide by 25.

If both sides of an inequality are positive, we are allowed to square it, because we do not have to worry about negative values.

$$\sqrt{n} > 25$$
$$(\sqrt{n})^2 > 25^2$$
$$n > 25^2$$

We should know that 25^2 is 625, but since we are not finished with the problem, avoid needless computation. Now divide both sides by 25:

$$\frac{n}{25} > \frac{25^2}{25}$$
$$\frac{n}{25} > 25$$

Note that $25^2/25$ equals 25 again.

As a result, our target expression $n/25$ must be greater than 25. The only choice that is greater than 25 is 26.

The correct answer is (E).

PS 177. <u>FDPs</u>: Percents
Difficulty: Devilish **OG Page:** 177

The problem tells us that the price per share of a stock increased by k percent and that the earnings per share of the stock increased by m percent, where k is greater than m. We are asked to compute the ***Percent Increase*** in the ratio of the price per share to earnings in terms of k and m.

This ***Percents*** problem is particularly confusing because we are given variable instead of numbers to work with. Since there are variables in the answer choices, a good way to solve this is to ***Choose Smart Numbers*** for the unknowns in the problem. Pick numbers for k and m, and also pick numbers for the original price of the stock (p) and the original earnings per share (e).

As is often the case, smart numbers are only effective if we can pick numbers that will make the computation as easy as possible. Use 100 for p and 10 for e, (powers of 10 are easy to use in percent problems).

Picking values for k and m so that the calculations are easy will be a bit more challenging. Remember, the question talks about the ratio of price to earnings. Ratios involve division, so we want to make sure that the new price per share is divisible by the new earnings per share.

Pick a value for m first. 50 is an attractive option. It will be easy to plug into the answer choices, and it makes the new earnings per share $10 \times 1.5 = 15$. This is nice, as division involving multiples of 5 is usually fairly painless.

Now we need to pick a value for k. Ultimately, we want the new price to be a multiple of 15, and we need k to be greater than 50. That means that the new price needs to be greater than 150. 180 is a multiple of 15, which makes k equal to 80.

Variable	Value picked
p	100
e	10
k	80
m	50

Now we're ready to answer the question. The original ratio of price per share to earnings per share is 100 : 10. Write the ratio as a fraction and simplify. This will make the percent change calculation easier. 100 : 10 $\longrightarrow$ 100/10 = 10.

The new ratio of price per share to earnings per share is 180 : 15. Write this as a fraction and simplify. 180 : 15 $\longrightarrow$ 180/15 = 12.

We could use the percent change formula, although the numbers we've used actually make the calculation quite easy. The percent change from 10 to 12 is 20%. Our ***Target Value*** is 20. Plug numbers into the answer choices and ***Find a Match***.

(A) $\frac{k}{m}\% = \frac{80}{50}\% \Leftarrow$ TOO SMALL!

(B) $(k-m)\% = 80 - 50 = 30\% \Leftarrow$ TOO BIG!

(C) $\frac{100(k-m)}{100+k}\% = \frac{100(30)}{180} = \frac{3{,}000}{180}\% = \frac{300}{18}$

$= \frac{150}{9} \Leftarrow$ NOT 20

(D) $\frac{100(k-m)}{100+m}\% = \frac{100(30)}{100+50} = \frac{3{,}000}{150} = \frac{300}{15}$

$= 20\% \Leftarrow$ YES!!

(E) $\frac{100(k-m)}{100+k+m}\% = \frac{100(30)}{100+80+50}$

$= \frac{3{,}000}{230}\% \Leftarrow$ NOT AN INTEGER!

Alternatively we could have done algebra to solve this, which is what the OG does, but that solution is very long and easy to mess up with a mechanical error because it is so complicated. Solving this problem in a mathematically simple way did require that we be smart about how we picked our numbers, but the time taken to do that was well spent because it made computation so much easier.

The correct answer is (D).

PS 178. <u>Word Problems</u>: Overlapping Sets
Difficulty: Devilish **OG Page:** 177

This rather unsettling problem talks about a study that involved a total of 300 subjects. 40% experienced sweaty palms, 30% experienced vomiting, and 75% experienced dizziness. We are also told that all of the subjects experienced at least one of these symptoms and that 35% of them experienced exactly two of these symptoms. We need to solve for the number of people who experienced only one symptom.

Although this is an ***Overlapping Sets*** problem, we cannot use a double-set matrix to solve it because we have three dimensions (each of the three symptoms) instead of two, so writing out the given information is a good next step.

Given Information:

total people = 300
two-symptom people = $0.35 \times 300 = 105$

sweaty people = $0.40 \times 300 = 120$
vomiting people = $0.30 \times 300 = 90$
dizzy people = 0.75 of 300 = 225

total symptoms = $120 + 90 + 225 = 435$

There are more symptoms than people because people who have two symptoms are counted twice, once for each symptom, and people with three symptoms are counted three times (again, once for each symptom). We need to create equations for the number of people and for the number of symptoms based on the number of one-symptom, two-symptom, and three-symptom people so we can solve for the number of one symptom people by ***Substitution***. x_1, x_2, and x_3 make good choices.

First, set up an equation for the total number of symptoms:

$$435 = x_1 + 2x_2 + 3x_3$$

Then we create one for the total number of people.

$$300 = x_1 + x_2 + x_3$$

Since we know that $x_2 = 105$, we can simplify both equations:

$$435 = x_1 + 2 \times 105 + 3x_3$$
$$435 = x_1 + 210 + 3x_3$$
$$225 = x_1 + 3x_3$$
$$300 = x_1 + 105 + x_3$$
$$195 = x_1 + x_3$$

Then we can subtract the second equation from the first to solve for x_3:

$$225 = x_1 + 3x_3$$
$$\underline{-(195 = x_1 + x_3)}$$
$$30 = 2x_3$$
$$15 = x_3$$

Then we just plug back in to one of the equations and solve for x_1.

$$195 = x_1 + (15)$$
$$180 = x_1$$

The correct answer is (D).

PS 179. FDPs: Ratios
Difficulty: Easy **OG Page:** 177

In this ***Ratios*** problem, we are given the ***Multiple Ratio*** 6 : 5 : 2, which indicates the relative weight of apples, peaches and grapes in a fruit salad. The ratio itself does not indicate the absolute quantity of any of the ingredients, but rather only the relative quantities. Therefore, we should introduce an ***Unknown Multiplier*** x in order to obtain the actual quantities. With this definition, the actual weights of apples, peaches and grapes in the salad are $6x$, $5x$, and $2x$, respectively. The total weight of the salad is given by

$$W = 6x + 5x + 2x = 13x = 39$$

We can now solve for x:

$$x = 3$$

The weight of the apples is $6x = 18$ pounds, and the weight of the grapes is $2x = 6$ pounds. Therefore, there are $18 - 6 = 12$ more pounds of apples than grapes.

The correct answer is (B).

PS 180. Algebra: Exponents & Roots
Difficulty: Easy **OG Page:** 177

This ***Exponents*** problem tells us $m^{-1} = -\frac{1}{3}$ and asks us to find the value of m^{-2}.

One way to solve this problem is to first find the value of m and then evaluate m^{-2}. We know that a ***Negative Exponent*** is just the reciprocal:

$$x^{-1} = \frac{1}{x}$$

If $m^{-1} = -\frac{1}{3}$, then $m = -3$. Now, we can evaluate m^{-2}:

$$m^{-2} = (-3)^{-2} = \left(-\frac{1}{3}\right)^2 = \frac{1}{9}$$

This is the **answer.**

Another approach to this problem is to use the following ***Rule of Multiplying Exponents*:**

$$(a^x)^y = a^{xy}$$

If we notice that $m^{-2} = (m^{-1})^2$, then we can answer the question simply by squaring both sides of the given equation:

$$m^{-1} = -\frac{1}{3}$$
$$(m^{-1})^2 = \left(-\frac{1}{3}\right)^2$$
$$m^{-2} = \frac{1}{9}$$

The correct answer is (D).

PS 181. <u>FDPs</u>: Percents
Difficulty: Hard **OG Page:** 177

This ***Percents*** problem asks us to express y as a percentage of x, if we know x as a percentage of y.

One option is to approach the problem using ***Direct Algebra***. Knowing that "of" means times and "percent" means division by 100, we can ***Translate*** the first relation as:

$$x = \frac{m}{100} \times y$$

We are asked to answer the question, "what percent of x is y?" The best approach is to ***Name a Variable*** w to stand for the "what" in "what percent." We can then answer the question by solving for w. Accordingly:

$$y = \frac{w}{100} \times x$$

Substituting for x from the first relation yields

$$y = \frac{w}{100} \times \frac{m}{100} \times y$$

Divide both sides by y and solve for w:

$$1 = \frac{w}{100} \times \frac{m}{100}$$
$$1 = \frac{wm}{10{,}000}$$
$$\frac{10{,}000}{m} = w$$ This is the **answer.**

An alternative approach is to ***Choose Smart Numbers***. Suppose we pick $m = 50$. In that case, x is 50%, or half, of y, and so y must be twice x, or 200% of x. Our ***Target Value*** is therefore 200.

Now substitute $m = 50$ into each answer choice to determine which one yields a value of 200.

(A) $100m = 100 \times 50 = 5{,}000$ INCORRECT

(B) $\frac{1}{100m} = \frac{1}{100 \times 50} = \frac{1}{5{,}000}$ INCORRECT

(C) $\frac{1}{m} = \frac{1}{50}$ INCORRECT

(D) $\frac{10}{m} = \frac{10}{50} = \frac{1}{5}$ INCORRECT

(E) $\frac{10{,}000}{m} = \frac{10{,}000}{50} = 200$ **CORRECT**

The correct answer is (E).

PS 182. <u>FDPs</u>: Percents
Difficulty: Devilish **OG Page:** 178

This problem tells us that a dealer ordered 60 cameras to be sold for $250 each, which represents a 20% markup over the dealer's cost per camera. We are also told that 6 cameras were never sold and were returned to the manufacturer for a 50% refund of the dealer cost.

The question asks for the deal's approximate profit or loss as a percent of the dealer's initial cost for the 60 cameras.

This is a ***Percents*** problem, and is about profit and total cost, so the following two relationships are relevant:

profit = revenue − cost

total price = unit price × quantity purchased

The information is provided in a confusing way, so try to organize all the information before solving.

First, if \$250 represents a 20% markup over the dealer cost, which we will call c, for one camera, then:

$$1.2c = \$250$$

$$c = \frac{\$250}{1.2} = \frac{\$2{,}500}{12} \approx \$210$$

Remember that the question used the word *approximate*. That means that you should round numbers where possible to make computation easier.

So the total cost for all of the cameras was about

$$60 \times \$210 = \$12{,}600.$$

The number of cameras sold for \$250 was 60 − 6 = 54. So the revenue from selling cameras was

$$54 \times \$250 = 50 \times \$250 + 4 \times \$250 = \$12{,}500 + \$1{,}000 = \$13{,}500.$$

The revenue from returning each of the unsold 6 cameras to the manufacturer was about \$210/2 = \$105. So the revenue from returning cameras was

$$6 \times \$105 = \$630.$$

So the total revenue from cameras was

$$\$13{,}500 + \$630 = \$14{,}130$$

So the total profit was

$$\$14{,}130 - \$12{,}600 \approx \$1{,}500$$

Now we just need to find the profit as a percent of the initial cost.

$$\frac{1{,}500}{12{,}600} = \frac{1{,}260}{12{,}600} + \frac{240}{12{,}600}$$

1,260/12,600 is 10%, so we know that the profit has to be a little more than 10% of the initial cost. Of the answer choices, 7% profit is too low, and 15% profit is too high. The best answer choice is (D) 13% profit.

The correct answer is (D).

PS 183. <u>Word Problems</u>: Statistics
Difficulty: Hard **OG Page:** 178

This problem tells that the ***Average*** length of seven pieces of rope is 68 cm and that the ***Median*** length among the seven pieces is 84 cm. We are asked what the ***Maximum*** possible length of the longest piece of rope is.

Before worrying about the maximum length, organize the information presented.

First, if we know the average length is 68 cm, then we know that the total length of all of the rope is $7 \times 68 = 476$ cm. Second, if the median length is 84 cm, then the 4th longest piece of rope is 84 cm.

We are also told that the length of the longest piece of rope is 14 centimeters more than 4 times the length of the shortest piece of rope. Call the shortest length s. That means the longest length is $4s + 14$.

When dealing with sets of numbers, it is often helpful to list out all the numbers in the set. Right now, we only have ways of expressing the shortest piece, the longest piece, and the median piece. Use the variables a, b, c, and d for the other 4 pieces:

$$s, a, b, 84, c, d, 4s + 14$$

Now we're ready to figure out the maximum length of the longest piece. First, ask yourself, what is limiting the length of the longest piece? We already figured out that the total length of the rope is 476 cm. That means that the lengths of the 7 pieces of rope have a fixed sum. If we want to maximize the length of the longest piece, we need to minimize the lengths of the other six pieces.

$s, a, b, 84, c, d,$ $4s + 14$

minimize maximize

So what are the minimum lengths for a, b, c, and d?

Since c and d have to be at least as long as the median, the minimum length for each is 84 cm. Remember, the problem didn't specify that each piece of rope has a different length. By a similar logic, a and b must be at least as long as s, but they don't have to be longer than s. The minimum length for a and b is s. Rewrite the numbers in the set:

$s, s, s, 84, 84, 84, 4s + 14$

Now everything is in terms of s. We can set the sum equal to 476 and solve for s:

$$s + s + s + 84 + 84 + 84 + 4s + 14 = 476$$
$$7s + 266 = 476$$
$$7s = 210$$
$$s = 30$$

If $s = 30$, then the length of the longest piece equals $4(30) + 14 = 134$.

The correct answer is (D).

PS 184. Word Problems: Algebraic Translations
Difficulty: Easy **OG Page:** 178

This problem specifies that Lois has x dollars more than Jim has and that they have a total of y dollars together. We can determine the number of dollars Jim has using ***Direct Algebra***.

First, translate the word problem into algebra. We can ***Name Variables*** to represent Lois's and Jim's amounts of money. Let's use L and J. Then we can relate those variables.

$$L = J + x$$
$$L + J = y$$
$$J = ?$$

The answer choices show only x and y, so we want to express J in terms of only those two variables. To do so, we will also need to get rid of L. Manipulate the equations and add them together so that we cancel out L. Begin by isolating J in each equation.

$$J = L - x$$
$$J = -L + y$$

Now we can add the equations and solve for J.

$$J = L - x$$
$$\underline{J = -L + y}$$
$$2J = y - x \rightarrow J = \frac{y-x}{2}$$

This is the **answer**.

Alternatively, we can ***Choose Smart Numbers***. Pick easy numbers and remember to follow any constraints given in the problem.

If $L = 10$ and $J = 6$, then Lois has $x = 4$ more dollars than Jim has, and together they have $y = 16$ dollars. Since we are asked to solve for J, we want an answer choice that equals 6, the number we chose, given that $x = 4$ and $y = 16$.

(A) $\frac{y-x}{2} = \frac{16-4}{2} = \frac{12}{2} = 6$ **CORRECT**

(B) $y - \frac{x}{2} = 16 - \frac{4}{2} = 16 - 2 = 14$ INCORRECT

(C) $\frac{y}{2} - x = \frac{16}{2} - 4 = 8 - 4 = 4$ INCORRECT

(D) $2y - x = 2(16) - 4 =$ too big INCORRECT

(E) $y - 2x = 16 - 2(4) = 16 - 8 = 8$ INCORRECT

The correct answer is (A).

PS 185. FDPs: Percents
Difficulty: Medium **OG Page:** 178

This ***Algebraic Translations*** problem involves several calculations. We can find the solution efficiently by organizing the information in a ***Table*** and setting up equations.

The rows correspond to the first 100 games, the remaining games, and the total number of games.

The columns are the "Win %," "Games Played," and "Games Won" (with Games Won = Win % × Games Played). Just as with an Rate-Time-Distance Table, the final column is equal to the product of the first two.

	Win %	Games Played	Games Won
First 100 games			
Remaining games			
Total			

The first step is to input the information provided in the problem. We know all of the winning percentages, and we know that there were 100 games originally played. Let's ***Name a Variable*** and call the number of remaining games n.

Fill in the table, multiplying across to get an expression or number for Games Won in each row.

	Win %	Games Played	Games Won
First 100 games	0.80	100	$0.80(100) = 80$
Remaining games	0.50	n	$0.50n$
Total	0.70	$100 + n$	$0.70(100 + n)$

Now use the "Games Won" column to create an equation. The games won in the first two rows must add up to total games won in the third row.

$$80 + 0.50n = 0.70(100 + n)$$
$$80 + 0.50n = 70 + 0.70n$$
$$10 = 0.20n$$
$$50 = n$$

Since $n = 50$, the number of remaining games was 50. The problem asks for the total number of games played, which is $100 + n$.

$100 + 50 = 150$ total games played.

The correct answer is (D).

PS 186. <u>Word Problems</u>: Overlapping Sets
Difficulty: Easy **OG Page:** 178

This standard ***Overlapping Sets*** problem presents two binary splits: four years of experience vs. less than four years of experience, and degree vs. no degree. Construct a ***Double-Set Matrix*** according to these criteria, filling in the information from the prompt and indicating the desired quantity with a question mark:

	At Least 4 Yrs	Less than 4 Yrs	Total
Degree	?		18
No Degree		3	
Total	14		30

Remembering that the first two elements of every row and column must add to the third element, we can fill in the rest of the chart:

	At Least 4 Yrs	Less than 4 Yrs	Total
Degree	***5***	***13***	18
No Degree	***9***	3	***12***
Total	14	***16***	30

There are 5 candidates with at least four years of experience and a degree.

The correct answer is (E).

PS 187. <u>Algebra</u>: Linear Equations
Difficulty: Easy **OG Page:** 178

To solve this ***Linear Equations*** problem, we will use ***Direct Algebra.*** We can tackle the algebra in several ways. For instance, we can cancel the denominators by multiplying both sides by x:

$$1+\frac{1}{x}=2-\frac{2}{x}$$
$$\left(1+\frac{1}{x}=2-\frac{2}{x}\right)x$$
$$x+1=2x-2$$
$$3=x$$

This is the **answer.**

Alternatively, we could subtract 1 from each side and add $2/x$ to each side. Note that $1/x$ and $2/x$ have the same denominator, so they add up to $3/x$.

$$1+\frac{1}{x}=2-\frac{2}{x}$$
$$\frac{1}{x}=1-\frac{2}{x}$$
$$\frac{3}{x}=1$$
$$3=x$$

We could also use x as a common denominator. This approach requires a little more fraction work:

$$1+\frac{1}{x}=2-\frac{2}{x}$$
$$\frac{x}{x}+\frac{1}{x}=\frac{2x}{x}-\frac{2}{x}$$
$$\frac{x+1}{x}=\frac{2x-2}{x}$$
$$x+1=2x-2$$
$$3=x$$

The correct answer is (E).

PS 188. <u>FDPs</u>: Ratios
Difficulty: Easy **OG Page:** 178

The first piece of information gives the ***Ratio*** of the number of vehicle accidents to the number of vehicles that traveled on a certain highway last year. This ratio can be used to calculate the actual number of accidents since we are given the actual number of vehicles that traveled on that highway. We can set up a proportion to do so:

$$\frac{96 \text{ accidents}}{100 \text{ million vehicles}}=\frac{x}{3 \text{ billion vehicles}}$$

We can simplify the calculations by using ***Powers of 10.*** 100 million = 100,000,000 = 10^8. 1 billion = 1,000,000,000 = 10^9.

$$\frac{96}{10^8}=\frac{x}{3\times 10^9}$$
$$96(3\times 10^9)=(10^8)x$$
$$\frac{96(3\times 10^9)}{10^8}=x$$
$$96(3\times 10)=x$$
$$2{,}880=x$$

This is the **answer.**

Alternatively, we can solve this problem using ***Mental Calculation.*** 1 billiosn is ten times 100 million, so the number of accidents for 1 billion motorists would be 96 × 10 = 960. The number of accidents then for 3 billion motorists would be 3 × 960 = 2,880.

The correct answer is (C).

PS 189. <u>Word Problems</u>: Overlapping Sets
Difficulty: Easy **OG Page:** 179

This ***Overlapping Sets*** problem calls for a ***Double-Set Matrix.*** The problem presents two criteria for the group, each of which splits the group in two. In this case, we have those who passed the test or did not and those who took the course or did not.

Begin by creating the Double-Set Matrix. It does not matter which yes/no option is on top and which is on the side.

	Passed test	**Did not**	**Total**
Took course			
Did not			
Total			

Next, insert the information from the problem carefully, keeping an eye out for internal algebra. Because real numbers are given, we cannot call the total 100. In fact, we are solving for this total. So we should ***Name a Variable*** and call the total t. "Thirty percent of the members" will be shown as $0.3t$. We can fill in the "Did Not Pass" column as well.

	Passed test	Did not	Total
Took course		12	
Did not		30	
Total	$0.3t$	42	$t = ?$

We can create an equation by summing across the bottom row. Then we solve algebraically.

$$0.3t + 42 = t$$
$$42 = 0.7t$$
$$42 = \frac{7}{10}t$$
$$42\left(\frac{10}{7}\right) = t$$
$$60 = t$$

The correct answer is (A).

PS 190. <u>Algebra</u>: Formulas
Difficulty: Easy **OG Page:** 179

The nth term of the given ***Sequence*** is $n + 2^{n-1}$, in which n represents that term's placement in the sequence. We are asked for the difference between the 6th and the 5th terms of the sequence. Because these terms are not numbered too high, the ***Exponents*** that we have to deal with are small.

Thus, the best way to solve this problem is to compute the needed terms, then subtract.

For the fifth term, $n = 5$. The term itself is $5 + 2^{5-1} = 5 + 2^4 = 5 + 16 = 21$.

For the sixth term, $n = 6$. The term itself would be $6 + 2^{6-1} = 6 + 2^5 = 6 + 32 = 38$.

The question is asking for the difference between 38 and 21, which is 17. This is the **answer.**

Often, in sequence problems, we extrapolate a pattern. However, the GMAT has set a trap pattern in this problem. The difference between the first and second terms is 2. The difference between the second and third terms is 3. If we thought that the differences simply grow with the integers 2, 3, 4, 5, 6, etc., then our answer would be 6 (choice (C)), which is incorrect.

The correct answer is (E).

PS 191. <u>Algebra</u>: Quadratic Equations
Difficulty: Medium **OG Page:** 179

In this ***Quadratic Equation,*** both the left side and the right side are perfect squares. Therefore, the simplest solution method is to take the ***Square Root*** of both sides. Remember that there will be two valid solutions, one positive and the other negative. This approach yields:

$$x - 1 = \pm\sqrt{400} = \pm 20$$

Positive solution: $x - 1 = 20$, in which case $x = 21$. Negative solution: $x - 1 = -20$, in which case $x = -19$.

The question asks not for x itself, but for $x - 5$. The positive solution, $x = 21$, leads to $21 - 5 = 16$. This number is not among the available choices. However, the negative solution $x = -19$ leads to $-19 - 5 = -24$. This is the **answer.**

An alternative approach for finding x is to multiply out the left side, collect all terms on that side, and then ***Factor*** the resulting quadratic. Indeed, if the given equation had not involved perfect squares, this approach would have been the only option. In this case, however, it requires cumbersome arithmetic, since we have to factor 399 into two numbers that differ by 2. We might think to try 21 and 19, since they are close to 20 (the square root of 400), but these numbers are much clearer in hindsight. The details are shown below for the sake of completeness:

$$(x - 1)^2 = x^2 - 2x + 1 = 400$$
$$x^2 - 2x - 399 = 0$$
$$(x - 21)(x + 19) = 0$$

The correct answer is (C).

PS 192. <u>Algebra</u>: Inequalities
Difficulty: Medium **OG Page:** 179

In this ***Inequalities*** problem, we need to find the range of all values for which $1 - x^2 \geq 0$. First, simply add x^2 to both sides:

$$1 \geq x^2$$

We can also flip the inequality and write $x^2 \leq 1$.

Now we can make use of ***Number Line Awareness***. Numbers whose squares are less than 1 are positive or negative proper fractions, and the numbers whose squares are actually equal to 1 are –1 and 1. Thus, the numbers we want are between –1 and 1, inclusive. We can write this range as a ***Compound Inequality***:

$-1 \leq x \leq 1$ This is the **answer**.

Another method is to ***Test Values*** that are inside or outside the ranges presented in the answer choices. For instance, we can try 2. Since 2 doesn't work (because 2^2 is NOT ≤ 1), we can eliminate answer choices (A) and (D), which allow 2.

Next, we can try –2. It also does not work, so we can eliminate B, which allows –2.

Only (C) and (E) are left. Pick a value allowed by one of the answer choices but not by the other. For example, try –1/2. Since $(-1/2)^2 = 1/4$, which is less than 1, –1/2 must be included in the range of answers for x. Thus, we can eliminate (C), which does not include –1/2.

The correct answer is (E).

PS 193. Number Properties: Probability
Difficulty: Medium **OG Page:** 179

This problem asks us to find the ***Probability*** of getting at least one tails when you flip a coin three times. The ***Basic Probability Formula*** is:

$$\text{Probability} = \frac{\text{Desired Outcomes}}{\text{Total Outcomes}}$$

One approach is to ***List All the Possibilities*** for the three tosses:

HHH HHT HTH THH
TTH THT HTT TTT

Out of the eight possible outcomes, seven of them show at least one tails. Thus, the probability of getting at least one tails in three tosses is 7/8. This is the **answer**.

Another approach to this problem is to use the ***1 – x Principle***. The idea is to focus on the failures, not the successes, when the failures are easier to count or otherwise measure. The question can be rephrased in this way: "*What is the probability of NOT showing ALL heads?*"

Since $P(\text{HHH}) + P(\text{not HHH}) = 1$, we can answer this question by finding $1 - P(\text{HHH})$.

If the probability of showing one head is 1/2, then the probability of showing heads on the first toss, heads on the second toss and heads on the third toss is:

$$\left(\frac{1}{2}\right)\left(\frac{1}{2}\right)\left(\frac{1}{2}\right) = \frac{1}{8}.$$

Thus, the answer to the problem is

$$1 - \frac{1}{8} = \frac{7}{8}.$$

The correct answer is (D).

PS 194. FDPs: Fractions
Difficulty: Easy **OG Page:** 179

The problem specifies the ***Fraction*** of students in a certain class who received A's, B's, and C's. The problem further specifies the actual number of students who received D's. The question asks us to determine the total number of students in the class. We can ***Name Variables*** and represent the unknown total as x and the unknown fraction of D students as y.

Let's organize the information in a ***Table:***

Grade	Fraction	Actual #
A	1/5	
B	1/4	
C	1/2	
D	y	10
Total	1	x

We can determine y, the fractional amount represented by D, because the fractions of all four grades must add up to 1. We can either use common denominators or ***Percentage Equivalents***. Let's take the second approach:

Grade	Fraction	Percentage	Actual #
A	1/5	20%	
B	1/4	25%	
C	1/2	50%	
D	y	z	10
Total	1	100%	x

Determine the percentage represented by a D grade:

$20 + 25 + 50 + z = 100$

$z = 5$

Therefore, 5% of the total equals 10 students, or

$$\frac{5}{100}x = 10$$

$$x = 10 \times \frac{100}{5} = {}^{2}\cancel{10} \times \frac{100}{\cancel{5}_{1}} = 200$$

The correct answer is (D).

PS 195. FDPs: Fractions
Difficulty: Medium **OG Page:** 179

This problem provides three expressions in terms of x and asks us to determine whether the value must increase for each of these as x increases from 165 to 166. The properties of ***Linear Equations*** and of ***Fractions*** can help to answer the question.

I. $2x - 5$

This expression is straightforward, so we can simply ***Plug In the Values*** 165 and 166 and see which one is bigger.

$2(165) - 5 = 330 - 5 = 325$
$2(165) - 5 = 332 - 5 = 327$

If we apply ***Algebraic Reasoning,*** we can avoid computation. If x goes up, so does $2x$, and so does $2x - 5$.

327 is bigger than 325, so $2x - 5$ increases.

II. $1 - 1/x$

The key here is to grasp numerator and denominator rules for fractions. We are dealing with positive values of x, and as the denominator of a positive fraction increases, the value of the fraction decreases. Therefore, as positive x increases, $1/x$ decreases. Since we are subtracting a smaller value from 1 as x increases, $1 - 1/x$ must increase.

III. $\frac{1}{x^2 - x}$

Factoring the denominator into $x(x - 1)$, we notice that as long as x is greater than 1, we are multiplying two positive consecutive integers in the denominator. Therefore, as x increases the value in the denominator must also increase, and the overall value of the fraction must decrease.

The only two expressions that must increase are I and II. This is the **answer.**

Note that we could also directly ***Test Values*** for x in this problem. The numbers 165 and 166 are arbitrary. As long as we choose numbers greater than 1, the fractions in Expressions II and III will remain positive. The same properties used above will hold. Thus, we can simplify the computations by using small numbers, such as $x = 2$ and $x = 3$.

The correct answer is (C).

PS 196. Algebra: Exponents & Roots
Difficulty: Devilish **OG Page:** 180

The problem tells us that 20 integers between −10 and 10 are chosen, with repetitions allowed, and asks us for the least possible product of those integers.

The answer choices can provide a hint as to what this value is. Because this problem involves negative numbers, it is reasonable to assume that the least possible value will be negative. We can confidently eliminate (A), (B), and (C).

Of the remaining answer choices, $-(10)^{20}$ is less than $-(10)^{19}$. If $-(10)^{20}$ is a possible value, then it will be the correct answer.

If we pick –10 an odd number of times, the product of those numbers will be a negative power of 10. If we then pick 10 for the rest of the numbers, the negative power of 10 would be multiplied by a positive power of 10, resulting in $-(10)^{20}$.

To see exactly how this works, try, for example, picking –10 once and then 10 nineteen times:

$$-10 \times (10)^{19} = -1 \times 10 \times (10)^{19} = -1 \times (10)^{20} = -(10)^{20}$$

The correct answer is (E).

PS 197. Geometry: Triangles & Diagonals
Difficulty: Medium **OG Page:** 180

The distance called for in this ***Diagonals*** problem is the main diagonal of the box, the diagonal that stretches between two opposite corners, through the interior of the box. Be sure to ***Draw a Picture:***

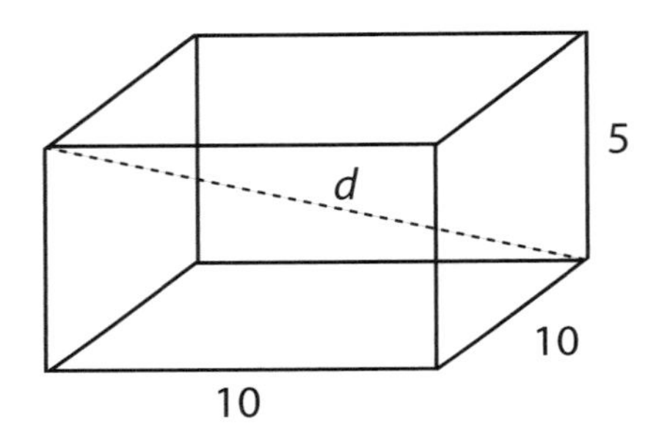

This problem can be solved most quickly and easily with the ***Deluxe Pythagorean Theorem***, which is especially designed to find distances like this one. That theorem states that, for any rectangular box with length l, width w, and height h, we know that $l^2 + w^2 + h^2 = d^2$, in which d is the length of the main diagonal.

Substituting the given length, width, and height into this formula yields $10^2 + 10^2 + 5^2 = d^2$, or $225 = d^2$. Therefore, $d = 15$ inches. This is the **answer**.

The other approach to this problem is to use the standard ***Pythagorean Theorem*** twice. Since d is not currently the hypotenuse of a triangle, construct *another* right triangle, in the *base* of the box, by drawing a diagonal across that base:

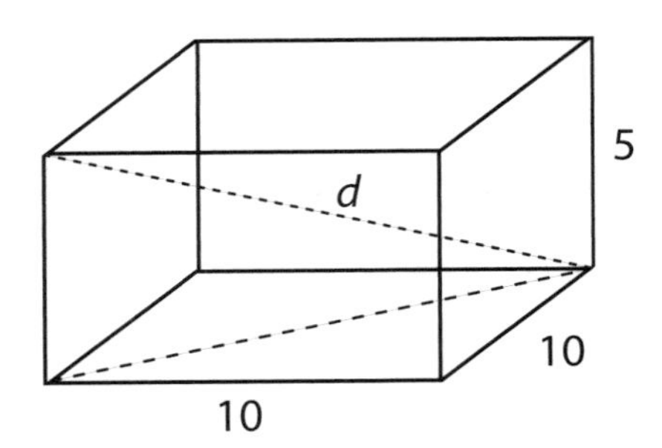

First, find the length of this new base diagonal. The fastest way to find its length is to realize that it creates a ***45–45–90*** triangle with the two sides of length 10.

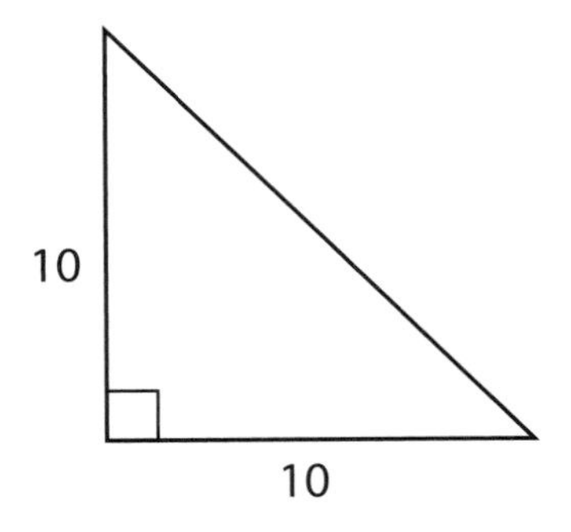

Since the ratio of side to hypotenuse in a 45°–45°–90° triangle is $1 : \sqrt{2}$, this triangle's sides are 10, 10, and $10\sqrt{2}$.

Alternatively, we can use the Pythagorean Theorem: $10^2 + 10^2 = (\text{new diagonal})^2$. Therefore, new diagonal $= \sqrt{200}$, or $10\sqrt{2}$.

Once this base diagonal has been found, consider the triangle that it forms with the main diagonal, d, and the height of the box (which is 5).

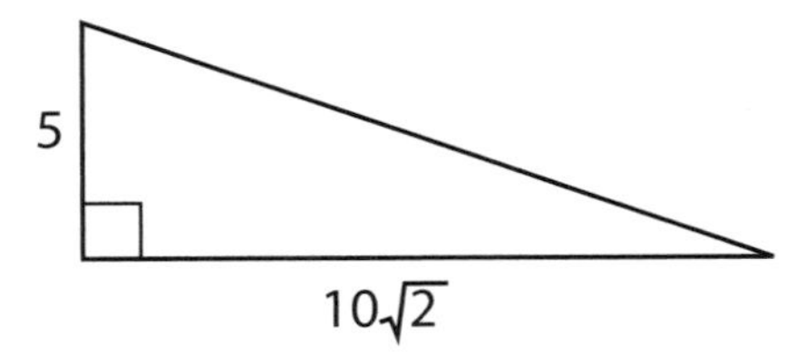

We can use the Pythagorean Theorem to solve for d:

$$5^2 + (10\sqrt{2})^2 = d^2 (\text{or, } 5^2 + (\sqrt{200})^2 = d^2)$$
$$25 + 200 = d^2$$
$$225 = d^2$$
$$15 = d$$

The correct answer is (A).

PS 198. FDPs: Percents
Difficulty: Devilish **OG Page:** 180

This challenging problem gives us some information about a store that sold only two types of newspapers. We are told that paper A was sold for \$1 each and paper B was sold for \$1.25 each. We are also told that r percent of the store's revenue from paper sales is from A and that p percent of the papers sold were paper A. Then we are asked which answer expresses r in terms of p.

The given information is complicated, so organizing it into a ***Table*** is a good idea. The percents are a bit tricky here, because instead of being given as decimals between 0 and 1, they are given as numbers between 0 and 100, so the percentage of paper B sold is $100 - p$, not $1 - p$, and the percentage of revenue from B is $100 - r$, not $1 - r$.

	Price per paper	Percentage sold	Percentage of revenue
Paper A	\$1.00	p	r
Paper B	\$1.25	$100 - p$	$100 - r$

Since we want to express r in terms of p, we want an equation for r that uses only p as a variable. Let's start by thinking about how r, the percentage of revenue from paper A, could be expressed in an equation and see if we can transform that equation to get it in terms of p.

$$r = \frac{\text{revenue from A}}{\text{total revenue}} \times 100$$

In order to calculate the revenue from A and the total revenue from the percentage sold and the price, we need to know the quantity of papers sold. Notice that there is no information given on the actual quantitiy of papers sold, so we could introduce a variable, Q, for it. However, since there is also no information on the actual amount of revenue either, and this problem is about the relationship between quantity sold and revenue, we could ***Choose a Smart Number*** for Q that makes the computations easier. Let's set up the equations with Q as a variable and then decide what to pick for it later:

$$\text{revenue from A} = \$1.00 \times \frac{p}{100} \times Q = \frac{pQ}{100}$$

$$\text{revenue from B} = \$1.25 \times \frac{100 - p}{100} \times Q$$

$$= \frac{(125 - 1.25p)Q}{100}$$

$$\text{total revenue} = \frac{pQ}{100} + \frac{(125 - 1.25p)Q}{100}$$

$$= \frac{pQ}{100} + \frac{125Q - 1.25pQ}{100} = \frac{125Q - 0.25pQ}{100}$$

It would be convenient to get rid of the 100 in the demonimators of revenue from A and total revenue. It would also simplify the math to get rid of the decimal coefficient, 0.25, in front of pQ. Picking 400 for Q would accomplish both of these goals.

We can then substitute back into the equation for r and get:

$$\text{revenue from A} = \frac{p(400)}{100} = 4p$$

$$\text{total revenue} = \frac{125Q - 0.25pQ}{100}$$

$$= \frac{Q(125 - 0.25p)}{100}$$

$$= \frac{400(125 - 0.25p)}{100}$$

$$= 4(125 - 0.25p)$$

$$= 500 - p$$

Now we can plug these values into our original equation for r:

$$r = \frac{\text{revenue from A}}{\text{total revenue}} \times 100$$

$$r = \frac{4p}{500 - p} \times 100$$

$$r = \frac{400p}{500 - p}$$

If we had tried to pick Q immediately, before we understood what the equations look like, we would have had a harder time with this problem because it would be very difficult to get both a percentage sold and a percentage of revenue that would be easy to work with integers.

Alternatively, a good backup approach to this problem is to eliminate answers. If all of the papers sold were paper A, then 100% of the sales would be from paper A and 100% of the revenue would be from paper A, so p and r would both be 100.

So if we plug in our value of p, which is 100, we should get 100 as the value of r:

(A) $\frac{100p}{125-p}=\frac{10{,}000}{125-100}=\frac{10{,}000}{25}\Leftarrow$ STOP! > 100

(B) $\frac{150p}{250-p}=\frac{15{,}000}{250-100}=\frac{15{,}000}{150}=100$

(C) $\frac{300p}{375-p}=\frac{30{,}000}{375-100}=\frac{30{,}000}{275}\Leftarrow$ STOP! > 100

(D) $\frac{400p}{500-p}=\frac{40{,}000}{500-100}=\frac{40{,}000}{400}=100$

(E) $\frac{500p}{625-p}=\frac{50{,}000}{625-100}=\frac{50{,}000}{525}\Leftarrow$ STOP! < 100

Both (B) and (D) work when $p = 100$, so we know that one of them has to be the correct answer. Generally speaking, anything as easy as picking 100% for an unknown percentage will lead to more than one correct answer, but this is a fast way to eliminate some answers on a tough problem and make an educated guess.

The correct answer is (D).

PS 199. Algebra: Quadratic Equations
Difficulty: Devilish **OG Page:** 180

This expression is just about impossible to compute in a straightforward way in less than two minutes, which tells us that there must be a pattern to see that will give us a clue about a way to rewrite it.

Notice that all of the answers include powers of 10 (either 10^{-4} or 10^{-8}), and that none of them contain fractions. That's a clue that we should try to rewrite the fractions in terms of powers of 10.

Additionally, notice that $10^{-4} = 0.0001$. The denominator of the first fraction is 1.0001. We can rewrite this as $1 + 10^{-4}$.

We can perform a similar manipulation on the numerator. $0.99999999 = 1 - 0.00000001$, which can be rewritten as $1 - 10^{-8}$. The first fraction now looks like this:

$$\frac{1-10^{-8}}{1+10^{-4}}$$

Why did this help? It helped because $1 - 10^{-8}$ is a ***Difference of Squares.*** 1 is a perfect square ($1^2 = 1$) and 10^{-8} is also a perfect square ($(10^{-4})^2 = 10^{-8}$). We can factor the numerator and then cancel with the denominator.

$$\frac{1-10^{-8}}{1+10^{-4}}=\frac{\cancel{(1+10^{-4})}(1-10^{-4})}{\cancel{1+10^{-4}}}=1-10^{-4}$$

At this point, we have to assume that we can perform a similar operation on the second fraction. 0.99999991 can be rewritten as $1 - 9 \times 10^{-8}$ and 1.0003 can be rewritten as $1 + 3 \times 10^{-4}$. Factor the top as a difference of squares and cancel out the denominator:

$$\frac{0.99999991}{1.0003}=\frac{1-9(10^{-8})}{1+3(10^{-4})}=\frac{\cancel{(1+3(10^{-4}))}(1-3(10^{-4}))}{\cancel{1+3(10^{-4})}}=(1-3(10^{-4}))$$

Now subtract $(1 - 3(10^{-4}))$ from $(1 - 10^{-4})$:

$$1 - 10^{-4} - (1 - 3(10^{-4})) = 1 - 10^{-4} - 1 + 3(10^{-4}) = 2(10^{-4})$$

The correct answer is (D).

PS 200. FDPs: Ratios
Difficulty: Hard **OG Page:** 180

In this ***Ratio*** problem, we are given a ***Multiple Ratio*** involving three ingredients in a solution. The problem further states that some of the ratios are altered from the original situation. We can write the original ratio of soap to alcohol to water as

$$(S: A: W)_{original} = 2 : 50 : 100.$$

Multiple ratios with more than two parts, such as this one, are a convenient way of expressing the relative sizes of more than two quantities. One way to attack this problem is to ***Break Up the Multiple Ratio*** into 2 typical two-part ratios. For example, the ratio of soap to alcohol, as well as the ratio of soap to water, can be extracted from the multiple ratio above:

$(S: A)_{original} = 2 : 50$
$(S: W)_{original} = 2 : 100$

Notice that the 2 is the same for the soap in the two ratios above. Now, we are told that the ratio of soap to alcohol is doubled, while that of soap to water is halved:

$(S: A:)_{new} = 2 \times (2 : 50) = 4 : 50$
$(S: W:)_{new} = 1/2 \times (2 : 100) = 1 : 100$

In order to actually ***Alter a Ratio,*** we change *just one* number in the ratio. To double the ratio of soap to alcohol, for instance, we change the ratio from 2 : 50 to 4 : 50. We should not double *both* numbers. If we do, we end up with 4 : 100, which is exactly the same as 2 : 50. This works just like fractions. Doubling 2/50 gives us 4/50, not 4/100.

Now that we have the new ratios 4 : 50 and 1 : 100, we need to ***Scale the Ratios*** before reassembling them into a new multiple ratio. That is, we need the common ingredient (soap) to have the same number in both ratios. To scale a ratio, we change *both* numbers by the same factor. For instance, we can scale 1 : 100 to 2 : 200 or 4 : 400. Since soap appears as 4 in one ratio and as 1 in the other, we scale 1 : 100 to 4 : 400. Now we can ***Recombine the Two-Part Ratios*** into a new multiple ratio:

$(S: A)_{new} = 4 : 50$
$(S: W)_{new} = 4 : 400$
$(S: A: W)_{new} = 4 : 50 : 400 = 2 : 25 : 200$

At this point, we can introduce an ***Unknown Multiplier*** x in order to go from relative to absolute quantities of the ingredients. Rewriting the ratio with this multiplier, we have:

$(S: A: W)_{new} = 2x : 25x : 200x$

If the amount of alcohol will be 100, then

$A = 100 = 25x$
$4 = x$

Thus, the amount of water in the solution will be

$W = 200x = 200 \times 4 = 800$ cubic centimeters

This is the **answer.**

Alternatively, as we become more comfortable with multiple ratios, we can avoid breaking the multiple ratio down into typical two-part ratios. We simply adjust one number at a time in a table, keeping track of what happens to the two-part ratios $S : A$ and $S : W$.

First, we try to double $S : A$, as follows.

	S	A	W
old	2	50	100
	×2 ↓		
	4	50	100

We have successfully doubled $S : A$. But we have also doubled $S : W$. That's bad. To fix the issue, we should leave S alone and change W. We want to reduce $S : W$, so we should make W bigger (as we would a denominator, which W effectively is). Let's try doubling W.

S	A	W
4	50	100
		×2 ↓
4	50	200

This step brings $S : W$ back to where it was originally (4 : 200 is the same as 2 : 100), but we need to cut the original ratio $S : W$ in half. So we keep going, doubling W again.

	S	A	W
	4	50	200
			↓ ×2
	4	50	400

Now we are all set with the two-part ratios. $S:A$ is double what it was, and $S:W$ is half what it was. Now we just need to scale the whole ratio up, so that there are actually 100 cubic centimeters of alcohol.

	S	A	W
new	4	50	400
	↓ ×2	↓ ×2	↓ ×2
	8	100	800

We are looking for the final amount of water, which is 800 cubic centimeters.

The correct answer is (E).

PS 201. FDPs: Percents
Difficulty: Medium **OG Page:** 180

In this ***Overlapping Sets*** problem that also involves ***Percents,*** students in a class are categorized by how they answered two questions on a test. Some students (75%) got the first question right, and the rest did not. Likewise, some students (55%) got the second question right, and the rest did not. Some students (20%) got neither question right. We are asked for the percentage of students who got both questions right.

One approach is to use a ***Double-Set Matrix***. Since we are dealing with percents only (no actual numbers of students), we choose the ***Choose the Smart Number*** 100 for the total number of students in the class. Shade the box we want.

	Q1 Right	Q1 Wrong	Total
Q2 Right			
Q2 Wrong			
Total			100

Now we fill in the numbers we know. Since 75 students got Q1 right, without regard to whether they got Q2 right, we put 75 at the bottom of the first column. Similarly, the 55 students who got Q2 right are placed in the first row's Total column. We also know that if 75 students got Q1 right, then $100 - 75 = 25$ students got it wrong. Likewise, $100 - 55 = 45$ students got Q2 wrong. Finally, the 20 students who got both questions wrong go in the middle box (Q1 Wrong and Q2 Wrong):

	Q1 Right	Q1 Wrong	Total
Q2 Right			55
Q2 Wrong		20	45
Total	75	25	100

Now, we fill in the rest of the table, making sure that all the rows and all the columns add up:

	Q1 Right	Q1 Wrong	Total
Q2 Right	50	5	55
Q2 Wrong	25	20	45
Total	75	25	100

50 students out of 100, or 50% of the class, got both questions right. This is the **answer**.

Alternatively, we can use a ***Quick Formula for Overlapping Sets:***

Total = Group 1 + Group 2 – Both + Neither

The logic behind this formula is that, since those who are in both groups have been counted twice, subtracting them once will count them correctly. Moreover, since those in neither group have not been counted at all, they are simply added.

Again, our total is 100 students. Thus:

$$100 = 75 + 55 - B + 20$$
$$100 = 150 - B$$
$$B = 50$$

The correct answer is (D).

PS 202. Geometry: Coordinate Plane
Difficulty: Medium **OG Page:** 180

This ***Coordinate Plane*** problem tells us that point A has coordinates (2,3), that the line $y = x$ is the perpendicular bisector of AB, and that the x-axis is the perpendicular bisector of BC. We are asked to find the coordinates of point C.

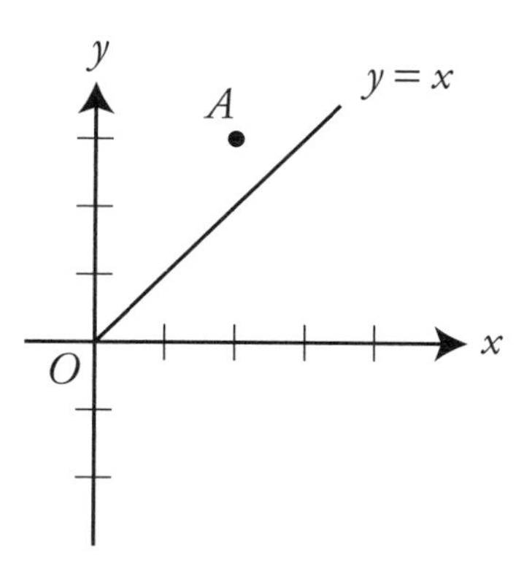

If $y = x$ is the ***Perpendicular Bisector*** of AB, then the line is perpendicular to AB, and intersects AB at its midpoint. This means the distance from point A to the line is equal to the distance from the line to point B. In other words, B is the ***Reflection*** of A through the line $y = x$. The word reflection is no accident: if A represents a person and the line $y = x$ represents a mirror, then B is the image of A "in the mirror."

We can sketch point B to lie to the right of and lower than point A, with coordinates of about (3,2). We can prove that these indeed are the coordinates of point B, since we know that perpendicular lines have slopes that are the negative reciprocal of one another. The slope of $y = x$ is 1. The slope of segment AB must be –1. However, in order to solve this problem, we do not need to take such a formal approach involving slopes.

If the x-axis is the perpendicular bisector of BC, we can also say that point C is the reflection of point B through the x-axis. We can sketch point C with coordinates of (3, –2).

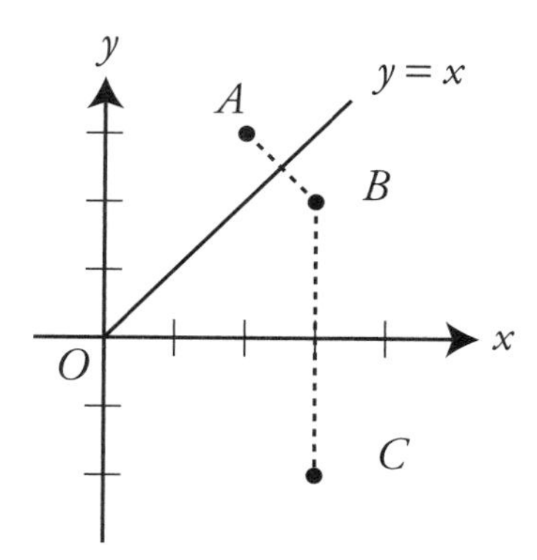

Thus, (3, –2) is the **answer**.

Even if we were unsure about the precise coordinates, using our reflection process we can ***Estimate*** the correct answer. With this analysis, we know that point C must be in quadrant IV, which eliminates (A), (B), and (E). We also know that point C must be to the right of point A, which eliminates (C).

The correct answer is (D).

PS 203. Word Problems: Algebraic Translations
Difficulty: Medium **OG Page:** 181

This problem specifies that a store charges the same price for each towel that it sells and that a certain (unspecified) number of towels can be purchased for \$120. If the current price of each towel were to increase by \$1, however, then ten fewer towels could be bought for that same \$120. The question asks for the current price of one towel.

Let's take a ***Direct Algebra*** approach and set up a ***Table*** to organize the information. We need to ***Name Variables***. Let x be the current price per towel, and let y be the current number of towels we can buy for \$120.

	Current	**New**
Price per towel	x	$x + 1$
# of towels for \$120	y	$y - 10$

We can now express the ***Cost Relationships*** that we know.

Current Total Cost: $xy = 120$

New Total Cost: $(x + 1)(y - 10) = 120$

The two equations are not linear, so solving for the variables will involve quadratics. It will take a fair amount of work to solve this way.

Instead, notice that the answers are almost all very small (1, 2, 3, 4, and 12). Let's switch approaches and try ***Working Backwards from the Answer Choices***.

Begin with the middle number. If 3 is the current price of each towel, then we could buy 120/3 = 40 towels for \$120. The new price would be 3 + 1 = \$4 per towel, and we could buy 120/4 = 30 towels for \$120. This fits the data, as we can see in our table.

	Current	**New**
Price per towel	$x = 3$	$x + 1 = 4$
# of towels for \$120	$y = 40$	$y - 10 = 30$

Thus, the current price of each towel is in fact \$3. This is the **answer**.

If (C) did not work out, we would be able to determine if we needed a larger or smaller number and would then test a corresponding answer choice.

Although it may seem hard to switch approaches mid-stream, this is a good overall strategy for certain tough problems. If the first path looks like a lot of work, we should see whether we can switch lanes to where the traffic is flowing faster.

If we had continued with the algebraic approach, we would have gotten the following:

$$xy = 120$$
$$y = 120/x$$
$$(x + 1)(y - 10) = 120$$
$$(x + 1)(120/x - 10) = 120$$
$$(x + 1)(120 - 10x) = 120x$$
$$120x - 10x^2 + 120 - 10x = 120x$$
$$-10x^2 - 10x + 120 = 0$$
$$x^2 + x - 12 = 0$$
$$(x + 4)(x - 3) = 0$$
$$x = 3 \text{ (must be > 0)}$$

The correct answer is (C).

PS 204. <u>Number Properties</u>: Divisibility & Primes
Difficulty: Devilish **OG Page:** 181

By far, the easiest approach is to ***Choose a Smart Number*** for p that follows the constraint that p is a prime number greater than 2.

Say that $p = 3$, so $p = (4)(3) = 12$.

The divisors of $n = 12$ are 1, 2, 3, 4, 6, and 12. There are four even divisors in this list (2, 4, 6, and 12).

The number picking approach is not only easy, but also mathematically safe. The answer *cannot* depend on which p we pick. No matter what prime number greater than 2 we choose, the answer must be the same. Thus, we are free to choose *any* convenient p and work out an answer.

The correct answer is (C).

PS 205. <u>Word Problems</u>: Algebraic Translations
Difficulty: Hard **OG Page:** 181

We can summarize the information given in this problem in the following ***Table:***

	Hours Worked	**Total Earned**
John	10 hours	$x + y$
Mary	8 hours	$x - y$

The problem essentially asks us to find x in terms of y. We can approach the problem using the ***Direct Algebra*** method.

First, express the hourly wage as:

$$\text{Hourly Wage} = \frac{\text{Total Earned}}{\text{Hours Worked}}$$

Since John's and Mary's hourly wages are the same, we can write an equation as follows:

$\frac{x+y}{10} = \frac{x-y}{8}$ Cross-multiply
$8(x + y) = 10(x - y)$ Distribute
$8x + 8y = 10x - 10y$ Subtract $8x$ and add $10y$
$18y = 2x$ Divide by 2
$x = 9y$

In this problem, it would be hard to ***Choose Smart Numbers***, because we have to select values for x and y that result in equal ratios. If we pick a value for y (say, $y = 1$), it is not immediately evident what value of x will result in an equal wage for both Mary and John. At this point, we would need to set up an equation:

$$\frac{x+1}{10} = \frac{x-1}{8}$$

This equation is not that much easier to solve than the equation that includes both x and y. Still, this approach will work.

The correct answer is (E).

PS 206. Geometry: Triangles & Diagonals
Difficulty: Easy **OG Page:** 181

The problem specifies that the area of ***Triangle*** *ORP* equals 12. This triangle lives in the ***Coordinate Plane.*** Point R is not drawn, but we are told that R is located somewhere on the y-axis. Point R's x-coordinate is therefore 0, but we do not know R's y-coordinate. We are asked to find it.

We should begin by ***Redrawing the Figure***, including point R. We should also draw the triangle specified by the question.

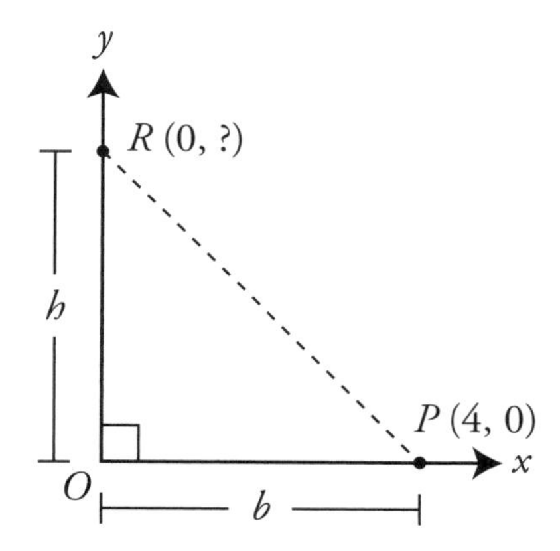

We know that the area of the triangle is 12. We also know that the base of the triangle has a length of 4. What we are missing is the height. The base and the height of any triangle are perpendicular. *OP*, the base of the triangle, runs along the x-axis. *OR*, which runs along the y-axis, is perpendicular to *OP*, so *OR* is the height of the triangle. This is true for any ***Right Triangle:*** the two shorter legs can be taken as a base and a height. And if *OR* is the height of the triangle, then the distance from the origin to point R is the height.

The ***Area of a Triangle*** is given by the formula $A = \frac{1}{2}bh$, where b and h are the base and height, respectively. Plug in the two givens and solve:

$$12 = \frac{1}{2}(4)h$$
$$6 = h$$

If the length of the height is 6, then the distance from the origin to point R must be 6. That means the y-coordinate of point R must be 6.

The correct answer is (B).

PS 207. Word Problems: Rates & Work
Difficulty: Medium **OG Page:** 181

This ***Rates*** problem asks us to determine how many hours it will take for Car A to overtake and drive 8 miles ahead of Car B, starting from 20 miles behind. Recall that when two bodies are traveling in the same direction, we subtract their rates. This gives us the effective rate at which Car A is gaining on Car B. We can use the following formula for ***Relative Rates:***

$$(\text{Rate}_A - \text{Rate}_B) \times t = (\text{difference in distance})$$

We are told that Car A is traveling at 58 mph and Car B is traveling at 50 mph. Car A must drive the same distance as Car B, plus the extra 20 miles to make up for the head start and the extra 8 miles after it overtakes Car B, as specified in the question. Therefore, Car A must drive 20 + 8 = 28 miles further than Car B. Substitute the known values into the formula and solve for t:

$$(58 - 50)t = 28$$
$$8t = 28$$
$$t = 28/8$$
$$t = 3.5 \text{ hours}$$ This is the **answer.**

We can also solve this problem using an ***Rate–Time–Distance Chart.***

Since the cars must travel for the same amount of time, we place a t in the Time for Car A and Car B. Car B will travel some distance d, and Car A will travel that same distance plus an extra 28 miles.

	Rate	Time	Distance
Car A	58	t	$d + 28$
Car B	50	t	d
Total			

We can now set up two equations:

$58t = d + 28$

$50t = d$

Use ***Substitution*** to replace d in the first equation with $50t$:

$58t = (50t) + 28$

$8t = 28$

$t = 3.5$ hours

The correct answer is (E).

PS 208. Word Problems: Statistics
Difficulty: Medium **OG Page:** 181

In this ***Statistics*** problem, we are told that the average production for a company was 50 units over n days. If we ***Name a Variable*** and assign t to total production over this period, we can represent this scenario using the ***Average Formula.***

$$\frac{t}{n} = 50$$

Today's production adds 90 units to the total production, 1 to the number of days, and 5 units to the average production.

$$\frac{t+90}{n+1} = 55$$

We are asked to solve for n. To do so, we can isolate t in the first equation, ***Substitute*** for it in the second equation, and solve:

$t = 50n$

$\frac{(50n)+90}{n+1} = 55$

$50n + 90 = 55(n+1)$

$50n + 90 = 55n + 55$

$35 = 5n$

$7 = n$ This is the **answer.**

Alternatively, we can solve this problem by ***Working Backwards from Answer Choices.*** Let's test answer choice (C). If $n = 10$, the average production over those 10 days was 50 units, so 50×10 represents the total number of units produced. 500 units were produced. The next day, 90 units were produced, so after 11 days, 590 units were produced. If the average production at that point was 55 units, then 590/11 should equal 55. It doesn't, so (C) can't be the right answer. Doing the same calculations for the other answer choices reveals that (E) works.

The correct answer is (E).

PS 209. FDPs: Fractions
Difficulty: Hard **OG Page:** 182

Although this question can be solved using ***Direct Algebra***, this method is inadvisable. The algebra is messy and prone to error, given the ***Negative Signs*** and ***Even Exponents.***

Moreover, we could perform the algebra correctly but be forced to go further, in order to match the particular form in the right answer choice.

As a result, this question is best solved by ***Choosing Smart Numbers.***

Let $x = 2$. Replace x with $1/x$ (i.e., 1/2) in the expression given and compute the ***Target Value:***

$$\left(\frac{x+1}{x-1}\right)^2 = \left(\frac{\frac{1}{2}+1}{\frac{1}{2}-1}\right)^2 = \left(\frac{\frac{3}{2}}{-\frac{1}{2}}\right)^2 = \left(\frac{3}{-1}\right)^2 = 9$$

The answer choice that yields a value of 9 when we plug in 2 for x is the correct answer.

(A) $\left(\frac{x+1}{x-1}\right)^2 = \left(\frac{2+1}{2-1}\right)^2 = \left(\frac{3}{1}\right)^2 = 9$

(B) $\left(\frac{x-1}{x+1}\right)^2 = \left(\frac{2-1}{2+1}\right)^2 = \left(\frac{1}{3}\right)^2 = \frac{1}{9}$

(C) $\frac{x^2+1}{1-x^2} = \frac{2^2+1}{1-2^2} = \frac{4+1}{1-4} = \frac{-5}{3}$

(D) $\frac{x^2-1}{x^2+1} = \frac{2^2-1}{2^2+1} = \frac{4-1}{4+1} = \frac{3}{5}$

(E) $-\left(\frac{x-1}{x+1}\right)^2 = -\left(\frac{2-1}{2+1}\right)^2 = -\left(\frac{1}{3}\right)^2 = -\frac{1}{9}$

The correct answer is (A).

PS 210. Geometry: Lines & Angles
Difficulty: Easy **OG Page:** 182

As there seems to be no direct relationship between x and y, which measure ***Angles,*** we must find the individual values of these variables and then sum them to answer the question.

As with any ***Geometry*** question that involves a picture, we should begin by ***Redrawing the Figure*** and filling in any known information. For ease of explanation, points in the figure have been labeled.

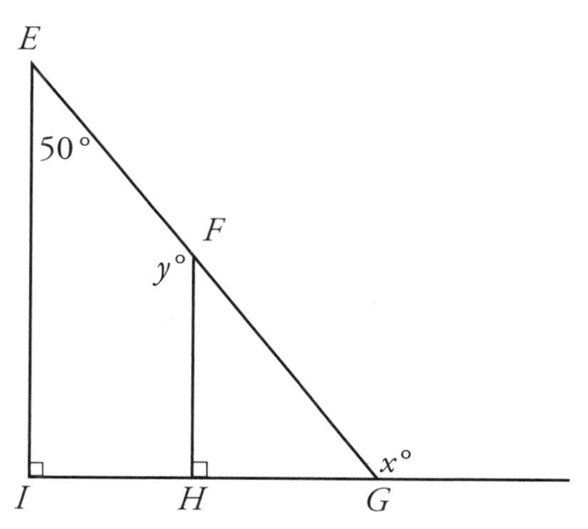

There are two ways we can find the value of y. We know that shape $EFHI$ is a ***Quadrilateral,*** and the internal angles of any quadrilateral must sum to 360. We also know that $\angle EIH$ and $\angle IHF$ are right angles. Therefore $90 + 90 + 50 + y = 360$. Solving for y gives us $y = 130$.

To find the value of x, we must think about how x relates to the rest of the figure. x is an ***Exterior Angle*** to the triangle EIG. Since the exterior angle of a triangle is equal to the sum of the two nonadjacent interior angles, we can solve. $\angle EIH$ is a right angle and $\angle IEF$ is 50.

$x = 90 + 50$
$x = 140$
$x + y = 140 + 130 = 270$

The correct answer is (D).

PS 211. Geometry: Coordinate Plane
Difficulty: Medium **OG Page:** 182

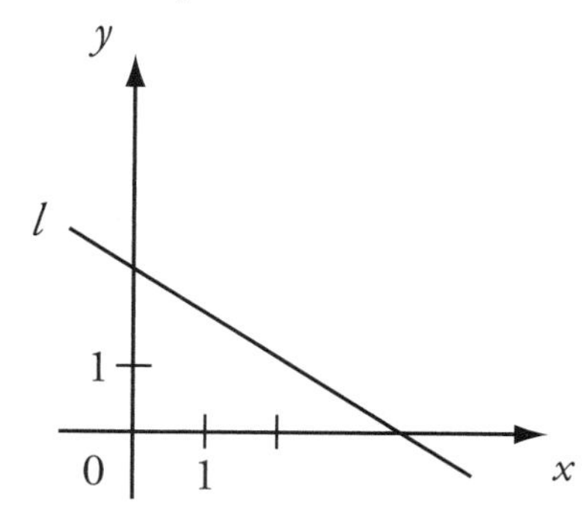

The primary way to solve this Coordinate Plane problem is to come up with the equation of the line. One way to do this is to use the ***Slope-Intercept Equation,*** $y = mx + b$, where m represents the slope of the line, and b the y-intercept.

This line has a y-intercept of 2, where the line crosses the y-axis. It has a slope of –2/3 because, as the line goes from left to right, it goes down by 2 units as it goes across by 3 units.

Therefore, we can write the equation as:

$y = (-2/3)x + 2$

Notice that none of the equations in the answer choices contain fractions. Therefore we need to multiply the equation by 3 in order to eliminate the fraction –2/3.

$3y = -2x + 6$
$2x + 3y = 6$ This is the **answer.**

Alternatively, we can ***Work Backwards from the Answer Choices*** by plugging in the two points on the line that we know of, namely (3, 0) and (0, 2), into the answer choices. This approach could take more time, but if we are organized, it will definitely work.

Note that both sets work for the equation in answer choice (B):

$2(3) + 3(0) = 6$
$2(0) + 3(2) = 6.$

None of the other equations work for both of the points.

The correct answer is (B).

PS 212. FDPs: Digits & Decimals
Difficulty: Easy **OG Page:** 182

In this ***Digits*** problem, we can take a ***Direct Algebra*** approach if we ***Name Variables*** for the digits of the two-digit number mentioned.

We can call the first two-digit number XY and the second two-digit number YX, where X and Y are the digits (not the product of X and Y). In the first number, X is in the 10's place and Y is in the 1's place. We can thus express XY as $10X + Y$. We can similarly express YX as $10Y + X$.

To illustrate with an actual number, consider the number 36. We can express 36 as 3(10) + 6(1), because 3 is in the 10's place and 6 is in the 1's.

We know that the difference between XY and YX is 27. Therefore, $XY - YX = 27$. We can substitute using the expressions above and simplify:

$(10X + Y) - (10Y + X) = 27$
$9X - 9Y = 27$
$9(X - Y) = 27$
$X - Y = 3$

Therefore, X and Y differ by 3.

We can also ***Test Numbers.*** This approach will take longer, because we have to find a number that fits the criterion by trial and error. However, once we hit upon any number that fits the criterion (e.g., 14), we can easily solve the problem.

The correct answer is (A).

PS 213. Geometry: Circles & Cylinders
Difficulty: Easy **OG Page:** 182

In this problem, we are told that a ***Circle*** in the ***Coordinate Plane*** with center C is tangent to both the x and y axes, such that the distance from the origin O to point C equals k. We are asked for the radius of the circle.

In order to solve for the radius, it is helpful to ***Redraw the Picture***, adding lines where necessary. Draw line segments from C to the points of tangency with the axes, as shown below:

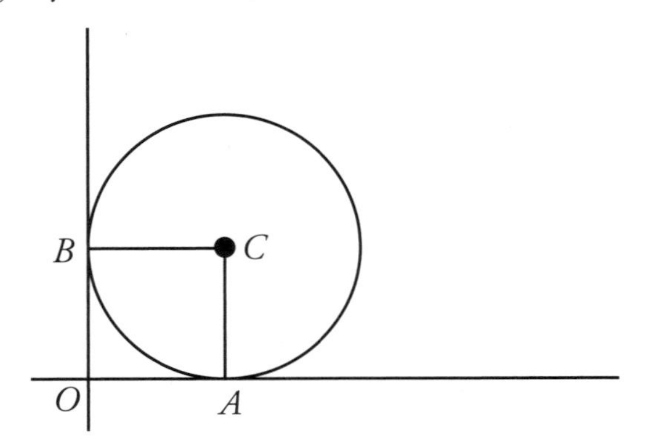

Because points A and B are on the circle, the distance from either of them to C must equal the radius r. Furthermore, a radius drawn to a point of tangency is perpendicular to the tangent at that point. Therefore, since all angles of quadrilateral $OACB$ equal 90°, and the side lengths are equal, $OACB$ is a ***Square,*** with OC as its diagonal. The length of the ***Diagonal of a Square*** is $\sqrt{2}$ times the side length:

$k = r\sqrt{2}$

Solving for r yields $r = \frac{k}{\sqrt{2}}$. This is the **answer**.

We could also have obtained this result by noticing that OAC and OBC are ***45–45–90*** triangles, or by using the ***Pythagorean Theorem*** on either of those right triangles:

$r^2 + r^2 = 2r^2 = k^2$ Square root both sides.
$r\sqrt{2} = k$ Solve for r.
$r = \frac{k}{\sqrt{2}}$

The correct answer is (B).

PS 214. <u>FDPs</u>: Fractions
Difficulty: Medium **OG Page:** 183

Notice that the verbal wind-up to this problem—everything having to do with resistors and circuits—is irrelevant. The question is simply, "The reciprocal of r is equal to the sum of the reciprocals of x and y. What is r in terms of x and y?"

The ***Reciprocals*** of r, x, and y are simply $1/r$, $1/x$, and $1/y$, respectively. Thus we can ***Algebraically Translate*** the words as follows:

$$\frac{1}{r} = \frac{1}{x} + \frac{1}{y}$$

If we take a ***Direct Algebra*** approach, it is tempting to simply "flip everything over" and conclude that $r = x + y$. However, this would be an illegal move: we can only invert both sides when each side consists entirely of a single fraction. That is, before we can "flip everything over," we must combine the right side into a single fraction. Multiply $1/x$ and $1/y$ by "convenient" forms of 1 in order to get a common denominator:

$$\frac{1}{r} = \frac{1}{x} \times \frac{y}{y} + \frac{1}{y} \times \frac{x}{x}$$

$$\frac{1}{r} = \frac{y}{xy} + \frac{x}{xy}$$

$$\frac{1}{r} = \frac{x+y}{xy}$$

NOW, we are permitted to do the "big flip":

$$r = \frac{xy}{x+y}$$ This is the **answer**.

Don't forget the final flip! One of the wrong answers is the correct expression for $1/r$.

We could also ***Choose Smart Numbers,*** but the algebraic route is relatively fast and straightforward, once we learn to avoid the traps.

The correct answer is (D).

PS 215. <u>Number Properties</u>: Probability
Difficulty: Medium **OG Page:** 183

In this ***Probability*** problem, we want to find the probability that:

Xavier solves the problem
AND
Yvonne solves the problem
AND
Zelda does *not* solve the problem.

This problem involves ***Multiple Outcomes.*** When we want outcomes A AND B both to happen, and A and B are independent events, we can multiply the probability of A by the probability of B to find the probability that both outcomes occur. (In probability problems, the word AND usually means to multiply, while the word OR usually means to add.)

We are given the probabilities of Xavier and Yvonne solving the problem, but not of Zelda NOT solving the problem. To find the probability of Zelda NOT solving the problem, we will use the ***1 – x Principle.*** We know that:

$$P\begin{pmatrix}\text{Zelda solves}\\\text{the problem}\end{pmatrix} + P\begin{pmatrix}\text{Zelda does NOT}\\\text{solve the problem}\end{pmatrix} = 1$$

so,

$$P\begin{pmatrix}\text{Zelda does NOT}\\\text{solve the problem}\end{pmatrix} = 1 - P\begin{pmatrix}\text{Zelda does NOT}\\\text{solve the problem}\end{pmatrix}$$

$$= 1 - \frac{5}{8} = \frac{3}{8}$$

In other words, if Zelda has a 5/8 chance of success, she has a 3/8 chance of failure.

Now we can answer the question by multiplying:

$$\left[P\begin{pmatrix}\text{Xavier}\\\text{solves the}\\\text{problem}\end{pmatrix}\right]\left[P\begin{pmatrix}\text{Yvonne}\\\text{solves the}\\\text{problem}\end{pmatrix}\right]\left[P\begin{pmatrix}\text{Zelda does}\\\text{NOT solve}\\\text{the problem}\end{pmatrix}\right]$$

$$= \left(\frac{1}{4}\right)\left(\frac{1}{2}\right)\left(\frac{3}{8}\right) = \frac{3}{64}$$ This is the **answer.**

Notice that if we had used Zelda's chance of *success* instead, we would have come up with wrong answer choice (D).

The correct answer is (E).

PS 216. Algebra: Quadratic Equations
Difficulty: Easy **OG Page:** 183

This problem specifies an equation and then asks what x "could" be. Note the word "could": this means that there is more than one possible value for x, but only one of the possible values will appear among the answer choices. As we will see, we will wind up with a ***Quadratic Equation.***

$$\frac{1}{x}-\frac{1}{x+1}=\frac{1}{x+4}$$

Combine the two fractions on the left by creating a ***Common Denominator***, which is $x(x + 1)$:

$$\frac{1}{x}-\frac{1}{x+1}=\frac{x+1}{x(x+1)}-\frac{x}{x(x+1)}=$$
$$\frac{x+1-x}{x(x+1)}=\frac{1}{x(x+1)}$$

Initially, this may seem complicated, but notice step 2: the x variables cancel each other out in the numerator.

Now we have the following:

$$\frac{1}{x(x+1)}=\frac{1}{x+4}$$

Take the reciprocal of each side and solve:

$$x(x + 1) = x + 4$$
$$x^2 + x = x + 4$$
$$x^2 + x - x - 4 = 0$$
$$x^2 - 4 = 0$$
$$(x + 2)(x - 2) = 0$$
$$x = -2 \text{ or } 2$$

Only -2 is among the choices. This is the **answer**.

Alternatively, we can answer this question by ***Working Backwards from the Answer Choices.*** This may initially seem like a lot of work, but there is a shortcut. We know that the denominators of fractions cannot equal 0 because we ***Cannot Divide by Zero.*** If we look at the three fractions in this equation, we see that x cannot equal 0, -1 or -4 respectively. But 0, -1 and -4 are all answer choices, which means there are only two possible values of x: -2 or -3.

Testing the surviving answer choices gives us:

(C) $\frac{1}{-2}-\frac{1}{-2+1}=\frac{1}{-2+4} \rightarrow -\frac{1}{2}-(-1)=\frac{1}{2}$

$$\frac{1}{2}=\frac{1}{2}$$

(D) $\frac{1}{-3}-\frac{1}{-3+1}=\frac{1}{-3+4} \rightarrow -\frac{1}{3}-\left(-\frac{1}{2}\right)=1$

$$\frac{1}{6}=1$$

The equation is true when $x = -2$.

The correct answer is (C).

PS 217. Algebra: Exponents & Roots
Difficulty: Easy **OG Page:** 183

When we simplify ***Exponential Expressions***, we should look for a ***Common Base***. Notice that all of the denominators are powers of 2. Start by breaking each base down into its ***Prime Factors:***

$$\left(\frac{1}{2}\right)^{-3}\left(\frac{1}{4}\right)^{-2}\left(\frac{1}{16}\right)^{-1}=\left(\frac{1}{2}\right)^{-3}\left(\frac{1}{2^2}\right)^{-2}\left(\frac{1}{2^4}\right)^{-1}$$

To simplify the given expression, remember that an expression with a negative exponent is the reciprocal of what the expression would be with a positive exponent. When we see ***Negative Exponents***, we should immediately think about ***Reciprocals.*** Now apply the negative exponents by taking the reciprocal of each term and making the exponent positive. Then we add exponents:

$$(2)^3(2^2)^2(2^4)^1 = 2^3 \times 2^4 \times 2^4 = 2^{3+4+4} = 2^{11}$$

Because all of the answer choices have negative exponents, we can perform the same transformations on them—simply take the reciprocal of each and change the exponent to a positive. Our answer matches that in choice (B):

$$2^{11} = \left(\frac{1}{2}\right)^{-11}$$ This is the **answer**.

Alternatively, we can solve the problem without changing the exponents to their positive forms. We can bring the outside exponent inside and apply it to both numerator and denominator:

$$\left(\frac{1}{2}\right)^{-3}\left(\frac{1}{2^2}\right)^{-2}\left(\frac{1}{2^4}\right)^{-1} =$$

$$\left(\frac{1}{2^{-3}}\right)\left(\frac{1}{2^{-4}}\right)\left(\frac{1}{2^{-4}}\right) =$$

$$\left(\frac{1}{2^{-11}}\right)$$

The correct answer is (B).

PS 218. FDPs: Digits & Decimals
Difficulty: Devilish **OG Page:** 183

This ***Digits & Decimals*** problem describes a list of 30 positive, non-integer decimals, whose exact sum is S.

An estimated sum, E, is then defined according to a rather strange rule. If the tenths digit of a decimal is even, the decimal is rounded *up* to the nearest integer, whereas if the tenths digit is odd, the decimal is rounded *down* to the nearest integer.

We are then told that 1/3 of the decimals in T have a tenths digit that is even, and asked whether each of the following numbers *is a possible value* of $E - S$.

(I) –16
(II) 6
(III) 10

The first thing to look at is the language of the question. The phrase "is a possible value of" tells us that we can't compute one specific value for an answer. There must be a range of values that makes sense because we are looking at the difference between the estimate and the actual value, and our task is to figure out which of –16, 6, and 10 are in that range. We need to figure out what the ***Minimum*** and ***Maximum*** values of $E - S$ are.

We know that 1/3 of the decimals, or 10 of them, have an even number in the tenths digit and so will be rounded up. That means that the other 20 of the decimals will be rounded down.

In order to figure out the minimum value of $E - S$, we need to make E as small as possible. To do this, we need to construct numbers whose estimates are as small as possible relative to the actual numbers.

Since the 10 numbers classified as even will always be rounded *up*, their estimated values will be larger than their actual values, so we want to minimize the difference between the actual and estimated values. The largest even digit is 8, so if we put 8 in the tenths digit, and make the other decimal digits 9's, each of the 10 decimals will look like this:

1.8999999999 rounds *up* to 2, so the estimate is no more than 0.1 more than the actual value.

Since the 20 numbers classified as odd are rounded *down*, their estimates will be smaller than their actual values, so we want to maximize the difference between actual and estimated values. The largest odd digit is 9, so put 9 in the tenths digit, and make the other decimal digits 9's:

1.9999999999 rounds down to 1, so the estimate is as much as 1 less than the actual value.

Taken together, that would make

$$E = S + 10(0.1) - 20(1) = S + 1 - 20 = S - 19$$

So the minimum value of $E - S$ is $(S - 19) - S = -19$.

We can use similar logic to figure out the maximum value of $E - S$, except that we now want to construct numbers whose estimates are as large as possible relative to the actual numbers.

Since the 10 numbers classified as even will always be rounded *up*, their estimated values will be larger than their actual values, so we want to maximize the difference between the actual and estimated values. The smallest even digit is 0, so we put 0 in the tenths digit, and make the other decimal digits

0's as well, except for an eventual 1 after a very large number of places (because the number can't be an integer):

1.0000000001 rounds *up* to 2, so the estimate is as much as 1 more than the actual value.

Since the 20 numbers classified as odd are rounded *down*, their estimates will be smaller than their actual values, so we want to minimize the difference between the actual and estimated values. The smallest odd digit is 1, so put 1 in the tenths digit, and make the other decimal digits 0's:

1.1000000000 rounds *down* to 1, so the estimate is no more than 0.1 less than the actual value.

Taken together, that would make

$$E = S + 10(1) - 20(0.1) = S + 10 - 2 = S + 8$$

So the ***maximum*** value of $E - S$ is $(S + 8) - S = 8$

The possible range is then anything greater than −19 and less than 8.

−16 and 6 are in the range, but 10 is not.

The correct answer is (B)

PS 219. Number Properties: Divisibility & Primes
Difficulty: Easy **OG Page:** 183

This problem, which presents a large product of prime numbers (2's, 3's, 5's, and 7's, multiplying to 147,000), can be identified as a ***Prime Factorization*** problem once we understand the strange rules of the bead game. If we factor the given product, 147,000, into primes, then we will be able to determine what beads were pulled.

$$147{,}000 = 147 \times 1{,}000$$

1,000 is easy to factor, but 147 is a less common number. However, we can use ***Divisibility Rules*** to find the factors of 147. The digits of 147 add up to a multiple of 3 ($1 + 4 + 7 = 12$), so 147 is divisible by 3.

$$147 \times 1{,}000 = (3 \times 49) \times (10 \times 10 \times 10)$$
$$= 3 \times 7 \times 7 \times 2 \times 5 \times 2 \times 5 \times 2 \times 5$$
$$= 2^3 \times 3 \times 5^3 \times 7^2$$

We know that prime factorizations are unique. In other words, the above factorization ($2^3 \times 3 \times 5^3 \times 7^2$) is the only way of breaking down the number 147,000 into 2's, 3's, 5's, and 7's—indeed, the only way of breaking that number down into primes at all.

Therefore, since the bead values correspond to these primes, we know that three blue beads (the 2's), one green bead (the 3), three yellow beads (the 5's), and two red beads (the 7's) must have been drawn. We only care about the red beads in the end, but we should complete the prime factorization to ensure there are no lurking 7's anywhere.

Thus, two red beads were removed from the container.

The correct answer is (D).

PS 220. Algebra: Linear Equations
Difficulty: Easy **OG Page:** 184

This ***Linear Equations*** question asks us to solve for y. This problem tests our ability to manipulate a ***Double Decker Fraction.*** First we should ***Cross-multiply,*** then solve for y:

$$\frac{2}{\left(1+\frac{2}{y}\right)} = 1$$

$$2 = \left(1+\frac{2}{y}\right)$$

$$1 = \frac{2}{y}$$

$$y = 2$$

This is the **answer.**

Alternatively, we can use ***Algebraic Reasoning*** to "think" our way to a correct answer. If the fraction on the left side of the given equation is equal to 1, the numerator and denominator must be equal, and therefore the sum in the denominator must equal 2. That means that $1 + 2/y = 2$. Solving for y, we get $2/y = 1$, which means that $y = 2$.

The correct answer is (D).

PS 221. Word Problems: Consecutive Integers
Difficulty: Easy **OG Page:** 184

The set of three integers $\{a, b, c\}$ is defined as a set of consecutive positive integers in ascending order. Using our rules for ***Consecutive Integers*** and ***Divisibility,*** we can tackle scenarios I, II and III.

I. $c - a = 2$ ALWAYS TRUE

By definition, a set of three consecutive integers is one that can be expressed as n, $n + 1$, $n + 2$. The third member of the set, which, in this case, is c, must be 2 more than the first member of the set, a.

$(n + 2) - (n) = 2$

II. abc is an even integer ALWAYS TRUE

Any product of integers that includes at least one even number will always be even. A set of three consecutive numbers must contain at least one even, and therefore will always have an even product.

III. $\frac{a+b+c}{3}$ is an integer ALWAYS TRUE

This statement is asserting that the sum of three consecutive integers is divisible by 3. For any set of consecutive integers with an odd number of items, the sum of all of the integers is ALWAYS a multiple of the number of items. Since this is the sum of 3 consecutive integers, it will be divisible by 3. This could also be proven algebraically:

$\frac{n+(n+1)+(n+2)}{3} = \frac{3n+3}{3} = n+1$, which is not only an integer, but also the middle term of the sequence, b.

Thus, all three statemens are definitely true. This is the **answer.**

It is also possible to ***Test Scenarios*** to prove each of the three statements. However, since we must find which statement(s) MUST be true, it is important to try more than one case. With consecutive integers, it makes the most sense to at least try both a case that begins with an odd integer and a case that begins with an even. Set up a ***Table*** to track these cases.

a, b, c	$c - a = 2$?	abc is even ?	$(a + b + c)/3 =$ integer?
2, 3, 4	$4 - 2 = 2$	$(2)(3)(4) = 24$	$(2 + 3 + 4)/3 = 3$
3, 4, 5	$5 - 3 = 2$	$(3)(4)(5) = 60$	$(3 + 4 + 5)/3 = 4$

The questions can all be answered Yes in both cases.

The correct answer is (E).

PS 222. Word Problems: Overlapping Sets
Difficulty: Medium **OG Page:** 184

This ***Overlapping Sets*** question asks us to determine both the minimum and maximum numbers of students who could be majoring in both chemistry and biology. We must therefore consider both cases as we think about ***Optimization*** both ways.

The maximum number of students who could be majoring in both subjects cannot be greater than the number majoring in the less numerous group. In other words, if 130 students major in chemistry and 150 in biology, the maximum number who could be majoring in both cannot be greater than 130. It could equal 130 (if all chemistry majors are also biology majors), but it cannot be greater.

Determining the minimum number requires a bit more thought. The question tells us that at least 30 students of the 200 total major in neither subject, then at most $200 - 30 = 170$ students are majoring in one or the other or both. Since the sum of 130 and 150 is greater than 170, the "extra" students must have been counted in both groups. Thus, at least $(130 + 150) - 170 = 110$ students must be majoring in both subjects.

Thus, we conclude that the number of double-majors can be any integer between 110 and 130. This is the **answer.**

Notice that we've used a ***Hidden Constraint***: the number of people in any category cannot be less than zero.

A less theoretical approach to calculating the minimum involves the use of a ***Double-Set Matrix.***

We can define the sets as

(1) those who major in chemistry/those who don't
(2) those who major in biology/those who don't

and fill in the matrix with the given information as follows (and shade the box in question):

	Chem	No Chem	Total
Bio			150
No Bio		≥ 30	
Total	130		200

Because every row and column must add up to the total, we have enough information to figure out what can go in the rest of the boxes.

For the sake of the explanation, let's fill in the remaining information in phases. The newly added terms are indicated using **bold**.

	Chem	No Chem	Total
Bio			150
No Bio		≥ 30	**50**
Total	130	**70**	200

	Chem	No Chem	Total
Bio		$\leq$ **40**	150
No Bio	$\leq$ **20**	≥ 30	50
Total	130	70	200

Now we can use either the "Chem" column or the "Bio" row to calculate the minimum number of those who majored in both:

	Chem	No Chem	Total
Bio	$\geq$ **110**	≤ 40	150
No Bio	≤ 20	≥ 30	50
Total	130	70	200

If we wanted to calculate the maximum using the matrix, we could do so by considering the minimums (0) for the "No Chem/Bio" and "No Bio/Chem" boxes:

	Chem	No Chem	Total
Bio	$\leq$ **130**	≥ 0	150
No Bio	≥ 0	≥ 30	50
Total	130	70	200

The number of students majoring in both subjects must be between 110 and 130.

The correct answer is (D).

PS 223. Algebra: Quadratic Equations
Difficulty: Easy **OG Page:** 184

In this ***Algebra*** problem, we are asked to determine the number of possible values of x that satisfy a given equation. We can begin by multiplying the entire equation by x in order to eliminate the fraction. This turns the equation into a ***Quadratic:***

$$5-\frac{6}{x}=x$$
$$5x-6=x^2$$

We can ***Factor*** this quadratic after bringing all terms to one side:

$$x^2-5x+6=0$$
$$(x-2)(x-3)=0$$

The solutions to the equation are 2, and 3, which are distinct. Therefore, x has two possible values. This is the **answer**.

Even if we were unable to factor the quadratic equation correctly, we would still be able to determine how many solutions are possible for x. As a secondary method, we can use the piece of the ***Quadratic Formula*** know as the ***Discriminant***—b^2-4ac. This is the part under the square root in the formula. If the discriminant is positive, there are 2 solutions for x. If it's 0, there is 1 solution, and if it's negative there are no solutions.

We assign the coefficient of the x^2 term the variable a, assign the coefficient of the x term the variable b, and the coefficient of the constant term the variable c. For this equation, $a = 1$, $b = -5$ and $c = 6$. So $b^2 - 4ac = (-5)^2 - 4(1)(6) = 25 - 24 = 1$. The discriminant is positive so there are two possible solutions for x.

The correct answer is (C).

PS 224. FDPs: Percents
Difficulty: Hard **OG Page:** 184

In this ***Percents*** problem, we are told that ***Mixture*** X is 40% ryegrass, mixture Y is 25% ryegrass, and a mixture of X and Y is 30% ryegrass. We are asked to find what percent of the mixture by weight comes from mixture X.

One approach is to write an equation to relate the amounts of ryegrass. ***Naming Variables,*** we can let x be the amount of mixture X, while y can be the amount of mixture Y. Converting ***Percents to Decimals,*** we can write $0.40x$ as the amount of ryegrass in mixture X. Similarly, $0.25y$ is the amount of ryegrass in mixture Y, and $0.30(x + y)$ is the amount of ryegrass in the combined mixture.

$$0.40x + 0.25y = 0.30(x + y)$$
$$0.40x + 0.25y = 0.30x + 0.30y$$
$$0.10x = 0.05y$$

We can multiply both sides by 100 to get rid of the decimals:

$$10x = 5y$$
$$2x = y$$

Now we can find the ratio of x to y:

$$\frac{x}{y} = \frac{1}{2}$$

If x and y are in a 1 to 2 ratio, then x is 1/3 of the total and y is 2/3 of the total. Since the total is 100%, x is therefore $33\frac{1}{3}$%. This is the **answer.**

Alternatively, we can look at this problem as a ***Weighted Averages*** problem. The percent of ryegrass in the combined mixture of X and Y, 30%, is between the ryegrass percents in the separate mixtures (40% and 25%).

Because the resulting 30% is closer to 25% that to 40%, we must have more of the 25% ryegrass (Y) than of the 40% ryegrass (X). This intuition can help us eliminate (D) and (E).

More specifically, 25% is 5% less than 30%, and 40% is 10% more than 30%. In order to balance the two, we need twice as much y as we do x:

2(5%) = 1(10%)

Therefore, the ratio $y:x$ is 2 : 1, and x is 1/3 of the mixture.

The correct answer is (B).

PS 225. Word Problems: Consecutive Integers
Difficulty: Easy **OG Page:** 184

This ***Consecutive Integers*** problem asks us about the product $n(n + 1)(n + 2)$ which is the product of three consecutive integers. Looking at our answer choices, we want to know whether the product will be odd or even.

We should first consider ***Even & Odd Rules.*** If we have consecutive integers, at least one will be even. Also, any product with an even number will be even.

If n is even, then (even)(odd)(even) = even
If n is odd, then (odd)(even)(odd) = even

The product is even regardless of whether n is even or odd, so we can eliminate (A) and (B). (Notice that in (A) and (B) the key word *only* means that the product cannot be even in any other situation.) We can also eliminate (C) because the product is never odd.

We can also ***Test Scenarios*** for n and see whether we spot any patterns.

Suppose $n = 2$ (here, n is an even integer),
(2)(3)(4) = 24 This is an even product.
Suppose $n = 3$ (here, n is an odd integer),
(3)(4)(5) = 60 This is an even product.

In (D), we want to find whether the product is divisible by 3. By ***Consecutive Integer Rules,*** the product of p or more consecutive integers is always divisible by p. This is true because in a group of p consecutive integers, at least one is a multiple of p. Thus, the product of 3 consecutive integers will always be divisible by 3, whether n is even or odd. So we can eliminate (D), which demands that the product be divisible by 3 *only* when n is odd.

Looking at (E), we cannot automatically conclude that the product of 3 consecutive integers is divisible by 4. However, when n is even, $n + 2$ is also even. Because two of the factors in the product are divisible by 2, the entire product is definitely divisible by 4 whenever n is even. This is the **answer.**

Again, we can test values for n to confirm. Reusing the examples above, we see that the output numbers (24 and 60) are *both* divisible by 3, whether n is even or odd. Thus, (D) cannot be correct, and we are left with only one choice.

The correct answer is (E).

PS 226. FDPs: Fractions
Difficulty: Easy **OG Page:** 184

This ***Fractions*** problem specifies that a straight pipe is 1 yard long and is marked off in fourths and thirds. Start by drawing a diagram:

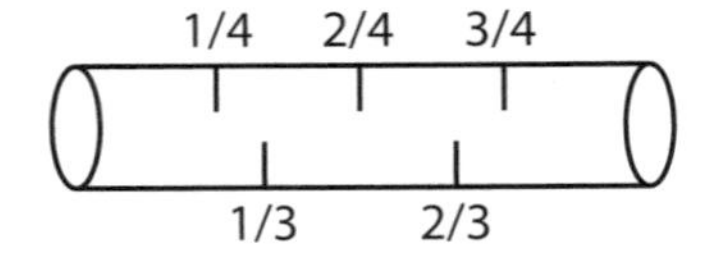

Remember that 1/3 > 1/4, so 1/3 should be placed to the right of 1/4. To clarify, think of the ***Decimal Equivalents:*** 1/3 is approximately 0.33 and 1/4 is 0.25.

The pipe is then cut at each of the above marks. We need to calculate a complete list of the lengths of pipe that result. Calculate one length and use ***Process of Elimination*** to get rid of any choices that do not include that length. Repeat until only one answer choice remains.

We can see immediately that one piece runs from the beginning to the first mark: 1/4. So one piece must be 1/4 in length. Eliminate answer (E).

Next, there is a length between the 1/4 mark and the 1/3 mark. The length is equal to the distance between these two numbers: 1/3 – 1/4 = 4/12 – 3/12 = 1/12. Eliminate (A), (B), and (C). Only (D) remains. This is the **answer.**

Alternatively, we could consider all possible lengths. To do so, we can think of thirds and fourths in terms of their ***Common Denominator,*** 12:

1/3 = 4/12, and 1/4 = 3/12. Then we can mark off every 3/12th and every 4/12th.

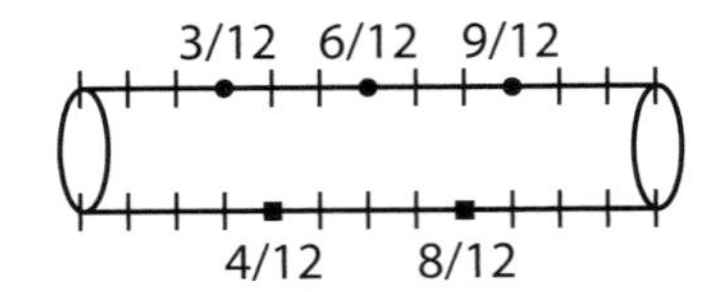

We can see that the differences are 3/12 (=1/4), 1/12, and 2/12 (=1/6).

The correct answer is (D).

PS 227. FDPs: Digits & Decimals
Difficulty: Medium **OG Page:** 185

In this difficult ***Digits & Decimals*** problem, we are asked to determine the value of $m - k$. Since m and k are both located on the left side of the equation, we must simplify this side. When dividing powers with the same base, we subtract exponents, so dividing 10^m by 10^k will result in 10^{m-k}.

However, we must also divide 0.0015 by 0.03, which is more easily accomplished if we convert these numbers to the integers 15 and 3. In order to do so, we can ***Trade Decimal Places for Powers of Ten.***

In the numerator, move the decimal point four places to the right in order to change 0.0015 to 15. We compensate for the shift by decreasing the exponent of 10 by 4. Our new numerator is thus 15 $\times 10^{m-4}$.

Similarly, to convert 0.03 to the integer 3, we move the decimal point two places to the right. Trade these two places for two powers of 10 by decreasing the exponent by 2. Our new denominator is $3 \times 10^{k-2}$.

The problem now reads:

$$\frac{15\times10^{m-4}}{3\times10^{k-2}}=5\times10^7$$

$$\frac{15}{3}\times\frac{10^{m-4}}{10^{k-2}}=5\times10^7 \quad \text{Subtract exponents}$$

$$5\times10^{(m-4)-(k-2)}=5\times10^7 \quad \text{Divide by 5}$$

$$10^{(m-4)-(k-2)}=10^7$$

Since both sides of this equation share the same base (10), we can set the exponents equal to each other.

$(m - 4) - (k - 2) = 7$ Distribute the negative sign
$m - 4 - k + 2 = 7$ Combine like terms
$m - k - 2 = 7$ Add 2 to both sides
$m - k = 9$

The correct answer is (A).

PS 228. Geometry: Coordinate Plane
Difficulty: Hard **OG Page:** 185

To construct a possible ***Triangle*** *PQR* in the ***Coordinate Plane,*** we must make three selections/decisions: the point *P*, the point *Q*, and the point *R*. Because we need to count up triangles, we are dealing with a ***Disguised Combinatorics*** problem.

According to the ***Fundamental Counting Principle***, we can find the number of ways to make each individual decision and multiply those to find the total number of triangles that can be constructed.

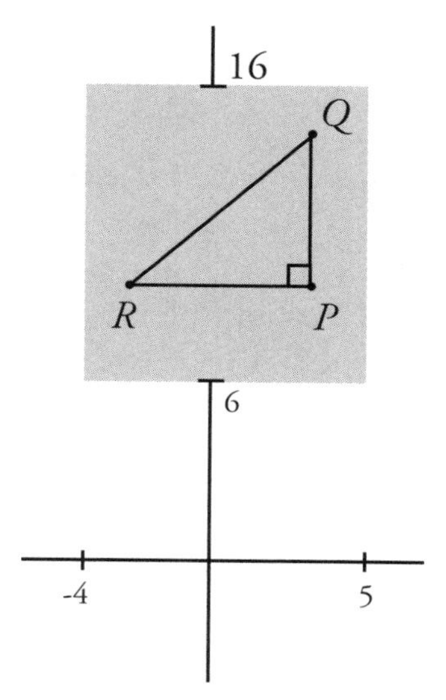

Since $\overline{PR}$ is parallel to the x-axis and the right angle is at *P*, the triangles formed must resemble the triangle pictured above. Note that point *Q* can be above point *P* (as pictured) or below point *P*, and point *R* can be left of point *P* (as pictured) or right of point *P*.

The number of potential points for *P* can be found using the Fundamental Counting Principle (also known as the ***Slot Method***).

# of potential *P* points = (number of potential x-coordinates for *P*) × (number of potential y-coordinates for *P*)

The x-coordinate of *P* can be any integer between −4 and 5, inclusive, so there are $5 - (-4) + 1 = 10$ possibilities for x. We "add 1 before we're done" because we are ***Counting a Consecutive Integer Set,*** namely, −4 through 5.

The y-coordinate of *P* can be any integer between 6 and 16, inclusive, so there are $16 - 6 + 1 = 11$ possibilities for y. Now we can count possible positions for *P:*

# of possible *P* points = $10 \times 11 = 110$

To find the number of potential *R* points, given a particular *P*, we simply need to count the number of possible x-coordinates for *R*, since the y-coordinate for *R* must be the same as the y-coordinate for

P. (We know this because $\overline{PR}$ must be parallel to the x-axis.)

Since R cannot occupy the same space as P, there is one fewer possibility for the x-coordinate of R than there were possibilities for P. Thus, there are $10 - 1 = 9$ possible x-coordinates for R, but only 1 possible y-coordinate. As a result, there are $9 \times 1 = 9$ possible positions for R.

# of possible R points = 9

To find the number of potential Q points, given a particular P and a particular R, we simply need to count the number of possible y-coordinates for Q since the x-coordinate for Q must be the same as the x-coordinate for P (as the right angle must be at point P).

Q cannot occupy the same space as P, because then if it did, PQR would not be a triangle. So Q has one fewer possibility for its y-coordinate than P had. There are $11 - 1 = 10$ possible y-coordinates for Q, but only 1 possible x-coordinate. As a result, there are $10 \times 1 = 10$ possible positions for Q.

# of possible Q points = 10

The total number of triangles can be found by using the Fundamental Counting Principle one additional time:

# of possible Triangles = (# of possible P points) × (# of possible R points) × (# of possible Q points)

# of possible Triangles = $110 \times 9 \times 10 = 9{,}900$

The correct answer is (C).

PS 229. Number Properties: Positives & Negatives
Difficulty: Devilish **OG Page:** 185

This ***Inequalities*** problem asks us to figure out how many integers less than 5 make the following expression either zero or a positive number.

$$\frac{(x+2)(x+3)}{x-2}$$

A straightforward way to solve this problem is to start testing integers that are less than 5, starting with the number 4. There can't possibly be more than five of these integers because the largest answer choice is five.

4 and 3 both work because they make the numerator and the denominator positive, resulting in a positive value overall.

2 does not work because it makes the denominator zero, which is a math error.

1, 0, and –1 do not work because they both make the numerator positive, but the denominator negative.

–2 and –3 work because they make the numerator zero, but not the denominator, resulting in an overall value of zero.

–4 and any integer less than –4 will not work because they make the numerator positive (product of two negative numbers) and the denominator negative, resulting in a negative value overall.

So there are a total of four integers: 4, 3, –2, and –3 that make the expression either zero or a positive number.

The correct answer is (D).

PS 230. Algebra: Exponents & Roots
Difficulty: Hard **OG Page:** 185

We must begin this complicated ***Exponents*** and ***Fractions*** problem by properly simplifying the sum in the numerator. We approach this sum by finding a ***Common Factor*** of the various terms and placing that factor outside parentheses. The remaining factors of each element of the sum will then be added together.

This question wants to know how many times 2^{-17} the fraction is. Moreover, each term in the numerator a power of 2 near 2^{-17}. If we factor out 2^{-17} from each term we will have 2^{-17} in the numerator, which will help us make a direct comparison. Notice that this problem is more straight forward if we keep the ***Negative Exponents*** as they are, rather than change them to a positive exponent and move them to the other part of the fraction.

Factoring out 2^{-17} gives us:

$$\frac{2^{-17}(2^3+2^2+2^1+2^0)}{5}$$

We can now simplify the interior of the parentheses:

$$\frac{2^{-17}(8+4+2+1)}{5}=\frac{2^{-17}(15)}{5}$$

We can further reduce this to $2^{-17}(3)$. In other words, our fraction is 3 times 2^{-17}.

The correct answer is (C).

Chapter 4

of

The Official Guide Companion

Data Sufficiency Explanations

In This Chapter...

Data Sufficiency Explanations

DS 1. Algebra: Linear Equations
Difficulty: Hard **OG Page:** 275

In this problem involving ***Linear Equations*** and ***Absolute Value,*** we are asked to determine the value of $|x|$. There is no need to rephrase this question, so we can go straight to the statements.

(1): INSUFFICIENT. If $x = -|x|$, then we know that x must be negative or zero, since it equals the negation of an absolute value, which will always be positive or zero. This does not tell us anything about the specific numeric value of $|x|$, however.

(2): SUFFICIENT: If $x^2 = 4$, then x must equal either 2 or -2. Since $|2| = 2$ and $-|2| = 2$, it must be true that $|x| = 2$. This is sufficient to answer the question. If you know a variable's ***Square,*** you know its absolute value.

Note that the trap in this question is to think that both statements are needed in order to determine whether $x = 2$ or $x = -2$. Since the absolute value of either solution is the same, and we are asked only about the absolute value, we do not need to know the exact value of x.

The correct answer is (B): Statement (2) alone is sufficient, but statement (1) alone is not sufficient.

DS 2. FDPs: Percents
Difficulty: Easy **OG Page:** 275

In this ***Percents*** problem, we are asked to determine the percentage of red-haired women in a group of people.

$$\frac{\text{red-haired women}}{\text{number of people in group}}(100) = ?$$

We would be able to answer this question if we knew the number of red-haired women and the total number of people in the group. Also, we could answer the question if we are given the relevant proportion directly.

(1): INSUFFICIENT. Even if we know that 5% of the women in the group have red hair, we do not know how many women there are, nor do we know how many people there are in the group as a whole.

(2): INSUFFICIENT. This statement tells us nothing about women with red hair.

(1) AND (2): INSUFFICIENT. Even with these combined pieces of information, we do not know the number of women with red hair, the number of people in the group as a whole, or the fraction of red-haired women in the group.

The correct answer is (E): Statements (1) and (2) TOGETHER are not sufficient.

DS 3. Number Properties: Probability
Difficulty: Easy **OG Page:** 275

The probability that a boy will be selected to read is equal to the number of boys divided by the total number of students. The ***Rephrased*** question is therefore "What is B/T?"

We will have sufficient information if we are given the actual amounts, or told the proportion directly.

(1): SUFFICIENT. If boys are two-thirds of the class, $B/T = 2/3$. The probability of selecting a boy is 2/3.

(2): INSUFFICIENT. Knowing that 10 students are girls does not tell us the number of boys or the total number of students.

The correct answer is (A): Statement (1) ALONE is sufficient, but statement (2) alone is not sufficient.

DS 4. Geometry: Polygons
Difficulty: Medium **OG Page:** 275

In this ***Polygons*** problem, we are given the distance between floors. We need to know how many steps there are between the first and second floors. We ought to consider ***Test Possible Scenarios***: either the steps have a uniform height, or they don't.

If each step has a uniform height, we can write an equation: (Height of each stair) × (# of stairs) = 9 feet. In this scenario, knowing the height of each stair will be sufficient to solve the problem.

If each step does NOT have a uniform height, we will need more information to determine how many steps there are.

(1): SUFFICIENT. This statement tells us the steps have a uniform height, and tells us the height of each step. The statement is sufficient. The number of stairs may be found by dividing the total height (9 feet) by the height of each stair.

(2): INSUFFICIENT. The width of the stairs is irrelevant to the question at hand.

The correct answer is (A): Statement (1) ALONE is sufficient, but statement (2) alone is not sufficient.

DS 5. Word Problems: Overlapping Sets
Difficulty: Easy **OG Page:** 275

In this ***Overlapping Sets*** problem, students are enrolled in chemistry and/or biology. Some students may be enrolled in both courses, and some students may be enrolled in neither course.

If we use a ***Double-Set Matrix***, we can let x be the number of students enrolled in both biology and chemistry, and y be the number of students enrolled in neither class.

		Chemistry?		
		Yes	No	Total
Biology?	Yes	x		
	No		y	
	Total			

We can ***Rephrase*** this question as, "What is $x - y$?"

(1): INSUFFICIENT. Knowing 60 people took chemistry does not provide enough information to find $x - y$.

		Chemistry?		
		Yes	No	Total
Biology?	Yes	x		
	No		y	
	Total	60		

(2): INSUFFICIENT. Knowing 85 people took biology does not provide enough information to find $x - y$.

		Chemistry?		
		Yes	No	Total
Biology?	Yes	x		85
	No		y	
	Total			

(1) AND (2): INSUFFICIENT. Even with the total enrollment numbers for both biology and chemistry, we still cannot find $x - y$.

		Chemistry?		
		Yes	No	Total
Biology?	Yes	x		85
	No		y	
	Total	60		

The correct answer is (E): Statements (1) and (2) TOGETHER are not sufficient.

DS 6. Word Problems: Extra Problem Types
Difficulty: Medium **OG Page:** 275

The problem, which involves ***Number Line*** thinking, specifies that an expressway has the following four exits in order: J, K, L, and M. The problem asks for the value of the distance from K to L. There is no simple rephrasing of this question. We have to know something about the relationship between K and L.

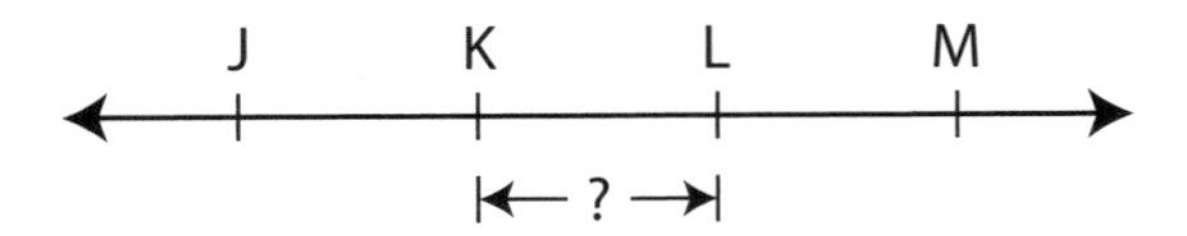

(1): INSUFFICIENT. We can add this information to our diagram, but we cannot calculate the distance from K to L.

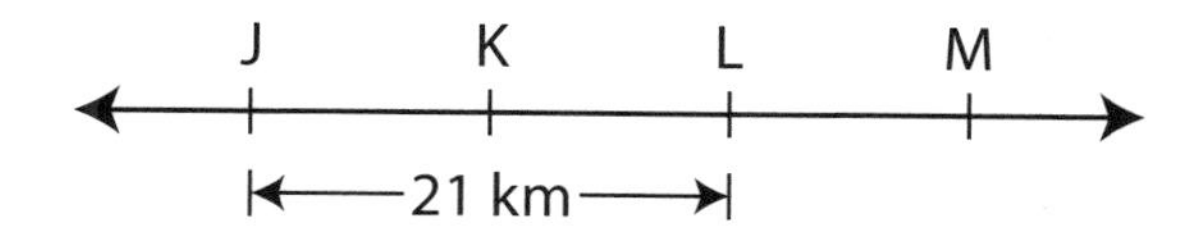

(2): INSUFFICIENT. We can add this information to our diagram, but we cannot calculate the distance from K to L.

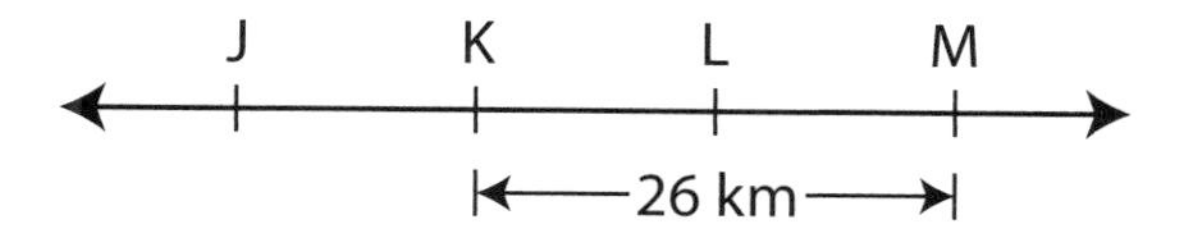

(1) AND (2): INSUFFICIENT. Even with both statements, there are multiple possible values for the distance from K to L. Here are two possibilities:

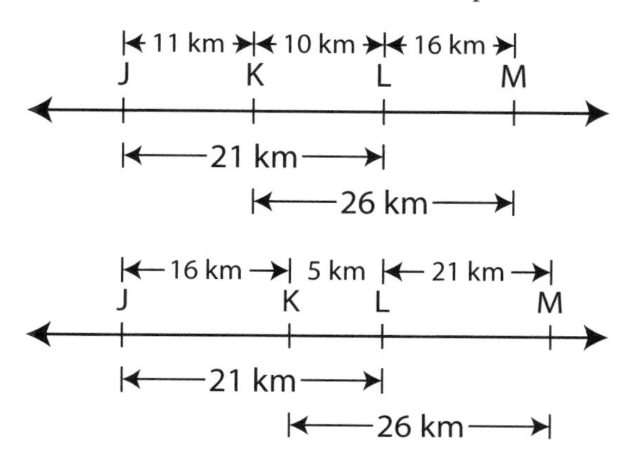

In essence, the fixed distances (21 and 26 km) can slide past each other, changing the K-to-L distance.

The correct answer is (E): Statements (1) and (2) TOGETHER are not sufficient.

DS 7. Number Properties: Odds & Evens
Difficulty: Easy **OG Page:** 275

This ***Odds & Evens*** question asks whether $n + 1$ is odd. Since the integer n must be even in order for $n + 1$ to be odd, we can ***Rephrase*** the question as "Is n even?"

(1): SUFFICIENT. If $n + 2$ is an even integer then n must also be even. Only an even integer added to another even (2, in this case) can equal another even integer. Here, we are applying ***Properties of Odds & Evens.***

(2): SUFFICIENT. Since odds and evens alternate, we know that if $n - 1$ is odd, n must be even.

The correct answer is (D): each statement ALONE is sufficient.

DS 8. FDPs: Percents
Difficulty: 300–500 **OG Page:** 275

This ***Percents*** problem requires an understanding of the term "rate of return," which refers to the average return, in dollars, of the investment *per dollar invested.* (Remember that all rates are expressed as one unit *per* another unit.) This type of rate may be expressed either as a ***Fraction*** or as a ***Percent.***

(1): SUFFICIENT. The annual rate of return for investment type J is \$115 per \$1,000, or \$(115/1,000) per dollar invested. Likewise, the annual rate of return for investment type K is \$300 per \$2,500, or \$(300/2,500) per dollar invested. Since these are both definite numerical figures, we will be able to determine which of them is greater. No further calculation is necessary.

(2): INSUFFICIENT. This statement provides the rate of return of investment type K. However, we know nothing about investment type J.

The correct answer is (A): Statement (1) ALONE is sufficient, but statement (2) alone is not sufficient.

DS 9. Word Problems: Algebraic Translations
Difficulty: Easy **OG Page:** 275

In this ***Algebraic Translations*** problem, we can first ***Name Variables:***

r = # of crates of oranges
g = # of crates of grapefruit

We are told the prices of crates of oranges and grapefruit, and we need to find the number of crates containing oranges. In other words, we are looking for the value of r.

(1): INSUFFICIENT. This statement translates into the following equation:

$r = 2g + 20$

Using only this equation, we cannot figure out the value of r.

(2): INSUFFICIENT. Since we are given a total cost, we can combine it with the information in the question stem about price to set up the following equation, which expresses a ***Cost Relationhip:***

$$15r + 18g = 38{,}700$$

Using only this equation, we cannot figure out the value of r.

(1) AND (2): SUFFICIENT. We can ***Substitute*** for r and solve for g:

$$15(2g + 20) + 18g = 38{,}700$$

or substitute for g and solve for r:

$$15r + 18(r - 20)/2 = 38{,}700.$$

In either equation, we have one variable and no exponents, so we will be able to find unique values for both variables. We can solve for r.

In fact, even before substituting, we should recognize that when we have ***Two Different Linear Equations*** and ***Two Unknowns,*** we can solve for the unknowns.

The correct answer is (C): BOTH statements TOGETHER are sufficient, but NEITHER statement ALONE is sufficient.

DS 10. <u>FDPs</u>: Fractions
Difficulty: Easy **OG Page:** 275

This question involves both ***Fractions*** and ***Algebraic Translations***. To get started, we can ***Name Variables*** representing various quantities.

s = amount that Pat saved last month
e = amount that Pat earned last month

From the given information, we know that $s = 600$.

We are asked to find e.

(1): SUFFICIENT. Knowing that Pat spent 1/2 of his earnings last month for living expenses while saving 1/3 of the remainder means that Pat saved 1/3 of the remaining 1/2 of his earnings or $\left(\frac{1}{3}\right)\left(\frac{1}{2}\right) = \frac{1}{6}$ of his earnings.

We can use this information, in conjunction with the given to solve for e:

$$s = \frac{1}{6}(e)$$
$$600 = \frac{1}{6}(e)$$
$$e = 3{,}600$$

(2): INSUFFICIENT. We know that Pat paid twice as much in taxes as he saved, so he paid $1,200 in taxes. However, this tells us nothing about his earnings.

The correct answer is (A): Statement (1) ALONE is sufficient, but statement (2) alone is not sufficient.

DS 11. <u>Geometry</u>: Coordinate Plane
Difficulty: Easy **OG Page:** 275

This ***Coordinate Plane*** question asks whether angle QPR is a right angle.

In the picture provided, it looks like QPR is a right angle, but geometry pictures are often misleading. We need to look to the statements for more information.

Since angle QPR would be a right angle if line segments QP and PR were perpendicular, we can rephrase this question as "Are QP and PR perpendicular to each other?"

(1): INSUFFICIENT. This statement tells us that Q and P have the same x-coordinate, which tells us that QP is a vertical line segment, parallel to the y-axis. However, it tells us nothing about line segment PR.

(2): INSUFFICIENT. This statement tells us that P and R have the same y-coordinate, which tells us that PR is a horizontal line segment, parallel to the x-axis. However, it tells us nothing about line segment QP.

(1) AND (2): SUFFICIENT. Taken together, the two statements tell us that *QP* is a vertical line segment, parallel to the *y*-axis and that *PR* is a horizontal line segment, parallel to the *x*-axis. This means *QP* and *PR* must be perpendicular to each other. *QPR* is a right angle.

The correct answer is (C): BOTH statements (1) and (2) TOGETHER are sufficient to answer the question asked, but NEITHER statement ALONE is sufficient.

DS 12. Word Problems: Rates & Work
Difficulty: Easy **OG Page:** 276

This problem describes a tank of water into which water is being pumped and out of which water is being drained. This is actually a variation of the ***Working Together: Add the Rates*** problem type. In this case, the two pipes are working *against* each other, so we ***Subtract the Rates.*** The inlet rate minus the outlet rate will give us the effective rate. We need both the inlet and outlet rates, or the difference between the two, in order to solve.

(1): INSUFFICIENT. This statement does not provide us with either the inlet or the outlet rate. Moreover, knowing the original amount of water in the tank is of no use whatsoever, as we are only concerned with the rate of increase, not with any actual amount in the tank.

(2): SUFFICIENT. This statement alone gives us both of the rates that we need. We do not need to actually subtract to find the overall rate of increase, as we know that we have enough information to do so.

The correct answer is (B): Statement (2) ALONE is sufficient, but statement (1) alone is not sufficient.

DS 13. Algebra: Inequalities
Difficulty: Easy **OG Page:** 276

In this ***Inequalities*** problem, we are asked whether x is negative. There is no need to rephrase this question, so we can proceed directly to the statements.

(1): SUFFICIENT. If $9x > 10x$, it must be true that x is negative.

One way to verify this is to subtract $9x$ from both sides:

$9x > 10x$
$9x - 9x > 10x - 9x$
$0 > x$

If 0 is greater than x, then x is negative by definition.

Alternatively, we can ***Test Scenarios:*** specifically, both a positive value for x and a negative value. Then we can contrast the outcomes. For example, if $x = 2$, then $9x = 18$ and $10x = 20$. It is NOT true that $9x > 10x$ if $x = 2$, so this case does not fit the statement.

However, if $x = -2$, then $9x = -18$ and $10x = -20$. In this case, it is true that $9x > 10x$. We can see that only negative values of x will fit this statement.

(2): INSUFFICIENT. Here, knowing that $x + 3$ is positive does not tell us whether x itself is positive or negative.

We can express this statement as $x + 3 > 0$ and then subtract 3 from both sides: $x > -3$. There are both positive and negative values that will satisfy this inequality.

The correct answer is (A): Statement (1) ALONE is sufficient, but statement (2) alone is not sufficient.

DS 14. Number Properties: Odds & Evens
Difficulty: Easy **OG Page:** 276

In this ***Odds & Evens*** problem, we are asked if the sum of the two integers i and j is even. The sum of two even integers would be even, as would the sum of two odd integers. Therefore, a good ***Rephrasing*** of the question is, "Are i and j both even or both odd?"

(1): INSUFFICIENT. This statement does not allow us to determine if i is even or odd. Moreover, it tells us nothing about j.

(2): SUFFICIENT. If $i = j$, then either both variables will be even or both will be odd. The sum will be even in either case. Notice that we must ***Test Scenarios,*** but we wind up at the same destination.

The correct answer is (B): Statement (2) ALONE is sufficient, but statement (1) alone is not sufficient.

DS 15. Algebra: Exponents & Roots
Difficulty: Easy **OG Page:** 276

This ***Exponents & Roots*** question asks us for the cubed root of w, which does not look easy to calculate. However, if we knew the value of w, it would certainly be possible to calculate its cubed root, so we can rephrase this questions as "What is w?"

(1): SUFFICIENT. This statement tells us that the 5th root of w is 64, so in order to calculate w, we would just multiply 64 times itself five times.

(2): SUFFICIENT. This statement tells us that the 15th root of w is 4, so in order to calculate w, we would just multiply 4 times itself fifteen times.

A typical DS time saving technique used here is to not compute either w or the cubed root of w. This extra work can be avoided because this data sufficiency problem is not asking us for a value for the cubed root of w, but rather is asking us if we have enough information to compute the cubed root of w.

The correct answer is (D).

DS 16. Word Problems: Rates & Work
Difficulty: Easy **OG Page:** 276

In this ***Rates*** problem, we are asked to find the time it takes for Car X to cross a bridge that is 1/2 mile long. We can use the ***Rate–Time–Distance Formula*** to find the time:

$$\text{Time} = \frac{\text{Distance}}{\text{Rate}}$$

$$\text{Time} = \frac{\left(\frac{1}{2}\text{ mile}\right)}{\text{Rate}}$$

Given that we are looking for time, there are three legitimate ***Rephrasings*** of the question that we can consider:

What is Car X's rate?

What is Car X's time?

What is another relationship between Car X's rate and time?

(1): INSUFFICIENT. All we know from this statement is that Car X was on the bridge one second less than Car Y. Without knowing how long Car Y was on the bridge, we do not know how long Car X was on the bridge. This does not answer any of our rephrased questions.

(2): INSUFFICIENT. With Car Y's rate, we can find how long Car Y was on the bridge.

$$\text{Time} = \frac{\text{Distance}}{\text{Rate}}$$

$$= \frac{\left(\frac{1}{2}\text{ mile}\right)}{(30\text{ miles per hour})} = \frac{1}{60}\text{hour} = 1\text{ minute}$$

Knowing how long Car Y was on the bridge tells us nothing about Car X, thus this statement is insufficient.

(1) AND (2): SUFFICIENT. With both statements, we know Car Y was on the bridge for 1 minute, or 60 seconds, and Car X was on the bridge for 1 second less than Car Y, or 59 seconds.

The correct answer is (C): BOTH statements TOGETHER are sufficient, but NEITHER statement ALONE is sufficient.

DS 17. Algebra: Linear Equations
Difficulty: Medium **OG Page:** 276

This ***Basic Equations*** problem tells us that $n + k = m$ and asks for the value of k. This is a ***Combined Expression*** or ***Combo*** problem in disguise. We do not need the values of the individual variables, but rather a value for an arithmetic combination of them. For Combo problems, we should determine everything that would be sufficient before looking at the statements.

In this case, solve the given equation for the desired variable, k. If $n + k = m$, then $k = m - n$. Determining the value of k is sufficient, but it is also sufficient to determine the value of $m - n$. We can ***Rephrase*** the question as "What is k, or what is $m - n$?"

(1): INSUFFICIENT. This does not provide us with values for either k or $m - n$.

(2): SUFFICIENT. The given equation, $m + 10 = n$, does not contain k at all, but it does contain both m and n. It can be rearranged to yield a value for $m - n$. We get $m - n = -10$. Therefore $k = -10$.

The correct answer is (B): Statement (2) ALONE is sufficient, but statement (1) alone is not sufficient.

DS 18. Word Problems: Consecutive Integers
Difficulty: Easy **OG Page:** 276

This ***Consecutive Integers*** question says that the number of seats in the first row is 18 and that each subsequent row has 2 more seats than the previous row. The question then asks for the total number of seats.

Since knowing the number of seats in a row tells us the number of seats in the next row (just add 2 seats per each additional row), knowing the number of rows would allow us to figure out how many seats there are in each row. We could then sum to find the total number of seats. Therefore, this question can be rephrased as "How many rows of seats are there?"

(1): SUFFICIENT. This statement tells us that there are 27 rows of seats; this is enough to calculate the number of seats. Don't waste time by actually finding the sum.

(2): SUFFICIENT. This statement tells us that the last row has 70 seats. The total number of seats in the auditorium is the sum of all the even numbers from 18 to 70. This is sufficient to answer the question.

The correct answer is (D): EACH statement ALONE is sufficient to answer the question asked.

DS 19. Geometry: Triangles & Diagonals
Difficulty: Easy **OG Page:** 276

In this ***Triangles*** problem, we can begin by ***Drawing the Picture*** described:

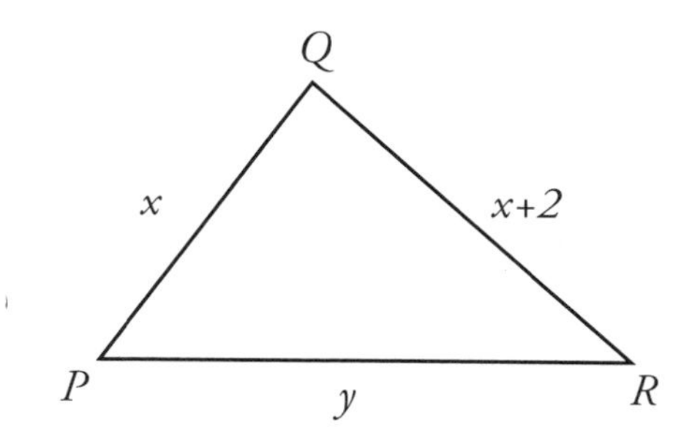

Note that, because we don't know actual values, the triangle cannot be drawn to scale.

We are asked which angle has the greatest measure. This will be the angle across from the longest side. We know that x can't be longest side, because it must be smaller than $x + 2$. Either the y side or the $x + 2$ side must be longest.

In order to find the longest side, and therefore the largest angle, we can ask the ***Rephrased*** question: "Is $y > x + 2$?"

(1): SUFFICIENT. $y = x + 3$. We can show this information in the drawing:

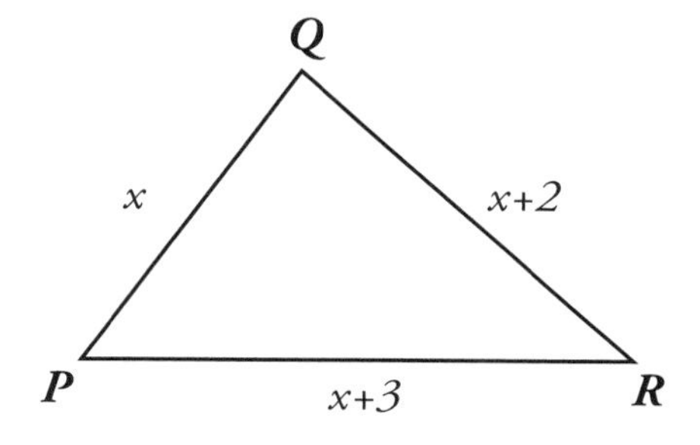

Although we do not know the value of x, we know that $\overline{PR}$ is longer than the other two side lengths. Thus, $\angle PQR$, which is opposite side length $\overline{PR}$, will be the largest angle.

(2): INSUFFICIENT. Although this statement gives us a value for x, we still do not know the value of y. Thus, we cannot determine whether the side of length y is longer or shorter than either of the other two sides.

The correct answer is (A): Statement (1) ALONE is sufficient, but statement (2) alone is not sufficient.

DS 20. Word Problems: Statistics
Difficulty: Easy **OG Page:** 276

This ***Statistics*** problem asks for the value of n. Without more information, it is hard to predict how the question will provide enough information. Go straight to the statements.

(1): INSUFFICIENT. There are many numbers that are greater than 12.

(2): SUFFICIENT. The ***Median*** of a list of numbers is defined as the middle number (or the average of the two middle numbers if there is an even number of numbers in the set) if the list is put into numerical order. Since 13 isn't already on this list of five numbers and 9 and 12 are both less than 13 and 15 and 20 are both greater than 13, this tells us that the missing number, n, must be 13.

The correct answer is (B): Statement (2) ALONE is sufficient, but statement (1) alone is not sufficient to answer the question asked.

DS 21. Word Problems: Overlapping Sets
Difficulty: Medium **OG Page:** 276

In this ***Overlapping Sets*** problem, we are asked to determine the percent of drama club members who are female. There are several ways to figure this out without knowing any specific numbers (e.g., using *Ratios, Percents* or *Fractions*), so we should not worry about finding specific values. However, we will still need either a percent or a ratio of female members of the drama club to total members of the drama club.

(1): INSUFFICIENT: Knowing the percent of female students who are drama club members does not tell us the percent of drama club members who are female. For example, say there are 100 female students and 40%, or 40, of them are in the drama club. If the drama club has 200 members, then the percent would be 40/200 = 4/5 = 20%. But if the club has 400 members, then the percent would be 40/400 = 1/10 = 10%.

(2): INSUFFICIENT. Knowing the percent of male students who are members of the club does not tell us anything about the percent of drama club members who are female. Keep in mind that this statement is NOT telling us that 25% of the club is male but rather that 25% of male students are in the club. Since we do not know the percent of the club that is male, we cannot deduce the percent that is female.

(1) AND (2): INSUFFICIENT. 40% of the female students in the school are in the drama club, and 25% of the male students in the school are in the drama club. However, without knowing how many male and female students are in the school, we have no way of knowing what percent of the drama club is female. Different ratios of male to female students in the school will make different ratios of male to female students in the drama club.

Thus, even using both statements together, we cannot determine the percent of drama club members who are female.

The correct answer is (E): Statements (1) and (2) TOGETHER are not sufficient.

DS 22. Word Problems: Rates & Work
Difficulty: Easy **OG Page:** 276

This ***Rates & Work*** question asks if we can calculate Mary's average rate. First, recall the formula for ***Average Rate***, which is:

$$\text{average rate} = \frac{\text{total distance}}{\text{total time}}$$

We know that the total distance was 50 miles, so we can rephrase this question as "What was the total time?"

(1): SUFFICIENT. This statement provides enough information to let us calculate the total time that the trip took using the rate equation. We're looking for time, so isolate t:

$$r \times t = d$$

$$t = \frac{d}{r}$$

Now we can calculate the times for the 30 mile and 20 mile legs of the trip:

$$\text{time for 30 mile leg} = \frac{30 \text{ miles}}{60 \text{ miles/hr}} = \frac{1}{2} \text{ hours}$$

$$\text{time for 20 mile leg} = \frac{20 \text{ miles}}{50 \text{ miles/hr}} = \frac{2}{5} \text{ hours}$$

We could add the fractions to calculate the total time, but we want to stop as soon as we know that the information given is sufficient.

(2): SUFFICIENT. This statement says that the total time is 54 minutes. This will allow us to solve for the average rate.

The correct answer is (D): EACH statement ALONE is sufficient to answer the question asked.

DS 23. FDPs: Ratios
Difficulty: Easy **OG Page:** 276

This ***Ratios*** question does not need rephrasing. The only thing to note is that we do not need the exact numbers of boys and girls, just the ratio of boys to girls.

(1): SUFFICIENT. The phrase "3 times as many girls as boys" can be rephrased directly: the ratio of boys to girls is 1 : 3.

(2): SUFFICIENT. ***Translate*** this statement into an equation, using b for the number of boys and g for the number of girls. We're looking for the ratio of boys to girls, or b/g:

$$b = \frac{1}{4}(b + g)$$

$$b = \frac{1}{4}b + \frac{1}{4}g$$

$$\frac{3}{4}b = \frac{1}{4}g$$

$$3b = g$$

$$\frac{3b}{g} = 1$$

$$\frac{b}{g} = \frac{1}{3}$$

So the ratio of boys to girls is 1 : 3. Remember that a part to whole ratio, such as $b : (b + g)$ can always be converted to a part to part ratio, such as $b : g$, and vice versa.

The correct answer is (D): EACH statement ALONE is sufficient to answer the question asked.

DS 24. Algebra: Formulas
Difficulty: Easy **OG Page:** 276

In order to figure out the 293rd term of this ***Sequence,*** we either need a general formula for the sequence, or the value of a certain term in the sequence, such as the 1st one, and a mathematical rule, such as "add 2 to each term to get the next term."

(1): SUFFICIENT. This statement gives us the value of the 298th term and a rule for getting to the next term. If each term is 2 less than the preceding term, then each preceding term is 2 more than a later term. For instance, if the 298th term is −616, then the 297th term must be 2 more, or −614. We can proceed in this way to find the value of the 293rd term.

(2): INSUFFICIENT. This statement tells us only the value of the first term. There is no rule given, so it is not enough.

The correct answer is (A): Statement (1) ALONE is sufficient, but statement (2) alone is not sufficient to answer the question asked.

DS 25. FDPs: Percents
Difficulty: Medium **OG Page:** 277

We know that Hannah earned x percent simple annual interest on \$5,000 and y percent simple annual interest on another amount of money, which we will call m, and the problem asks if we have enough information to determine m. Before trying to rephrase this ***Interest*** problem, it is a good idea to ***Translate*** the given information. Note that statement (1) introduces the quantity "total interest earned", which we will call t. This variable is helpful as it will let us translate the given information into an equation that uses m.

$$5{,}000 \times \frac{x}{100} + m \times \frac{y}{100} = t$$

This equation has four unknowns: x, m, y, and t, so it can't be solved. But it could be solved if the only unknown were m. We can rephrase the question as "what are the values of x, y, and t?"

(1): INSUFFICIENT. This statement tells us that $t = 900$, but does not tell us anything about x or y.

(2): INSUFFICIENT. This statement tells us that $x = 6$, but does not tell us anything about m or y.

(1) AND (2): INSUFFICIENT. Taken together, the statements give us t and x, but do not tell us y.

The correct answer is (E): Statements (1) and (2) TOGETHER are NOT sufficient to answer the question asked, and additional data are needed.

DS 26. FDPs: Ratios
Difficulty: Medium **OG Page:** 277

In this ***Ratios*** problem, we are told that profit increases, *though not proportionally*, with the number of units sold.

This tells us that "more means more"—but we do not know *how much* more. For instance, if 5 units generate \$5 in profit, 6 units could generate \$5.01, \$10, or \$1 million—all we know is that selling more than 5 units would generate more than \$5 in profit. Put another way, if we graphed units vs. profits, the graph would always go up, but it would not be a straight line through the origin.

To answer the question, "Did the profit exceed \$4 million on sales of 380,000 units?", we would need to know that \$4 million in profit had already been exceeded by some smaller number of units. Even knowing that 379,999 units generated \$3,999,999.00 would not be enough (for instance, maybe that last unit generated only one penny of profit). To answer the question with a *Yes*, we need to know that *less than* 380,000 units generated *at least* \$4 million in profit.

(1): INSUFFICIENT. If 200,000 units generated at least \$2 million in profit, then all we know is that more than 200,000 units must generate more than \$2 million in profit. This is not enough to tell us whether 380,000 units generated more than \$4 million in profit.

(2): SUFFICIENT. If 350,000 units generated \$5 million in profit, then more than 350,000 units must generate more than \$5 million in profit. Even without knowing *how much more*, this is enough to tell us that 380,000 units would generate more than \$4 million in profit.

The correct answer is (B): Statement (2) ALONE is sufficient, but statement (1) alone is not sufficient.

DS 27. Number Properties: Odds & Evens
Difficulty: Medium **OG Page:** 277

There is no particular rephrasing of this question, which asks whether n is even.

(1): SUFFICIENT. We can use ***Properties of Odds & Evens*** to rephrase this statement. If $n^2 - 1$ is an odd number, then n^2 must be an even number. n^2 is an even number only if integer n is even.

n	n^2	$n^2 - 1$
~~Odd~~	~~Odd~~	~~Even~~
Even	Even	Odd

(2): SUFFICIENT. We can again use ***Properties of Odds & Evens*** to rephrase this statement. If $3n + 4$ is an even integer, then $3n$ must be even. The only way for (ODD) × (n) to be even is if n is even.

n	$3n$	$3n + 4$
~~Odd~~	~~Odd~~	~~Odd~~
Even	Even	Even

The correct answer is (D): EACH statement ALONE is sufficient.

DS 28. Word Problems: Algebraic Translations
Difficulty: Easy **OG Page:** 277

This ***Algebraic Translations*** problem specifies that Carmen works 30 hours per week but it does not specify her hourly pay. We can now ***Name a Variable*** and call her hourly pay x. Her total weekly pay would be $30x$, according to her ***Wage Relationship.***

If Carmen's hourly wage is increased by \$1.50, then her new hourly wage is $x + 1.5$, but the number of hours she works will not stay the same. Call her new number of hours y. Her total weekly pay after the wage increase would be $(x + 1.5)y$.

The problem specifies that Carmen wants to earn the *same* weekly pay, so we can set the two total weekly pays equal to each other:

$$30x = (x + 1.5)y.$$

The question asks how many fewer hours she could work to earn the same pay. That would be represented by $30 - y$. If we can find y, then we can find $30 - y$, so we can ***Rephrase*** the question to "what is the value of y?"

If we know what x is, then we can solve for y. If we can find either the value of x or the value of y, then the information is sufficient.

(1): SUFFICIENT. If her current weekly pay is \$225, then $225 = 30x$. We can solve for x. Therefore, we can solve for y.

(2): SUFFICIENT. If \$1.50 represents 20% of her current hourly wage, then $1.5 = 0.2x$. We can solve for x. Therefore, we can solve for y.

The correct answer is (D): EACH statement ALONE is sufficient.

DS 29. FDPs: Fractions
Difficulty: Medium **OG Page:** 277

From the question and the statements, we know that both boys and girls auditioned and were accepted. Call the number of boys who auditioned b and the number of girls who auditioned g so we can *Translate* the given information:

$$90 = b + g$$

The question asks how many students were accepted, which will call a.

(1): INSUFFICIENT. Translate the statement:

$$a = \frac{2}{3}b + \frac{1}{3}g$$

We can get b in terms of g by rewriting the given information as:

$$g = 90 - b$$

We could substitute this value of g into the equation for a, but since we don't know b, we can't solve for a.

$$a = \frac{2}{3}b + \frac{1}{3}(90 - b)$$

Also note that, with 3 variables and only 2 equations, it is unlikely that we could solve for the value of a without more information.

(2): INSUFFICIENT. Translate the statement:

$$b = 26$$

However, since we don't know g, we can't solve for a.

(1) AND (2): SUFFICIENT. Taken together, we could plug 26 in for b in the equation we came up with in (1) and calculate a.

$$a = \frac{2}{3}(26) + \frac{1}{3}(90 - 26)$$

The correct answer is (C): BOTH statements (1) and (2) TOGETHER are sufficient to answer the question asked, but NEITHER statement ALONE is sufficient.

DS 30. Geometry: Circles & Cylinders
Difficulty: Easy **OG Page:** 277

For this ***Cylinders*** problem, we should first ***Redraw the Picture:***

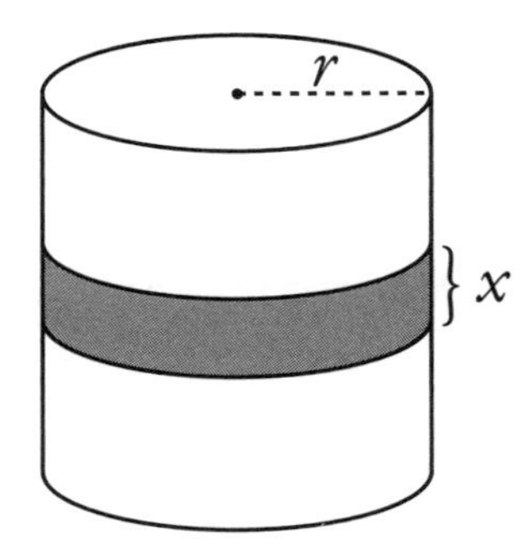

To crack this problem, consider how to calculate the surface area of a band that goes around the circumference of a cylinder.

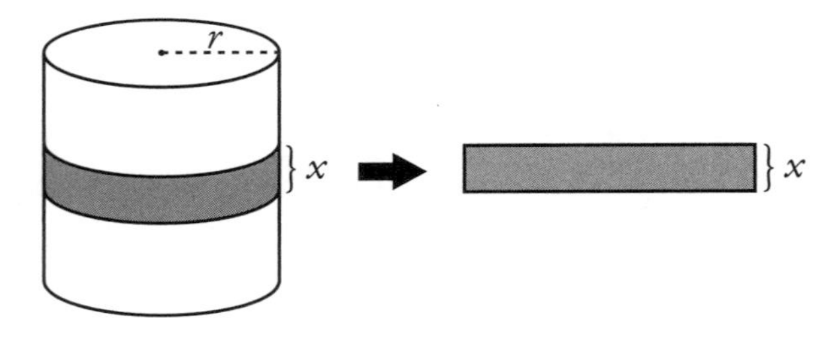

As we can see from the picture, once we unwrap the band from the cylinder, the band is actually a ***Rectangle.*** So the surface area of the band is actually the area of the rectangle. The width of the rectangle is x, while the length of the rectangle is the circumference of the circle.

To find the surface area of the painted stripe, we need either the circumference of the base (our length), or the radius of the base, which will allow us to calculate the circumference. We also need x (our width).

(1): INSUFFICIENT. This statement just gives us the value of x, the height of the cylindrical band.

(2): INSUFFICIENT. This statement provides us with no information about the height of the cylindrical band or the radius of the base. The height of the entire cylindrical tub is irrelevant.

(1) AND (2): INSUFFICIENT. With both statements we are still lacking information about the radius of the cylinder, and therefore cannot calculate circumference.

The correct answer is (E): Statements (1) and (2) TOGETHER are not sufficient.

DS 31. FDPs: Digits & Decimals
Difficulty: Easy **OG Page:** 277

In this ***Decimals*** problem, we are told that $d = 0.43t7$, where t is a ***Digit.*** We are then asked to determine the value of t. There is no need to rephrase, and we can go to the statements.

(1): INSUFFICIENT. When d is ***Rounded*** to the nearest hundredth, $d = 0.44$. We should ***Test Scenarios*** for d. We cannot determine the value of t from this information, because several possible values of d, namely 0.4357, 0.4367, 0.4377, 0.4387, and 0.4397, all yield 0.44 when rounded to the nearest hundredth.

(2): SUFFICIENT. When d is rounded to the nearest thousandth, $d = 0.436$. The only value of t that will yield 0.436 when d is rounded to the nearest thousandth is 5. If $t = 5$, then $d = 0.4357$. Rounding this decimal to the nearest thousandth yields 0.436, since the digit in the ten-thousandths place (in this case, 7) is greater than or equal to 5. Therefore, we must round up by 1 in the thousandths place.

The correct answer is (B): Statement (2) ALONE is sufficient, but statement (1) alone is not sufficient.

DS 32. Number Properties: Odds & Evens
Difficulty: Medium **OG Page:** 277

This ***Odds & Evens*** problem asks whether the product AB will be even. If either A is even or B is even, the product will also be even. This question can be ***Rephrased*** as, "is either A or B even?

(1): SUFFICIENT. Since A and B are both integers, each one is either even or odd. We need to ***Test Scenarios.*** List out all the possibilities and eliminate the ones that make the statement not true (i.e., make $A + B$ even).

A	B	$A + B$	$A \times B$
E	O	E + O = O	E × O = E
~~E~~	~~E~~	~~E + E = E~~	~~E × E = E~~
~~O~~	~~O~~	~~O + O = E~~	~~O × O = O~~
O	E	O + E = O	O × E = E

$A + B$ is only odd when either A or B is even. Therefore one of them must be even and the product AB must be even.

(2): SUFFICIENT. A is even. AB will also be even.

The correct answer is (D): EACH statement ALONE is sufficient to answer the question asked.

DS 33. Algebra: Inequalities
Difficulty: Medium **OG Page:** 277

This ***Inequalities*** question asks whether the weight of a dish of type X is greater than the weight of a dish of type Y. If we define the variable x as the weight of a dish of type X and y as the weight of a dish of type Y, this question can be rephrased as "Is $x < y$?"

(1): INSUFFICIENT. ***Translate*** the statement:

$$3x + 2y < 2x + 4y$$

Simplify this by gathering like variables:

$$3x + 2y < 2x + 4y$$
$$x + 2y < 4y$$
$$x < 2y$$

Knowing that x is less than $2y$ is not enough to guarantee that x is less than y.

(2): SUFFICIENT. ***Translate*** the statement:

$$4x + 3y < 3x + 4y$$

Simplify the inequality by gathering like variables:

$$4x + 3y < 3x + 4y$$
$$x + 3y < 4y$$
$$x < y$$

The correct answer is (B): Statement (2) ALONE is sufficient, but statement (1) alone is not sufficient to answer the question asked.

DS 34. Word Problems: Overlapping Sets
Difficulty: Medium **OG Page:** 277

From the question and the statements, we know that each student attended the science fair for either 0, 1, 2, or 3 days. We can ***Name Variables*** d_0, d_1, d_2, and d_3 such that d_0 is the number who attended for no days, d_1 is the number who attended for 1 day, d_2 is the number who attended for 2 days, and d_3 is the number who attended for 3 days. We can then translate the given information as:

$$d_0 + d_1 + d_2 + d_3 = 900$$

and rephrase the question as "What is d_3?"

(1): INSUFFICIENT. Since we know that the total number of students enrolled in the school is 900, and that the total number who attended on two or more days is just the sum of the number who attended on 2 days and the number who attended on 3 days, this statement can be rephrased as:

$$30\% \text{ of } 900 = d_2 + d_3$$
$$0.30 \times 900 = d_2 + d_3$$
$$270 = d_2 + d_3$$

We can't solve for d_3 because we do not know d_2.

(2): INSUFFICIENT. The hardest part of rephrasing this statement is understanding the language; "the students who attended on at least one day" means the sum of the students who attended on 1 day, 2 days, and 3 days. So this statement can be rephrased as:

$$10\% \text{ of } d_1 + d_2 + d_3 = d_3$$
$$0.10(d_1 + d_2 + d_3) = d_3$$
$$0.10d_1 + 0.10d_2 + 0.10d_3 = d_3$$
$$0.1d_1 + 0.1d_2 = 0.9d_3$$
$$d_1 + d_2 = 9d_3$$

We can't solve for d_3 because we do not know d_1 or d_2. We can't solve by plugging this equation into the given equation either, because we don't know the value of d_0.

(1) AND (2): INSUFFICIENT. Even taking the two statement equations together, we still can't solve because neither of them gives us the value of d_0, so we have no way to eliminate it from the given equation.

given: $d_0 + d_1 + d_2 + d_3 = 900$
(1): $270 = d_2 + d_3$
(2): $d_1 + d_2 = 9d_3$

The correct answer is (E): Statements (1) and (2) TOGETHER are NOT sufficient to answer the question asked, and additional data are needed.

DS 35. Geometry: Circles & Cylinders
Difficulty: Medium **OG Page:** 278

We are asked to find k, the number of 15-centimeter high ***Cylindrical*** cans that can fit into a ***Rectangular*** box. Because the height of both the box and the cans is 15 cm, we only care about how many circles (from the base of the cans) fit into the 48 cm × 32 cm rectangular base of the box. In this way, we can reduce a ***3-D Geometry*** question to a ***2-D Geometry*** question.

If we can find out how many cans can fit along the length and the width of the box, we can find k.

We can figure out how many cans fit if we know the diameter of each can. Additionally, if we know the radius or the circumference of a circle, we can find the diameter. This is true because

$$\text{Diameter} = 2 \times \text{Radius} = \frac{\text{Circumference}}{\pi}$$

So we can finally ***Rephrase*** the question as "What is any key dimension (radius, diameter, circumference, or area) of the circular base of a can?"

(1): SUFFICIENT. We are provided with the radius, which allows us to calculate the diameter, and therefore the number of cans. We know that the diameter is 8 cm, so 6 cans fit along the length and 4 cans fit along the width of the box, totaling 24 cans.

(2): SUFFICIENT. Knowing how many cans fit alongside the length allows us to calculate the diameter of each can and thus the number of cans in the box. If 6 cans fit exactly along the 48 cm length, then each can's diameter is 8 cm. We can now determine that 4 cans fit along the width, for a total of 24 cans.

Note: If the word *exactly* were not in statement (2), then the statement would not have been sufficient. With possible space left over along the length, the diameter could be shorter, and we might be able to add another cylinder along the width.

The correct answer is (D): EACH statement ALONE is sufficient.

DS 36. Algebra: Linear Equations
Difficulty: Easy **OG Page:** 278

This ***Linear Equations*** problem gives us a system of equations and asks for the value of z. This is a ***Combined Expression*** or ***Combos*** problem in disguise, since a combination of variables could be sufficient to solve for z. For Combo problems, we should figure out what knowledge would be sufficient before we look at the statements. Let's examine the given system of equations:

$$\begin{cases} x - 4 = z \\ y - x = 8 \\ 8 - z = t \end{cases}$$

Equation #1: if we can find x, we can find z.

Equation #2: if we can find y, we can find x. Therefore, if we can find y, we can find z.

Equation #3: if we can find t, we can find z.

In short, if we can find x, y, or t, then we can find z. Our ***Rephrased*** question is "What is the value of any given variable?"

(1): SUFFICIENT. This statement gives us the value of x. No further work is required.

(2): SUFFICIENT. This statement gives us the value of t. No further work is required.

The correct answer is (D): EACH statement ALONE is sufficient.

DS 37. Word Problems: Statistics
Difficulty: Medium **OG Page:** 278

This problem is tricky to rephrase! If we ***Name Variables***, a, b, and c, for the prices of the three items, we can translate the first sentence as:

$$\frac{a+b+c}{3}=50$$
$$a+b+c=150$$

Since the problem says that sales tax is only charged on items that cost more than \$80, and asks whether the total sales tax can be determined, we need to know "Which of a, b, and c are greater than 80 and what are the values of the prices greater than 80?"

(1): SUFFICIENT. The statement tells us that $c = 100$, which we can plug into the given equation to get:

$$a + b + 100 = 150$$
$$a + b = 50$$

Since the prices of items cannot be negative numbers, a and b must both be less than 80. The sales tax only applies to the highest priced item, which costs \$100. We can calculate the sales tax.

(2): INSUFFICIENT. The statement tells us that $a = 10$, which we can plug into the given equation to get:

$$10 + b + c = 150$$
$$b + c = 140$$

There are at least two sets of values that make the statement true but result in different amounts for the sales tax.

Statement is true if...	Sales tax would be
$b = 70$, $c = 70$	0
$b = 40$, $c = 100$	6% of 100

The correct answer is (A): Statement (1) ALONE is sufficient, but statement (2) alone is not sufficient to answer the question asked.

DS 38. Word Problems: Statistics
Difficulty: Easy **OG Page:** 278

Conceptually, the ***Standard Deviation*** is a measure of spread: how *wide* does our data spread from the average? The closer the values are to each other, the smaller the standard deviation. If the values are scattered, then the standard deviation might be large.

Because computing standard deviation is tedious, the GMAT will probably not require an actual calculation. To find the standard deviation without doing a computation, however, we need to know how far each number is from the mean.

(1): INSUFFICIENT. Knowing the ***Average*** does not give us information about how spread out the individual values are. Thus, the statement is insufficient.

(2): SUFFICIENT. If all the nests have the same number of eggs, then the values are not spread out at all. They have zero spread.

Looking at this issue computationally, we can see that if all the nests have the same number of eggs, then the average *is* the number of eggs in each basket. Therefore the difference between each term and the average is 0. The standard deviation must be 0.

The correct answer is (B): Statement (2) ALONE is sufficient, but statement (1) alone is not sufficient.

DS 39. Number Properties: Probability
Difficulty: Medium **OG Page:** 278

The question asks whether the probability that the card selected will be either red or white is less than 1/2. This can be rephrased using the definition of ***Probability***:

$$\text{Probability} = \frac{\text{Sucessful Outcomes}}{\text{Total Outcomes}}$$

Use the letters R, W, G, and B to represent the number of red, white, green, and blue cards respectively. Since we know that there are 12 cards total, this question can be rephrased as:

Given that $R + W + B + G = 12$,

Is $\frac{R+W}{12} > \frac{1}{2}$?, or Is $R + W > 6$?

(1): INSUFFICIENT. This statement tells us that:

$$\frac{B}{12} = \frac{1}{3}$$
$$B = 4$$

Think about different possibilities. If $B = 4$, then we know that $R + W + G = 8$, but that still doesn't tell us whether $R + W > 6$.

If $G = 1$, then $R + W > 6$.
If $G = 4$, then $R + W < 6$

(2): INSUFFICIENT. The statement tells us that:

$$\frac{R}{12} = \frac{1}{6}$$
$$R = 2$$

Without more information, this does not tell us whether $R + W > 6$.

(1) AND (2): INSUFFICIENT. Even if both statements are true, we still have the same problem.

$$R + W + B + G = 12$$
$$2 + W + 4 + G = 12$$
$$W + G = 6$$

We don't know the value of W, so we don't know whether $R + W > 6$.

The correct answer is (E): Statements (1) and (2) TOGETHER are NOT sufficient to answer the question asked, and additional data are needed.

DS 40. FDPs: Percents
Difficulty: Hard **OG Page:** 278

This ***Percents*** problem involves ***Algebraic Translation.***

First, we should ***Name Variables***, so that we can translate the ***Cost Relationship.*** Make the following assignments:

Selling price = S
Cost = C
Markup = M

The first sentence of the problem can be translated into an equation: $S = C + M$:

We are looking for the markup as a percent of the selling price. If we name another variable and designate the desired percent as x, then we can write an equation: $M = \frac{x}{100}S$. This equation can be solved to yield $x = \frac{M}{S} \times 100$. If we know the markup and the selling price, we will have enough information to answer the question.

Notice that the question only asks for the percent of the markup, not the actual markup. If that is the case, then the ***Ratio*** of the markup to the selling price would also be enough information to answer the question.

(1): SUFFICIENT. If the markup is 1/4 of the cost then the cost is 4 times the markup. Thus, we can ***Substitute*** in the above equation, plugging in $4M$ for C:

$$S = 4M + M$$
$$S = 5M$$

This equation gives the ratio of the markup to the selling price. The markup is 1/5, or 20%, of the selling price.

(2): INSUFFICIENT. This statement tells us that the *sum* of the cost and markup is \$250, but the cost and markup could be any two numbers summing to that amount. Thus, the markup could be anywhere from 0% to 100% of the cost. The markup-price ratio is not fixed.

The correct answer is (A): Statement (1) ALONE is sufficient, but statement (2) alone is not sufficient.

DS 41. Algebra: Exponents & Roots
Difficulty: Hard **OG Page:** 278

Since 4 and 8 are both powers of 2, we can rewrite the question as:

Is $(2^2)^{x+y} = (2^3)^{10}$?

Distribute the exponent:

Is $2^{2x+2y} = 2^{30}$?

Since the bases are the same, the two values will be the same if the exponents are equal, so we can rewrite as

Is $2x + 2y = 30$?
Is $x + y = 15$?

The simplest rephrase of this question is "What is $x + y$?"

(1): INSUFFICIENT. Manipulate the equation to get $x + y$ on the left

$$x - y = 9$$
$$x - y + 2y = 9 + 2y$$
$$x + y = 9 + 2y$$

We can't get a value for $x + y$ from this equation.

(2): INSUFFICIENT. Manipulate the equation to get $x + y$ on the left

$$\frac{y}{x} = \frac{1}{4}$$
$$4y = x$$
$$x + y = 5y$$

Again, we just can't get a value for $x + y$ from this equation.

(1) AND (2): SUFFICIENT. Taken together, we could plug the second equation into the first one to solve for y and then solve for x.

$$(4y) - y = 9$$
$$3y = 9$$
$$y = 3$$

Plug $y = 3$ into $x - y = 9$ to solve for x. We can stop working as soon as we see that we can solve for both x and y.

The correct answer is (C): BOTH statements (1) and (2) TOGETHER are sufficient to answer the question asked, but NEITHER statement ALONE is sufficient.

DS 42. Geometry: Polygons
Difficulty: Hard **OG Page:** 278

The question tells us about a rectangular sheet of glass and a rectangular tabletop, but does not give us the dimensions of either. It asks if the sheet of glass can be placed on top of the tabletop so that it covers the entire tabletop and has edges parallel to the tabletop's edges. The wording is a bit confusing, but a picture makes it clear:

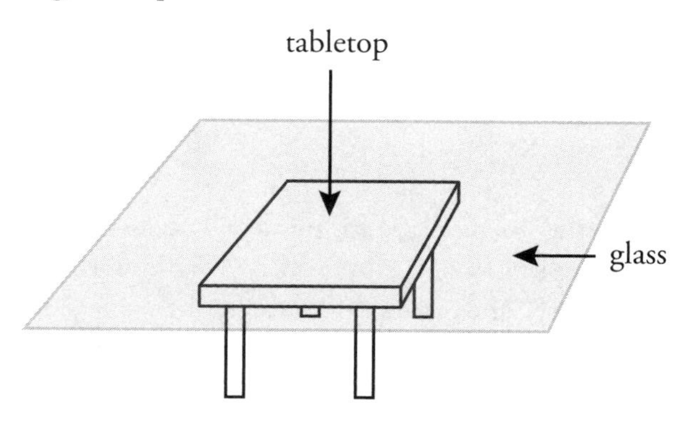

A simple rephrase for this question is "Are the length and width of the glass rectangle both greater than or equal to the length and width, respectively, of the tabletop rectangle?"

(1): INSUFFICIENT. This statement tells us nothing about the size of the glass.

(2): INSUFFICIENT. This statement tells us nothing about the size of the tabletop.

(1) AND (2): INSUFFICIENT. If the glass is 2,400 square inches, then it could be 40 inches wide and 60 inches long, since $40 \times 60 = 2,400$, so its dimensions could be greater than or equal to those of the tabletop. However, the glass rectangle could also be 24 inches wide by 100 inches long, since $24 \times 100 = 2,400$, which would mean that its width would be smaller than the tabletop's width.

The correct answer is (E): Statements (1) and (2) TOGETHER are NOT sufficient to answer the question asked, and additional data are needed.

DS 43. Algebra: Inequalities
Difficulty: Medium **OG Page:** 278

We can set up a ***Table*** to keep track of the variables and the question.

District	Population	# of reps.	Ratio (pop. to reps.)
1	p_1	r_1	p_1/r_1
2	p_2	r_2	p_2/r_2

This ***Inequalities*** problem asks "which ***Ratio*** is greater?" Since the answer is either one or the other (a binary response) we can ***Rephrase*** this question as the Yes/No question, "Is $\frac{p_1}{r_1} > \frac{p_2}{r_2}$?" (also a binary response).

Further manipulation is possible by cross-multiplication: "Is $p_1r_2 > p_2r_1$?" We did not have to worry about flipping the sign of the inequality, as all the variables represent numbers of people, which cannot be negative. To answer the question, we need to know something about the values of the products p_1r_2 and p_2r_1, or the values of all four variables individually.

(1): INSUFFICIENT. This gives us a relationship between the populations (p_1 and p_2), but no information about the number of representatives (r_1 and r_2).

(2): INSUFFICIENT. This gives us a relationship between the number of representatives (r_1 and r_2), but no information about the populations (p_1 and p_2).

(1) AND (2): SUFFICIENT. We can think about the situation using ***Algebraic Reasoning.*** If the District 1 population is *greater* than the District 2 population, but the number of representatives for District 1 is *less* than the number of representatives for District 2, then the District 1 ratio (p_1/r_1) is definitely greater than the District 2 ratio (p_2/r_2).

Alternatively, we can combine the inequalities for the two statements. Because we know that all the variables are positive, we can line the inequalities up and safely multiply them together. This gives us:

$$p_1 > p_2$$
$$\times\ r_2 > r_1$$
$$p_1r_2 > p_2r_1$$

The new equations matches the rephrasing we did at the beginning of the question.

Notice that we know the variables are all positive because there is a ***Hidden Constraint.*** All the variables count people, so the variables cannot be negative.

The correct answer is (C): BOTH statements TOGETHER are sufficient, but NEITHER statement ALONE is sufficient.

DS 44. Word Problems: Algebraic Translations
Difficulty: Easy **OG Page:** 278

In this ***Algebraic Translations*** question, we know that there are 80 adults, some of whom are college graduates and some of whom are not. Let's ***Name Variables:***

n = not college graduates
c = number of college graduates
$n + c = 80$

The question asks us to find the number of college graduates, or c. Using the given information, we can ***Rephrase*** the question as "What is $80 - n$?" or simply "What is n?"

Notice that we have a ***Linear Equation*** ($n + c = 80$) in the question stem. All we need is one more distinct linear equation containing n and c.

(1): SUFFICIENT. There are 3 times as many non-college graduates as graduates, so $n = 3c$.

We now have ***Two Different Linear Equations*** relating n and c. Thus, we will be able to find a unique value for c. No further work is required.

To solve for c, ***Substitute*** $3c$ for n into the stem equation.

$$n + c = 80$$
$$(3c) + c = 80 \quad \textbf{\textit{Substitute}}\ n = 3c$$
$$4c = 80$$
$$c = 20$$

(2): SUFFICIENT. Since the number of non-college graduates is 40 more than the number of college graduates, $n = c + 40$.

Once again, we have two distinct linear equations relating n and c. We know that we can find a unique value for c. No further work is required.

The correct answer is (D): EACH statement ALONE is sufficient.

DS 45. Word Problems: Extra Problem Types
Difficulty: Easy **OG Page:** 279

The given table lists the distances between four different cities. Looking at the ***Table***, we can determine that we are looking for the value of x, which represents the distance between city R and city T.

(1): INSUFFICIENT. This statement tells us that the distance from S to T, which is known to be 56, is twice the distance from S to R, labeled y. Thus, we can create an equation:

$$56 = 2y$$

This allows us to solve for y. However, knowing y does not allow us to solve for x.

(2): SUFFICIENT. This statement tells us that the distance between T and U, known to be 69, is 1.5 times the distance between R and T, labeled x. Thus, we can create an equation:

$$69 = 1.5x$$

This is a straightforward ***Linear Equation,*** which will result in only one value for x.

The correct answer is (B): Statement (2) ALONE is sufficient, but statement (1) alone is not sufficient.

DS 46. FDPs: FDPs
Difficulty: Easy **OG Page:** 279

What is the tenths ***Digit*** in the ***Decimal*** representation of a certain number? The question does not require rephrasing.

(1): INSUFFICIENT. The number is less than 1/3. Since the decimal representation of 1/3 is $0.\overline{3}$, a number less than 1/3 could have a tenths digit of 3, 2, 1, or 0 (and, if it is a negative number, 9, 8, 7, 6, 5, or 4).

(2): INSUFFICIENT. The number is greater than 1/4. Since the decimal representation of 1/4 is 0.25, a number greater than 1/4 could have a tenths digit of 2, 3, 4, 5, 6, 7, 8, or 9 (and, if the number is greater than 1, 0 or 1).

(1) AND (2): INSUFFICIENT. A number between 1/4 and 1/3 is between 0.25 and $0.\overline{3}$. Therefore, its tenths digit could be 2 or 3. Therefore, we cannot answer the question.

The correct answer is (E): Statements (1) and (2) TOGETHER are not sufficient.

DS 47. FDPs: Ratios
Difficulty: Medium **OG Page:** 279

In this problem, we can ***Name Variables*** to represent the ***Work Rates*** of each robot:

x = rate of Robot X
y = rate of Robot Y
z = rate of Robot Z

In this case, $r_x = x/z$, and $r_y = y/z$. We want to find out whether z is the largest. Notice the ***Hidden***

Constraint that all variables must be positive, because work rates must be positive.

Rephrasing the question leads to:

Is $z > x$ and $z > y$?

Notice that the word *and* means that both parts need to be true, if we are to answer *Yes*.

(1): INSUFFICIENT. We can replace the ratio with the rates:

$$\frac{x}{z} < \frac{y}{z}$$

Multiply both sides of the inequality by z (because z cannot be negative) and get $x < y$. However we do not know how z compares to either x or y.

(2): INSUFFICIENT. We can replace the ratio with the rates:

$$\frac{y}{z} < 1$$

When we multiply both sides by z, which must be positive, we get $y < z$. However, this does not provide any information about how z compares to x.

(1) AND (2): SUFFICIENT. From (1), we know that $x < y$. From (2), we know that $y < z$. Putting these relationships together, we get:

$x < y < z$

Here, we see that $z > x$ and $z > y$, and we can answer our rephrased question.

The correct answer is (C): BOTH statements TOGETHER are sufficient, but NEITHER statement ALONE is sufficient.

DS 48 Algebra: Inequalities
Difficulty: Easy **OG Page:** 279

No rephrasing is required. This ***Inequalities*** question is asking whether $x < y$.

(1): INSUFFICIENT. If $a < c$, we know that the lower range of possibilities for x is smaller than the lower range for y. Using only this information, we cannot say with certainty that x itself is smaller than y.

We can ***Test Numbers*** to verify our thinking. For instance, suppose $a = 0$ and $c = 2$. If $x = 2$ and $y = 3$, $x < y$. However, if $x = 4$ and $y = 3$, then $y < x$.

(2): SUFFICIENT. If $b < c$, the upper limit for x is smaller than the lower limit for y. What this means is that the biggest x can be is smaller than the smallest y can be. Therefore, x must be smaller than y.

We could test numbers, but this ***Algebraic Reasoning*** is both solid and quick.

The correct answer is (B): Statement (2) ALONE is sufficient, but statement (1) alone is not sufficient.

DS 49. Word Problems: Overlapping Sets
Difficulty: Medium **OG Page:** 279

For this ***Overlapping Sets*** problem, we can create a ***Double-Set Matrix***. We are looking for the number that goes in the upper-left box—people who are directors of both Company R and Company K.

		Director of K?		
Director of R?		**Yes**	**No**	**Total**
	Yes			
	No			
	Total			

(1): INSUFFICIENT. Plug in this information as follows:

		Director of K?		
Director of R?		**Yes**	**No**	**Total**
	Yes			
	No		0	
	Total			17

Note that we have placed a 0 in the center box. This is because the 17 represents the total number of directors. Thus, each of the 17 people is a member of at least 1 board. No one is on *neither* board. This "0 in Neither" represents an important insight. Nonetheless, we cannot arrive at a value for the upper-left box.

(2): INSUFFICIENT. Plug in this information as follows:

Director of R?		Director of K?		
		Yes	No	Total
	Yes			8
	No			
	Total	12		

This is not enough to solve for the value of the upper-left box.

(1) AND (2): SUFFICIENT. Now place all of the information into the same matrix:

Director of R?		Director of K?		
		Yes	No	Total
	Yes		5	8
	No	9	0	9
	Total	12	5	17

From here, we can easily fill in every other box. 3 people are directors of both Company R and Company K.

Notice that *without* the "0 in Neither," we would not have sufficiency at this point.

The correct answer is (C): BOTH statements TOGETHER are sufficient, but NEITHER statement ALONE is sufficient.

DS 50. <u>Algebra</u>: Inequalities
Difficulty: Easy **OG Page:** 279

In this ***Inequalities*** problem, we are asked whether $x/y > 1$. In order for this to be true, given that both x and y are positive, x must be greater than y. We can thus ***Rephrase*** the question as "Is $x > y$?"

(1): INSUFFICIENT. Knowing that the product of x and y is greater than 1 does NOT establish whether $x > y$.

(2): SUFFICIENT. If $x - y > 0$, then we can add y to both sides and get $x > y$. This result satisfies our rephrased question.

The correct answer is (B): Statement (2) ALONE is sufficient, but statement (1) alone is not sufficient.

DS 51. <u>FDPs</u>: FDPs
Difficulty: Medium **OG Page:** 279

In this problem, we are told that a store bought an item for x dollars and sold it for y dollars. We are asked to determine the profit on the sale as a percentage of the initial cost.

Because we are being asked for a value that can be represented algebraically, our first step should be to ***Translate*** the question into an expression. Calculate Percent Profit by dividing the dollar profit by the dollar cost and multiplying the result by 100. By the ***Profit Relationship,*** Profit = Revenue − Cost = $y - x$. Cost is x, so Percent Profit $= \frac{y-x}{x} \times 100$.

Before moving on to the statements, we should see whether we can simplify this expression:

$$\frac{y-x}{x} \times 100 = \left(\frac{y}{x} - \frac{x}{x}\right) \times 100 = \left(\frac{y}{x} - 1\right) \times 100$$

This problem involves a ***Combined Expression***, or Combo. To find the Combo y/x, we don't necessarily need the value of x and the value of y. We will be able to answer the ***Rephrased*** question if we can find the ***Ratio*** of y to x.

(1): INSUFFICIENT. This statement tells us that the dollar amount of the profit was equal to 20. However, without knowing the cost x, we cannot determine a profit percentage.

(2): SUFFICIENT. From this statement, we learn that the ratio y/x is equal to 5/4. This answers our rephrased question.

We can also ***Substitute*** this value into the equation for percent profit to obtain

$$\text{Percent profit} = \left(\frac{5}{4} - 1\right) \times 100 = \frac{1}{4} \times 100 = 25$$

The correct answer is (B): Statement (2) ALONE is sufficient, but statement (1) alone is not sufficient.

DS 52. Algebra: Inequalities
Difficulty: Medium **OG Page:** 279

The question asks whether $x < 10 < y$.

(1): SUFFICIENT. The numbers in this question give us a valuable clue about how to start thinking about this problem. Note the 100's in the statements and the 10 in the question and remember that $100 = 10^2$.

Since $xy = 100$ and both x and y are positive, either $x = y = 10$, or one of the variables is greater than 10 and the other one is less than 10. Think about this. If both x and y were greater than 10, then their product would be greater than 100, and if both x and y were less than 10, their product would be less than 100.

Since this statement also tells us that $x < y$, we know that $x < 10$ and $y > 10$, so:

$$x < 10 < y$$

(2): SUFFICIENT. Since we know that x and y are both positive, we can square root this inequality.

$$x^2 < 100 < y^2$$
$$\sqrt{x^2} < \sqrt{100} < \sqrt{y^2}$$
$$x < 10 < y$$

The correct answer is (D): EACH Statement ALONE is sufficient.

DS 53. Algebra: Exponents & Roots
Difficulty: Medium **OG Page:** 279

We cannot easily rephrase this question, which involves ***Equations*** and ***Exponents***.

(1): SUFFICIENT. The equation contains a ***Square Root*** sign. Our first move should be to square both sides:

$$3^x + 3^{-x} = \sqrt{b+2}$$
$$(3^x + 3^{-x})^2 = b + 2$$

Recognize that the left side of the equation is a ***Special Product Quadratic***. Distribute and simplify. Note that we will have to make liberal use of ***Exponent Rules:***

$$(3^x)(3^x) + 2(3^x)(3^{-x}) + (3^{-x})(3^{-x}) = b + 2$$
$$3^{2x} + 2(3^0) + 3^{-2x} = b + 2$$
$$3^{2x} + 2 + 3^{-2x} = b + 2$$
$$3^{2x} + 3^{-2x} = b$$

At this stage, the terms on the left have a base of 3, but the terms in the question stem have a base of 9. We need to use exponent rules again to make the final leap.

$$3^{2x} + 3^{-2x} = (3^2)^x + (3^2)^{-x}$$
$$(3^2)^x + (3^2)^{-x} = b$$
$$9^x + 9^{-x} = b$$

This equation directly answers the question.

(2): INSUFFICIENT. This statement provides no information about the value of b. Therefore, we cannot determine whether the equation is true.

The correct answer is (A): Statement (1) ALONE is sufficient, but statement (2) alone is not sufficient.

DS 54. Word Problems: Algebraic Translations
Difficulty: Easy **OG Page:** 279

To find the charge for a 10-mile ride in terms of f and m, we need to ***Translate*** the ***Cost Relationship*** in the question stem. Specifically, the charge for a 10-mile ride is $f + 9m$.

We can answer this question if we know both f and m, or if we know the value of the ***Combined Expression*** $f + 9m$.

(1): INSUFFICIENT: From this statement, we can derive the following equation:

$$f + m = 90$$

(Since f and m are in cents, our total should also be in cents.)

We cannot arrive at values for either f or m. Likewise, we cannot determine the value of the Combo $f + 9m$.

(2): INSUFFICIENT: We can rephrase this statement by translating it:

$$f + 3m = 120$$

We cannot determine the value of f, the value of m, or the value of the combined expression $f + 9m$.

(1) AND (2): SUFFICIENT. We can use both equations to find the values of both variables. Right away, notice that we have ***Two Different Linear Equations*** and ***Two Unknowns***, so the information is sufficient.

If we really want to find the values of the variables, we can use ***Elimination***.

$$\begin{array}{r} f + 3m = 120 \\ -(f + m = 90) \\ \hline 2m = 30 \\ m = 15 \\ f \quad\quad = 75 \end{array}$$

Knowing the values of f and m is sufficient to answer the question.

The correct answer is (C): BOTH statements TOGETHER are sufficient, but NEITHER statement ALONE is sufficient.

DS 55. <u>FDPs</u>: Percents
Difficulty: Hard **OG Page:** 279

In order to know the ***Percent Change*** of Guy's net income, we must know his original net income and the change in his net income, or at least the ***Ratio*** of these quantities.

Percent change is calculated by the following formula:

$$\frac{\text{Dollar change in net income}}{\text{Starting net income in dollars}}$$

Without these two values, we cannot calculate percent change.

Note that we also have a ***Profit Relationship***:

Gross Income – Deductions = Net Income

This relationship behaves mathematically just like the normal profit relationship (Revenue – Cost = Profit).

(1): INSUFFICIENT. Guy's gross income increased by 4% on the specific date in question. This does not allow us to calculate either the change in net income or the starting net income.

(2): INSUFFICIENT. Guy's deductions increased by 15% on the specific date in question. This does not allow us to calculate either the change in net income or the starting net income.

(1) AND (2): INSUFFICIENT. Guy's gross income increased by 4% and his deductions increased by 15%. We do not know the starting or ending values for the actual dollar amounts, so we cannot calculate either the change in net income or the starting net income. Thus, both statements together are insufficient.

Note that if both gross income and deductions grew by 4%, then so would his net income. If two percent changes are the same in a profit relationship, then the third percent change will equal the other two.

Because the percent changes are different for the gross income and the deductions, we cannot tell what percent change will happen to the net income. We can prove this by creating two ***Scenarios***:

	Example 1	Example 2
starting gross income	\$100	\$50
starting deduction	\$10	\$30
starting net income	100 – 10 = 90	50 – 30 = 20
new gross income (+4%)	\$104	\$52
new deductions (+15%)	\$11.50	\$34.50
new net income	104 – 11.5 = 92.5	52 – 34.50 = 17.5
percentage change	(92.5 – 90)/90 = 2.5/90 = 2.78%	(20 – 17.5)/20 = 2.5/20 = 12.5%

In the last step, notice that the first example returns 2.5/90 and the second example returns 2.5/20. We do not need to calculate the actual percentages in order to see that these numbers are not equal.

The correct answer is (E): Statements (1) and (2) TOGETHER are not sufficient.

DS 56. Geometry: Triangles & Diagonals
Difficulty: Easy **OG Page:** 279

The sum of the ***Angles of a Triangle*** is 180. Therefore, $x + y + z = 180$. Since the problem asks for the value of z, we start by isolating z:

$z = 180 - (x + y)$

In order to find the value of z, we need to answer the question "What is the value of $180 - (x - y)$?" More simply, we can ask the ***Rephrased*** question "What is the value of $x + y$?" Here, $x + y$ is a ***Combined Expression,*** or Combo.

(1): SUFFICIENT. We are given the value of $x + y$, directly matching our rephrasing, so we can stop here.

If we know the value of $x + y$, we can solve for the value of z (though it is unnecessary to do so).

$z = 180 - (x + y)$
$z = 180 - (139)$
$z = 41$

(2): INSUFFICIENT. Knowing the value of $y + z$ is neither sufficient to calculate $x + y$ nor sufficient to calculate z itself.

The correct answer is (A): Statement (1) ALONE is sufficient, but statement (2) alone is not sufficient.

DS 57. Word Problems: Algebraic Translations
Difficulty: Medium **OG Page:** 280

The question tells us that there are two types of gift certificates, one that sold for \$10 and another that sold for \$50, and that the bookstore sold more than 5 of the \$50 gift certificates. It asks what the total number of gift certificates sold was.

If we ***Name a Variable*** t for the number of \$10 gift certificates sold and another variable f for the number of \$50 gift certificates sold, the given information can be ***Translated*** as:

$f > 5$,
t and f are both integers

The question can also be translated as

$t + f = ?$

(1): INSUFFICIENT. Translate the statement:

$t < 9$

Although we already know that $f > 5$, this is not enough information to tell us the value of $t + f$.

(2): INSUFFICIENT. Translate the statement:

$10t + 50f = 460$

If this were a simple two variable, linear equation problem, it wouldn't be solvable. However, the ***Integer Constraints*** (t and f must both be integers) and the fact that $f > 5$ suggest that there may only be one solution that works. In general, the constraint that variables must be integers often greatly reduces the number of possible solutions.

Since f must be at least 6, we know that at least $6 \times \$50 = \$300$ worth of \$50 gift certificates were sold, leaving \$160 worth of gift certificates to account for. However \$160 worth of gift certificates could be three \$50 certificates and one \$10 certificate, two \$50 certificates and six \$10 gift certificates, or one \$50 certificate and eleven \$10 certificates. This means that there is more than one possible answer to the question.

(1) AND (2): INSUFFICIENT. Even if we assume that both statements are true, more than one example from **(2)** matches the information. There could be three \$50 certificates and one \$10 certificates, or two \$50 and six \$10 gift certificates.

The correct answer is (E): Statements (1) and (2) TOGETHER are NOT sufficient to answer the question asked, and additional data are needed.

DS 58. <u>Number Properties</u>: Divisibility & Primes
Difficulty: Hard **OG Page:** 280

The question asks for the ***Tens Digit*** of positive integer x. The topic of ***Divisibility*** will come into play in the statements.

(1): SUFFICIENT. Often, the simplest way to deal with ***Remainder*** questions is to ***Test Numbers***. We know that when x is divided by 100, the remainder is 30. This means that every possible x will be 30 more than a multiple of 100. Recast language such as "*when x is divided by 100, the remainder is 30*" in terms of multiples ("*x is 30 more than a multiple of 100*"), since multiples make more intuitive sense to most people.

Let's set up a ***Table*** to find the pattern.

Possible values for x	The tens digit of x?
$100(0) + 30 = 30$	3
$100(1) + 30 = 130$	3
$100(2) + 30 = 230$	3

The tens digit of all such possible x values is 3.

We can actually start with (100)(0) as the first multiple of 100, since zero is technically a multiple of all numbers.

(2): INSUFFICIENT. We can again generate a list of possible x values. Each x must be 30 more than a multiple of 110.

Possible values for x	The tens digit of x?
$110(0) + 30 = 30$	3
$110(1) + 30 = 140$	4
$110(2) + 30 = 250$	5

The results show three different values for the tens digit of x, although two are enough to prove insufficiency.

The correct answer is (A): Statement (1) ALONE is sufficient, but statement (2) alone is not sufficient.

DS 59. <u>Word Problems</u>: Algebraic Translations
Difficulty: Hard **OG Page:** 280

This ***Algebraic Translations*** problem involves a disguised ***Cost Relationship.*** The number of bills, multiplied by the worth or "cost" of each bill, equals the total value (in dollars).

To represent this relationship algebraically, we can ***Name Variables.*** If we let f stand for the number of five-dollar bills, and t the number of twenty-dollar bills, then the cost relationship translates to $5f + 20t = 125$.

There is also a ***Hidden Constraint*** in this problem. We know that f and t must be positive integers, since it is impossible for Max to have fractional or negative numbers of bills. This integer constraint will greatly restrict the number of possible combinations of f and t.

For problems involving linear equations with integer constraints, ***Testing Scenarios*** is often the most efficient method of solution.

(1): SUFFICIENT. Since $5f + 20t$ must equal 125, we may find $20t$ in each case by subtraction: $20t =$

$125 - 5f$. We are looking for values of f that allow t to be a positive integer.

We know that f is less than 5, so let's test only values less than 5. Make a ***Table*** to organize the job.

$125 - 5f = 20t$. Therefore, if $125 - 5f$ is not a multiple of 20, then t can't be an integer.

f	$125 - 5f$	$\div 20 = t$
4	105	not an integer
3	110	not an integer
2	115	not an integer
1	120	6
0	125	not an integer

The only possible solution is 1 five-dollar bill and 6 twenty-dollar bills.

(2): SUFFICIENT. Since $5f + 20t$ must equal 125, we may find $5f$ in each case by subtraction: $5f = 125 - 20t$.

We know that t is greater than 5, so only test values that are greater than 5. Make another table to organize the job:

t	$125 - 20t$	$\div 5 = f$
6	5	1
7	Negative	negative
8	Negative	negative

All values of t greater than 6 will produce negative values for f. These values are impossible. Again, 1 five-dollar bill and 6 twenty-dollar bills is the only solution.

Notice that, in both statements, an ***Inequality*** turned out to be sufficient information for precise values of f and t. This is frequently the case in problems with hidden integer constraints.

The correct answer is (D): EACH statement ALONE is sufficient.

DS 60. Algebra: Linear Equations
Difficulty: Medium **OG Page:** 280

We can begin by manipulating the given ***Linear Equation*** to isolate n:

$$-25 + 19 + n = s$$
$$-6 + n = s$$
$$n = s + 6$$

The question asks us for the value of n. We can answer if we know the value of either n or s. Thus, we can ***Rephrase:*** "What is the value of n or s?"

(1): SUFFICIENT. We are given the value of s. This satisfies our rephrased question.

(2): SUFFICIENT. Combining this statement with the information from the question stem, we have ***Two Different Linear Equations*** with ***Two Unknowns.*** We can stop here, since we have sufficient information to solve for either unknown.

If we really want to know what n is, we can solve by ***Substitution***.

Begin by putting s in terms of n:

$$n/s = 4$$
$$n = 4s$$
$$s = 1/4n$$

Next, plug this value for s into the first equation:

$$n = (1/4n) + 6$$
$$3/4n = 6$$
$$n = 8$$

Of course, the calculations are unnecessary, once we are certain that we can arrive at a definite value for n.

The correct answer is (D): EACH statement ALONE is sufficient.

DS 61. FDPs: Percents
Difficulty: Medium **OG Page:** 280

In this ***Percents*** problem, which also involves ***Algebraic Translations***, we are asked to determine the number of guests who received double scoops of ice cream. Because we can approach the solution in many different ways, we should go to the statements without a specific rephrase.

(1): INSUFFICIENT. Knowing the percent of guests who received double scoops is not enough, if we do not know the total number of guests.

(2): INSUFFICIENT. Knowing the total number of scoops does not tell us how many guests received double scoops.

(1) AND (2): SUFFICIENT. If we know that 60% of the guests received a double scoop, then we know the ratio of single-scoop guests to double-scoop guests. If we know the total number of scoops, we can use the ratio to determine the number of guests who received double scoops.

First, ***Name a Variable*** x for the total number of guests at the picnic. If 60% of the guests received a double scoop, then $0.6x$ people received double scoops. The total number of scoops received by these guests was $2 \times 0.6x$. Similarly, 40% of the guests, or $0.4x$, received a single scoop, so the number of single scoops received by these guests was $1 \times 0.4x$. We know the total number of scoops served, so $0.4x + 2 \times 0.6x = 120$.

This equation will allow us to solve for the total number of guests at the picnic. Once we know the total number of guests, we will be able to determine the number of guests who were served a double scoop.

A ***Table*** can help us stay organized, if we're having trouble keeping track of all the pieces. Here's what a table could look like for statements (1) and (2) together:

	Guests	**Scoops per Guests**	**Total Scoops**
Single Scoop	$0.4x$	1	$0.4x$
Double Scoop	$0.6x$	2	$1.2x$
Total	x		$1.6x$

Since we know $1.6x = 120$, we can solve for x and calculate every cell, in theory.

The correct answer is (C): BOTH statements TOGETHER are sufficient, but NEITHER statement ALONE is sufficient.

DS 62. FDPs: Percents
Difficulty: Medium **OG Page:** 280

In this ***Percents*** problem, we are asked "Is the discount price at Store M less than the discount price at Store L?" For both stores, we need either the discount price or the original price AND the amount (or percent) of the discount.

This problem also involves a ***Discount Relationship:***

Original Price − Discount = Discount Price

This relationship is mathematically similar to a profit or markup relationship.

(1): INSUFFICIENT. Knowing the *percent* discount at each store does not tell us whether the discount *price* at Store M is less than the discount price at Store L, because we do not know the original prices of the items. For instance, if Store M's original price is much higher than Store L's, Store M's discount price could be higher even with a larger percent taken off the original price.

(2): INSUFFICIENT. Store L gives \$5 off and Store M gives \$6 off. Without knowing the original prices for the product at both stores, we cannot answer the question.

(1) AND (2): SUFFICIENT. Combining both statements, we know that Store L's discount is 10%, which is equal to \$5.

Thus, $\$5 = 0.1 \times$ Store L's original price. This equation allows us to calculate the original price (\$50) and the discount price ($\$50 - \$5 = \$45$).

Store M's discount is 15%, which is equal to \$6. We are given the same type of information for Store M as for Store L, so we will also be able to calculate the discount price at Store M. No further calculation is required.

The correct answer is (C): BOTH statements TOGETHER are sufficient, but NEITHER statement ALONE is sufficient.

DS 63. FDPs: Digits & Decimals
Difficulty: Medium **OG Page:** 280

There is no rephrasing needed for this ***Decimals*** question, which also involves ***Inequalities.***

(1): INSUFFICIENT. When ***Rounding a Decimal*** to the nearest tenth, we have to look at the hundredths digit and ***Test Scenarios.***

If d is rounded *down* to 0.5 (for example, 0.53), then $d > 0.5$. Here, the answer to the question is *Yes*. If d is rounded *up* to 0.5 (for example, 0.47), then $d < 0.5$. Here, the answer to the question is *No*.

As we can create two different scenarios, this statement is insufficient.

Alternatively, we can ***Translate*** this statement. According to this statement, the values for d are defined as $0.45 \leq d < 0.55$. This clearly shows that it is only sometimes true that $d \leq 0.5$.

(2): SUFFICIENT. When rounding a number to the nearest units digit, we have to look at the tenths digit. We can translate this statement, saying that the values for d are defined as $0.5 \leq d < 1.5$. This clearly shows that it is always the case that $d \geq 0.5$.

The correct answer is (B): Statement (2) ALONE is sufficient.

DS 64. Word Problems: Consecutive Integers
Difficulty: Medium **OG Page:** 280

If we know the values of r and s, we can calculate the number of integers between them. These integers will form a ***Consecutive Integer*** set.

Furthermore, if we know the difference between r and s—that is, how far apart they are on a number line—then we can also calculate the number of integers between them, even if we do not know what the specific values are. It does not matter whether s or r is larger.

(1): SUFFICIENT. If $s - r = 10$, then s and r are 10 units apart on a number line. Therefore, there must be nine integers between them on a number line. For example, if s is 3 and r is 13, then the nine integers 4, 5, 6, 7, 8, 9, 10, 11, and 12 are between the two. This is true no matter where we place s and r.

By the way, the problem specifies "between, but not including." This definition may seem unusual, because with consecutive integer sets, we more typically include the endpoints. But for this problem, it does not matter which way we define "between," as long as the definition stays consistent through the problem.

(2): SUFFICIENT. If there are 9 integers between, but not including, $r + 1$ and $s + 1$, then $r + 1$ and $s + 1$ are 10 units apart on a number line. As a result, r and s must also be 10 units apart on a number line.

Again, this is true no matter where we place s and r. For example, if $r + 1$ is 11, then the 9 integers are 12, 13, 14, 15, 16, 17, 18, 19 and 20. Therefore $s + 1$ is 21. That means that r is 10 and s is 20. We can determine how many integers are between r and s.

The correct answer is (D): EACH statement ALONE is sufficient.

DS 65. Word Problems: Algebraic Translations
Difficulty: Medium **OG Page:** 280

If we create a variable b for the number of coins that Bert has and another variable c for the number of coins that Claire has, the question can be ***Translated*** as

$$b + c = ?$$

Since b and c are numbers of coins, we also know that they are integers. This kind of ***Integer Constraint*** often greatly reduces the total number of possible solutions.

(1): INSUFFICIENT. Translate:

$$b = 1.5c$$

There are many numbers that could satisfy this, such as 3 and 2 or 6 and 4.

(2): INSUFFICIENT. Translate:

$21 < b + c < 28$

$b + c$ could be any number between 21 and 28, so again, there are many numbers b and c that could work, such as 10 and 12 or 12 and 15.

(1) AND (2): SUFFICIENT. If we were to treat this as a simple two-variable, linear equation problem, we might assume it wasn't solvable. However, the additional integer constraint (b and c must both be integers) and the fact that $b + c$ is one of 22, 23, 24, 25, 26, or 27 suggest that there may only be one solution that works.

We can substitute the value of b given in **(1)** into the inequality in **(2).** Replace b with $(1.5c)$:

$21 < (1.5c) + c < 28$
$21 < 2.5c < 28$

The next step is to get rid of the ugly decimal 2.5. We can do that by multiplying the inequality by 2.

$42 < 5c < 56$

Since c has to be an integer, and the only two multiples of 5 between 42 and 56 are 45, 50, and 55, this tells us that c is 9, 10, or 11.

However, since b also has to be an integer and $b = 1.5c$, the only one of these possibilities that works for b is $c = 10$, which makes $b = 15$.

$9 \times 1.5 = 13.5 \leftarrow$ NOT an integer
$11 \times 1.5 = 16.5 \leftarrow$ NOT an integer

The correct answer is (C): BOTH statements (1) and (2) TOGETHER are sufficient to answer the question asked, but NEITHER statement ALONE is sufficient.

DS 66. Word Problems: Overlapping Sets
Difficulty: Medium **OG Page:** 280

This standard ***Overlapping Sets*** problem presents two binary criteria: student loans vs. no student loans, and scholarship vs. no scholarship. Construct a ***Double-Set Matrix*** according to these criteria, filling in the information from the prompt and circling the desired quantity.

Note that, since we know the total number of students surveyed (200), we can multiply the given ***Percents*** by 200 to yield concrete numbers.

As is customary on all double-set matrix problems, we fill in the third entry in any row that contains two existing entries (in italics).

	Student Loans	No Loans	Total
Sch.			80
No Sch			*120*
Total	60	*140*	200

(1): SUFFICIENT. According to this statement, 50 students received scholarships but no loans. Add this number into the matrix (in bold), and then fill in the third entry in all rows and columns containing two existing entries (in italics):

	Student Loans	No Loans	Total
Sch.	*30*	**50**	80
No Sch	*30*	*90*	120
Total	60	140	200

The desired answer is thus 90 students.

(2): SUFFICIENT. According to this statement, 50 percent *of the 60 students who had received loans* said that they had also received scholarships. Therefore, 30 students had received both loans and scholarships. Add this number into the matrix (in bold), and then fill in the third entry in all rows and columns containing two existing entries (in italics):

	Student Loans	No Loans	Total
Sch.	**30**	*50*	80
No Sch	*30*	*90*	120
Total	60	140	200

The desired answer is thus 90 students.

The correct answer is (D): EACH statement ALONE is sufficient.

DS 67. Algebra: Quadratic Equations
Difficulty: Medium **OG Page:** 280

We are asked for the value of n. Finding one and only one value of n will be sufficient.

(1): INSUFFICIENT. As we have been told that n is an integer, many people will see that the expression $n(n + 1)$ is the product of two consecutive integers. Because this product is equal to 6, it is easy to assume that the integers in question are 2 and 3 (thus $n = 2$). No other positive integers fit.

However, we do not know that n is positive. In fact, this equation is ***Quadratic.*** We need to solve for the two solutions of n:

$$\begin{aligned} n(n+1) &= 6 \\ n^2 + n &= 6 \\ n^2 + n - 6 &= 0 \\ (n+3)(n-2) &= 0 \\ n &= 2, -3 \end{aligned}$$

If $n = -3$, then $n + 1 = -2$, and $n(n + 1) = 6$. Since two possible values of n satisfy $n(n + 1) = 6$, the statement is insufficient.

(2): SUFFICIENT. We can simplify the given ***Equation with Exponents*** as follows:

$$\begin{aligned} 2^{2n} &= 16 \\ 4^n &= 16 \\ 4^n &= 4^2 \\ n &= 2 \end{aligned}$$

The correct answer is (B): Statement (2) ALONE is sufficient, but statement (1) alone is not sufficient.

DS 68. Word Problems: Rates & Work
Difficulty: Medium **OG Page:** 280

Survey this ***Rates & Work*** question to see what we need to keep track of: three machines (K, M, and P), as well as Rate, Time, and Work for each and every machine. Set up an ***Rate–Time–Work Chart*** to stay organized.

When they work together, the machines can complete the task in 24 minutes. Using the property that $R = W/T$, we can fill in the entire bottom row of the chart.

Machine	Rate	Time	Work
K	a.	?	1 task
M	b.	c.	1 task
P			1 task
All (together)	1/24 task/min.	24 min.	1 task

The question asks for the time it takes Machine K to complete the task, so we place a question mark in the chart to represent that time.

We would be able to solve for K's time if we had some other information, namely any of the following:

- K's rate, because

$$T = \frac{W}{R} = \frac{1 \text{ task}}{\text{rate at which K works}}$$

- M and P's combined rate, because the three machines in this problem work together, meaning that we can ***Add the Rates*** (i.e., the rate for the three machines working together is equal to the sum of their individual rates). Let's Name Variables as simply as we can, and call K's rate k, M's rate m, and P's rate p. (This differs from the way the OG explanation uses these letters, by the way.) Thus, $k + m + p$ = Total Rate = 1/24.

- The time it takes M and P working together to complete the task, because $R = W/T$ so

$$m + p = \frac{1 \text{ task}}{\text{time for M \& P}}.$$

Therefore, we can ***Rephrase*** the original question to "What is k?" or "What is the combined rate of m and p?" OR "How long does it take m and p working together to complete the task?" These questions are represented by "a." "b." and "c." respectively in the chart above.

(1): SUFFICIENT. This statement provides the time it takes M and P together to complete the task, the answer to one of our rephrased questions.

It is not necessary to fill in the entire chart, though we can do so here:

Machine	Rate	Time	Work
K	a.	?	1 task
M	1/36	36	1 task
P			1 task
All (together)	1/24	24	1 task

We know that $k + m + p$ = Total Rate = 1/24. So k + (1/36) = 1/24. This allows us to solve for the rate at which K works and thus find the amount of time it takes for K to complete the task.

Notice that $m + p$, a ***Combined Expression*** or Combo, is sufficient to answer the question. The GMAT loves this kind of trick: it gives us a relationship among *three* variables ($k + m + p$ = Total Rate = 1/24) and asks us for the value of one of the variables (k = ?). The right Combo of the other variables will do the trick.

Specifically, since $k = 1/24 - (m + p)$, we needed $m + p$, the combined rates of machines M and P.

(2): INSUFFICIENT. This statement gives the time necessary for K and P to complete the task when working together. This time could be used to compute the *combined* rate of K and P($k + p$). However, we cannot determine the *individual* rate of K.

The correct answer is (A): Statement (1) ALONE is sufficient, but statement (2) alone is not sufficient.

DS 69. <u>Number Properties</u>: Positives & Negatives
Difficulty: Medium **OG Page:** 281

By asking whether r is the closest to zero of the four numbers on the ***Number Line,*** this ***Positives & Negatives*** question is really asking about the positioning of zero on the number line. In the number line below, the four numbers have been intentionally placed with uneven spacing, since the question says nothing about even spacing. Sometimes, it is good to ***Exaggerate the Picture*** somewhat to ensure that we don't find unjustified features, such as even spacing.

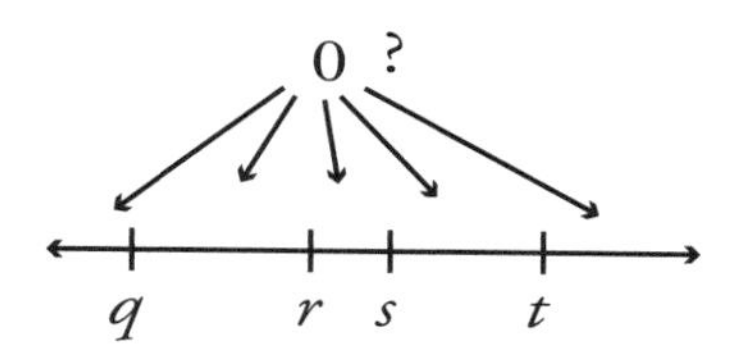

(1): SUFFICIENT. If $q = -s$, then q and s are equally spaced on opposite sides of zero. That is to say, zero is *halfway* between q and s. To prove this, we can ***Test Numbers.*** If $s = 5$, then $q = -5$. If $s = 3$, then $q = -3$, etc. In all cases, 0 is halfway between q and s.

If zero is *halfway* between q and s, r must be closer to zero than either one of them because it is definitely somewhere between q and s. If r is between 0 and s, then it is closer to 0 than s is. But s and q are equidistant from 0, which means that r is also closer to 0 than q. The logic is the same if r is between q and 0. Finally, t is definitely farther from zero than s since t is to the right of s (and thus a larger positive number). Therefore, r is the closest to zero.

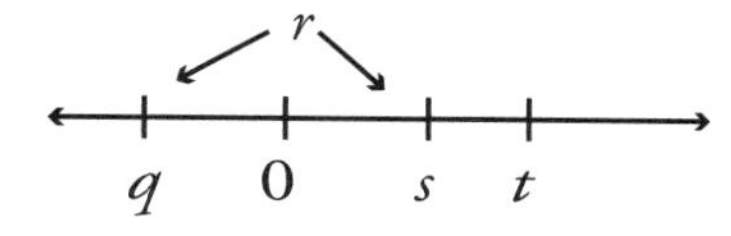

(2): INSUFFICIENT. If $-t < q$, then all we know is that $-t$ is left of q. That means t is farther from zero than q, so zero is to the left of the halfway point between t and q. But this is not enough to tell us whether r is closest to zero.

The correct answer is (A): Statement (1) ALONE is sufficient, but statement (2) alone is not sufficient.

DS 70. <u>Word Problems</u>: Statistics
Difficulty: Medium **OG Page:** 281

We know that a test was given to a group of men and women and that the average score of the group was 80. The question asks if the average score of the women was greater than 85.

In order to rephrase this question, we have to think about what we would need to know to answer it. The overall average of the men and women together must be between the average of the men and the average of the women. If there are more women than men, the overall average will be closer to the women's average than to the men's average, and vice versa.

So, if we knew whether there were more women or more men, and we knew what the average of either the women or the men was, we would know whether the overall average of 80 was closer to the men's average or to the women's average.

(1): INSUFFICIENT. Let's look at some simple scenarios. Suppose there were only 1 man and 1 woman in the group. If the man has a score of 74, then the woman must have a score of 86 for the average to be 80.

Now suppose there is still 1 man but now there are 2 women in the group. If the man has a score of 74, the women must have an average score of 83 for the total average to be 80.

This information isn't enough by itself to tell whether the women's average score is above 85.

(2): INSUFFICIENT. This statement does tell us that there are more men than women, so we know that the overall average of 80 is closer to the men's average than to the women's average.

However, this statement tells us nothing about the men's average, so we can't infer anything about the women's average from it and cannot answer the question.

(1) AND (2): SUFFICIENT. If we know that the number of men is greater than the number of women, we know that 80, the overall average, is closer to the men's average than it is to the women's average. Another way of phrasing this is to say that 80 must be farther away from the women's average than it is from the men's average.

Suppose the men's average is 74. Even though we don't know the women's average, we do know that it must be farther away from 80 than 74 is. 74 is 6 less than 80. That means that the women's average must be at least 6 greater than 80. So the women's average must be greater than 86.

No matter what the women's average turns out to be, it must be greater than 85.

The correct answer is (C): BOTH statements (1) and (2) TOGETHER are sufficient to answer the question asked, but NEITHER statement ALONE is sufficient.

DS 71. Word Problems: Algebraic Translations
Difficulty: Hard **OG Page:** 281

In this ***Algebraic Translations*** problem, we know that n people each donated \$500, for a total of \$500n. Each of these n people, in turn, convinced n more people to donate \$500. Thus, the number of people donating in the second round will be n times n, or n^2, for a total of \$500n^2 raised in the second round. The total amount raised will therefore be equal to \$500n + \$500n^2. This expression is a variation of the ***Cost Relationship.***

We can answer this question if we are given the total amount raised (***Rephrasing*** the question), or if we can create an equation to solve for the value of n directly.

(1): SUFFICIENT. ***Translate*** the statement:

$$500n = \frac{1}{16}(500n + 500n^2)$$
$$500n = \frac{1}{16}(500)(n + n^2)$$
$$n = \frac{1}{16}(n + n^2)$$
$$16n = n + n^2$$
$$15n = n^2$$
$$n^2 - 15n = 0$$
$$n(n - 15) = 0$$
$$n = 0, 15$$

There are two solutions. However, 0 is invalid: there is an implicit constraint that n is positive. (Mary must have found at least *some* people to donate or else there could not have been a second round of fundraising.) Thus, $n = 15$.

(2): SUFFICIENT. If given the total raised, we can create and solve the following equation:

$$\$500n + \$500n^2 = \$120,000$$
$$\$500(n + n^2) = \$120,000$$
$$(n + n^2) = 240$$
$$n + n^2 = 240$$
$$n^2 + n - 240 = 0$$

We can stop at this point. This is a ***Quadratic Equation*** that will result in one positive and one negative solution for n. However, given the implicit constraint that n must be positive (Mary could not have encouraged a negative number of people to donate), there is only one valid solution.

Of course, we can finish the computation as well:

$$(n + 16)(n - 15) = 0$$
$$n = 15, -16$$

Only the positive solution is valid. Thus, $n = 15$.

The correct answer is (D): EACH statement ALONE is sufficient.

DS 72. Number Properties: Odds & Evens
Difficulty: Hard **OG Page:** 281

If m is an integer, is m odd? The question is obviously about ***Odds & Evens,*** but no rephrasing is needed.

(1): INSUFFICIENT. We are told that $m/2$ is NOT an even integer. This does NOT mean that $m/2$ is an odd integer! Rather, it may be that $m/2$ is not an integer at all.

Let's set up a quick ***Table*** to ***Test Scenarios.***

m	$m/2$ = not even	m = odd int?
1	1/2	No
2	1	Yes

Since both examples conform to the condition "$m/2$ is NOT an even integer" yet give different answers to the question, the statement is not sufficient.

(2): SUFFICIENT. Apply ***Properties of Odds & Evens.*** If $m - 3$ is an even integer, then m – Odd = Even. That means that m = Even + Odd, which is *always* Odd.

The correct answer is (B): Statement (2) ALONE is sufficient, but statement (1) alone is not sufficient.

DS 73. Geometry: Triangles & Diagonals
Difficulty: Medium **OG Page:** 281

The ***Area of a Triangle*** can be found with the following formula:

$$\text{Area} = \frac{1}{2}(\text{base})(\text{height})$$
$$\text{Area} = \frac{1}{2}(AC)(BD)$$

Thus, we can ***Rephrase*** the question as "What is the product $(AC)(BD)$?" We need either the lengths of the two segments or their product.

(1): SUFFICIENT. This statement tells us that $(BD)(AC) = 20$, directly answering the rephrased question.

(2): INSUFFICIENT. Knowing the measure of x without any lengths does not help us find either AC or BD.

The correct answer is (A): Statement (1) ALONE is sufficient, but statement (2) alone is not sufficient.

DS 74. Geometry: Coordinate Planes
Difficulty: Hard **OG Page:** 281

The question asks whether point R is equidistant from points $(-3, -3)$ and $(1, -3)$. A picture is helpful for most geometry problems. Note that the two lines on the plane correspond to the two statements:

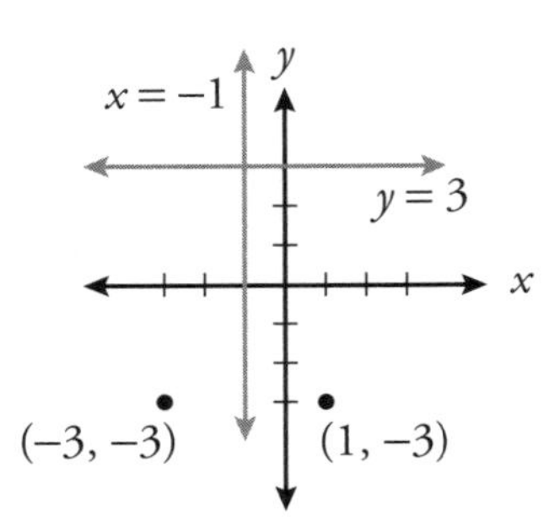

(1): SUFFICIENT. If the x-coordinate of point R = −1, R is somewhere on the vertical line with the equation $x = -1$. Since the midpoint between the x-coordinates of the two points is −1, that line is the same distance from (−3, −3) and (1, −3), so any point on it is as well.

(2): INSUFFICIENT. If point R is on the horizontal line $y = 3$, then it could be the point (1, 3), which is directly above (1, −3) and so closer to (1, −3) than to (−3, −3) or it could be the point (−1, 3), which is on the line $x = -1$ and so the same distance from both (−3, −3) and (1, −3).

The correct answer is (A): Statement (1) ALONE is sufficient, but statement (2) alone is not sufficient to answer the question asked.

DS 75. <u>FDPs</u>: Digits & Decimals
Difficulty: Hard **OG Page:** 281

The question asks whether N is less than 40.

(1): SUFFICIENT. If N is a positive two-digit integer, the first digit has to be at least 1 and the second digit can't be more than 9, so we can list out all of the possibilities. They are 17, 28, and 39. All of them are less than 40.

(2): SUFFICIENT. The largest that the units digit of N could be is 9. 4 less than 4 times 9 is 36 − 4 = 32. If the maximum possible value of N is 32, then N is definitely less than 40.

The correct answer is (D): EACH statement ALONE is sufficient to answer the question asked.

DS 76. <u>FDPs</u>: Percents
Difficulty: Hard **OG Page:** 281

We can rewrite the opening sentence in this ***Percents*** problem using ***Algebraic Translations.***

The salesman is paid a fixed sum of $300, plus 5% of all sales *over* $1,000. If we ***Name Variables*** and designate the salesman's total sales for the week as x, then the amount on which the commission is paid is given by $x - 1{,}000$ (which is the amount of sales *over* 1,000). This is a typical ***Cost Relationship.*** We therefore have:

$$300 + 0.05(x - 1{,}000) = ?$$

If we can determine the amount of sales made by the salesman last week, we can answer the question.

We can therefore ***Rephrase*** the question as "What is x?"

(1): SUFFICIENT. This statement declares that the salesman's total pay, represented by $300 + 0.05(x - 1{,}000)$, equals 10 percent of the total sales. Since x represents the total sales, we can write an equation:

$$300 + 0.05(x - 1{,}000) = 0.10x$$

This ***Linear Equation*** has one unknown. We can definitely solve for a unique value of x.

(2): SUFFICIENT. This statement gives us the value of x directly.

The correct answer is (D): EACH statement ALONE is sufficient.

DS 77. <u>Word Problems</u>: Statistics
Difficulty: Devilish **OG Page:** 281

In this ***Statistics*** problem, which also involves ***Simple Interest***, a total of $60,000 was invested. Some of this money was invested at x% simple annual interest, and the rest was invested at y% simple annual interest. By the end of the year, $4,080 was earned in interest overall.

Remember the ***Simple Interest Formula***:

Interest Rate (%) × Original Investment (\$) = Interest Paid (\$)

We can use this formula to calculate the overall interest rate. (It turns out that this quick ***Decimals and Percents*** calculation is not absolutely necessary, but it's a good first step toward understanding the real meaning of this problem. The most important thing to know is that this overall interest rate is a fixed, given number.)

Overall Interest Rate = Interest Paid/Original Investment = \$4,080/\$60,000 = 0.068 = 6.8%

Conceptually, this 6.8% is a ***Weighted Average*** of x% and y%. The number 6.8 will be somewhere between x and y. Where exactly it falls will depend on how much money is invested at each interest rate. For instance, if almost all the \$60,000 is invested at x%, then 6.8 has to be much closer to x than to y. The money invested at each rate is the weight of that investment.

Let's now ***Name a Variable*** and designate P as the amount invested at x% (P stands for "Principal.") Then $60{,}000 - P$ = the amount invested at y%. (At this point, with three variables, let's not name a fourth.)

We can now write a master equation to represent the Total Interest Paid (\$) as the sum of the interest paid on each of the two investments:

$$4{,}080 = \left(\frac{6.8}{100}\right)(60{,}000) = \left(\frac{x}{100}\right)P + \left(\frac{y}{100}\right)(60{,}000 - P)$$

We are asked for the value of x. One viable option is to rearrange this equation to isolate x. However, that would be a lot of work. At this point, we can stop and say that if we know the values of the other variables P and y, we can plug them into the master equation and find x.

(1): INSUFFICIENT. This statement gives us a specific relationship between x and y. In fact, we should notice that x and y have a ***Constant Ratio***, according to this statement. Such relationships can typically take us far on Data Sufficiency.

Rearranging to solve for y, we get $y = 4x/3$, which we can plug into our master equation:

$$4{,}080 = \left(\frac{x}{100}\right)P + \left(\frac{4x/3}{100}\right)(60{,}000 - P)$$

Although we can combine the terms somewhat, there's no way to cancel out the P, so we cannot get a number for x with this information alone. This time, a Constant Ratio was not in fact sufficient by itself.

(2): INSUFFICIENT. ***Translate*** this information into an equation. A ratio can be written as a fraction:

$$\frac{\text{amount at } x\%}{\text{amount at } y\%} = \frac{P}{60{,}000 - P} = \frac{3}{2}$$

We should recognize that we can get a value for P, because we have a ***Linear Equation with One Unknown.***

If necessary, we can actually solve for P. The earlier we can stop, however, the better. Remember that on Data Sufficiency problems, we do not need to report the specific numbers we find. We just need to know *when* we can find those numbers.

Here is the algebra to solve for P. The first step is to ***Cross-Multiply*** the equation above.

$$2P = 3(60{,}000 - P)$$
$$2P = 180{,}000 - 3P$$
$$5P = 180{,}000$$
$$P = 36{,}000$$

Since $60{,}000 - P = 60{,}000 - 36{,}000 = 24{,}000$, our master equation now looks like this:

$$4{,}080 = \left(\frac{x}{100}\right)(36{,}000) + \left(\frac{y}{100}\right)(24{,}000)$$

However, without knowing y, we cannot solve for x. This statement by itself is not enough.

(1) AND (2): SUFFICIENT. Statement (1) gives us y as a constant (4/3) times x, and statement (2) gives us the value of P. Together, they provide enough information to solve for x, so we can stop here.

If necessary, we can substitute information from both statements into our master equation and solve to confirm. Again, we should stop as soon as we are confident that we see the rest of the path toward a particular value for x.

$$4{,}080 = \left(\frac{x}{100}\right)(36{,}000) + \left(\frac{4x/3}{100}\right)(24{,}000)$$

This equation may seem complex, but it is actually just a linear equation in x. For this reason, we can solve for a unique value of x. It matters now that x and y are related by a Constant Ratio. For instance, if y were instead equal to x^2, we would now have a quadratic equation, which would not necessarily have just one solution.

Here's the algebra to find x:

$$4{,}080 = 360x + \left(\frac{4x}{100}\right)(8{,}000)$$
$$4{,}080 = 360x + 4x(80)$$
$$4{,}080 = 360x + 320x$$
$$4{,}080 = 680x$$
$$6 = x$$

The correct answer is (C): BOTH statements TOGETHER are sufficient, but NEITHER statement ALONE is sufficient.

DS 78. Word Problems: Algebraic Translations
Difficulty: Medium **OG Page:** 281

In this ***Algebraic Translations*** problem, we have a typical ***Cost Relationship*** involving prices and quantities of two baked goods.

Name Variables, letting d be the price of a doughnut and b be the price of a bagel. The ***Rephrased*** question is asking for a ***Combined Expression,*** or a Combo:

What is $5d + 3b$?

As in other Combo problems, finding the values of the individual variables (in this case b and d) is unnecessary.

(1): SUFFICIENT. This statement specifies the value of $10d + 6b$, which is exactly twice the desired combo. Therefore, dividing the given price in half will yield the price for the desired Combo: $5d + 3b = (12.90/2) = 6.45$.

(2): INSUFFICIENT. This statement tells us that $d = b - 0.15$. However, we have no information about the actual prices of either bagels or doughnuts and are thus unable to come up with a total cost. The statement gives us the value of $b - d$, but we cannot get the desired Combo.

The correct answer is (A): Statement (1) ALONE is sufficient, but statement (2) alone is not sufficient.

DS 79. Geometry: Triangles & Diagonals
Difficulty: Devilish **OG Page:** 282

The question asks whether the area of Triangle ABC is equal to the area of Triangle DBA.

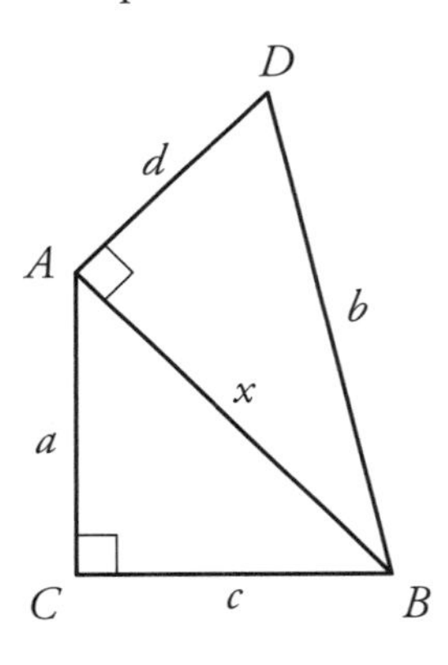

Introducing variables for the lengths of the sides makes it easier to rephrase this question. Since both triangles are right triangles, the area of Triangle ABC is $\frac{ac}{2}$ and the area of Triangle DBA is $\frac{dx}{2}$. This question can be rephrased as "Is $ac = dx$?"

(1): INSUFFICIENT. ***Translate*** using the variables we introduced:

$a^2 = 2d^2$

Since triangle side lengths have to be positive, we can square root both sides:

$$a = d\sqrt{2}$$

This is not enough because we don't know anything about the values of c and x.

(2): INSUFFICIENT. Translate using the variables we introduced:

$$a = c$$

This means that Triangle ABC must be a 45–45–90 right triangle, so we also know that $x = c\sqrt{2}$.

This is also not enough because we don't know anything about the value of d.

(1) AND (2): SUFFICIENT. If we know that both statements are true, we can solve for dx in terms of ac by substitution. From the first statement, we know that $a = d\sqrt{2}$, and from the second statement, we know that $x = c\sqrt{2}$. Start by replacing a with $d\sqrt{2}$:

$$ac = \left(d\sqrt{2}\right)c$$

Then we can rewrite the equation relating x and c in terms of c:

$$x = c\sqrt{2} \rightarrow \frac{x}{\sqrt{2}} = c$$

Replace c with $\frac{x}{\sqrt{2}}$:

$$ac = \left(d\sqrt{2}\right)\left(\frac{x}{\sqrt{2}}\right)$$

$$ac = dx$$

The correct answer is (C): BOTH statements (1) and (2) TOGETHER are sufficient to answer the question asked, but NEITHER statement ALONE is sufficient.

DS 80. FDPs: Digits & Decimals
Difficulty: Hard **OG Pages:** 282

The question asks whether r/s can be expressed as a ***Terminating Decimal***. Although there isn't an obvious rephrase here, think about whether knowing r or $1/s$ alone is enough information.

If $1/s$ is a terminating decimal, then $r \times 1/s$ must be a terminating decimal because r is an integer. If we don't know whether $1/s$ is a terminating decimal, then we need to know something about both s and r to figure this out.

(1): SUFFICIENT. Since $100 = 2^2 5^2$, it has $3 \times 3 = 9$ factors. A reasonable approach to this problem is to list these factors systematically in a table and look at all 9 possible values of $1/s$ to see if they are terminating.

s (factor of 100)	$1/s$	terminating?
$2^0 5^0 = 1$	1	Y
$2^1 5^0 = 2$	0.5	Y
$2^2 5^0 = 4$	0.25	Y
$2^0 5^1 = 5$	0.2	Y
$2^1 5^1 = 10$	0.1	Y
$2^2 5^1 = 20$	0.05	Y
$2^0 5^2 = 25$	0.04	Y
$2^1 5^2 = 50$	0.02	Y
$2^2 5^2 = 100$	0.01	Y

Since all of the possible values of $1/s$ are terminating, the answer to the question is always yes.

An even more clever way to see that this is sufficient is to realize that all of the factors of 100 are powers of 2, powers of 5, or multiplicative combinations of powers of 2 and 5. Since $1/2 = 0.5$ and $1/5 = 0.2$, both terminating decimals, $1/s$ is either 1 or a product of terminating decimals, so it must also be a terminating decimal.

(2): INSUFFICIENT. Since we already created a table of the factors of 100, a good strategy here is just to look at a few of those factors and try to come up with possible values of s that will let us prove insufficiency.

If $r = 1$ and $s = 1$, the answer to the question is yes.

However, if $r = 1$ and $s = 3$, the answer is no.

The correct answer is (A): Statement (1) ALONE is sufficient, but statement (2) alone is not sufficient to answer the question asked.

DS 81. FDPs: Ratios
Difficulty: Hard **OG Page:** 282

The question tells us that the ***Ratio*** of the number of students to the number of teachers in school districts M and P is the same, but notably does not give any actual quantities. It then asks for the ratio of the number of students in district M to the number in district P.

(1): INSUFFICIENT. We can't get a value for the number of students in either district because all we know is that the number of students in M is 10,000 more than the number of students in P, which tells us nothing about the ratio.

This can be seen by ***Testing Numbers*** and trying to prove insufficiency. District M could have 10,000 students and district P could have 20,000 students, for a ratio of 1:2. Or district M could have 20,000 students and district P could have 30,000 students, for a ratio of 2:3.

(2): INSUFFICIENT. We can't get a ratio for the number of students in district M to the number in district P because all we know is that the ratio of teachers to students is 1:20 in both districts.

This can also seen by testing numbers and trying to prove insufficiency. District M could have 5 teachers and 100 students and district P could have 50 teachers and 1,000 students, for a ratio of 1:10. But district P could also have 100 teachers and 2,000 students, for a ratio of 1:20.

(1) AND (2): INSUFFICIENT. Knowing the ratio of students to teachers doesn't actually restrict the information in statement (1). Both examples mentioned in (1) are still possible, meaning we can't determine the ratio of students in district M to the students in district P.

The correct answer is (E): Statements (1) and (2) TOGETHER are NOT sufficient to answer the question asked, and additional data are needed.

DS 82. Algebra: Inequalities
Difficulty: Medium **OG Page:** 282

Because we are told that r and s are both positive, we can ***Cross-Multiply*** the given ***Inequality*** without flipping the sign:

Is $r/s > s/r$?
Is $r^2 > s^2$?

Furthermore, because we know that r and s are both positive, we can take the square root of both sides without altering the meaning of the inequality. Thus, our ***Rephrased*** question is really:

Is $r > s$?

(1): SUFFICIENT. Begin by cross-multiplying:

$$\frac{r}{3s} = \frac{1}{4}$$
$$4r = 3s$$

Next, simplify for r:

$$r = \frac{3s}{4}$$

Because r is a fraction of s and both are positive, r must be less than s.

(2): SUFFICIENT. s is 4 greater than r. Thus, $s > r$.

The correct answer is (D): EACH statement ALONE is sufficient.

DS 83. Number Properties: Divisibility & Primes
Difficulty: Hard **OG Page:** 282

This ***Remainders*** question tells us that k is one of the numbers 57, 58, 59, 60, 61, 62, 63, 64, or 65 and asks for the value of k.

(1): INSUFFICIENT. This statement can be rephrased as "k is not a multiple of 2" because all multiples of 2, otherwise known as even numbers, have a remainder of 0 when divided by 2. Since any integer that is not an even number is an odd number, the simplest possible rephrase of this statement is "k is an odd number".

We can prove insufficiency by looking at the possible values of k and seeing that there are several odd numbers on the list, so this is not enough to determine a single value for k.

(2): INSUFFICIENT. Since only multiples of 3 have a remainder of 0 when divided by 3, this statement can be rephrased as "$k + 1$ is a multiple of 3".

We can prove insufficiency by looking at the possible values of k and seeing that $59 + 1 = 60$ and $62 + 1 = 63$ are both multiple of 3, so this statement allows more than one possible value for k.

(1) AND (2): INSUFFICIENT. In order to combine both statements, we can make a table of the odd numbers in the range and determine whether $k + 1$ is divisible by 3 for more than one of them.

Possible odd k	$k + 1$	Is $k + 1$ divisible by 3?
57	58	N
59	60	Y
61	62	N
63	64	N
65	66	Y

If both statements are true, k could be either 59 or 65, so we do not have enough information to determine the value of k.

The correct answer is (E): Statements (1) and (2) TOGETHER are NOT sufficient to answer the question asked, and additional data are needed.

DS 84. Word Problems: Statistics
Difficulty: Medium **OG Page:** 282

In this ***Statistics*** problem, we are given the set $\{k, n, 12, 6, 17\}$ and asked for the value of n. There is no useful way to rephrase this question, so we must proceed directly to the statements.

(1): INSUFFICIENT. Knowing that n is greater than k does not tell us the value of n.

(2): INSUFFICIENT. Knowing that the ***Median*** is 10 tells us that either n or k must equal 10. This is true because in a set containing an odd number of terms, as we have here, the median will always be one of the terms of the set. Since none of the given values is 10, either k or n must be 10. But since we cannot tell whether n is the median from this information, this statement is insufficient.

(1) AND (2): SUFFICIENT. In a set with an odd number of terms, the median will be the term exactly in the middle. If k is less than n, we know that the elements of the set, written in numeric order, would look either like this:

$\{6, k, n, 12, 17\}$ or like this:

$\{k, 6, n, 12, 17\}$

There is remaining uncertainty about whether k is smaller than or greater than 6, but that is of no consequence for the question at hand. n is in the middle regardless, so n is the median and $n = 10$.

The correct answer is (C): BOTH statements TOGETHER are sufficient, but NEITHER statement ALONE is sufficient.

DS 85. Algebra: Inequalities
Difficulty: Easy **OG Page:** 282

This ***Inequalities*** question asks for the value of $x + y$.

(1): SUFFICIENT. This inequality already contains $x + y$, but in fraction form, so multiply the inequality by 2 to get rid of the fraction:

$$3 < \frac{x+y}{2} < 4$$
$$6 < x + y < 8$$

Since both x and y are integers, the value of $x + y$ must be 7.

(2): SUFFICIENT. Since the only two integers that are greater than 2 but less than 5 are 3 and 4, and $x < y$, we know that x must be 3 and y must be 4, so $x + y = 7$.

The correct answer is (D): EACH statement ALONE is sufficient to answer the question asked.

DS 86. Algebra: Linear Equations
Difficulty: Medium **OG Page:** 282

In this ***Linear Equations*** problem, we are asked for the value of the ***Combined Expression*** $b + c$, also known as a Combo. No rephrasing is needed.

(1): INSUFFICIENT. It is not possible to manipulate $ab + cd + ac + bd = 6$ to get a numeric value for $b + c$.

(2): INSUFFICIENT. This tells us nothing about $b + c$.

(1) AND (2): SUFFICIENT. We will take a ***Direct Algebra*** approach.

Since we do have a value for $a + d$, we can manipulate $ab + cd + ac + bd = 6$ to isolate $a + d$. Begin by re-ordering the terms to make factoring easier:

$$ab + cd + ac + bd = 6$$
$$ab + ac + cd + bd = 6$$
$$a(b + c) + d(c + b) = 6$$

Now ***Factor*** out the common term $(b + c)$:

$$(b + c)(a + d) = 6$$

Plug in statement (2): $a + d = 4$:

$$(b + c)(4) = 6$$

At this point we see that we can solve for $b + c$, which equals 6/4, or 1.5.

Notice that we never find out what b or c is individually. As it turns out, we do not need the values of the separate variables. This is why we do not rephrase a question about a Combo, such as $b + c$, into a question about b and c separately.

The correct answer is (C): both statements TOGETHER are SUFFICIENT.

DS 87. Word Problems: Statistics
Difficulty: Easy **OG Page:** 282

According to the ***Average Formula,*** the average of j and k is:

$$\text{Average} = \frac{\text{Sum of Terms}}{\text{Number of Terms}} = \frac{j+k}{2}$$

If we know the values of j and k, or of the ***Combined Expression*** $j + k$, we will have enough information to answer the question.

(1): SUFFICIENT. This statement allows us to find the sum of the two variables. We can ***Translate*** the statement and use the average formula:

$$\frac{(j+2)+(k+4)}{2} = 11$$

We should be able to tell that we can theoretically solve for the Combo $j + k$.

If necessary, actually do the algebra:

$$j + 2 + k + 4 = 22$$
$$j + k = 16$$

(2): SUFFICIENT. We can translate this statement using the average formula and solve for the sum of $j + k$:

$$\frac{j+k+14}{3} = 10$$

Again, we should be able to tell that we can theoretically solve for the Combo $j + k$.

If necessary, actually do the algebra:

$$j + k + 14 = 30$$
$$j + k = 16$$

Notice that we never find out what j or k is individually. As it turns out, we do not need the values of the separate variables. This is why we do not rephrase a question about a Combo, such as $j + k$, into a question about j and k separately.

The correct answer is (D): EACH statement ALONE is sufficient.

DS 88. <u>FDPs</u>: FDPs
Difficulty: Medium **OG Page:** 282

We are given one equation, $P + S = 100$, and asked to find P. In order to do so, we must know the value of S or a relationship between P and S such that we can solve for P. Notice that we already have one ***Linear Equation***, so if we get another, we will be able to solve for P.

This problem involves both ***Fractions*** and ***Percents*** along the way.

(1): SUFFICIENT. Combine the equation given in this statement, $S = (2/3)P$, with the equation given in the question stem.

We now have ***Two Different Linear Equations*** with ***Two Variables,*** so it is possible to solve for the value of P. We should stop now to save time.

If we really want to do the algebra for practice, here it is:

$$S + P = 100$$
$$\left(\frac{2}{3}P\right) + P = 100$$
$$\frac{5}{3}P = 100$$
$$P = 60$$

(2): INSUFFICIENT. This statement does not provide any information about the number of tickets Sandy sold, because we don't know the total number of tickets sold. We can't figure out how many tickets Paula sold.

Be careful of the problem's wording. We may incorrectly assume that Paula and Sandy were the *only* people who sold tickets, but we are not told this. Moreover, the numbers in the statements do not support that assumption.

The correct answer is (A): Statement (1) ALONE is sufficient, but statement (2) alone is not sufficient.

DS 89. <u>Word Problems</u>: Extra Problem Types
Difficulty: Easy **OG Page:** 282

This is a ***Grouping*** problem that also involves ***Inequalities.*** Each person has 30 integers to choose from. Thus, if there are fewer than 30 people, everyone can choose a different number. But if there are more than 30 people but only 30 integers to choose from, at least two people will have to write down the same number. Some number (or numbers) will have to be repeated.

If we have fewer than 30 people, we cannot guarantee that everyone will write down a different number. But if we have more than 30 people, we can guarantee that they *will not* all write down different numbers.

Therefore, we can usefully ***Rephrase*** the question as "Were there more than 30 people?"

(1): SUFFICIENT. We know that there were more than 40 people. Therefore, there were more than 30 people as well. This answers our rephrased question.

In other words, at least one of the numbers *must* have been written down more than once.

(2): INSUFFICIENT. We do not know whether there were more than 30 people. We are told that there were fewer than 70 people. There could have been 50 people or 10 people.

The correct answer is (A): Statement (1) ALONE is sufficient, but statement (2) alone is not sufficient.

DS 90. <u>Word Problems</u>: Rates & Work
Difficulty: Hard **OG Page:** 283

This rate question tells us very little really. We are asked if $t_1 > t_2$.

Since the statements tell us about the rates and distances, but not about the times, rephrase this question in terms of rates and distances:

$$D = R \times T \rightarrow T = D/R$$

So $t_1 = d_1/r_1$ and $t_2 = d_2/r_2$. We can rephrase the question as "Is $\frac{d_1}{r_1} > \frac{d_2}{r_2}$?"

Alternatively, since all of the numbers must be positive (traveling is not done at negative rates or for negative distances) we can further simplify by cross-multiplying to get rid of the denominators and have a fraction free rephrase:

"Is $\frac{d_1}{r_1} > \frac{d_2}{r_2}$?"

"Is $d_1r_2 > d_2r_1$?"

(1): INSUFFICIENT. We can ***Substitute*** $d_2 + 30$ for d_1 in either version of the prompt question:

$$\text{Is } \frac{d_2+30}{r_1} > \frac{d_2}{r_2}? \text{ or Is } (d_2+30)r_2 > d_2r_1?$$

We can't determine an answer because we don't know anything about the rates.

(2): INSUFFICIENT. We can substitute $r_2 + 30$ for r_1 in either version of the prompt question:

$$\text{Is } \frac{d_1}{r_2+30} > \frac{d_2}{r_2}? \text{ or Is } d_1r_2 > d_2(r_2+30)?$$

We can't determine an answer because we don't know anything about the distances.

(1) AND (2): INSUFFICIENT. This is harder to see intuitively. Algebraically, we can substitute $(r_2 + 30)$ for r_1, and $(d_2 + 30)$ for d_1, in either version of the prompt question and see that we still have more than one unknown and can't cancel them out:

$$\text{Is } \frac{d_2+30}{r_2+30} > \frac{d_2}{r_2}? \text{ or Is } (d_2+30)r_2 > d_2(r_2+30)?$$

However, an easier way to see that we just don't have enough information is to ***Test Numbers***.

If $d_2 = 36$ and $r_2 = 3$, then $d_1 = 66$ and $r_1 = 33$. So $t_1 = 66/33 = 2$ and $t_2 = 36/3 = 12$, which makes $t_1 < t_2$.

But, if $d_2 = 30$ and $r_2 = 30$, then $d_1 = 60$ and $r_1 = 60$. So $t_1 = 60/60 = 1$ and $t_2 = 30/30 = 1$, so $t_1 = t_2$, and we know that there is not enough information to know whether $t_1 > t_2$.

The correct answer is (E): Statements (1) and (2) TOGETHER are NOT sufficient to answer the question asked, and additional data are needed.

DS 91. <u>FDPs</u>: Percents
Difficulty: Medium **OG Page:** 283

In this ***Percents*** problem, we can set up a ***Table*** to keep track of the money Arturo spent last year:

Expense	Amount
Real Estate Taxes	?
Home Insurance	
Mortgage Payments	
Total	\$12,000

We should be on the lookout for statements that give information about home insurance and mortgage payments or about the two as a combined sum. In other words, if we know the ***Combined Expression*** $H + M$, then we can answer the question.

(1): INSUFFICIENT. This statement gives us neither the combined mortgage payments and home insurance expenses, nor these expenses individually.

If the sum of real estate taxes and home insurance equals $33\frac{1}{3}$% of the mortgage payments, then the sum of real estate taxes and home insurance is 1/3 the total mortgage payments. ***Naming a Variable,*** we can let x be the amount spent on real estate taxes and M be the amount spent on mortgage payments. The amount spent on real estate taxes and home insurance has to add up to 1/3 the amount spent on mortgage payments, or $M/3$.

Expense	Amount	
Real Estate Taxes	x	} Sum = $M/3$
Home Insurance	$M/3 - x$	
Mortgage Payments	M	
Total	\$12,000	

We can extract the following equation:

$$x+\left(\frac{M}{3}-x\right)+M=12{,}000$$
$$\frac{4}{3}M=12{,}000$$
$$M=9{,}000$$

This statement gives us M, the mortgage payments, but the real estate taxes could be any value less than or equal to 1/3 of \$9,000, or \$3,000.

(2): SUFFICIENT. This statement relates the combined mortgage payment and home insurance expenses to the real estate taxes. Let y be the total amount spent on home insurance and mortgage payments. In other words, $y = H + M$.

Expense	Amount
Real Estate Taxes	$0.2y$
Home Insurance	y
Mortgage Payments	
Total	\$12,000

$$0.2y+y=12{,}000$$
$$1.2y=12{,}000$$
$$y=\frac{12{,}000}{1.2}$$
$$y=10{,}000$$

Therefore, Arturo paid 0.2(\$10,000) = \$2,000 in real estate taxes.

The correct answer is (B): Statement (2) ALONE is sufficient, but statement (1) alone is not sufficient.

DS 92. FDPs: Fractions
Difficulty: Medium **OG Page:** 283

Although we usually can't cross-multiply variables across an inequality, this question tells us that all of the variables are positive. That means that we can rewrite the question as "Is $ad < bc$?"

(1): INSUFFICIENT. In this statement, we are told that the fraction on the right-hand side of the inequality is positive. It must then be true that the numerator and the denominator are either both positive or both negative. Make note of the two scenarios:

If they are both positive, then $c > a$ and $d > b$
If they are both negative, then $a > c$ and $b > d$

If $c > a$ and $d > b$, we don't know whether $ad < bc$ because it depends on how much greater c is than a versus d is than b. We can prove insufficiency with numbers.

If $c = 4$, $a = 1$, $d = 2$, and $b = 1$, then the answer to the question is NO.

However, if $c = 2$, $a = 1$, $d = 4$, and $b = 1$, the answer is YES.

(2): SUFFICIENT. In this statement, we are told that a number, $\left(\frac{ad}{bc}\right)$ squared is less than the number itself. This is something that is only true of positive fractions. Any positive fraction is greater than 0 and less than 1:

$$0<\left(\frac{ad}{bc}\right)<1$$
$$0<ad<bc$$

ad must be less than bc.

The correct answer is (B): Statement (2) ALONE is sufficient, but statement (1) alone is not sufficient to answer the question asked.

DS 93. Word Problems: Overlapping Sets
Difficulty: Hard **OG Page:** 283

This question asks about the number of members of two clubs, Club X and Club Y. We can consider this an ***Overlapping Sets*** problem, since the question also describes people who are members of both Club X and Club Y.

The stem does not give us much information for the ***Double Set Matrix***. All we can really do is ***Name Variables***. Designate the total number of members in Club X as x and the total number of members in Club Y as y. In these terms, the question asks whether $x > y$.

We cannot ***Rephrase*** any further, but we can observe that ***Inequalities*** are involved.

		Club X?		
		Yes	No	Total
Club Y?	Yes			y
	No			
	Total	x		

(1): INSUFFICIENT. This statement tells us that 20% of the members of Club X are actually members of both Y and X. We can place a $0.2x$ in the "Yes-Yes" cell at the upper left (Yes to both clubs). This does not help us to decide whether $x > y$.

		Club X?		
		Yes	No	Total
Club Y?	Yes	$0.2x$		y
	No			
	Total	x		

(2): INSUFFICIENT. This statement tells us that 30% of the members of Club Y are actually members of both X and Y. We can place a $0.3y$ in the Yes-Yes cell. This does not help us to decide whether $x > y$.

		Club X?		
		Yes	No	Total
Club Y?	Yes	$0.3y$		y
	No			
	Total	x		

(1) AND (2): SUFFICIENT. Both statements gave us an expression for the Yes-Yes cell. This is the key step: we can set these two expressions equal to each other and solve for x in terms of y:

$$0.2x = 0.3y$$
$$2x = 3y$$
$$x = 1.5y$$

Since x is 1.5 times the value of y, x is in fact greater than y. Even though we do not know the value of either x or y, we know that x is greater than y. This is true because y is definitely positive: it represents a number of people. Any positive number multiplied by 1.5 becomes larger.

The correct answer is (C): BOTH statements TOGETHER are sufficient, but NEITHER statement ALONE is sufficient.

DS 94. FDPs: Percents
Difficulty: Medium **OG Page:** 283

In this ***Percents*** problem, we are told that 30% of the employees at a certain office who are over 40 years old have master's degrees. We are asked for the actual *number* of employees over 40 who have master's degrees. In order to answer this question, we need to determine the number of employees at the office who are over 40.

Since the problem involves ***Overlapping Sets***, we can visualize the given data in the form of a ***Double Set Matrix***, as shown below, with the desired number shaded. ***Name a Variable*** x to indicate the total number of people at the office:

		Over 40?		
		Yes	No	Total
College?	Yes			$0.5x$
	No			$0.5x$
	Total	$0.6x$	$0.4x$	x

If we can determine how many people are in the office, we can find out how many people in the office are over 40. Once we know how many people are over 40, we can figure out how many of them have master's degrees.

A good ***Rephrasing*** of the question is simply "What is x?"

(1): SUFFICIENT. This statement tells us that $0.5x = 100$. From this, we can solve for x and for $0.6x$. Remember that we do not actually need to find that value.

(2): INSUFFICIENT. This statement does not give us any hard numbers. Instead, it only specifies a percent, making it impossible to solve for x.

The correct answer is (A): Statement (1) ALONE is sufficient, but statement (2) alone is not sufficient.

DS 95. Word Problems: Statistics
Difficulty: Medium **OG Page:** 283

In this ***Statistics*** problem, we are told that p, q, r, s, and t are five consecutive even integers in increasing order. Notice that the number line is beside the point. The question asks for the ***Average*** of the five integers.

In any ***Evenly Spaced Set*** (such as a list of consecutive integers, consecutive even integers, etc.), the average is simply the middle number (or the average of the two middle numbers if there is an even number of terms). Thus, the average of this list is equal to the value of r. We can ***Rephrase*** this question as "What is the value of r?"

Since p, q, r, s, and t are evenly spaced and in increasing order, knowing any one of them would allow us to find r. For example, we know that r is 4 greater than p. So if we knew the value of p, we would know the value of r.

Therefore, we can rephrase even further: "What is the value of any of the variables?"

(1): SUFFICIENT. If $q + s = 24$, the average of q and s is 12. Since the list is evenly spaced, and q and s are equidistant from the average, we know that r simply equals 12.

Alternatively, we can use ***Substitution***. Note that q equals $r - 2$ (because q is the next lower even number) and s equals $r + 2$ (because s is the next higher even number).

Therefore, $q + s = 24$ can be rewritten as follows:

$$(r - 2) + (r + 2) = 24$$
$$2r = 24$$
$$r = 12$$

(2): SUFFICIENT. If the average of q and r is 11, then q and r sum to 22. Since r is 2 more than q, we know that q and r are simply 10 and 12, respectively. To verify, we can substitute $(r - 2)$ for q and solve:

$$\frac{(r-2)+r}{2} = 11$$
$$2r - 2 = 22$$
$$2r = 24$$
$$r = 12$$

The correct answer is (D): each statement ALONE is sufficient.

DS 96. Algebra: Formulas
Difficulty: Devilish **OG Page:** 283

The question defines an odd looking function in order to ask whether 0 is the smallest integer that is greater than or equal to x. For this to be true, x would have to be less than or equal to 0, but greater than -1.

The question can be rephrased as "Is $-1 < x \leq 0$?"

(1): INSUFFICIENT. If $x = -0.5$, then the smallest integer that is greater than x is 0.

However, if $x = 0.5$, then the smallest integer that is greater than x is 1.

(2): INSUFFICIENT. There is no way to solve for an exact x here, so a good approach is to try to prove insufficiency by ***Testing Numbers***.

We already know that if $x = -0.5$, then the smallest integer that is greater than x is 0.

However, if $x = -3.5$, then the smallest integer that is greater than x is -3.

(1) AND (2): SUFFICIENT. Statement (2) tells us that x is a negative number. Combined with statement (1), the two together tell us that $-1 < x < 0$. The smallest integer that is greater than every number in that range is 0.

The correct answer is (C): BOTH statements (1) and (2) TOGETHER are sufficient to answer the question asked, but NEITHER statement ALONE is sufficient.

DS 97. **Number Properties:** Positives & Negatives
Difficulty: Devilish **OG Page:** 283

The questions asks if $x > y$.

(1): INSUFFICIENT. There is no information here about the relative values of x and y. They could be equal, y could be greater than x, or x could be greater than y and this could still be true.

(2): INSUFFICIENT. In order for y^x to be a negative number, y must be a negative integer and x must be an odd integer. This isn't sufficient because x could be a negative odd integer, which doesn't have to be greater than y.

We can prove this by ***Testing Numbers***.

x	y	$y^x < 0$	Is $x > y$?
−1	−1	$(-1)^{-1} = -1$	N
−1	−3	$(-3)^{-1} = -1/3$	Y

(1) AND (2): SUFFICIENT. Statement (2) tells us that y is a negative number. Look at the inequality in Statement (1). If $x + y > 0$, and y is negative, then x must be positive.

Alternatively, rewrite the equation by moving y over:

$$x + y > 0$$
$$x > -y$$

If y is negative, then $-y$ is positive. x must be greater than a positive number, so x must be positive. Either way, we know that y is negative and x is positive, so $x > y$.

The correct answer is (C): BOTH statements (1) and (2) TOGETHER are sufficient to answer the question asked, but NEITHER statement ALONE is sufficient.

DS 98. **Algebra:** Linear Equations
Difficulty: Hard **OG Page:** 283

There is no rephrasing to be done for this ***Linear Equations*** question, which asks whether the product rst equals 1.

(1): INSUFFICIENT. If $rs = 1$, t could be any number. We can ***Test Numbers*** to confirm. If t is also 1, then we have a *Yes* answer. If t is 42, then we have a *No* answer. Thus, the statement is insufficient.

(2): INSUFFICIENT. If $st = 1$, then r could be anything, just as in statement (1).

(1) AND (2): INSUFFICIENT. We can combine the equations, trying to put rst on one side of the resulting equation.

$$(rs)(st) = (1)(1)$$
$$rs^2t = 1$$
$$rst = 1/s$$

We cannot isolate rst on one side of the equation and have a number by itself on the other side. Therefore, we cannot find a specific value for rst, and we cannot confirm or deny that $rst = 1$.

Alternatively, we can prove this point with real numbers. If $r = s = t = 1$, then $rs = 1$, $st = 1$, and $rst = 1$. We have a *Yes* answer to our question.

On the other hand, if $r = t = 42$ and $s = 1/42$, then $rs = 1$, $st = 1$, but $rst = 42$. We have a *No* answer. Thus, the statements are insufficient.

The correct answer is (E): Statements (1) and (2) TOGETHER are not sufficient.

DS 99. **Algebra:** Quadratic Equations
Difficulty: Devilish **OG Page:** 283

The roots of a ***Quadratic Equation*** are the solutions to that equation, so this question tells us that:

$$(x - r)(x - s) = x^2 + bx + c = 0$$

We are asked if $rs < 0$.

It is helpful to multiply out $(x - r)(x - s)$ to see what we know about the constants b and c, since the statements tell us about them:

$$(x - r)(x - s) = x^2 - rx - sx + \underline{rs}$$
$$= x^2 + (-r - s)x + \underline{rs}$$

So we know that:

$b = -r - s = -(r + s)$
$c = rs$

(1): INSUFFICIENT. If b is negative, we know that $-(r + s)$ is negative, so $r + s$ must be positive. We can prove this statement insufficient by ***Testing Numbers***.

If $r = 1$ and $s = 2$, the statement will be true and the answer to the question will be NO. However, if $r = -1$ and $s = 2$, the answer to the question will be YES.

(2): SUFFICIENT. If c is negative, we know that either r is negative and s is positive or vice versa. Either way, rs would have to be less than 0.

The correct answer is (B): Statement (2) ALONE is sufficient, but statement (1) alone is not sufficient to answer the question asked.

DS 100. Geometry: Circles & Cylinders
Difficulty: Easy **OG Page:** 283

In a ***Pie Chart*** representing total expenses, the number of degrees in each ***Sector*** is proportional to the expenses for the corresponding division. For example, if a sector occupies 90 degrees of the circle, then the corresponding division accounts for 90/360 = 1/4 of the total expenses.

We know that the total expenses for Company H are $5,400,000. Thus, to determine the expenses for Division R, we only need to know the value of x, the number of degrees in the Division R sector.

The ***Rephrased*** question is therefore "What is x?"

(1): SUFFICIENT. We are given the value of x.

(2): INSUFFICIENT. We can conclude that the sectors corresponding to Divisions S and T take up twice as much of the circle as Division R, but we do not have enough information to solve for x.

The correct answer is (A): Statement (1) ALONE is sufficient, but statement (2) alone is not sufficient.

DS 101. Algebra: Inequalities
Difficulty: Devilish **OG Page:** 284

The important constraint here is that we are told that x is a negative number.

(1): SUFFICIENT. Remember that x^2 hides the sign of the base. Therefore there are positive and negative solutions to this inequality. If $x^2 > 9$, then $x > 3$ *or* $x < -3$. Since we are told that x is negative, we know that $x < -3$.

(2): INSUFFICIENT. The tricky part about this statement is that the cube root of -9 is not an integer, so we can't easily calculate the upper bound of x. However, we know that the upper bound of x must be between -2 and -3 because $(-2)^3 = -8$ and $(-3)^3 = -27$.

This means that there are values greater than -3 that make the equation true. But it's also true that x can be less than -3. For instance $(-5)^3 = -125$, which is less than -9. Therefore the statement is insufficient.

The correct answer is (A): Statement (1) ALONE is sufficient, but statement (2) alone is not sufficient to answer the question asked.

DS 102. Geometry: Circles & Cylinders
Difficulty: Medium **OG Page:** 284

The problems asks for the number of cans that can be packed in a certain carton, but tells us nothing about the dimensions of either the carton or the cans.

(1): INSUFFICIENT. This statement tells us the volume of the carton, but nothing about the size of the cans.

(2): INSUFFICIENT. This statement tells us the size of the cans, but nothing about the size of the carton.

(1) AND (2): INSUFFICIENT. Although we know the volume of the carton is 2,304 cubic inches, we do not know its length, width, or height. We can prove insufficiency just by ***Testing Scenarios*** either in words, or by drawing pictures.

The carton could resemble a large pizza box say, and be only one inch tall, although very big in terms of length and width. In that case, 0 cans would fit in it.

Alternatively, the carton could be 6 inches high, by 4 inches wide, and then $2{,}304/(6 \times 4)$ inches long, which means that more than one can 6 inches high and 4 inches in diameter would fit in it.

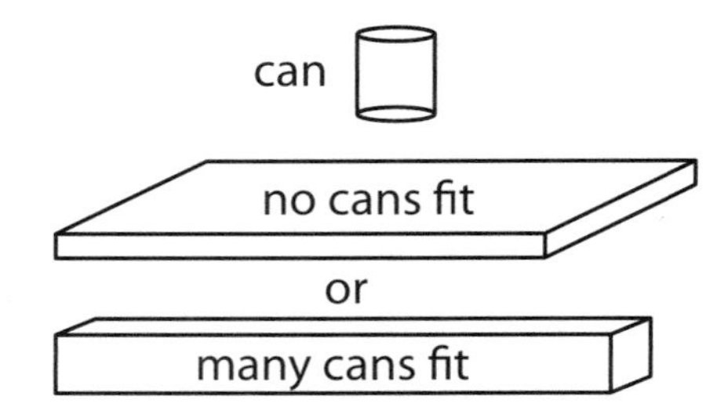

The correct answer is (E): Statements (1) and (2) TOGETHER are NOT sufficient to answer the question asked, and additional data are needed.

DS 103. <u>Word Problems</u>: Extra Problem Types
Difficulty: Hard **OG Page:** 284

r	s	t
u	v	w
x	y	z

This is Sudoku!

The key to this question is carefully following the rules set out in the question about the values of the 9 letters. Each of the 9 letters has a value of 1, 2 or 3, and neither a column nor a row can have more than one instance of a 1, 2 or 3.

This means that each digit must occur exactly once in each column and each row. This also means that there will be a total of three 1's, three 2's and three 3's.

The question asks us for the value of r, the letter in the top left cell.

(1): SUFFICIENT. If $v + z = 6$ both v and z must equal 3, since 3 + 3 is the only way to achieve 6 if only 1's, 2's and 3's can be used. If v and z are 3, then we know the other numbers sharing either a row or a column with v or z cannot be 3. We should record our thinking by crossing out rows and columns in the ***Table*** we've drawn.

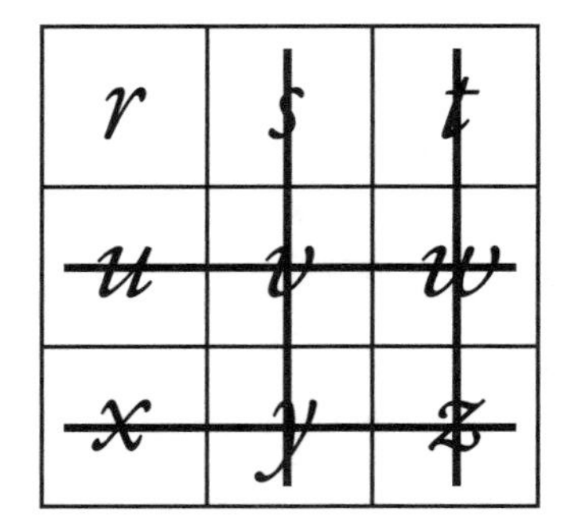

We know there must be a third 3 somewhere in the grid. The only remaining possibility is r, so $r = 3$.

(2): SUFFICIENT. We know that $s + t + u + x = 6$. Using only 1's, 2's and 3's, there are only two ways for four integers to sum to 6:

$1 + 1 + 1 + 3 = 6$
$1 + 1 + 2 + 2 = 6$

However, since u and x are in the same column they cannot have the same value, and since s and t are in the same row, they too cannot have the same value. The first scenario is not a possibility (three 1's would require either u and x or s and t to have the same value). Furthermore, s and t must be 1 and 2 (not necessarily in that order), and the same is true of u and x.

Therefore, we know that r, which is in the same row as s and t (and in the same column as u and x) must be 3.

Again, we should ***Test Scenarios*** by putting them on paper in our table.

3	1 2	2 1
1 2		
2 1		

The correct answer is (D): EACH statement ALONE is sufficient.

DS 104. FDPs: Digits & Decimals
Difficulty: Easy **OG Page:** 284

This ***Decimals*** problem defines a ***Strange Symbol Formula*** for us: $[x]$ is the greatest integer less than or equal to x. For $[x]$ to be 0, x must be greater than or equal to 0 but less than the integer 1.

Thus, our ***Rephrased*** question becomes this:

Is $0 \le x < 1$?

Notice that our rephrased question involves a ***Compound Inequality***.

(1): SUFFICIENT. Here we are given a ***Linear Equation*** for x. We do not actually need to solve it. We already know that we will be *able* to solve for x, from which we can determine the value of $[x]$. Thus we would be able to answer the question definitively.

If we do decide to solve for x, we get:

$$5x + 1 = 3 + 2x$$
$$5x = 2 + 2x$$
$$3x = 2$$
$$x = 2/3$$

Because x is between 0 and 1, the greatest integer less than x will be 0.

(2): SUFFICIENT. The range given falls completely within the range in our rephrased question. If we choose to consider the original question, we can see that because x is between 0 and 1, the greatest integer less than x will be 0.

The correct answer is (D): EACH statement ALONE is sufficient.

DS 105. Word Problems: Statistics
Difficulty: Devilish **OG Page:** 284

We are told in this ***Statistics*** problem that Material A costs \$3 per kilogram and Material B costs \$5 per kilogram. We are also told that 10 kilograms of Material K is composed of x kilograms of Material A and y kilograms of Material B. We are then asked whether $x > y$.

Since $x + y = 10$, we know that $y = 10 - x$. We can ***Rephrase*** the question:

Is $x > 10 - x$?
Is $2x > 10$?
Is $x > 5$?

At this point, we may recognize that the ***Cost Relationship*** will become important, but we do not have enough information about it yet.

(1): INSUFFICIENT. If y is greater than 4, it could equal 5, in which case $x = y$, since $x + y = 10$ from the question stem. Or y could equal 6, in which case x would equal 4 and $y > x$. Or it could even equal 4.1, in which case x would equal 5.9 and $y < x$. Since we cannot tell which of these scenarios we have, we cannot answer the question.

(2): SUFFICIENT. We know from the question stem that $x + y = 10$. Thus, $x = 10 - y$. We also know from this statement that the total cost is less than \$40. ***Translating*** the cost relationship, we can write $3x + 5y < 40$.

Now we can ***Substitute*** and simplify:

$$3x + 5y < 40$$
$$3(10 - y) + 5y < 40$$
$$30 - 3y + 5y < 40$$
$$-3y + 5y < 10$$
$$2y < 10$$
$$y < 5$$

If $y < 5$, then $x > 5$, and we can answer the question.

We might also recognize ***Weighted Averages*** in this statement. The average cost per kilogram of mixture K is a weighted average of \$3 (the cost per kg of Material A) and \$5 (the cost per kg of Material B).

The weights are the literal weights of A and B in mixture K. For instance, the per-kilogram cost of K will be closer to \$3 (that is, lower than \$4, the mid-point between \$3 and \$5) if there is more 3-dollar A in K than there is 5-dollar B. In effect, statement (2) tells us exactly this. The per-kilogram cost of K is below \$4, so we must be using more of the cheap stuff (x kilograms of A) than of the expensive stuff (y kilograms of B). Thus $x < y$.

The correct answer is (B): Statement (2) ALONE is sufficient, but statement (1) alone is not sufficient.

DS 106. <u>Word Problems</u>: Rates & Work
Difficulty: Medium **OG Page:** 284

In this ***Rates*** problem, we are told that two cars are traveling on the same road at constant rates. Car X is now 1 mile ahead of Car Y. The question is when (in terms of minutes from now) Car X will be 2 miles ahead of Car Y. It may be helpful to ***Draw a Picture*** to ensure that you can visualize the problem. Exaggerate the differences so you can see what's happening.

NOW LATER

Car Y Car X Car Y Car X

We could answer this question with an ***Rate-Time-Distance Chart***. However, we are interested in *relative* distances (how far one car is ahead of the other), not absolute distances along the road. Thus, a better approach is to use ***Relative Rates***. Because these cars are moving in the same direction, their rates can be subtracted. It is the *difference* of the rates (speeds) of Cars X and Y that determines how rapidly the distance between them grows.

The general ***Rate-Time-Distance Formula*** states that distance equals the product of rate and time.

In this problem, we are given the change in distance (1 mile) and asked for the time.

Therefore, a good ***Rephrasing*** is, "What is the difference between the rates (speeds) of Cars X and Y?"

(1): SUFFICIENT. This statement gives us the speeds of Cars X and Y directly, so we can compute the difference of their speeds through subtraction.

(2): SUFFICIENT. This statement tells us that 3 minutes ago, the distance between the two cars was 1/2 mile. Therefore, in those three minutes, the distance grew by $1 - 1/2 = 1/2$ mile.

We can substitute this intermediate result into the rate equation to solve for the rate R, which is really the difference of the speeds of Cars X and Y:

$$R \times 3\,\text{min} = \frac{1}{2}\,\text{mi}$$

Once we obtain a value for R, we can solve for the time (in minutes) that it would take for the distance to grow an additional mile, that is, from 1 mile to 2 miles. Incidentally, this time is 6 minutes, as we would suspect.

The correct answer is (D): EACH statement ALONE is sufficient.

DS 107. <u>Word Problems</u>: Rates & Work
Difficulty: Easy **OG Page:** 284

In this ***Rates & Work*** problem, we are told that an animated cartoon consists of 17,280 frames. We want to know how many minutes it will take to run the cartoon.

We can determine this time using the ***Rate–Time–Work Formula*** ($RT = W$) if we know the rate (R) at which the cartoon runs, since we already know the work (W).

The question can be ***Rephrased*** as "What is the cartoon's running time, OR what is the rate at which the cartoon runs?"

(1): SUFFICIENT. This statement gives us the rate explicitly, although this rate is in frames per second. The question seems to require frames per *minute*, but we could easily convert the units. This statement provides enough information to find the unknown time.

(2): SUFFICIENT. It takes six times as long to run the cartoon as to rewind it, and it takes 14 minutes to complete both acts. Express this 6 to 1 ***Ratio*** with an ***Unknown Multiplier*** x:

$$6x + 1x = 14$$
$$7x = 14$$
$$x = 2$$

Since $x = 2$, it takes $6x$, or 12 minutes, to run the cartoon.

The correct answer is (D): EACH statement ALONE is sufficient.

DS 108. Word Problems: Rates & Work
Difficulty: Medium **OG Page:** 284

The first thing to consider in this ***Rates*** problem is whether the speed of the train was constant. Unless the speed was constant, we can only determine ***Average Speed*** between two points, not the instantaneous speed at a specific point.

(1): INSUFFICIENT. With the total distance and total time, we can compute the average speed for the entire trip, using the ***Rate–Time–Distance Formula*** ($RT = D$). However, we do not know whether the train was traveling at a *constant* speed through the entire trip.

(2): INSUFFICIENT. This gives us the average speed through the trip, but we still do not know whether the speed was constant.

(1) AND (2): INSUFFICIENT. Both statements essentially provide the same information: the average speed. Thus, we get nothing new when we put them together, and we cannot determine whether the speed was constant.

The correct answer is (E): Statements (1) and (2) TOGETHER are not sufficient.

DS 109. Word Problems: Statistics
Difficulty: Devilish **OG Page:** 284

This ***Statistics*** problem looks much worse than it is. It tells us about list M, which consists of 8 of the 10 integers in the given list. The question asks for the ***Standard Deviation*** of list M.

In order to answer this, we need to know what is required to calculate the standard deviation of a list of numbers. The standard deviation is just a measure of how spread out the numbers on the list are relative to the mean. To calculate it, we first compute the mean, and then we calculate the square of the value of each number on the list minus the value of the mean. Finally, we take the square root of the average of those squares of differences of each term from the mean.

Fortunately, this is far more work than the GMAT would ever make you do. The important takeaway from how to compute a standard deviation is that we need to know the values of all of the numbers on the list in order to compute the list's standard deviation. So we can rephrase this question as "Which 8 of the 10 numbers in the given list are on list M?" or "Which 2 of the 10 numbers on the given list are *not* on list M?"

(1): INSUFFICIENT. We know that the average of a list of ***Consecutive Integers*** such as the given list is just (*last* + *first*)/2, which is $(22 + 4)/2 = 13$.

However, knowing that M's average value is 13 is not enough. As long as we remove two integers whose average value is 13 from the list, such as either 4 and 22 or 12 and 14, the average value of the remaining numbers will also be 13, but the actual numbers of the list will be different, so the standard deviations will be different.

(2): INSUFFICIENT. This statement only tells us the value of one of the two numbers removed from the given list to create list M. We have no way of knowing what the second number removed is.

(1) AND (2): SUFFICIENT. If 22 is not on list M and M's average is 13, the removed number must be 4, because the only way to keep *M*'s average the same as the given list's average is to remove numbers with an average value of 13. Thus, the two statements together allow us to figure out the values of all of the numbers on list *M*.

The correct answer is (C): BOTH statements (1) and (2) TOGETHER are sufficient to answer the question asked, but NEITHER statement ALONE is sufficient.

DS 110. Word Problems: Statistics
Difficulty: Hard **OG Page:** 284

This ***Statistics*** problem tells us that the ***Mean*** price of the three homes is $120,000. We are asked to find the ***Median*** (middle) price of the three houses.

(1): INSUFFICIENT. Knowing that Tom's house cost $110,000 allows us to determine that Tom's house was not the most expensive. If it were, then the average price could not be $120,000. However, we do not know whether Tom's house was the least expensive house or the "middle" house.

We should ***Test Scenarios***. If Tom's house is the least expensive, then the middle house would cost more than $110,000, and the median would be some number greater than $110,000. If Tom's house is the middle house, however, then the median would be $110,000.

(2): SUFFICIENT. We know that Jane's house cost $120,000. Again, consider different scenarios. Jane's house cannot be less expensive than both of the others, or else the average would have been higher than $120,000. By the same token, we know that Jane's house cannot be more expensive than both of the others. Otherwise, the overall average would have to be less than $120,000.

There are only two viable scenarios. One is that the three houses are worth different amounts, and Jane's house (worth $120,000) is in the middle. The second scenario is that all three houses are worth $120,000. In either case, the median is $120,000.

The correct answer is (B): Statement (2) ALONE is sufficient, but statement (1) alone is not sufficient.

DS 111. Number Properties: Odds & Evens
Difficulty: Medium **OG Page:** 284

In this ***Odds & Evens*** problem, we are asked whether xy is even. In order for this to be true, just one of the two integers needs to be even. By the ***Properties of Odds & Evens***, an even integer multiplied by any other integer produces an even product.

Therefore, we can ***Rephrase*** the question as "Is x OR y even?"

(1): SUFFICIENT. If $x = y + 1$, then we are dealing with two ***Consecutive Integers***. In any pair of consecutive integers, one of the integers must be even. The answer to the rephrased question is *Yes*.

(2): SUFFICIENT. If x/y is an even integer, x must be even. An odd number contains only odd prime factors, so if x were odd and divided by y, the quotient would be either an odd integer or a fraction.

Since x is definitely even, the answer to the rephrased question is *Yes*.

Alternatively, we can do ***Direct Algebra*** with Odds & Evens rules:

$x/y = \text{Even}$

$x = (y)(\text{Even}) = \text{Another even}$

The correct answer is (D): EACH statement ALONE is sufficient.

DS 112. Word Problems: Consecutive Integers
Difficulty: Hard **OG Page:** 285

On the ***Number Line*** shown, x is at the third tick mark to the right of 0, and y is at the seventh tick mark to the right of 0. The tick marks are equally spaced, so let's ***Name a Variable*** and call the constant spacing k.

Thus, by looking at the number line, we can write the following relationships:

$$x = 3k$$
$$y = 7k$$
$$y - x = 4k$$

The question asks "What is y?" We can ***Rephrase*** this question in any of several ways:

"What is k?" (because y is determined by k)

OR "What is x?"

OR "What is $y - x$?" (because these two questions will also give us a value for k).

(1): SUFFICIENT. This provides the value of x, answering one of the rephrased questions.

If $x = 1/2 = 3k$, then $k = 1/6$ and $y = 7/6$.

(2): SUFFICIENT. This statement gives us the value of $y - x$, answering one of the rephrased questions.

If $y - x = 2/3 = 4k$, then $k = 1/6$ and $y = 7/6$.

The tick marks in this problem turn out not to be ***Consecutive Integers***, in fact. However, the tick marks represent an ***Evenly Spaced Set***, of which consecutive integer sets are a special example.

The correct answer is (D): EACH statement ALONE is sufficient.

DS 113. Geometry: Triangles & Diagonals
Difficulty: Devilish **OG Page:** 285

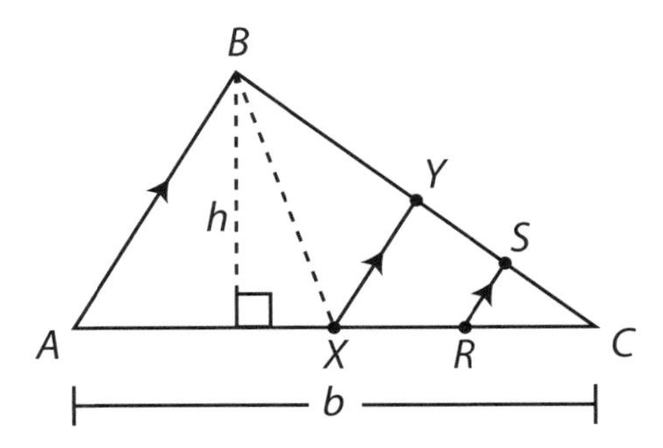

This is a complicated ***Triangles*** problem. First ***Draw a Diagram*** carefully.

As shown above, $\overline{XY}$ is drawn by connecting the midpoints of $\overline{AC}$ and $\overline{BC}$. Because points X and Y are the midpoints of $\overline{AC}$ and $\overline{BC}$, respectively, we can draw certain conclusions about ΔXYC. First, the base of triangle XYC will be half the base of ΔABC. Second, because Y is halfway between B and C, we also know that the height of ΔXYC will be half the height of ΔABC. Finally, we should notice that $\overline{AB}$ is parallel to $\overline{XY}$, so ΔABC and ΔXYC are ***Similar Triangles***.

Now we can compare the areas of ΔABC and ΔXYC. The ***Triangle Area Formula*** multiplies together the base AND the height $(A = \frac{1}{2}bh)$. If the base and height of ΔXYC are each half the base and height of ΔABC, respectively, then the area of ΔXYC will be $(1/2)^2$ or 1/4 that of ΔABC. This follows a general rule for any two similar figures (not just triangles). If one figure has lengths that are 1/2 those of a second similar figure, then the first figure will have 1/4 the area of the second.

Using this same reasoning, ΔRSC will also be similar to ΔXYC and have an area that is 1/4 that of ΔXYC.

$$\text{Area}_{\Delta RSC} = \frac{1}{4}\text{Area}_{\Delta XYC}$$

$$\text{Area}_{\Delta XYC} = \frac{1}{4}\text{Area}_{\Delta ABC}$$

$$\text{Then Area}_{\Delta RSC} = \frac{1}{4}\left(\frac{1}{4}\right)\text{Area}_{\Delta ABC} = \frac{1}{16}\text{Area}_{\Delta ABC}.$$

We are directly asked for the area of ΔRSC. We can ***Rephrase*** the question as "What is the area of ΔABC?"

(1): SUFFICIENT. This statement tells us the area of ΔABX. While this triangle was not discussed above, this triangle can be related to the larger ΔABC. Since X is the midpoint of $\overline{AC}$, this triangle has a base that is exactly half that of ΔABC. (If the base of ΔABC is b as pictured above, the base of ΔABX will be $\frac{1}{2}b$).

Both ΔABX and ΔABC have a height of h, as shown in the diagram above. This means that the area of ΔABX is 1/2 that of ΔABC, so $\text{Area}_{\Delta ABC} = 64$. While it is unnecessary to do so, from this we can calculate the area of $\Delta RSC = \frac{1}{16}\text{Area}_{\Delta ABC} = \frac{1}{16}(64) = 4$.

(2): INSUFFICIENT. Knowing the length of one of the heights (altitudes) of ΔABC tells us nothing about the area of ΔABC. We would need to know the length of the corresponding base to which the height is drawn. In fact, we don't even know which side of the triangle to consider the base for the given height of 8.

The correct answer is (A): Statement (1) ALONE is sufficient, but statement (2) alone is not sufficient.

DS 114. FDPs: Ratios
Difficulty: Devilish **OG Page:** 285

In this ***Ratios*** problem, we are told that the manager distributed x pens, y pencils, and z pads to each staff member. We are asked how many staff members are in the department.

All we really know here is that all of the numbers have to be integers and the number of employees must evenly divide each of x, y, and z. Otherwise, it would not be possible to evenly split x pens, y pencils, and z pads between the employees.

(1): INSUFFICIENT. The ***Ratio*** of pens to pencils to pads that each employee received does not tell us the number of employees. If we wanted to use an ***Unknown Multiplier***, say w, we could write

$x = 2w$

$y = 3w$

$z = 4w$

But this doesn't get us very far.

(2): INSUFFICIENT. 18, 27, and 36 are all divisible by 9, 3, and 1. So the 18 pens, 27 pencils, and 36 pads could have been divided evenly among 9, 3, or 1 employees.

We can see this with cases as well:

# employees	# pens per employee	# pencils per employee	# pads per employee
9	2	3	4
3	6	9	12
1	18	27	36

(1) AND (2): INSUFFICIENT. Although this looks at first like it might be sufficient, notice that 2 : 3 : 4, 6 : 9 : 12, and 18 : 27 : 36 from statement (2) all reduce to the same ratio, which is 2 : 3 : 4, so statement (1) gives us no new information beyond what statement (2) already gave us. We still don't have enough information to figure out whether there are 9, 3, or 1 employees.

# employees	# pens per employee	# pencils per employee	# pads per employee
9	2	3	4
3	$6 = 2 \times 3$	$9 = 3 \times 3$	$12 = 4 \times 3$
1	$18 = 2 \times 9$	$27 = 3 \times 9$	$36 = 4 \times 9$

The correct answer is (E): Statements (1) and (2) TOGETHER are NOT sufficient to answer the question asked, and additional data are needed.

DS 115. Word Problems: Rates & Work
Difficulty: Hard **OG Page:** 285

This ***Rates & Work*** problem involves two machines X and Y that produce identical bottles at different constant rates. We want to know how many hours it would take Machine X to fill a production lot by itself.

The general equation governing such situations is the ***Rate-Time-Work Formula***, which states that work equals the product of rate and time. Typically the amount of work is left in vague terms, such as a production lot. In such cases we can just regard the total work as 1, as in "one lot" or "one job." This leaves the rate as the only variable we need to determine the time it would take to complete the work.

We can ***Rephrase*** the question as "What is the rate at which Machine X fills the production lot?"

(1): INSUFFICIENT. This statement tells us the rate at which Machine X produces bottles. However, without knowing how many bottles constitute one lot, we cannot determine how long it would take Machine X to fill the lot.

(2): SUFFICIENT. From the problem statement, we know that Machine X working alone for 4 hours, followed by Machine Y working alone for 3 hours, filled one production lot. This statement further tells us that Machine X produced *twice* as much as Machine Y.

Therefore, Machine X produced 2/3 of the lot, and Machine Y produced 1/3 of the lot, since 2/3 + 1/3 = 1.

If Machine X produces 2/3 of the lot in 4 hours, we can solve for the rate R of Machine X, using the relationship $RT = W$ as follows:

$$R(4) = 2/3$$
$$R = 2/12$$
$$R = 1/6$$

If we know the rate of Machine X, we can calculate how long it would take for Machine X to fill the lot by itself (6 hours).

Alternatively, we could have picked numbers or set up a chart. However, by not picking numbers, we avoid being distracted by irrelevant information such as the number of bottles in a lot or an actual rate of production in bottles per minute.

The correct answer is (B): Statement (2) ALONE is sufficient, but statement (1) alone is not sufficient.

DS 116. FDPs: Fractions
Difficulty: Easy **OG Page:** 285

In this ***Fractions*** problem, we are given a situation in which a group is split into two binary categories. Each person is an employee or a guest, and furthermore each person is a manager or a non-manager (with the caveat that no guests are managers).

One way to handle this situation is to consider ***Overlapping Sets*** and set up a ***Double-Set Matrix*** with a zero in the Manager-Guest box:

Manager?		Employee?		
		Yes	No	Total
	Yes		0	
	No	?		
	Total			

Since we do not yet know a total, we have to fill in the givens by ***Naming a Variable***. The problem is overrun with fractions, so let t stand for the total.

Manager?		Employee?		
		Yes	No	Total
	Yes	$1/2\ t$	0	
	No	$1/6\ t$		
	Total	$2/3\ t$	$1/3\ t$	t

Using the givens that 2/3 of the passengers are employees and 3/4 of those employees are managers, we can determine that 3/4 of 2/3, or $3/4 \times 2/3 = 1/2$, of the total are employees who are managers.

Also, $2/3 - 1/2 = 1/6$, so $(1/6)t$, is the number of employees who are *not* managers.

Since the number of employees who are not managers is equal to $(1/6)t$, the question can now be ***Rephrased*** as "What is $(1/6)t$?" or more simply, "What is t?"

(1): SUFFICIENT. The value of t is 690.

(2): SUFFICIENT. There are 230 guests, or:

$$(1/3)t = 230$$

This ***Linear Equation*** can be quickly solved for t.

The correct answer is (D): EACH statement ALONE is sufficient.

DS 117. Geometry: Circles & Cylinders
Difficulty: Easy **OG Page:** 285

We know that both gardens are ***Circular***.

As a first step, ***Translate*** the phrase "*length of edging that surrounds circular garden...*" into ***Circumference.*** Thus, we can simply write:

Circumference of K = 1/2 (Circumference of G)

We can use r_K and r_G to represent the radii of circles K and G, respectively. The formula for the circumference of a circle is $C = 2\pi r$. We can apply this formula to the equation above and simplify:

$$2\pi r_K = \frac{1}{2}(2\pi r_G)$$
$$2\pi r_K = \pi r_G$$
$$r_K = \frac{1}{2} r_G$$

We now have a relationship between the radii of the two circles. In order to find the area of garden K, we need r_K, because $A = \pi r^2$.

Moreover, because we have a relationship between r_K and r_G, knowing r_G will also be enough information to answer this question. Furthermore, knowing the diameter, the area or the circumference of garden G will also be sufficient, because any of those values could be used to solve for r_G.

Essentially, we can ***Rephrase*** this question as "What is any dimension of either circular garden?" If we know one number, we know them all.

(1): SUFFICIENT. This statement provides us with the area of circle G. With this area, we can find its radius, and thus the radius and area of circle K.

(2): SUFFICIENT. This statement provides the perimeter of circle G. With this perimeter, we can find its radius, and thus the radius and area of circle K.

Although unnecessary, we can find the actual area of circle K. From each of the statements, $r_G = 5$, so $r_K = 2.5$. Then $A_K = \pi(2.5)^2 = 6.25\pi$ square meters.

The correct answer is (D): EACH statement ALONE is sufficient.

DS 118. Algebra: Formulas
Difficulty: Devilish **OG Page:** 285

This ***Strange Symbol*** problem defines min(x, y) and max(x, y) functions, which respectively return the smaller, or min, of x and y and the larger, or max, of x and y. Although this problem is confusing because of these long-winded function definitions, these functions are actually not very difficult in and of themselves. The min of two numbers is the smaller of the numbers and the max of two numbers is the larger of the numbers.

This problem is asking us to figure out whether w or 10 is smaller. If w is greater than 10, then min(10, w) = 10. If w is less than 10, min(10, w) = w.

(1): SUFFICIENT. To deal with this statement, we need to think about possible values of z. Specifically, we need to consider values of z that are less than and greater than 20 (because that will change the value of max(20, z).)

If $z = 15$, max(20, z) = 20. That means that $w = 20$. If $w = 20$, then min(10, w) = 10.

If $z = 25$, max(20, z) = 25. That means that $w = 25$. If $w = 25$, then min(10, w) = 10.

No matter what value we pick for z, the value of w will have to be at least 20, which means the value of min(10, w) = 10.

(2): SUFFICIENT. The max of 10 and w must be *at least* 10 (if $w \leq 10$, the max is 10, and if $w > 10$, the max would be even bigger), so this tells us that $w \geq 10$. If w is greater than or equal to 10, then min(10, w) must be 10.

The correct answer is (D): EACH statement ALONE is sufficient to answer the question asked.

DS 119. Geometry: Triangles & Diagonals
Difficulty: Hard **OG Page:** 285

A preliminary note about this problem: the problem is clearly intended to be difficult, yet the answer to the actual question, "What is the length of PR?" is very easy to get to using both statements: 4 + 1 = 5. This should be an excellent clue that answer choice (C) might be too simple. Incidentally, this clue also completely rules out (E), since we actually can answer the question with the two statements together. The question is whether we can answer the question with even less.

Now we should study the figure. A ***Triangle Inscribed in a Semicircle*** is necessarily a right triangle, so mark the angle at Q as 90 degrees.

Note that each of the smaller triangles (the one with one side of a and the one with one side of b) has a right angle, and that they "share" the right angle at Q. This means that all three triangles (the two smaller and the larger one that encompasses them both) are ***Similar***. Similar triangles have the same angles and, thus, their legs are in proportion.

To see this point, let's ***Name a Variable*** and label an unknown angle as x. It follows that the other unmarked angle in that triangle must be $90 - x$, since the angles in any triangle must add to 180.

Moreover, the two angles that add up to the 90 degree angle at Q must also be x and $90 - x$, since together they must sum to 90. Since the triangles each have angles of 90, x, and $90 - x$, the triangles are similar.

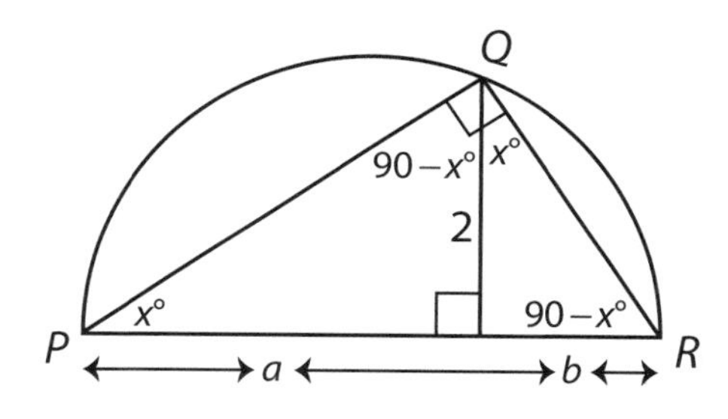

Redraw the two smaller similar triangles so that they are facing the same direction:

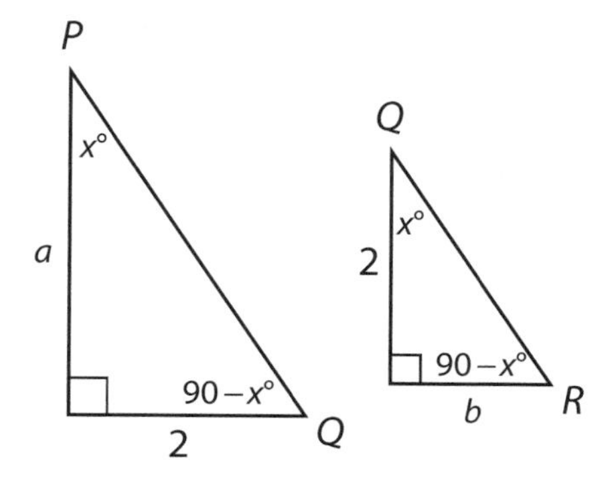

As the sides of similar triangles are in proportion:

$$a/2 = 2/b$$
$$ab = 4$$

Thus, if we know a, we know b. If we know b, we know a.

We can ***Rephrase*** the question as "What is a OR what is b?"

(1): SUFFICIENT. $a = 4$. From $ab = 4$, $b = 1$.

(2): SUFFICIENT. $b = 1$. From $ab = 4$, $b = 4$.

These relationships can be derived from repeated application of the ***Pythagorean Theorem*** within the three triangles, but the process is more cumbersome.

The correct answer is (D): EACH statement ALONE is sufficient.

DS 120. <u>Word Problems</u>: Statistics
Difficulty: Medium **OG Page:** 285

This ***Statistics*** problem also involves ***Algebraic Translations***. We must interpret a complicated scenario.

From the information presented in the prompt, we can determine that *any* book on the lower shelf will have more pages than *any* book on the upper shelf. This must be so because the *shortest* book on the lower shelf has more pages than the *longest* book on the upper shelf.

We are asked for the ***Median*** number of pages among the books on the shelves. Keep careful track of the relative numbers of books on each shelf.

(1): INSUFFICIENT. This statement provides no information about the number of books on the lower shelf and is thus insufficient.

If there are *more* books on the lower shelf than on the upper shelf, then the median number of pages will be that of some book on the lower shelf, or halfway between two such books (and will thus be 475 pages or more).

If there are *fewer* books on the lower shelf than on the upper shelf, then the median number of pages will be that of some book on the upper shelf, or halfway between two such books (and will thus be less than or equal to 400 pages).

Finally, if the two shelves are holding an equal numbers of books, then the median number of pages will be halfway between 400 and 475 (the two middle numbers).

(2): INSUFFICIENT. This statement provides no information about the number of books on the upper shelf, and is thus insufficient for the same reasons statement (1) is.

(1) AND (2): SUFFICIENT. If there are a total of 49 books, then the median number of pages is that of the 25th book in either increasing or decreasing order (halfway between 1st and 49th). Since the upper shelf contains all of the 25 shortest books, the longest book on that shelf determines the median: 400 pages.

The correct answer is (C): BOTH statements TOGETHER are sufficient, but NEITHER statement ALONE is sufficient.

DS 121. Word Problems: Statistics
Difficulty: Medium **OG Page:** 286

If the average number of people registered for the 6 days of the trade show is to be greater than 90, then from the ***Average Formula*** *(Average × number of terms = Sum)*, we know that the sum of all the registrants must be greater than 90 × 6, or 540.

We can ***Rephrase*** the question as "Were there more than 540 registrants in total, over all 6 days?" This question involves ***Inequalities***, as do the statements.

(1): SUFFICIENT. For the 4 days with the greatest number of people registered, the average number registered per day was 100. Therefore, the sum over these 4 days was 4 × 100 = 400.

Now let's ***Test Extreme Values*** that we are given. The question tells us that the least number of people registered in a single day was 80, so the smallest possible sum for the 6 days is 400 + 80 + 80 = 560. We can guarantee that there were more than 540 registrants.

(2): INSUFFICIENT. For the three days with the smallest number of registrants per day, there were 85 × 3 = 255 registrants. Since we know that the lowest number of people registered for one day was 80, we know that the next two smallest numbers must have totaled 255 − 80 = 175.

The problem is that we don't know how many people were registered on the three days with the largest number of participants.

Suppose that the second and third days had 87 and 88 registrants, respectively. 87 + 88 = 175, so that matches the statement.

If the number of registrants on the six days were 80, 87, 88, 200, 200, and 200, the average per day would be much greater than 90.

However, if the number of registrants on the six days were 80, 87, 88, 89, 89, and 89, the sum of the first three numbers would be 255, the second and third would be 175, and the average per day would be less than 90.

The correct answer is (A): Statement (1) ALONE is sufficient, but statement (2) alone is not sufficient to answer the question asked.

DS 122. Geometry: Circles & Cylinders
Difficulty: Devilish **OG Page:** 286

In this ***Circles*** problem, it will be helpful to ***Name Variables*** as follows. Let R ("big R") be the radius of the larger circle, and let r ("little r") be the radius of the smaller circle. We are asked for the difference in ***Areas*** of these circles, i.e., $\pi R^2 - \pi r^2$.

Dividing by π, we can ***Rephrase*** the question as "What is $R^2 - r^2$?" We can loosely rephrase even further: "What are R and r?"

(1): SUFFICIENT. AB is a radius of the smaller circle, so $r = 3$. Furthermore, AC is a radius of the larger circle, so $R = 3 + 2 = 5$. We thus have the values of both R and r directly.

(2): SUFFICIENT. CE is a radius of the larger circle, so $R = CD + DE = 1 + 4 = 5$. Using the fact that all radii of a circle are equal, we can also establish that $AC = 5$. Since $CD = 1$, we know that the diameter of the small circle, AD, equals $AC + CD = 5 + 1 = 6$. Therefore, $r = 3$, and again, we have both R and r.

This statement wound up being harder to figure out than the first statement, but it is also sufficient.

The correct answer is (D): EACH statement ALONE is sufficient.

DS 123. Word Problems: Statistics
Difficulty: Medium **OG Page:** 286

This ***Statistics*** problem is confusing! The given information tells us that the ***Range***, defined as *max* – *min*, of S is x and that the range of T is y. We are also told that all of the numbers in set T are also in set S, which means that T is a subset of S.

The question asks whether x is greater than y.

At first, it seems as if the range of S must be greater than the range of T because T is a subset of S. But the range of S will be the same as the range of T as long as S's *min* and *max* are in T.

For instance, if Set S is composed of the number (1, 2, 3) and T is composed of the numbers (1, 3) the sets will have the same range.

So the question can be rephrased as "Are S's *min* and *max* in T?"

(1): INSUFFICIENT. This tells us nothing about whether S's *min* and *max* are in T.

(2): INSUFFICIENT. This also tells us nothing about whether S's *min* and *max* are in T.

(1) AND (2): INSUFFICIENT. Even taking these two statements together, we still have no information about whether S's *min* and *max* are in T.

The correct answer is (E): Statements (1) and (2) TOGETHER are NOT sufficient to answer the question asked, and additional data are needed.

DS 124. Word Problems: Algebraic Translations
Difficulty: Medium **OG Page:** 286

To attack this problem, which involves a complicated ***Wage Relationship***, we should ***Name Variables***:

R = regular hourly rate
W = hours worked on "weekdays" (i.e., not Sunday)
S = hours worked on Sunday

Next, ***Translate*** the information in the question stem. If the employee worked 40 hours or fewer on the weekdays, plus some hours on Sunday, then the employee was paid as follows:

(Regular Hourly Wage) × (Weekday Hours) + (2 × Hourly Wage) × (Sunday Hours)

$= RW + 2RS$

If the employee worked more than 40 hours on the weekdays, plus some hours on Sunday, then the employee was paid as follows:

(Regular Hourly Wage) × (40 Hours) + (1.5× Hourly Wage) × (Overtime Hours) + (2 × Hourly Wage) × (Sunday Hours)

$40R + (1.5R)(W - 40) + 2RS$

To figure out how much the employee was paid last week, we need to know the actual values of R, W, and S. If $W \leq 40$, then we use the first wage relationship. If $W > 40$, then we use the second.

(1): INSUFFICIENT. $R = \$10$, but we do not know the value of W or S.

(2): INSUFFICIENT. The total hours worked last week is $W + S = 54$. The constraint that the employee did not work more than 8 hours per day can be expressed as $S \leq 8$ and $W \leq 48$ (that is, 6 days × 8 hours/day).

Not only is the value of R unknown, but also there are several possibilities for S and W.

We can ***Test Numbers*** to confirm our understanding. For instance, S could equal 6 and W could equal 48, or S could equal 7 and W could equal 47.

(1) AND (2): INSUFFICIENT. The value of R is known, but there are still several possible values for S and W.

Intuitively, the lack of sufficiency should make sense. Since the employee is paid a different amount for Sunday hours than he or she is for "weekday" hours (whether regular or overtime), we need to know the exact value of S (Sunday hours) to determine the total amount paid.

The correct answer is (E): Statements (1) and (2) TOGETHER are not sufficient.

DS 125. Number Properties: Probability
Difficulty: Medium **OG Page:** 286

This question asks for the ***Probability*** of selecting a chip that is either white or blue. Since there are only three chips—white, blue, and red—we can use the ***1 – x Principle*** to simplify the question. The only chips that are *not* white or blue are red, so the question can be ***Rephrased*** as "What is the probability that the chip is red?"

(1): INSUFFICIENT. This statement gives us two pieces of information. First, we know the literal content: the probability that the chip is blue (1/5). Second, by the $1 - x$ Principle, this statement also gives us the probability that the chip is either white *or* red (4/5).

However, we do not have any way of determining the probability that the chip is red. All we know is that this probability is between 0 and 4/5.

(2): SUFFICIENT. This statement provides the answer to our rephrased question above. If the probability that the chip will be red is 1/3, the probability that the chip will be white or blue is 2/3.

The correct answer is (B): Statement (2) ALONE is sufficient, but statement (1) alone is not sufficient.

DS 126. Word Problems: Algebraic Translations
Difficulty: Easy **OG Page:** 286

In this problem, which involves ***Algebraic Translations***, we can ***Name Variables*** as follows:

x = number of tickets sold at full price
$400 - x$ = number of tickets sold at reduced price
p_1 = price of tickets sold at full price
p_2 = price of tickets sold at reduced price

The question asks us for the ***Total Revenue*** of tickets sold (both at full and reduced price). Using our new variables, we can ***Rephrase*** the question as "What is the value of $xp_1 + (400 - x)p_2$?" Notice that this expression contains three separate variables.

(1): INSUFFICIENT. Since the number of tickets sold at full price was 1/4 of the total number of tickets sold, the number of tickets sold at full price was $\frac{1}{4}(400) = 100$. Likewise, the number of tickets sold at the reduced price was $400 - 100 = 300$.

This does not provide us with enough information, since we still need the values of p_1 and p_2 to find the total revenue, which can now be written as $100p_1 + 300p_2$.

(2): INSUFFICIENT. Knowing that the full price of the ticket is \$25 would not be enough to solve the expression above. We still need the values of p_2 and x to find the total revenue, which can now be written as $x(25) + (400 - x)p_2$.

(1) AND (2): INSUFFICIENT. Combining the two statements still fails to provide an answer, since we do not know the reduced ticket price, p_2. The total revenue is $100(25) + 300p_2$, but we still have one variable lurking.

The correct answer is (E): Statements (1) and (2) TOGETHER are not sufficient.

DS 127. FDPs: Percents
Difficulty: Devilish **OG Page:** 286

In this difficult ***Percent Changes*** problem, we can manipulate these changes to simplify the question drastically.

First, ***Name Variables*** and assign r to the rent in 1997. Since the rent in 1998 is x% more, the 1998 rent is $r\left(1+\frac{x}{100}\right)$.

Likewise, since the rent in 1999 is y% less, the 1999 rent is $r\left(1+\frac{x}{100}\right)\left(1-\frac{y}{100}\right)$. Thus, our question becomes:

$$\text{Is } r\left(1+\frac{x}{100}\right)\left(1-\frac{y}{100}\right) > r?$$

We shouldn't stop here. Because we know that the rent must have been some positive amount, we can divide by r without flipping the ***Inequality*** sign:

$$\left(1+\frac{x}{100}\right)\left(1-\frac{y}{100}\right) > 1?$$

Next, express each term with a ***Common Denominator***. This continued simplification may seem like a lot of work, but it will pay off.

$$\left(\frac{100+x}{100}\right)\left(\frac{100-y}{100}\right) > 1?$$
$$\frac{(100+x)(100-y)}{10{,}000} > 1?$$
$$(100+x)(100-y) > 10{,}000?$$
$$10{,}000 + 100x - 100y - xy > 10{,}000?$$
$$100x - 100y - xy > 0?$$
$$100(x-y) > xy?$$

This question cannot be ***Rephrased*** any further, and we can move on to the statements.

(1): INSUFFICIENT. Given that $x > y$, we know that $x - y$ will be positive. Thus, for our rephrased question, we know that $100(x - y)$ will be positive. However, we do not know whether this amount will be greater than xy.

(2): SUFFICIENT. If we have manipulated properly, as shown above, this is now an easy statement to evaluate.

$$\frac{xy}{100} < x - y$$
$$xy < 100(x - y)$$

This inequality perfectly matches our rephrased question, which we can now answer with a definitive *Yes*.

This problem is difficult to solve by picking numbers, especially since the final inequality is not intuitive. In this case, the algebraic approach is faster, easier, and more secure.

The correct answer is (B): Statement (2) ALONE is sufficient, but statement (1) alone is not sufficient.

DS 128. Geometry: Triangles & Diagonals
Difficulty: Devilish **OG Page:** 286

In this ***Triangles*** problem, we can ***Name Variables*** and assign x and y to the lengths of the two legs of the triangle.

We are told that we have a ***Right Triangle***. Using the ***Pythagorean Theorem***, which applies to all right triangles, we can determine from the prompt that $x^2 + y^2 = 100$.

The prompt question asks for the sum $x + y$. This is a ***Combined Expression***, or Combo. No rephrase is necessary.

(1): SUFFICIENT. Since the triangle is a right triangle, the legs x and y are also the base and height of the triangle.

Therefore, the area of the triangle is $\frac{1}{2}xy$. We have $\frac{1}{2}xy = 25$. Therefore, $xy = 50$.

To finish the calculations, we can rearrange this new equation: $y = 50/x$.

Next, substitute for y in the equation from the question:

$$x^2 + (50/x)^2 = 100, \text{ or } x^2 + 2{,}500/x^2 = 100$$

Multiply by the denominator, x^2, on both sides to produce $x^4 + 2{,}500 = 100x^2$, which can be rearranged into a ***Quadratic Equation:***

$$x^4 - 100x^2 + 2{,}500 = 0$$

This equation factors to

$$(x^2 - 50)(x^2 - 50) = 0 \text{ or } (x^2 - 50)^2 = 0$$

x^2 must equal 50. Thus x has the unique value $\sqrt{50}$.

Note that we don't need to consider negative solutions, because x represents a positive length. Moreover, we can plug this value back into $y = 50/x$ to determine a unique value for y (which will also be $\sqrt{50}$, as it turns out).

Since we have unique values of both x and y, the sum $x + y$ is uniquely determined.

Alternatively, we might recognize that we nearly have a ***Special Product*** with $x^2 + y^2 = 100$. The form on the left is not quite the same as $(x + y)^2$, which expands as follows:

$$(x + y)^2 = x^2 + 2xy + y^2$$

All we are missing is the xy cross-term. This statement supplies it. Since $xy = 50$, we also know that $2xy = 100$. Hence, we have the right side of the equation:

$$\begin{aligned}(x + y)^2 &= x^2 + 2xy + y^2\\ &= (x^2 + y^2) + 2xy\\ &= 100 + 100\\ &= 200\end{aligned}$$

Taking the square root, we find that $x + y$ is $\sqrt{200}$.

(2): SUFFICIENT. If the right triangle has two legs of equal length, then it must be a ***45–45–90*** triangle. The sides of such triangles are in the fixed ratio $1:1:,\sqrt{2}$ so the length of the legs may be found from that of the hypotenuse. Therefore, the length of each leg can be determined, and the sum of the two legs can likewise be determined.

The correct answer is (D): EACH statement ALONE is sufficient.

DS 129. Geometry: Coordinate Plane
Difficulty: Devilish **OG Page:** 286

This problem tells us that region R consists of all of the points in the half plane determined by $2x + 3y \leq 6$ and asks if a particular point (r, s) is in region R.

A picture makes this easier to understand. First, put the inequality in point-slope form so we can graph the line that marks the boundary of region R.

$$\begin{aligned}2x + 3y &\leq 6\\ 3y &\leq -2x + 6\\ y &\leq -\frac{2}{3}x + 2\end{aligned}$$

So the dividing line $y = -\frac{2}{3}x + 2$ has a slope of $-2/3$ and a y-intercept of 2.

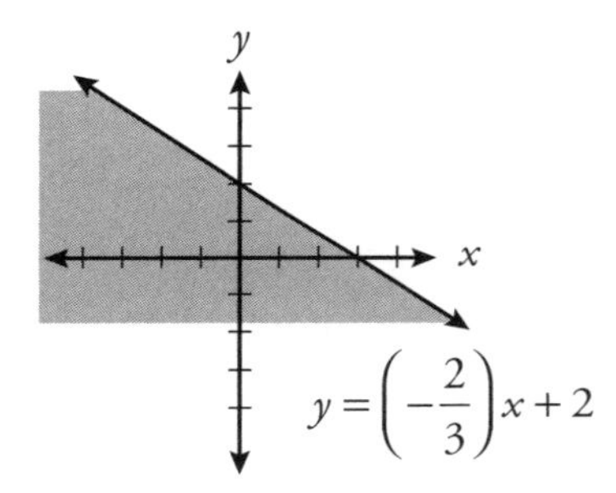

(1): INSUFFICIENT. Since this equation determines a line where r is the x value and s is the y value, we can put it into point–slope form and graph it as well.

$$\begin{aligned}3x + 2y &= 6\\ 2y &\leq -3x + 6\\ y &\leq -\frac{3}{2}x + 3\end{aligned}$$

Since the slope of this line is not the same as the slope of the line $y = -\frac{2}{3}x + 2$ that defines the edge of the half plane, the two lines must intersect as shown. So some points on the line $y = -\frac{2}{3}x + 3$

are to the left of the dividing line (in the shaded region) and some points are to the right.

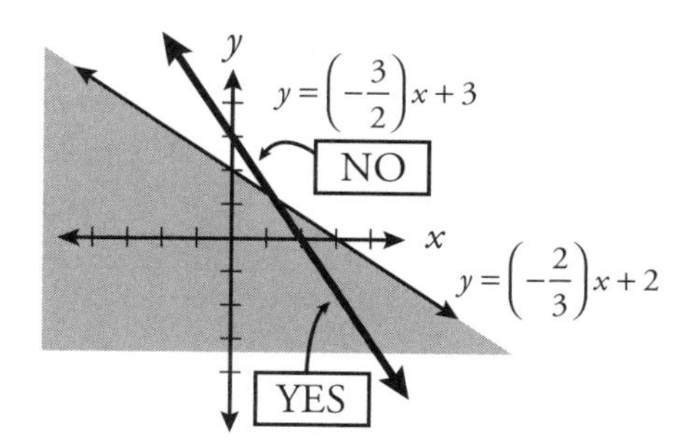

(2): INSUFFICIENT. Since r is the x value and s is the y value in the coordinate pair, we can quickly graph both of these inequalities. This statement tells us that (r, s) lies below the line $y = 3$ and to the left of the line $x = 2$. Looking at the graph, we see that part of this region is to the left of the dividing line $y = -\frac{2}{3}x + 2$ and part is to the right, so we don't know which side of the line (r, s) is on.

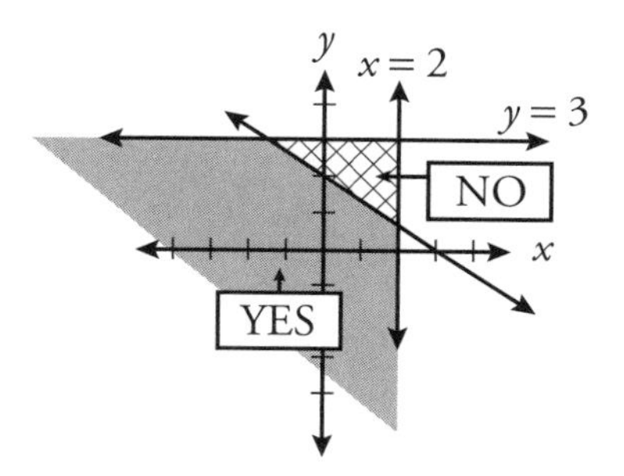

(1) AND (2): INSUFFICIENT. If we drew accurate graphs, we can see that even together the two statements are insufficient because there is a small region (shaded in the diagram) that makes both statements true but is not in region R.

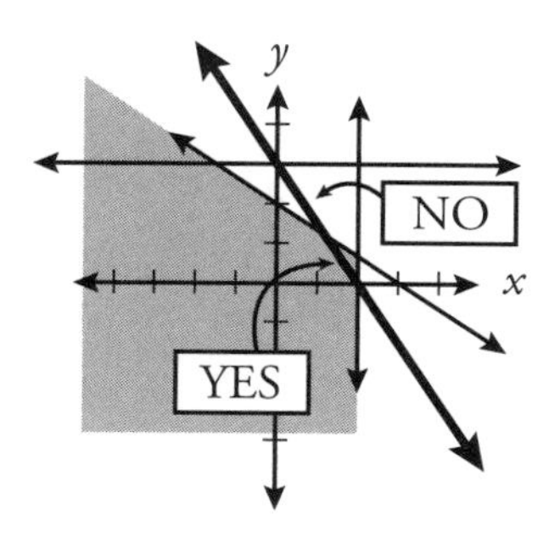

However, if we don't trust our graphs, we can see that such a region exists by solving for the intersection of the dividing line for half plane R and the line given by (1) and see that the intersection is below $y = 3$ and to the left of $x = 2$.

$$-\frac{2}{3}x+2=-\frac{3}{2}x+3$$
$$-\frac{2}{3}x=-\frac{3}{2}x+1$$
$$6\left(-\frac{2}{3}x\right)=6\left(-\frac{3}{2}x+1\right)$$
$$-4x=-9x+6$$
$$5x=6$$
$$x=\frac{6}{5}$$

Now plug $x = 6/5$ into the equation given in (1) to get the y value of the intersection:

$$y=-\left(\frac{2}{3}\right)\left(\frac{6}{5}\right)+2$$
$$=-\frac{4}{5}+2$$
$$=-\frac{4}{5}+\frac{10}{5}$$
$$=\frac{6}{5}$$

The correct answer is (E): Statements (1) and (2) TOGETHER are NOT sufficient to answer the question asked, and additional data are needed.

DS 130. Geometry: Polygons
Difficulty: Devilish **OG Page:** 286

In this ***Polygons*** problem, we are asked for the ***Volume of a Rectangular Solid.*** This volume is equal to the area of its base times its height or, put differently, it is the product of the three different side lengths (length × width × height).

(1): INSUFFICIENT. This statement gives us the areas of two adjacent rectangular faces of the solid. We can regard one of those areas as the base, but we cannot get a unique value for the height.

Two adjacent faces share one edge. ***Name Variables*** and assign x to the length of that edge, assigning y and z to the lengths of the other sides of the box. Thus we know

$xy = 15$

and

$xz = 24$

However, more than one rectangular solid can be constructed with these measurements. Two possibilities are shown below:

1.

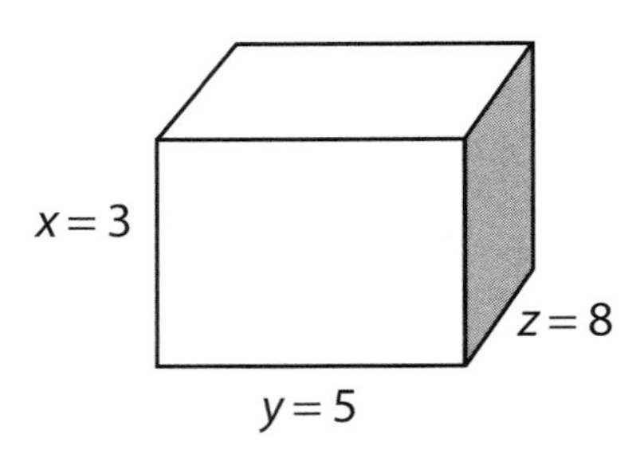

2.

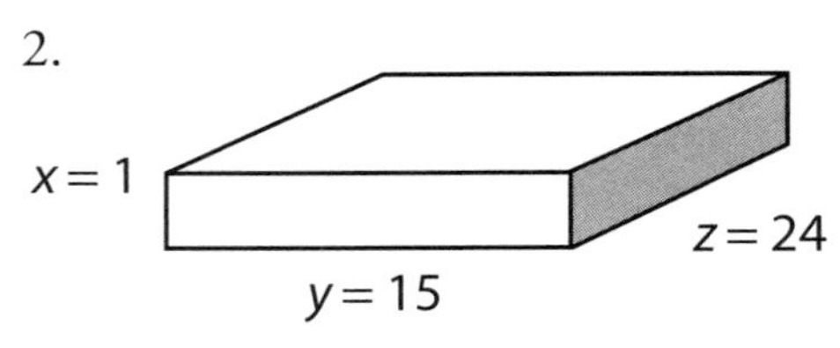

(2): INSUFFICIENT. This statement tells us that the area of two opposite faces of the solid is 40. By the logic we used in (1) we can say that

$yz = 40$

But we do know nothing about the height of the solid and so cannot determine its volume.

(1) AND (2): SUFFICIENT. We know that the volume of the solid is xyz and the two statements taken together give us something about each of the dimensions x, y, and z, so the trick to this is figuring out how to get xyz by combining what we know from (1) and (2):

$xy = 15$
$xz = 24$
$yz = 40$

With the addition of $yz = 40$, we now know that the second set of dimensions discussed in (1) is now impossible, but the first set does indeed match.

However, we can also prove that the first set of dimensions is the only possibility.

Notice that if we look at what we know, the dimensions are already being multiplied by each other and each of x, y, and z appear twice. This suggests that we multiply the three equations by each other and see if we can find a way to take a square root.

$$(xy)(xz)(yz) = 15 \times 24 \times 40$$
$$x^2y^2z^2 = 15 \times 24 \times 40$$
$$\sqrt{x^2y^2z^2} = \sqrt{15 \times 24 \times 40}$$
$$xyz = \sqrt{15 \times 24 \times 40}$$

At this point, we can stop, because we know that we could compute the square root and we don't want to spend any extra time.

The correct answer is (C): BOTH statements (1) and (2) TOGETHER are sufficient to answer the question asked, but NEITHER statement ALONE is sufficient.

DS 131. <u>FDPs:</u> Fractions
Difficulty: Devilish **OG Page:** 287

We are told that there are two trucks and that each of the 6 shipments, S1, S2, S3, S4, S5, and S6, is entirely on one of those two trucks. The table shows us the fraction of the total value of the 6 shipments that each individual shipment is worth. We are also told that more than half of the total value of the 6 shipments is in the shipments on the first truck.

The question asks if S3 is on the first truck. In order to answer this, we need think about what conditions would require S3 to be on the first truck. All we know about the first truck is that more than half of the total value of the shipment is on it. So all of the shipments could be on it, which isn't very helpful.

However, if more than half of the value of the total value of the shipment must be on the first truck, we know that less than half of the total value of the shipment must be on the second truck. This is promising, because many combinations of the individual shipments (such as S1 + S2 + S3) add up to more than half of the total value and so could not be on the second truck together.

So we can rephrase the question as "Would putting S3 on the second truck push the value of the shipments on the second truck over 1/2 of the total value of the shipment?"

(1): INSUFFICIENT. If S2 and S4 are on the first truck, S3 could be on the first truck with them, or it could be alone on the second truck, which would be fine since its value is only 1/6th of the total.

Test Scenarios to prove this statement insufficient.

	S3 on Truck 1	**S3 on Truck 2**
Truck 1	S2, S3, S4	S1, S2, S4, S5, S6
Value on Truck 1	$\frac{1}{5}+\frac{1}{6}+\frac{3}{20}=\frac{31}{60}$	5/6
Truck 2	S1, S5, S6	S3
Value on Truck 2	$\frac{1}{4}+\frac{2}{15}+\frac{1}{10}=\frac{29}{60}$	1/6

(2): SUFFICIENT. If S1 and S6 are on Truck 2, then we need to check and see if adding S3 to Truck 2 to would push its total value over 1/2.

$$\frac{1}{4}+\frac{1}{10}+\frac{1}{6}=\frac{15}{60}+\frac{6}{60}+\frac{10}{60}=\frac{31}{60}$$

Since 31/60 > 1/2, S3 cannot be on Truck 2 and so must be on Truck 1.

The correct answer is (B): Statement (2) ALONE is sufficient, but statement (1) alone is not sufficient to answer the question asked.

DS 132. Word Problems: Algebraic Translations
Difficulty: Devilish **OG Page:** 287

A way to ***Rephrase*** this ***Algebraic Translations*** problem may not be immediately clear. But consider what would happen if Joanna spent exactly \$0.44 on stamps. If she spent \$0.44 on stamps, then she bought one of each—\$0.15 stamps and \$0.29 stamps cannot add up to \$0.44 in any other way.

There is an ***Integer Constraint*** in this question. We cannot have fractional or negative amounts of stamps.

If we ***Name Variables,*** we can write down the ***Cost Relationship***. Let x be the number of \$0.15 stamps, and let y be the number of \$0.29 stamps. Then the total cost = $\$0.15x + \$0.29y$. We are looking for x.

(1): SUFFICIENT. Joanna bought \$4.40 worth of stamps. Note that \$4.40 ends in 0. Any multiple of \$0.15 must end in 5 or 0. Therefore, whatever multiple of \$0.29 stamps Joanna bought must also end in 5 or 0 (so that the value of the \$0.15 stamps plus the value of the \$0.29 stamps can add to \$4.40).

If Joanna must have bought \$0.29 stamps in multiples of 5, there are only a few possibilities before the \$0.29 stamps alone add up to more than \$4.40. Thus, we can simply test which combination(s) are possible:

Number of \$0.29 stamps	**Actual Value**	**Amount Left for \$0.15 Stamps**
5	\$1.45	\$2.95
10	\$2.90	\$1.50
15	\$4.35	\$0.05

Only one of these combinations leaves an "Amount Left for \$0.15 Stamps" that is actually divisible by \$0.15. Joanna must have purchased 10 \$0.29 stamps and 10 \$0.15 stamps.

This is a very tricky problem. Consider the cost equation in x and y:

$$\$0.15x + \$0.29y = \$4.40$$

Normally, a solitary linear equation with two unknowns x and y cannot be solved for a definite value for either unknown.

However, if x and y are restricted to positive integers, and if the other numbers in the equation are chosen carefully, there may only be one possible solution for the equation.

(2): INSUFFICIENT. Knowing only that Joanna bought equal numbers of each type of stamp does not tell us how many $0.15 stamps she bought. For instance, she could have bought one of each or one million of each.

The correct answer is (A): Statement (1) ALONE is sufficient, but statement (2) alone is not sufficient.

DS 133. <u>FDPs</u>: Digits & Decimals
Difficulty: Devilish **OG Page:** 287

We are told that x, y, and z are three-digit positive integers and that $x = y + z$.

The question asks if the hundreds digit of x is equal to the sum of the hundreds digits of y and z.

In order to answer this question, we have to think about how the addition of three digit integers works. In order to calculate the hundred's digit of x, we add the hundreds digits of y and z, plus any carry left over from adding the tens and ones digits of y and z.

If there is no carry, then the hundreds digit of x equals the sum of the hundreds digits of y and z. For instance, $300 + 400 = 700$. The hundreds digits of y and z (3 and 4) sum to the hundreds digit of x (7).

However, that is not always the case. It is also true that $360 + 450 = 810$. In this case, the hundreds digits of y and z (3 and 4) do not sum to the hundreds digit of x (8). That is because of the tens digits of y and z. $60 + 50 = 110$, which carries 1 over to the hundreds.

Therefore, to determine whether the hundreds digits add up, we really need to know about the tens digits of y and z. If the tens digits of y and z sum to more than 10, then the hundreds digits of y and z will not sum to the hundreds digit of x.

(1): SUFFICIENT. This statement tells us that the tens digits of y and z sum to the tens digit of x.

What this tells us is that the tens digits of y and z must sum to less than 10. Otherwise the tens digit of x would not equal their sum. For instance, in the sum $360 + 450 = 810$, the tens digits don't add up $(6 + 5 \neq 1)$.

No matter what numbers we pick, as long as the tens digits of y and z sum to less than 10, the hundreds digits of y and z will sum to the hundreds digit of x.

$220 + 660 = 880$ $(2 + 6 = 8)$
$166 + 529 = 695$ $(1 + 5 = 6)$
$435 + 564 = 999$ $(4 + 5 = 9)$

(2): INSUFFICIENT. This statement tells us that summing the ones digits of y and z results in a number that is less than 10. However, this is not enough because the tens digits of y and z could still be big enough to create a carry into the hundreds digits when they are summed.

Examples can be used to illustrate this and to prove insufficiency.

$245 + 324 = 569$ $(2 + 3 = 5)$
$470 + 150 = 620$ $(4 + 1 \neq 6)$

The correct answer is (A): Statement (1) ALONE is sufficient, but statement (2) alone is not sufficient to answer the question asked.

DS 134. <u>Word Problems</u>: Overlapping Sets
Difficulty: Devilish **OG Page:** 287

This is an advanced version of the standard ***Overlapping Sets*** question type, so we want to adapt our overlapping sets strategy.

One approach might be to set up a ***Triple-Set Matrix***, which is similar to the ***Double-Set Matrix***. The only difference is that there is an extra row and column to take care of the additional choices. The shaded box represents the answer to the question.

Candidate N	Candidate M			
	Fav.	Unfav.	Not Sure	Total
Fav.	?			30
Unfav.				35
Not Sure				35
Total	40	20	40	100

Since we are only finding voters who had responded "Favorable" to the candidates, we can also simplify this into a ***Double-Set Matrix*** by combining the "Unfavorable" and "Not Sure" responses:

Candidate N	Candidate M		
	Fav.	Unfav./Not Sure	Total
Fav.	?		30
Unfav./Not Sure			70
Total	40	60	100

(1): SUFFICIENT. Since this statement deals with voters that responded with "Favorable," insert this information into the Double-Set Matrix. We find that 10 voters had responded "Favorable" for both candidates.

Candidate N	Candidate M		
	Fav.	Unfav./ Not Sure	Total
Fav.	10	20	30
Unfav./ Not Sure	***30***	***40***	70
Total	40	60	100

(2): INSUFFICIENT. Since this statement deals with voters that responded with "Unfavorable," we will use our Triple-Set Matrix. This does not provide enough information to answer the question.

Candidate N	Candidate M			
	Fav.	Unfav.	Not Sure	Total
Fav.	?			30
Unfav.		10		35
Not Sure				35
Total	40	20	40	100

The Triple-Set Matrix is useful conceptually, but when we break it out in its full glory, we will almost never have enough information to fill it out completely. There are just too many boxes.

The correct answer is (A): Statement (1) ALONE is sufficient, but statement (2) alone is not sufficient.

DS 135. Number Properties: Divisibility & Primes
Difficulty: Devilish **OG Page:** 287

This is a very confusing problem! We need to figure out what it is really asking before we know what to do with the given information.

We are told that each of n students will be assigned to one of m classrooms and asked if it is possible to do this in such a way that each classroom will have the same number of students. In other words, we want to know if n students can be divided evenly into m classrooms. We know that m and n must both be integers because they are quantities, so this must be a ***Divisibility*** problem!

This question can be rephrased as, "Is n divisible by m?"

The other information that we are given about m and n is that $3 < m < 13$ and $n > 13$.

(1): INSUFFICIENT. This statement tells us that $3n$ is divisible by m.

The theory behind this problem is confusing, so a good approach here is to ***Choose Smart Numbers***. Maybe by picking numbers we can figure out what's really going on here.

Now the question is, do we pick a number for n first, or for m? If we pick a number for n first, it seems more straightforward to figure out what m could be (because m can only be between 3 and 13).

The question states that $n > 13$, so let's try $n = 14$. The question states that $3n$ is divisible by m. If n is 14, then $3n = 3 \times 14 = 42$.

If $3n$ is 42, what could m be? Of the numbers between 3 and 13, 42 is divisible by 6 and 7.

Now we know that, when $n = 14$, m can be 6 or 7. Now let's go back to the original question, "Is n divisible by m ?"

If $n = 14$ and $m = 6$, then n is not divisible by m, and the answer to the question is NO.

If $n = 14$ and $m = 7$, then n is divisible by m and the answer to the question is YES.

Before looking at Statement (2), let's figure out why this statement is insufficient. Let's look at the smart numbers we picked using prime factors. Prime factors are important to many divisibility problems, and this is no exception.

When $n = 14$, $3 \times 14 = 3 \times 2 \times 7$.

For $(3 \times 2 \times 7)$ to be divisible by m, it must have all the prime factors that m has. That's why the only two possible values for m are 6 (2×3) and 7.

Now we can see why $3n$ being divisible by m did not guarantee that n would be divisible by m. m is able to have a 3 as a prime factor that did not originally come from n.

(2): SUFFICIENT. Now that we have a sense of why Statement (1) was insufficient, we can use that understanding to see why Statement (2) *is* sufficient.

This statement tells us that $13n$ is divisible by m. The difference between the two statements is that there are possible values of m that are divisible by 3, but there are no possible values of m that are divisible by 13. Therefore, the only way that $13n$ can be divisible by m is if n contains all the prime factors of m. And that is just another way of saying that n must be divisible by m.

A quick look at a few numbers confirms that this statement is sufficient:

If $n = 14$, $13n = 13 \times 2 \times 7$. Possible values of m: 7 (14 is divisible by 7)

If $n = 15$, $13n = 13 \times 3 \times 5$. Possible values of m = 5 (15 is divisible by 5)

If $n = 16$, $13n = 13 \times 2^4$. Possible values of m = 4, 8. (16 is divisible by 4 and 8)

The correct answer is (B): Statement (2) ALONE is sufficient, but statement (1) alone is not sufficient to answer the question asked.

DS 136. Algebra: Linear Equations
Difficulty: Medium **OG Page:** 287

This problem looks worse than it actually is. We are told that "$\circ$" is one of the standard arithmetic operations +, –, or × and asked if the strange looking expression holds for all numbers. If we knew which of the operations $\circ$ represented, we could figure this out by testing numbers, so we can rephrase this question as "Is $\circ$ addition, subtraction, or multiplication?"

Alternatively, we might recognize the expression

$$k \circ (l + m) = (k \circ l) + (k \circ m)$$

as the *distributive property*, which only holds for multiplication and is normally written as:

$$k \times (l + m) = (k \times l) + (k \times m)$$

If so, we would rephrase this question as "Is $\circ$ multiplication?"

(1): SUFFICIENT. If $k \circ 1 \neq 1 \circ k$ for only some values of k, then $\circ$ cannot represent multiplication, because $k \times 1 = 1 \times k$ for all values of k. This means that we can answer the question with a definitive *No*.

Incidentally, we can show that $\circ$ cannot represent addition either, because $k + 1 = 1 + k$ is also true for all values of k. Therefore, $\circ$ must represent subtraction.

Alternatively, we can test numbers. $2 \times 1 = 1 \times 2$ and $2 + 1 = 1 + 2$, but $2 - 1 \neq 1 - 2$. So we know we are looking at subtraction and:

$$k - (l + m) = k - l - m$$
$$(k - l) + (k - m) = 2k - l - m$$

The answer to the question is a definite *No.*

(2): SUFFICIENT. This statement indicates that $\circ$ must be subtraction. Thus, we can answer the question with a definitive *No.*

We don't have to test numbers because we already showed this was the case for subtraction when we worked on the precious statement.

The correct answer is (D): EACH statement ALONE is sufficient to answer the question asked.

DS 137. Word Problems: Overlapping Sets
Difficulty: Easy **OG Page:** 287

This ***Overlapping Sets*** problem describes cars that either have power windows or do not, and that either have a stereo or do not. The question is how many cars have *neither* power windows *nor* a stereo?

To structure the problem, we can use a ***Double-Set Matrix;*** the question is shaded below:

		Power Windows?		
		Yes	No	Total
Stereo?	Yes			
	No			
	Total			60

(1): INSUFFICIENT. Knowing that 20 cars had a stereo but not power windows does not help us calculate the number of cars that have neither power windows nor a stereo.

		Power Windows?		
		Yes	No	Total
Stereo?	Yes		20	
	No			
	Total			60

(2): INSUFFICIENT. Knowing that 30 cars had a stereo *and* power windows does not help us calculate the number of cars that have neither power windows nor a stereo.

		Power Windows?		
		Yes	No	Total
Stereo?	Yes	30		
	No			
	Total			60

(1) AND (2): INSUFFICIENT. With these combined pieces of information, we know that 50 cars had a stereo, so 10 did not. However, we do not know exactly how many of those cars had power windows.

The number is now bounded between 0 and 10, but we need to know the precise value.

		Power Windows?		
		Yes	No	Total
Stereo?	Yes	30	20	50
	No			10
	Total			60

The correct answer is (E): Statements (1) and (2) TOGETHER are not sufficient.

DS 138. Word Problems: Overlapping Sets
Difficulty: Hard **OG Page:** 287

This standard ***Overlapping Sets*** problem presents two binary criteria: French vs. no French, and Spanish vs. no Spanish. Construct a ***Double-Set Matrix*** according to these criteria, filling in the information from the prompt and circling the desired quantity. Note that the problem deals only with students who take French or Spanish or both, so that there are 0 students taking *neither* course. This subtle but critical piece of information is easy to miss.

As is customary on all Double-Set Matrix problems, *immediately* fill in the third entry in any row that contains two existing entries (in italics).

	French	No French	Total
Spanish	?	*100*	
No Spanish		0	
Total	*200*	100	300

(1): SUFFICIENT. According to this statement, 60 students do *not* study Spanish. Add this number into the matrix (in bold), and then fill in the third entry in all rows and columns containing two existing entries (in italics):

	French	No French	Total
Spanish	*140*	100	*240*
No Spanish	*60*	0	**60**
Total	200	100	300

140 students are taking both languages.

(2): SUFFICIENT. According to this statement, 240 students study Spanish. Add this number into the matrix (in bold), and then fill in the third entry in all rows and columns containing two existing entries (in italics):

	French	No French	Total
Spanish	*140*	100	**240**
No Spanish	*60*	0	*60*
Total	200	100	300

140 students are taking both languages.

The correct answer is (D): EACH statement ALONE is sufficient.

DS 139. Word Problems: Statistics
Difficulty: Hard **OG Page:** 287

This ***Statistics*** question asks for the ***Median*** number of employees assigned per project for the projects at Company Z. The median of a set is the value that falls in the middle of the set, when the set is arranged in increasing order.

(1): INSUFFICIENT. Knowing that 25% of the projects at Company Z have 4 *or more* employees assigned to each project tells us that 75% have less than 4 (i.e., 3 or less). While the median will definitely be less than 4 (i.e., in the 75% region), it could be 1, 2, or 3.

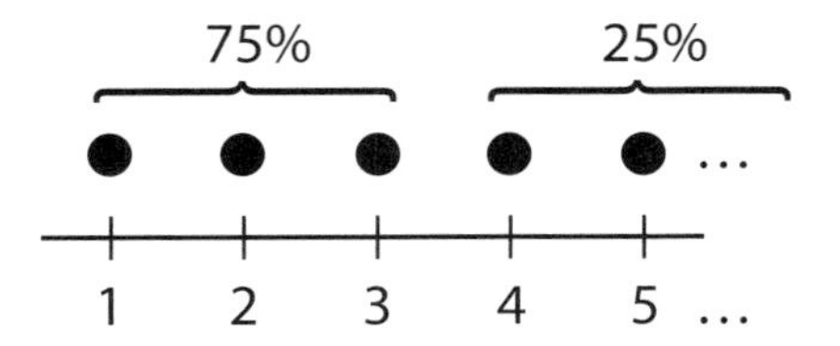

At this point, the problem has introduced both ***Percents*** and ***Inequalities*** as relevant issues.

(2): INSUFFICIENT. Knowing that 35% of the projects at Company Z have 2 or fewer employees assigned to each project tells us that 65% have more than 2 (i.e., 3 or more). While the median will definitely be greater than 2, it could be 3, 4, 5, etc.

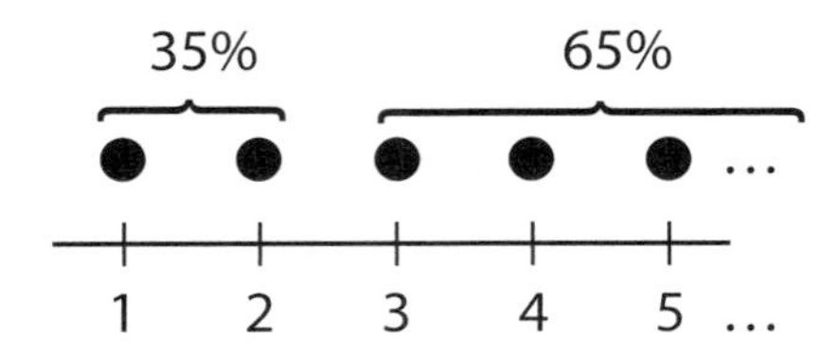

(1) AND (2): SUFFICIENT. Combining the two statements gives us enough information to locate the median. If 35% of the projects have 2 or fewer employees and 25% of projects have 4 or more employees, the median value will be in the middle 40% of projects.

The number of employees assigned to any project must be an integer, and there is only one integer value between 2 and 4, namely 3.

Therefore the median number of employees assigned per project for the projects at Company Z must be 3.

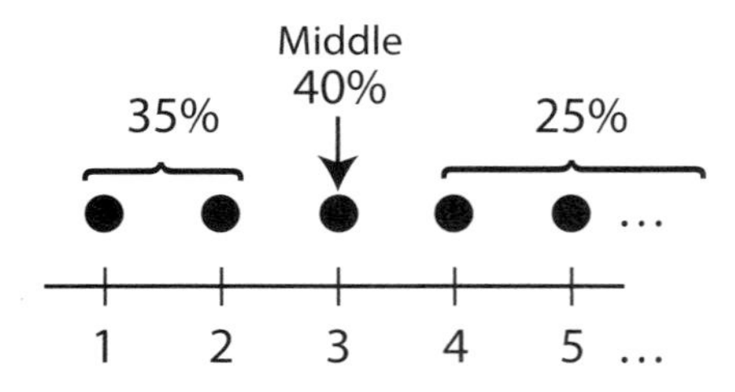

Notice how the ***Hidden Constraint*** on the number of employees (there must be a whole number of employees) operates to create sufficiency. There are many numbers between 2 and 4, but only one *integer*.

The correct answer is (C): BOTH statements TOGETHER are sufficient, but NEITHER statement ALONE is sufficient.

DS 140. Word Problems: Extra Problem Types
Difficulty: Medium **OG Page:** 287

This is a yes/no question about a ***Scheduling*** issue. Was the appointment on a Wednesday?

(1): INSUFFICIENT. 60 hours is exactly $2\frac{1}{2}$ days. Knowing that two and a half days before the appointment it was Monday does not tell us what day the appointment was. The appointment could have been on Wednesday or Thursday and still satisfied this condition.

To verify, we can ***Test Extreme Values***: early Monday morning and late Monday night. If 60 hours prior to the appointment it was 12:01am Monday morning, then the appointment was at 12:01pm Wednesday afternoon. At the other extreme, if 60 hours prior to the appointment was midnight Monday, then the appointment was at noon on Thursday.

We can see that the appointment could have been on a Wednesday or a Thursday.

(2): INSUFFICIENT. This tells us nothing about the day of the week.

(1) AND (2): SUFFICIENT. The second statement tells us that the appointment was in the latter half of the day. Therefore, Thursday is no longer an option. We cannot reach from Monday into the latter half of Thursday in only 2.5 days, no matter how late we start on Monday. The appointment must have been on a Wednesday.

The correct answer is (C): BOTH statements TOGETHER are sufficient, but NEITHER statement ALONE is sufficient.

DS 141. Word Problems: Algebraic Translations
Difficulty: Devilish **OG Page:** 288

We are told that a company's total cost for manufacturing some number of units of product X last year was \$100,000 plus 5% of the total revenue from the sales of that number of units of product X. We are also told that the company made a profit on product X. Finally, we are asked if more than 21,000 units of product X were sold last year.

There is a lot of information here and we need to ***Translate*** it. First, think about variables we will need. We know that we need a variable for the number of units of product X sold because that is what the question is about, so call that variable n. The other big unknown seems to be the total revenue from sales of product X, so call the total revenue r.

We can then translate the given information about the costs as

$$\text{total costs} = 100{,}000 + 0.05r$$

So

$$\text{Profit} = r - (100{,}000 + 0.05rn)$$
$$= 0.95r - 100{,}000$$

There's also something very important the question tells us about the profit, even if it may not initially seem important. We know the company made a profit on product X, which means the profit is positive. Consequently, the profit is greater than 0:

$$0.95r - 100{,}000 > 0$$
$$0.95r > 100{,}000$$

And we want to use this to figure out whether $n > 21{,}000$.

(1): INSUFFICIENT. Translate the statement:

$$r > 110{,}000$$

Without knowing the price per unit of product X, it will be impossible to tell how many units of product X were sold.

For instance, if product X costs \$1, then the company sold at least 110,000 units. But if product X costs \$10,000, then we only know that at least 11 units were sold.

(2): SUFFICIENT. Translate the statement. If the per-unit revenue (that is, the sale price) of product X is \$5, then the total revenue must equal 5 times the total number of units sold:

$$r = 5n$$

Combine this with the given inequality:

$$0.95r > 100{,}000$$
$$0.95(5n) > 100{,}000$$

To make the math easier, change 0.95 to $\frac{19}{20}$:

$$\frac{19}{20} \times 5n > 100{,}000$$
$$\frac{19n}{4} > 100{,}000$$
$$19n > 400{,}000$$

Unfortunately, we do have to solve this all the way because it is an inequality, and it could be possible that n is greater than a number less than 21,000, which would make the answer to the question MAYBE, which would mean that the statement was insufficient.

$$\begin{array}{r} 21 \\ 19\overline{)400,000} \\ \underline{38} \\ 20 \end{array}$$

Fortunately, we can stop the long division here. No matter what the actual quotient is, it will definitely be greater than 21,000. Thus, $n > 21{,}000$.

The correct answer is (B): Statement (2) ALONE is sufficient, but statement (1) alone is not sufficient to answer the question asked.

DS 142. Word Problems: Algebraic Translations
Difficulty: Medium **OG Page:** 288

In this ***Algebraic Translations*** problem, we are told that there were 4 more heads than tails. Thus, $h = t + 4$, where h is the number of heads and t is the number of tails.

If we have one more distinct ***Linear Equation*** with h and t, we can solve for both variables.

(1): SUFFICIENT. This statement tells us that $h + t = 24$. We now have ***Two Different Linear Equations*** and ***Two Unknowns.*** Knowing that we could solve for h with these two equations, we can stop at this point.

To illustrate that we could indeed solve for h, we can ***Substitute*** $t + 4$ for h in this equation and get

$$(t + 4) + t = 24$$
$$2t + 4 = 24$$
$$2t + 4 = 24$$
$$2t = 20$$
$$t = 10$$

Since $h = t + 4$, we know $h = 14$.

(2): SUFFICIENT. This statement gives us another equation: $3h + t = 52$. Again, we have a second distinct equation and can solve for h.

If we really want, we can substitute $t + 4$ for h and get:

$$3(t + 4) + t = 52$$
$$4t + 12 = 52$$
$$4t = 40$$
$$t = 10$$

Since $h = t + 4$, $h = 14$.

The correct answer is (D): EACH statement ALONE is sufficient.

DS 143. Word Problems: Statistics
Difficulty: Devilish **OG Page:** 288

In this ***Statistics*** problem, we are told that Carl deposited $120 into his account on the 15th of every month for several consecutive months, starting in January, and then withdrew $50 on the 15th of every month for the remainder of the year. We are also told that his balance at the end of May was $2,600.

We are asked for the range of monthly closing balances for the year. In order to know this range, we need to know for how many months Carl deposited $120 and for how many months he withdrew $50 or, in other words, the month in which he switched from deposits to withdrawals.

To work through this problem, we need a clear understanding of Carl's strange story (how his deposits and withdrawals work in sequence). As we proceed, we will have to ***Test Scenarios*** logically. We will also have to think about ***Inequalities***, since these are the constraints imposed by the statements.

(1): INSUFFICIENT. We know that Carl could not have withdrawn $50 in April, because his closing balance for April would need to have been at least $50 greater than it was in May. From this statement, we know that this was not the case.

So Carl did not begin withdrawing from the account until at least June 15. (We know he did not withdraw in May, since he would have needed $2,650 in his account in April to afford such a withdrawal and still have a balance of $2,600.)

Thus, Carl must have deposited $120 into his account every month through at least May. If he had $2,600 in the account in May, the fifth month, he must have made 5 deposits of $120 apiece, for a total of $600 in deposits. So he began the year with $2,000 in the account.

But we do not know when he began withdrawing, so we cannot say what the range of balances was for the whole year.

(2): INSUFFICIENT. Again, we must consider possible scenarios. If Carl had deposited into his account in June, his balance would have been $2,720. Since his balance for June was less than that, he must have withdrawn on June 15. But we cannot tell whether June was the first month in which Carl withdrew or the second, third, etc.

(1) AND (2): SUFFICIENT. We know from statement (1) that Carl did not begin withdrawing until at least June. We know from statement (2) that he definitely did withdraw in June.

If June was the first possible month in which Carl could have withdrawn and he actually did withdraw in June, then we know in how many months Carl deposited and in how many months he withdrew.

We can thus figure out the range of balances for the entire year.

The correct answer is (C): BOTH statements TOGETHER are sufficient, but NEITHER statement ALONE is sufficient.

DS 144. Word Problems: Statistics
Difficulty: Medium **OG Page:** 288

We want to know if all of the numbers in a certain list of 15 numbers are equal. The question cannot be usefully rephrased, but we should recognize that we are dealing with ***Sets*** and may need to run ***Statistics*** on the members of the set.

(1): INSUFFICIENT. The sum of the 15 numbers is 60. Each of the numbers *could* be 4, but there are many other possibilities. For instance:

$$4 + 4 + 4 + 4 + 4 + 4 + 4 + 4 + 4 + 4 + 4 + 4 + 4 + 4 + 4 = 60$$

$$4 + 4 + 4 + 4 + 4 + 4 + 4 + 4 + 4 + 4 + 4 + 4 + 4 + 7 + 1 = 60$$

(2): SUFFICIENT. The sum of *any* 3 of the numbers is 12. While it is possible to use this statement to prove that each of the numbers is therefore 4, it is reasonable to simply ***Test Scenarios.*** Go ahead and try to make a list of numbers of which any 3 sum to 12. It will quickly become apparent that this is impossible unless each number is equal to 4.

Even if we construct a list such that only two numbers are not 4, we cannot guarantee that *any* three numbers in the list sum to 12.

4, 4, 4, 4, 4, 4, 4, 4, 4, 4, 4, 4, 4, 5, 3

Example 1: 4 + 5 + 3 = 12

Example 2: 4 + 4 + 5 = 13

Although we did not wind up computing any statistics, for other problems we should recognize the consequences of having all the numbers in the set be equal. For instance, the standard deviation will be zero.

The correct answer is (B): Statement (2) ALONE is sufficient, but statement (1) alone is not sufficient.

DS 145. Geometry: Polygons
Difficulty: Medium **OG Page:** 288

This ***Polygons*** problem provides a diagram of a ***Trapezoid*** with certain information given:

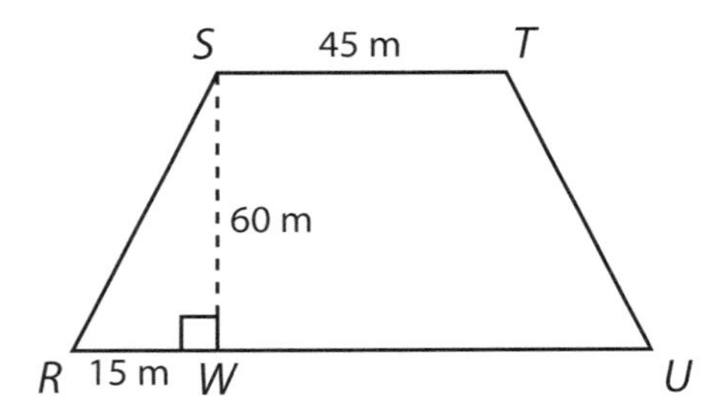

The ***Area of the Trapezoid*** is represented by the following formula:

$$A=\frac{1}{2}(b_1+b_2)h$$

In this formula, b_1 and b_2 represent the lengths of the parallel sides and h represents the height of a perpendicular line drawn between the two parallel sides.

The base *ST* and the height *SW* are given. To determine the area of the trapezoid, we need to find the value for b_2, which is *RU* in the diagram.

Thus, we can ***Rephrase*** the question as "What is the length of *RU*?"

(1): SUFFICIENT. This statement directly answers our question. We can stop here, knowing that $RU = 80$.

(2): SUFFICIENT. Given that $TU = 20\sqrt{10}$, we can find *RU*. First, we ***Draw a Line*** parallel to *SW*, starting at point *T* and dropping to line *RU*. Label this line 60 m, since it the same length as *SW*. We label the new point at which this new line crosses *RU*. Let's call it *X*. Finally, we can label line *WX* 45 m, since it is the same length as *ST*.

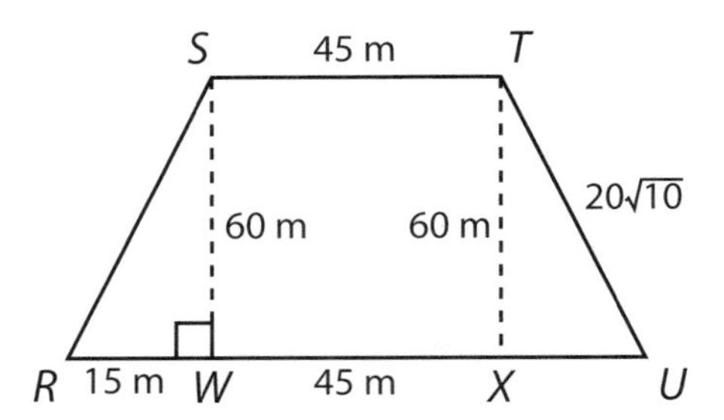

The only missing information to determine the length of line *RU* is the length of line *XU*. This can be calculated using the ***Pythagorean Theorem:***

$$(60)^2+XU^2=(20\sqrt{10})^2$$

Since *XU* is a positive length, we know that we can solve this equation for *XU* and therefore compute *RU*. At this point, we should stop.

For extra practice, calculate *XU:*

$$(60)^2+XU^2=(2\sqrt{10})^2$$
$$3{,}600+XU^2=4{,}000$$
$$XU^2=400$$
$$XU=20$$

The correct answer is (D): EACH statement ALONE is sufficient.

DS 146. Word Problems: Statistics
Difficulty: Easy **OG Page:** 288

This ***Statistics*** problem asks us about the makeup of a set of six numbers with a predetermined ***Average*** or mean.

The strategy of using ***Residuals*** works well here. Residuals are the differences between a set's data points and its average—in other words, the "overs" and "unders" relative to the mean. For any set, the residuals sum to zero. The positive residuals and negative residuals must cancel out.

For example, in the set {10, 20, 30, 40} the mean is 25 and the residuals are {−15, −5, +5, +15}. Notice that the sum of the residuals is zero.

All this is a fancy way of saying that numbers *over* the mean must be balanced out by numbers *under* the meant, and vice versa.

Since the set in question has a mean of 75 and we are asked how many of the numbers are equal to 75, we can ***Rephrase*** this question as "How many of the six numbers have a residual of zero?"

(1): SUFFICIENT. If none of the six numbers is less than 75, there can be no negative residuals. There are no numbers *under* the mean. Thus, there cannot be any numbers *over* the mean.

With no positive or negative residuals, all of the numbers must be equal to the mean, so all 6 of the numbers are equal to 75.

(2): SUFFICIENT. Similarly, if none of the six numbers is greater than 75, there are no numbers *over* the mean. Thus, there cannot be any numbers *under* the mean.

All six of the numbers must again be equal to 75.

The correct answer is (D): EACH statement ALONE is sufficient.

DS 147. <u>Word Problems</u>: Algebraic Translations
Difficulty: Easy **OG Page:** 288

This problem has many moving parts, including ***Algebraic Translations*** and ***Percents.*** To get started, let's ***Name Variables*** and list all the relevant quantities:

F = Full ticket price

x = percent of full price paid for discount tickets

$\frac{x}{100}F$ = discount price

d = number of discounted tickets sold

$400 - d$ = number of full-price tickets sold, since 400 tickets in all were sold.

Now we can set up the following equation for the ***Cost Relationship***:

$$\text{Revenue} = \left(\frac{x}{100}F\right)d + F(400 - d)$$

Notice that this equation expresses revenue in terms of three variables. Moreover, the relationship is complicated.

To determine the total revenue for the theater, we most likely will need the values of x, F, and d individually.

(1): INSUFFICIENT. $x = 50$, but we do not know the values of F and d. We cannot compute the total revenue.

(2): INSUFFICIENT. F = \$20, but we do not know the values of x and d. Again, we cannot compute the total revenue.

(1) AND (2): INSUFFICIENT. We still know the values of both x and F, but we do not know the value of d.

The lack of sufficiency should make sense intuitively. For one thing, we have an equation with three unknowns, but we are only given two of the needed values in the statements.

Putting those values in, we can see that the full price tickets sold for \$20 and discounted tickets for 50% of that, or \$10. Even with both statements, we don't know how many tickets were sold at a discount. If no tickets sold at a discount, the revenue would be 400(\$20) = \$8,000. If all the tickets sold at a discount, the revenue would be 400(\$10) = \$4,000.

The correct answer is (E): Statements (1) and (2) TOGETHER are not sufficient.

DS 148. FDPs: FDPs
Difficulty: Hard **OG Page:** 288

This problem involves ***Connections between Fractions and Decimals***. Specifically, we have to deal with a very specific kind of decimal: a ***Terminating Decimal***.

A terminating decimal is one that ends, such as 0.1 or 0.77. These decimals have a finite number of nonzero digits after the decimal. Integers count as terminating decimals, too.

All fractions with integers on top and bottom can be expressed *either* as terminating decimals *or* as infinitely repeating decimals—e.g., $0.\overline{6}$. (By the way, a decimal that continues infinitely *without* a repeating pattern, on the other hand, is irrational and *cannot* be expressed as a fraction. $\sqrt{2}$ or π are two examples of non-terminating, non-repeating decimals.)

Note that in determining whether a fraction will be equivalent to a terminating or non-terminating decimal, the most important element is the divisor. Certain divisors, such as 2, will always create a terminating decimal when divided into an integer (e.g. 3/2 = 1.5, and 4/2 = 2), but others, such as 3, will only do so in certain situations. For instance, 2/3 = 0.66666666...(non-terminating), but 6/3 = 2 (terminating).

The crucial test is whether the denominator has only 2's and/or 5's as Prime Factors, after we cancel common factors with the numerator. Denominators containing *only* 2's and 5's will always produce terminating decimals when divided into integers.

(1): INSUFFICIENT. This only tells us that the numerator r is an integer between 90 and 100. We are given no information about the denominator. Thus, we don't know whether the denominator only contains 2's and 5's as prime factors, and we cannot answer the question.

We can ***Test Numbers*** to see what happens with different combinations of numbers. For instance, 93/6 will be a terminating decimal (15.5), but 92/3 will not ($30.\overline{6}$).

(2): SUFFICIENT. This tells us that the denominator is 4. Any integer divided by 4 will produce a finite terminating decimal. We can confirm this by trying out a few numbers:

1/4 = 0.25
2/4 = 0.5
3/5 = 0.75
4/4 = 1
5/4 = 1.25
6/4 = 1.5 and so on.

We can also see that 4 only has 2 as a prime factor. 4 fits our criteria for creating terminating decimals.

The correct answer is (B): Statement (2) ALONE is sufficient, but statement (1) alone is not sufficient.

DS 149. Geometry: Triangles & Diagonals
Difficulty: Medium **OG Page:** 289

For ***Geometry*** questions in Data Sufficiency, we should assume that the given drawings are NOT to scale. In this ***Triangles*** problem, it seems as though point D lies at a point equidistant from A, B, and C. However, this is not guaranteed.

We are asked for the value of $x + y$, a ***Combined Expression*** or Combo.

(1): INSUFFICIENT. We are given the value of x. But can we find the value for y? We know that y must be larger than x, and thus greater than 70. However, we do not know where point D is within the triangle. Thus, we cannot know the value of y. Therefore, we do not know the value of $x + y$.

(2): INSUFFICIENT. Because the triangles are each ***Isosceles,*** we might assume that $AB = BC$ and $AD = DC$. However, we know nothing about the length of AC, nor do we know the height of B or D above segment AC. It might be helpful for us to ***Draw Pictures*** displaying two possible variations of the triangle, to show what we know *and* what we do not know:

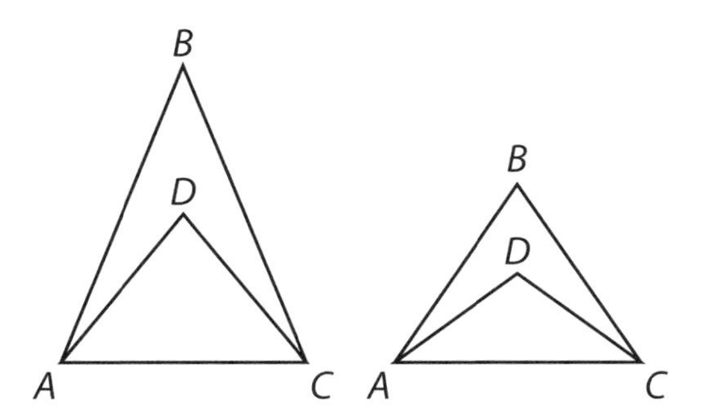

Each of the above triangles fits the current parameters. However, we can clearly see that the angles have changed. Moreover, both angles are larger in the second triangle. Thus, we know for certain that their sum has grown as well.

In fact, we do not technically know which sides of each triangle are meant to be equal. The explanation in the Official Guide assumed that the "sides of each mountain" are meant to be equal, but this assumption is unwarranted. It could certainly be the case that $AB = AC$ rather than $AB = BC$. Remember, the pictures are not necessarily drawn to scale. We already know that this statement is insufficient, but we should be careful about making unjustified assumptions.

(1) AND (2): INSUFFICIENT. We still do not know the value of y (because we have not learned the position of point D). Again, we can show this by creating two separate drawings, each of which meets all of the current parameters (even going ahead and assuming $AB = BC$):

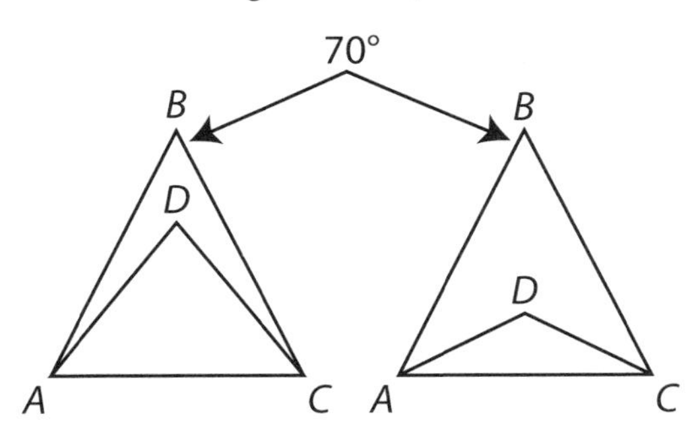

The correct answer is (E): Statements (1) and (2) TOGETHER are not sufficient.

DS 150. <u>FDPs</u>: Percents
Difficulty: Easy **OG Page:** 289

This ***Percents*** problem, which involves a ***Salary Relationship,*** asks for the dollar amount that Jean earned as commission from her sales in the first half of 1988.

In order to know this dollar amount, we need to know her sales and her rate of commission during that time period, or we need enough information to recreate this data.

(1): INSUFFICIENT. This statement tells us that Jean earned a commission of 5% from her total sales in 1988, but without knowing how much she sold in dollar terms, we cannot determine the actual amount of her commission.

Furthermore, we do not know how much of her yearly commission she earned in the first half of the year.

(2): INSUFFICIENT. From this statement, we learn that Jean's average monthly sales in the second half of 1988 were $10,000 more than her average monthly sales in the first half of the year.

However, we do not know how much she sold in either half of the year, or for the whole year. We also do not know how much commission Jean earned on her sales.

(1) AND (2): INSUFFICIENT. Even with both pieces of information, we do not know how much Jean sold in the first half of the year in dollar terms.

As a further subtlety, we do not know that Jean's commission was a *uniform* 5% of sales throughout the year. We only know that what she earned in commission was an amount equal to 5% of her *total* sales for the year.

We can ***Translate*** the information we have and place it in a ***Table***. This way, we can see how big the gaps are. ***Name a Variable*** and let x be the average monthly sales in the first half of the year.

	Sales ($)	Commission Rate (%)	Commission ($)
First half of 1988	$6x$	?	
Second half of 1988	$6x +$ 60,000	?	
All of 1988	$12x +$ 60,000	5%	5%($12x +$ 60,000)

The correct answer is (E): Statements (1) and (2) TOGETHER are not sufficient.

DS 151. FDPs: FDPs
Difficulty: Medium **OG Page:** 289

This problem, which involves ***Connections Between Percents & Fractions*** and ***Percent Change,*** benefits from upfront analysis before we consider the statements.

The price per share of Stock X increased by 10%—that is, it went from x to $1.1x$. Meanwhile, the price of Stock Y decreased by 10%—that is, it went from y to $0.9y$. The question asks, "$0.9y$ is what percent of x?"

We can ***Name Variables*** and assign p as the percent we are seeking. The question may now be ***Translated*** to an equation:

$$0.9y = \frac{p}{100}x$$

Isolate p:

$$0.9y = px$$

$$p = \frac{90y}{x}$$

Thus, the question may be ***Rephrased*** as, "What is $90y/x$?" or simply, "What is y/x?"

Because the question asks us for a percentage and not the actual values, a ***Ratio*** of y to x will be sufficient to answer this question.

(1): SUFFICIENT. The increased price of X was equal to the original price of Y. This provides a ratio and is sufficient. Algebraically, we have:

$$1.1x = y$$

$$\frac{y}{x} = 1.1$$

(2): SUFFICIENT. The increase in X was 10/11 the decrease in Y. This also provides a ratio and is sufficient.

If we write out the algebraic steps, we get:

$$0.1x = \frac{10}{11}(0.1y)$$

$$x = \frac{10}{11}y$$

$$\frac{11}{10} = \frac{y}{x}$$

The correct answer is (D): EACH statement ALONE is sufficient.

DS 152. Geometry: Triangles & Diagonals
Difficulty: Easy **OG Page:** 289

Both ***Right Triangles*** and ***Squares*** are involved in this problem. To know the area of A, we need to find the length of a side of square A.

Name Variables to represent the sides of the three squares:

a = length of a side of square A
b = length of a side of square B
c = length of a side of square C

We can use the formula for the ***Area of a Triangle*** and set up an equation for the area of triangle D, which we know is 4.

Area = ½ (base)(height)
$4 = \frac{1}{2}bc$
$bc = 8$

Because triangle D is a right triangle, we also can use the ***Pythagorean Theorem*** to relate its sides:

$$b^2 + c^2 = a^2$$

Because $bc = 8$, if we know either b or c, we can find the other. We can then find out a^2 by using the Pythagorean Theorem equation.

Thus, we can ***Rephrase*** the question as "What is the value of either b or c?"

(1): SUFFICIENT. Use the formula for the ***Area of a Square*** to translate this statement:

$b^2 = 9$

$b = 3$

This directly answers the rephrased question.

Although it's unnecessary, we can compute the value of a for practice. We can use the value of b to solve for c because $bc = 8$.

$(3)c = 8$

$c = 8/3$

Now plug b and c into the Pythagorean Theorem to solve for a.

$$(3)^2 + \left(\frac{8}{3}\right)^2 = a^2$$

$$9 + \frac{64}{9} = a^2$$

$$\frac{145}{9} = a^2$$

$$\frac{\sqrt{145}}{3} = a$$

(2): SUFFICIENT. Use the formula for the area of a square to translate this statement:

$$c^2 = \frac{64}{9}$$

$$c = \frac{8}{3}$$

This directly answers the rephrased question.

Although it's unnecessary, we could solve for a using the same method we used for statement (1).

The correct answer is (D): EACH statement ALONE is sufficient.

DS 153. Word Problems: Algebraic Translations
Difficulty: Easy **OG Page:** 289

In this ***Algebraic Translations*** problem, we know that $S = 2B$. In order to solve for S, we need the value of B, or another ***Linear Equation*** involving just S and B.

(1): SUFFICIENT. We can create a linear equation from this statement. Since we will then have ***Two Different Linear Equations*** with ***Two Unknowns***, we can stop right here. Under exam conditions, we should certainly move on right now.

For algebra practice, we can continue solving. Four years ago, Sara was $S - 4$, whereas Bill was $B - 4$. At that time, Sara's age was three times Bill's age. Write a relationship:

$S - 4 = 3(B - 4)$.

Substitute the original equation ($S = 2B$) into this equation

$$(2B) - 4 = 3(B - 4)$$

$$2B - 4 = 3B - 12$$

$$8 = B$$

Now that we have the value for B, we can solve for S.

$$S = 2B$$

$$S = 2(8)$$

$$S = 16$$

(2): SUFFICIENT. Again, this relationship will produce a distinct linear equation relating Sara's age and Bill's age. With two different linear equations at our disposal, we know right now that we have sufficiency.

Again for practice, let's lay out the algebra. Eight years from now, Sara will be $S + 8$ and Bill will be $B + 8$. At that time, Sara's age will be 1.5 times Bill's age.

$S + 8 = 1.5(B + 8)$

Combine this with the original equation: $S = 2B$:

$$(2B) + 8 = 1.5(B + 8)$$

$$2B + 8 = 1.5B + 12$$

$$0.5B = 4$$

$$B = 8$$

Just as we did in Statement (1), we can use the value of B to solve for S.

The correct answer is (D): EACH statement ALONE is sufficient.

DS 154. <u>Word Problems</u>: Statistics
Difficulty: Medium **OG Page:** 289

In this ***Statistics*** problem, we are asked whether the average number of words per paragraph for 25 paragraphs is less than 120.

Using the ***Average Formula,*** Sum = Average × Number of Terms, we must actually determine whether the sum of the number of words in all 25 paragraphs is less than 120 × 25 = 3,000. We already know that the report originally consisted of 2,600 words. For the sum to be less than 3,000, the two new paragraphs must consist of less than 400 words in total.

The ***Rephrased*** question is therefore "Do the two new paragraphs in the preface contain less than 400 words in total?"

As is common for Yes-No questions on Data Sufficiency, this question involves ***Inequalities.***

(1): INSUFFICIENT. If each paragraph of the preface has more than 100 words, then the total number of words for the two new paragraphs is greater than 200. Knowing that the total number of words was greater than 200 does not tell us whether the total was less than 400.

(2): SUFFICIENT. If each paragraph of the preface has fewer than 150 words, the total number of words in these two new paragraphs is less than 300. Thus, we know that the new paragraphs have less than 400 words in total.

The correct answer is (B): Statement (2) ALONE is sufficient, but statement (1) alone is not sufficient.

DS 155. <u>Geometry</u>: Coordinate Plane
Difficulty: Hard **OG Page:** 290

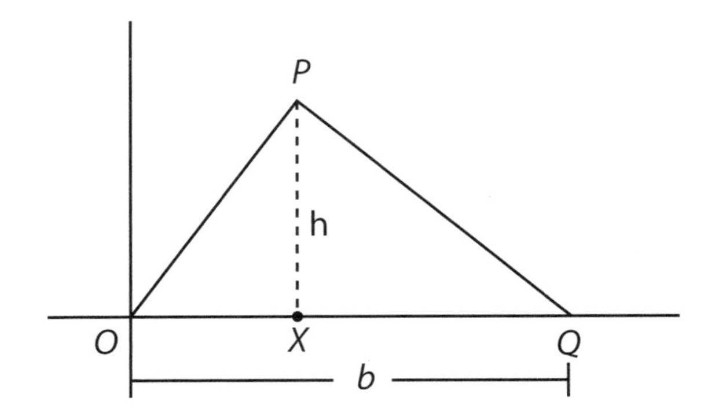

The question is asking whether the area of ΔOPQ is greater than 48, given that $OP < PQ$. We will need to consider the ***Area of a Triangle*** and ***Inequalities*** as well.

Redraw the Picture, adding labels and ***Naming Variables*** as necessary. We can label $\overline{OQ}$ as b, the base of the triangle. We can also drop a height from P to a point X and label this distance h, the height of the triangle.

We should also ***Exaggerate Constraints***. For instance, we are told that $OP < PQ$. In the diagram given, PQ is barely longer than OP, if at all. In our picture, we should make sure that PQ is *substantially* longer than OP. This way, our eyes will be working for us as we make sense of the diagram.

We can ***Rephrase*** the question as "Is $\frac{1}{2}bh > 48$?" or "Is $bh > 96$?"

(1): SUFFICIENT. Knowing the coordinates of point P tells us the value of $h = 8$, the y-coordinate of P. It also tells that $OX = 6$, the x-coordinate of P. This, however, is only *part* of the base b.

To understand why this statement is sufficient, first consider what would happen if $OP = PQ$. If $OP = PQ$, then ΔOPQ will be isosceles, and the height drawn to base OQ will be the perpendicular bisector of that base. Thus, we have $OX = XQ = 6$ (as shown below).

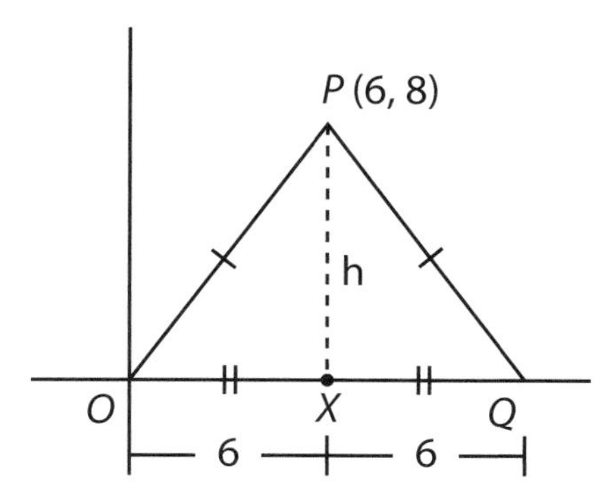

Since $OP < PQ$, however, PQ must extend further out, making $XQ > OX$ (shown below).

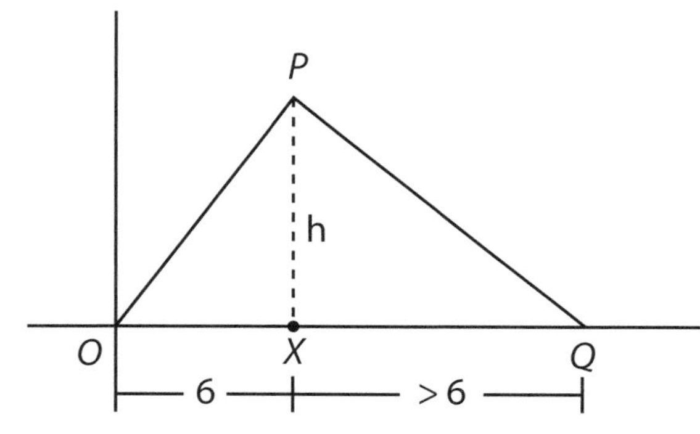

Therefore XQ must be greater than 6 and OQ must be greater than 12.

$$\text{Area}_{\Delta OPQ} = \frac{1}{2}bh$$
$$= \frac{1}{2}(\text{greater than } 12)(8)$$
$$= \text{greater than } 48$$

(2): INSUFFICIENT. Knowing the coordinates of point Q tells us nothing about the height of ΔOPQ.

The correct answer is (A): Statement (1) ALONE is sufficient, but statement (2) alone is not sufficient.

DS 156. Algebra: Linear Equations
Difficulty: Medium **OG Page:** 290

To attack this ***Linear Equations*** problem, we should first simplify this ***Double-Decker Fraction***, starting with the denominator:

$$S = \frac{\frac{2}{n}}{\frac{1}{x} + \frac{2}{3x}} = \frac{\frac{2}{n}}{\frac{3}{3x} + \frac{2}{3x}}$$
$$= \frac{\frac{2}{n}}{\frac{3+2}{3x}} = \frac{\frac{2}{n}}{\frac{5}{3x}} = \left(\frac{2}{n}\right)\left(\frac{3x}{5}\right) = \frac{6x}{5n}$$

Alternatively, we can simplify by using the universal ***Common Denominator***. This is the ***Least Common Multiple*** of each of the individual denominators within the fraction. Since the individual denominators are n, x, and $3x$, we know that $3xn$ is the universal common denominator:

$$S = \frac{\frac{2}{n}}{\frac{1}{x} + \frac{2}{3x}} = \frac{\left(\frac{2}{n}\right)(3xn)}{\left(\frac{1}{x} + \frac{2}{3x}\right)(3xn)} = \frac{6x}{3n + 2n} = \frac{6x}{5n}$$

Either way, we are asked for the value of S. Thus, we can ***Rephrase*** this question as "What is the value of $\frac{6x}{5n}$?

The key piece of information here is the ***Ratio*** x/n.

If we have the value for x/n, we can multiply it by 6/5 to solve for S.

Thus, we can rephrase further: "What is the value of x/n?"

(1): SUFFICIENT. This gives us a value for the ratio x/n. Namely, $x/n = 2$, so we can answer the rephrased question.

(2): INSUFFICIENT. This gives us a value for n, but we do not know the value for x.

A trap in this problem is that we might think we need both statements. After all, with both statements, we get values of both n and x. If we have both these values, we can solve for the value of any Combo of the two variables, including S.

However, it turns out that we only need the ratio of x to n, in order to find S.

The correct answer is (A): Statement (1) ALONE is sufficient, but statement (2) alone is not sufficient.

DS 157. FDPs: Digits & Decimals
Difficulty: Medium **OG Page:** 290

In this ***Digits & Decimals*** problem, we are told that $k = 5.1 \times 10^n$, with n as a positive integer. We are then asked for the value of k.

We will need to make use of ***Powers of Ten***. Since the value of n dictates the value of k, we can ***Rephrase*** the question as "What is n?"

(1): SUFFICIENT. If it is true that $6{,}000 < k < 500{,}000$ and that $k = 5.1 \times 10^n$, then it must be true that $k = 51{,}000$.

Since n is a positive integer, the only possible values of k are 51, 510, 5,100, 51,000, 510,000, etc. The only one of these values in the given range is 51,000.

(2): SUFFICIENT. If we know that $k^2 = 2.601 \times 10^9$, then we theoretically know the value of k, since 2.601×10^9 is a specific numeric value.

We do not need to compute the value of k. We simply need to recognize that we *could* find it.

We do not need to worry about the negative root of k^2, since we know that k must be positive. No matter the value of n, if $k = 5.1 \times 10^n$, then k is greater than zero.

The correct answer is (D): EACH statement ALONE is sufficient.

DS 158. Word Problems: Algebraic Translations
Difficulty: Hard **OG Page:** 290

In this ***Algebraic Translations*** problem, we are asked whether Carmen has fewer tapes than Rafael. We are given a relationship between the number of tapes that each person has.

Name Variables and assign C to the number of tapes that Carmen has. Likewise, assign R to the number of tapes that Rafael has.

The question stem states that $C + 12 = 2R$. We can solve this equation for C to yield $C = 2R - 12$. The question asks whether Carmen has fewer tapes than Rafael, which we can ***Rephrase*** as:

Is $C < R$?

If we replace C with $2R - 12$, we get:

Is $2R - 12 < R$?
Is $R < 12$?

Alternatively, we could simplify the expression in terms of C. If $C = 2R - 12$, then $R = \frac{C+12}{2}$. The inequality becomes:

Is $C < \frac{C+12}{2}$?
Is $2C < C + 12$?
Is $C < 12$?

We have two rephrasings for this question, either of which would be sufficient: "Is $R < 12$ OR is $C < 12$?"

Either way, the question involves ***Inequalities***.

(1): INSUFFICIENT. This statement tells us that $R > 5$. R could be either greater than or less than 12.

(2): SUFFICIENT. This statement tells us that C is less than 12. According to the work we did above, this is a direct answer to the second rephrasing of the original question.

The correct answer is (B): Statement (2) ALONE is sufficient, but statement (1) alone is not sufficient.

DS 159. Algebra: Inequalities
Difficulty: Easy **OG Page:** 290

This ***Inequalities*** problem involves ***Exponents*** and ***Absolute Values***.

Let's consider the possibilities for the given inequality when x is positive and when it is negative.

$|x|$ is always positive, regardless of whether x itself is positive. 2^x is also always positive, since we cannot take a positive base, raise it to some exponent, and get a negative number.

Therefore, the only quantity in $x|x| < 2^x$ that could be negative is x. Thus, if x is negative, then the answer to the question is definitely *Yes*, since a negative will always be less than a positive.

If x is zero, the answer to the question will be *Yes*, since 0 is less than 2^0, which is 1.

If x is positive, however, we will need more information, such as its exact value, in order to evaluate the statement.

Therefore, we can ***Rephrase*** the question in two parts: "Is x negative or zero? If *Yes*, we are done. If *No*, there is one more question: is $x|x| < 2^x$?"

(1): SUFFICIENT. x is negative. This answers the first part of the rephrased question. From the reasoning above, the answer to the question is *Yes*.

(2): SUFFICIENT. x is negative. This also answers the first part of the rephrased question. From the reasoning above, the answer to the question is *Yes*.

The correct answer is (D): EACH statement ALONE is sufficient.

DS 160. Algebra: Exponents & Roots
Difficulty: Medium **OG Page:** 290

This problem involves not only ***Equations with Exponents*** but also ***Inequalities***.

We can ***Rephrase*** the question, translating from words to symbols:

Is $b - a \geq 2(3^n - 2^n)$?

Go further by distributing the 2:

Is $b - a \geq 2(3^n) - 2(2^n)$?

(1): SUFFICIENT. We can manipulate the information in this statement to get $b - a$ on one side of an equation. To do so, ***Subtract Equations***: that is, subtract the equation for a from the equation for b.

The tricky step is that we have to rewrite 3^{n+1} as $(3^n)(3^1)$, which equals $(3)(3^n)$. This applies a very subtle ***Exponents Rule***.

Do the same thing for 2^{n+1} to get $(2)(2^n)$.

$$b - a = 3^{n+1} - 2^{n+1} = (3)(3^n) - (2)(2^n)$$

Now plug this equation into the rephrased question:

Is $b - a \geq (2)(3^n) - (2)(2^n)$?
Is $(3)(3^n) - (2)(2^n) \geq (2)(3^n) - (2)(2^n)$?
Is $(3)(3^n) \geq (2)(3^n)$?
Is $3 \geq 2$?

The answer to this question will always be *Yes*. Thus, this statement is sufficient.

(2): INSUFFICIENT. This statement does not tell us anything about a or b.

The correct answer is (A): Statement (1) ALONE is sufficient, but statement (2) alone is not sufficient.

DS 161. FDPs: Ratios
Difficulty: Easy **OG Page:** 290

In this ***Ratios*** problem, we are asked to find the price of the mixer in 1970, given the inflation index. If we ***Name Variables*** and label the 1970 price x, then the price of the mixer in 1989 will be $3.56x$. The question is "What is x?"

If we can find the price in 1970 or the price in 1989, then we can answer the question. We will also have enough information if we are given a relationship between the two prices that we can use to solve for x.

(1): SUFFICIENT. The difference between the two prices is $102.40. In other words, we know that the 1989 price – the 1970 price = 102.4.

We can now calculate the price in 1970. The 1989 price ($3.56x$) minus the 1970 price (x) equals $3.56x - x = 2.56x$. Therefore, $3.56x = 102.40$. We can stop here, because this is a ***Linear Equation*** in just one variable.

Remember, we don't have to actually solve for x. Once we know we can find the value of x, we know the statement is sufficient, and we can move on.

(2): SUFFICIENT. Knowing the price of the mixer in 1989 allows us to calculate the price of the mixer in 1970, using the following relationship.

$$3.56x = 142.4.$$

If we do compute x in either case, we get $x = \$40$. However, we should not take the time to do so under exam-like conditions.

The correct answer is (D): EACH statement ALONE is sufficient.

DS 162. Algebra: Exponents & Roots
Difficulty: Hard **OG Page:** 290

No rephrasing is required: "Is $5^k < 1{,}000$?"

In theory, we can rephrase to a more specific question about k itself. But we may as well leave the question in terms of 5^k and see where the statements lead.

This problem involves both ***Equations with Exponents*** and ***Inequalities***.

(1): INSUFFICIENT. Manipulate the inequality to isolate 5^k as shown:

$5^{k+1} < 3{,}000$	Write 5^{k+1} as $5^k \times 5^1 = 5^k \times 5$
$5^k \times 5 > 3{,}000$	Divide both sides by 5
$5^k > 600$	

We know that $5^k > 600$, but this information does not tell us whether 5^k is less than 1,000.

(2): SUFFICIENT. Manipulate the equation:

$5^{k-1} = 5^k - 500$	Move powers of 5 to one side
$5^{k-1} - 5^k = -500$	Write 5^{k-1} as $5^k \times 5^{-1} = \frac{5^k}{5}$ (very tricky!)
$\frac{5^k}{5} - 5^k = -500$	Factor out 5^k on the left side
$5^k(1/5 - 1) = -500$	
$5^k(-4/5) = -500$	Subtract 1 from 1/5
$5^k = 625$	Multiply both sides by $-5/4$

We can and should stop, once we know that we can arrive at a definite value for 5^k. After all, with a definite value for 5^k, we can answer any Yes-No question about 5^k.

The correct answer is (B): Statement (2) ALONE is sufficient, but statement (1) alone is not sufficient.

DS 163. Algebra: Quadratic Equations
Difficulty: Medium **OG Page:** 290

In this ***Quadratic Equations*** problem, which also involves ***Algebraic Translations***, we have the following relationship:

60 = (# of members)(contribution per person)

We can ***Name Variables:***

m = number of club members
c = dollars each member contributes

Thus, we can rewrite the equation as $60 = mc$.

The original question asks "What is m?" We can ***Rephrase*** this question as "What is $60/c$?" or simply "What is c?" Having the value of c will allow us to determine the value of m.

(1): SUFFICIENT. If $c = 4$, then we can answer the rephrased question. $m = 60/4 = 15$.

(2): SUFFICIENT. The gift certificate costs \$60 no matter how many members actually contribute. If 5 of the members do not contribute, then the rest of the members ($m - 5$ members) do contribute. The contributing members have to pay \$2 more than they otherwise would if everyone contributed. That is, they each pay $c + 2$.

Thus, we can set up a second equation for the (hypothetical purchase of the gift certificate:

$$60 = (m - 5)(c + 2)$$

Solve for m by combining the two equations. First, solve the equation from the question stem for c:

$60 = mc$

$c = \frac{60}{m}$

Substitute into the equation from (2):

$60 = (m - 5)(c + 2)$

$60 = (m-5)\left(\frac{60}{m}+2\right)$

$\left[60 = (m-5)\left(\frac{60}{m}+2\right)\right] \times m$

$60 = (m - 5)(60 + 2m)$

$60m = 60m + 2m^2 - 300 - 10m$

$0 = 2m^2 - 300 - 10m$

$0 = m^2 - 5m - 150$

$0 = (m - 15)(m + 10)$

$m = 15$ *or* -10

Since the number of club members most be positive, the only valid solution is $m = 15$.

Beware of assuming that a quadratic will always produce two solutions and thus fail to provide a sufficient answer for a value question. On difficult GMAT questions, one of the solutions may be either invalid or redundant, leaving only one (therefore sufficient) answer. The safest policy is to factor and solve any quadratic before answering the original question.

The correct answer is (D): EACH statement ALONE is sufficient.

DS 164. Number Properties: Positives & Negatives
Difficulty: Medium **OG Page:** 290

While this question may look like an ***Inequality*** question on the surface, it is really testing ***Positives & Negatives***. The question stem tells us that x is negative and asks us whether y is positive.

(1): SUFFICIENT. If $x/y < 0$, then by ***Rules of Positives & Negatives***, we know that x and y must have opposite signs (x positive and y negative, or vice versa). Since we already know that x must be negative from the question stem, y must be positive.

(2): INSUFFICIENT. We are told that $y - x > 0$. If we add x to both sides of the inequality we get $y > x$. While we know that x is negative, all we know is that y is greater than some negative number. y could be either negative or positive.

The correct answer is (A): Statement (1) ALONE is sufficient, but statement (2) alone is not sufficient.

DS 165. Geometry: Circles & Cylinders
Difficulty: Easy **OG Page:** 290

We know from the given drawing that triangle OXZ is a ***Right Triangle***. We also know (from the question stem) that O is the center of the ***Circle***. Thus, we know that the arc XYZ represents one quarter of the total ***Circumference***, because $90/360 = 1/4$.

We are asked for the total circumference. We can calculate the circumference if we know the radius of the circle, which is equal to the length of each of the legs of the right triangle. Thus, we can ***Rephrase*** the question as "What is the radius of the circle?"

(1): SUFFICIENT. We are told that the ***Perimeter*** of triangle OXZ is $20+10\sqrt{2}$. Because OX and OZ are each radii of the circle, $OX = OZ$. This means that triangle OXZ is ***Isosceles***.

Furthermore, because triangle OXZ is also a right triangle, it must be a ***45–45–90*** triangle. Such triangles have a special property: their sides must be in the ratio of $1:1:\sqrt{2}$.

We do not know the value of the radius, so let's ***Name a Variable*** and call it r. We know that $OX = OZ = r$, and that $XZ = \sqrt{2}r$. Thus, the perimeter of triangle OXZ must be $r+r+\sqrt{2}r$. Statement (1) gives us a value for that overall perimeter, from which we can create an equation:

$r+r+\sqrt{2}r = 20+10\sqrt{2}$

$2r+\sqrt{2}r = 20+10\sqrt{2}$

$r(2+\sqrt{2}) = 10(2+\sqrt{2})$

$r = 10$

Now that we know the value of r, we can easily determine the value of the overall circumference:

$$C = 2\pi r$$
$$C = 2\pi(10)$$
$$C = 20\pi$$

Of course, this final process is unnecessary. Once we know that we can compute r, we know that the statement is sufficient.

(2): SUFFICIENT. We are told that arc XYZ is 5π. We know that this arc is one fourth the overall circumference. Thus, the overall circumference is 20π.

The correct answer is (D): EACH statement ALONE is sufficient.

DS 166. Geometry: Lines & Angles
Difficulty: Hard **OG Page:** 291

In this problem, we need to determine what information, given the diagram of crisscrossing ***Lines & Angles,*** will be sufficient to find the sum of x and y. A quick glance at the statements reveals that we are given neither value directly. Thus, we need to figure out if there's any kind of relationship between one pair of variables, x & y, and either of the other two variables, w and z.

The key is the ***Quadrilateral*** formed by the four lines in the figure. While we do not initially know anything about any *individual* angle, we do know that the four interior angles of the quadrilateral must sum to 360°. We can ***Name Variables*** and label these four internal angles p, q, r and s.

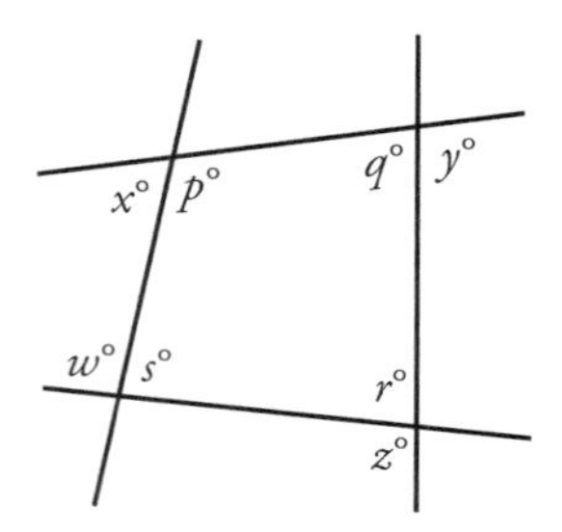

We also know that $x + p = 180$ and $y + q = 180$, because these angles pair up to form straight lines, Therefore, $x + p + y + q = 360$. That means $x + y = 360 - p - q$, which can be restated as $x + y = 360 - (p + q)$. We can ***Rephrase*** the question as "What is the value of $p + q$?"

(1): INSUFFICIENT. Knowing the value of w allows us to calculate the value of s, because $w + s = 180$. Unfortunately, this does not allow us to find the value of p or q, or the sum of p and q.

(2): INSUFFICIENT. Knowing the value of z allows us to calculate the value of r, because $z + r = 180$. Unfortunately, this does not allow us to find the value of p or q, or the sum of p and q.

(1) AND (2): SUFFICIENT. If $w = 95$, then $s = 85$. If $z = 125$, then $r = 55$. $s + r = 140$. That means that $p + q$ must equal 220, because $p + q + r + s = 360$. We can stop here, because we have answered our rephrased question.

If we really want to solve for $x + y$, we can do so easily:

$$x + y = 360 - (p + q) = 360 - 220 = 140$$

The correct answer is (C): BOTH statements TOGETHER are sufficient, but NEITHER statement ALONE is sufficient.

DS 167. Algebra: Inequalities
Difficulty: Medium **OG Page:** 291

In this problem, which involves both ***Inequalities*** and ***Roots,*** we are told that n and k are positive integers. We are asked whether $\sqrt{n+k}$ is greater than $2\sqrt{n}$. Because n and k must be positive, we can square both sides of the inequality without introducing any complications. We arrive at an equivalent question:

Is $\sqrt{n+k} > 2\sqrt{n}$?

Is $n+k > (2\sqrt{n})^2 = 4n$?

Simplifying further, we can ***Rephrase*** the question as "Is $k > 3n$?"

(1): SUFFICIENT. This gives a direct answer to the rephrased question.

(2): INSUFFICIENT. This statement tells us that $n + k > 3n$, or that $k > 2n$. However, we cannot determine whether k is greater than $3n$, even with the restriction that k and n are positive integers.

We can ***Test Numbers*** to confirm. For example, if we choose $n = 1$ and $k = 3$, then k is not greater than $3n$. However, for the same n, if $k = 4$, then k is greater than $3n$.

The correct answer is (A): Statement (1) ALONE is sufficient, but statement (2) alone is not sufficient.

DS 168. FDPs: Ratios
Difficulty: Medium **OG Page:** 291

In this ***Ratios*** problem, we are asked to find a value for p if $i = 70$. We are told that p is directly proportional to e, which is directly proportional to i. From this we can deduce that p is directly proportional to i.

To answer the question, we need to know both the relationship between p and e and between e and i (that is, a relationship between p and i using e as the "middleman"). Alternatively, because we know that p is directly proportional to i, the relationship between p and i would also be sufficient.

Any set of two values of p and i in proportion will tell us the constant by which they are proportional. Alternatively, any set of two values for p and e in proportion and e and i in proportion will also tell us the constant that relates p and i.

(1): INSUFFICIENT. This tells us the relationship between e and i, but we lack the relationship between p and e or p and i.

(2): SUFFICIENT. This tells us the relationship between p and i directly. It is not necessary to know anything about e to answer the question.

Although we may certainly stop here, a numeric solution can be found for practice. ***Name a Variable*** and call the proportionality constant m:

$$p = mi$$
$$2 = m(50)$$
$$m = 1/25$$

Thus, the proportionality constant is 1/25. If we know that $i = 70$:

$$p = \frac{1}{25}(70)$$
$$p = \frac{70}{25}$$
$$p = \frac{14}{5}$$

The correct answer is (B): Statement (2) ALONE is sufficient, but statement (1) alone is not sufficient.

DS 169. Algebra: Exponents & Roots
Difficulty: Medium **OG Page:** 291

In this ***Exponents*** problem, manipulate the ***Inequality*** in the question as much as possible before evaluating the statements.

Notice that both sides of the inequality can be expressed as ***Powers of Ten:***

$$(1/10)^n < 0.01?$$
$$(10^{-1})^n < 10^{-2}?$$
$$10^{-n} < 10^{-2}?$$

When both sides of an inequality share the same positive base (not equal to 1), we can drop the bases and compare the exponents:

Is $-n < -2$?

Is $n > 2$? This is our ***Rephrased*** question.

(1): SUFFICIENT. This statement matches our rephrasing directly.

(2): SUFFICIENT. Manipulate the inequality:

$$(1/10)^{n-1} < 0.1$$
$$(10^{-1})^{n-1} < 10^{-1}$$
$$10^{-n+1} < 10^{-1}$$
$$-n + 1 < -1$$
$$-n < -2$$
$$n > 2$$

The correct answer is (D): EACH statement ALONE is sufficient.

DS 170. <u>FDPs</u>: Digits & Decimals
Difficulty: Hard **OG Page:** 291

No rephrase is necessary for this ***Digits*** question.

(1): SUFFICIENT. If n is multiplied by 10 to produce $10n$, each digit moves "up" by one place. The ones (units) digit of n becomes the tens digit of $10n$, the tens digit of n becomes the hundreds digit of $10n$, and so on.

We can ***Test Numbers*** to verify these relationships. For instance, let $n = 352$, so that $10n = 3{,}520$. Note that the "2," which is the units digit of n, becomes the tens digit of $10n$. The "5," which is the tens digit of n, becomes the hundreds digit of $10n$. Finally, the "3," which is the hundreds digit of n, becomes the thousands digit of $10n$.

This statement gives us the hundreds digit of $10n$, which is exactly the same as the tens digit of n. Therefore, the tens digit of n is 6.

(2): INSUFFICIENT. The addition of 1 may or may not change the original tens digit of n.

We should ***Test Numbers.*** For instance, if $n + 1$ is 70, then n is 69. The tens digit of the original n would be 6.

On the other hand, if $n + 1$ is 71, then n is 70. The tens digit of the original n is 7.

Therefore, the tens digit of n could be either 6 or 7. This is not specific enough information.

The correct answer is (A): Statement (1) ALONE is sufficient, but statement (2) alone is not sufficient.

DS 171. <u>Algebra</u>: Linear Equations
Difficulty: Medium **OG Page:** 291

This ***Linear Equations*** problem contains a ***Double-Decker Fraction***. In this case, we can split the numerator. The common term of $t - x$ in both the numerator and denominator allows us to do strategic ***Direct Algebra:***

$$\frac{2t+t-x}{t-x} = \frac{(2t)+(t-x)}{(t-x)}$$
$$= \frac{2t}{(t-x)} + \frac{(t-x)}{(t-x)}$$
$$= \frac{2t}{(t-x)} + 1$$

The problem hinted at this manipulation by writing the numerator as $2t + t - x$, rather than as the more normal form $3t - x$.

The only value that is still unknown is $\frac{2t}{(t-x)}$. With that value, we will be able to determine the value of $\frac{2t+t-x}{t-x}$. Thus, the ***Rephrased*** question is "What is the value of $\frac{2t}{(t-x)}$?"

(1): SUFFICIENT. This answers the rephrased question directly. If $\frac{2t}{(t-x)} = 3$, then $\frac{2t+t-x}{t-x} = 3 + 1 = 4$.

(2): INSUFFICIENT. We cannot manipulate $t - x = 5$ to determine the value of $\frac{2t}{(t-x)}$.

The correct answer is (A): Statement (1) ALONE is sufficient, but statement (2) alone is not sufficient.

DS 172. <u>Algebra</u>: Exponents & Roots
Difficulty: Hard **OG Page:** 291

This deceptively simple question is asking whether n is an integer. As we shall see, this problem involves both ***Exponents*** and ***Roots***.

(1): INSUFFICIENT. It is crucial to read this statement *without* assuming that n is an integer, since that is actually the question at hand. This only tells us that n, when multiplied by itself, results in an integer.

One way to deal with this statement is to ***Test Numbers***. Be careful though. We need to make sure we pick numbers that make the statement true.

The easiest way to do that is not to pick values for n, but to pick values for n^2.

We know that n^2 must be an integer. Try $n^2 = 1$. If $n^2 = 1$, then $n = \pm 1$, which means n can be an integer.

Now try $n^2 = 2$. If $n^2 = 2$, then $n = \sqrt{2}$, which is not an integer. Therefore, n does not have to be an integer.

(2): SUFFICIENT. The statement tells us that $\sqrt{n}$ is an integer. Testing numbers is a little tricky here because it is tempting to pick n, but we should pick $\sqrt{n}$ instead because the statement tells us about $\sqrt{n}$, not n. If we pick $\sqrt{n}$ as an integer, such as 1, 2, or 3, we can see that n must also be an integer:

$$\sqrt{n} = 1 \rightarrow n = 1^2 = 1$$

$$\sqrt{n} = 2 \rightarrow n = 2^2 = 4$$

$$\sqrt{n} = 3 \rightarrow n = 3^2 = 9$$

We also can see this quickly with theory. Since $n = \sqrt{n} \times \sqrt{n}$ and we know that $\sqrt{n}$ is an integer,

(integer) × (integer) = integer.

The correct answer is (B): Statement (2) ALONE is sufficient, but statement (1) alone is not sufficient.

DS 173. Number Properties: Odds and Evens
Difficulty: Medium **OG Page:** 291

In this ***Odds & Evens*** problem, we are asked about the ***Combined Expression*** $x - y$.

For the Combo $x - y$ to be odd, one of these terms must be odd and the other even.

Thus, we can ***Rephrase*** the question somewhat clumsily as "Are x and y opposites in terms of Odds & Evens?"

(1): INSUFFICIENT. Create an ***Odd/Even Table***:

z	z^2	x
Odd	Odd	Odd
Even	Even	Even

x could be either odd or even. Moreover, we know nothing about y.

(2): INSUFFICIENT. Create an ***Odd/Even Table***:

z	$z - 1$	y
Even	Odd	Odd
Odd	Even	Even

y could be either odd or even. Moreover, we know nothing about x.

(1) AND (2): SUFFICIENT. Combine the tables:

z	$z - 1$	y	x
Even	Odd	Odd	Even
Odd	Even	Even	Odd

We can see that whenever x is even, y will be odd, and vice versa. Thus, x and y are opposites in terms of Odds & Evens, and $x - y$ must be odd.

Alternatively, we could do ***Direct Algebra***:

$$y = (z - 1)^2$$
$$y = z^2 - 2z + 1$$

Next, subtract the y equation from the x equation:

$$x = z^2$$
$$-[y = z^2 - 2z + 1]$$

$$x - y = z^2 - (z^2 - 2z + 1)$$

$$x - y = z^2 - z^2 + 2z - 1$$

$$x - y = 2z - 1$$

$2z$ must be even. Thus, $2z - 1$ is odd, and $x - y$ is odd as well.

The correct answer is (C): BOTH statements TOGETHER are sufficient, but NEITHER statement ALONE is sufficient.

DS 174. Word Problems: Algebraic Translations
Difficulty: Easy **OG Page:** 291

Questions such as this one require us to know either the dimensions of the vessel or how a particular volume relates to some portion of the overall capacity.

We must be ready to do ***Algebraic Translations***, but there is no upfront rephrasing needed.

(1): INSUFFICIENT. This statement tells us nothing about the total capacity of Marcia's bucket. All we know is that it can hold, at minimum, 9 liters.

(2): SUFFICIENT. There is enough information to set up a ***Linear Equation*** with the given ***Fractions***. We can then solve for the capacity of the bucket.

According to this statement, adding 3 liters to a half-full bucket will increase the volume by 1/3. Thus, we know that 3 liters is equal to 1/3 of a half-full bucket. We can ***Name a Variable*** and assign c to the capacity of the bucket.

$$3 = (1/3)(1/2)c$$

$$3 = (1/6)c$$

$$18 = c$$

Marcia's bucket has a capacity of 18 liters.

The correct answer is (B): Statement (2) alone is sufficient, but statement (1) alone is not sufficient.

Chapter 5

of

The Official Guide Companion

The Hot List

In This Chapter...

The Hot List

The Hot List

Welcome to the Hot List! If you've run into trouble on any of these problems—or with the explanations printed in the OG—relax. You're in good company. Thousands of other students have knocked their heads against these beauties, too. We've updated the list to reflect the "new nasties" in OG 13.

Below, we discuss typical issues that students face and highlight key takeaways. We'll also evaluate the quality of the answer explanations given in the OG. As previously mentioned, some of these explanations are fine; others should be avoided. In fact, certain problems are on this list in part because the relevant OG explanation is confusing.

Warning: ***spoilers ahead!*** Don't look at our commentary until you've given the problem a try.

Hot List Problem: D 10 (Diagnostic Test)
Beginning of Question: In the figure shown...
Page in OG: 21
Page in This Book: 25

Comments:
Don't forget that *Smart Numbers* are effective on some Geometry problems. The internal angles of a pentagon have a constant sum, so as long as the numbers you choose for those angles add up to 540, you will get the correct answer to the question.

Hot List Problem: D 11 (Diagnostic Test)
Beginning of Question: Of the three-digit integers...
Page in OG: 22
Page in This Book: 26

Comments:
Students frequently ask for a shortcut on this problem. Unfortunately, there's no one-step recipe. However, when faced with a counting problem, you should always ask yourself: should I directly count the outcomes that I *want*, or should I count the outcomes that I *don't* want and subtract from the total number of outcomes? You may be able to solve this problem more quickly with the latter approach.

The OG explanation counts the desired outcomes directly; this approach certainly works and is worth studying.

Hot List Problem: D 13 (Diagnostic Test)
Beginning of Question: If s and t are positive integers...
Page in OG: 22
Page in This Book: 27

Comments:
This is an infamous problem. Focus on the connection between integer remainders (8 divided by 5 leaves remainder 3) and the decimal part of a quotient (8 divided by 5 equals 1.6).

The OG explanation is cryptic. We would not do it that way ourselves.

Hot List Problem: D 15 (Diagnostic Test)
Beginning of Question: The product of all the...
Page in OG: 22
Page in This Book: 29

Comments:
Focus on the phrase "closest to" and the large spread in the answer choices. You only need to estimate the product. Find ways to round off your computations. You'll save lots of time.

The OG says that you should go ahead and multiply all the numbers up and get 9,699,690. That's downright insane. Do not do this.

Hot List Problem: D 16 (Diagnostic Test)
Beginning of Question: If $\sqrt{3-2x}$...
Page in OG: 22
Page in This Book: 29

Comments:
Many people find roots daunting—especially since squaring both sides of the given equation does *not* immediately eliminate all the roots. Also, you may feel a chill when you realize that you can't easily isolate x in this equation. But notice that three of the answer choices have x in them. Since you are asked for $4x^2$, isolate *that* expression on one side of the equation and see what you get on the other side.

The process given in the OG is fine; we would perform the same algebra. It just requires some perseverance.

Hot List Problem: D 24 (Diagnostic Test)
Beginning of Question: Aaron will jog home...
Page in OG: 23
Page in This Book: 33

Comments:
This tough Rates & Work problem has variables in the answer choices, making it extra-difficult. Notice that the problem gives you three variables (x, y, and t), but the quantity you're asked for (the distance) doesn't have a letter. Go ahead and make one up. Or pick a number for that distance. But don't ignore it.

The OG explanation is hard to follow because it doesn't create a letter or pick a number for the distance.

Hot List Problem: D 30 (Diagnostic Test)
Beginning of Question: The only gift certificates...
Page in OG: 25
Page in This Book: 37

Comments:
Be careful whenever word problems in Data Sufficiency involve unknowns that must be integers. There tend to be far fewer solutions than when unknowns are not so constrained.

On these problems, at least one of the statements is very likely to be sufficient on its own. It's easy to think you need both statements; (C) is a very common wrong answer on this problem. Even if you end up guessing, choose (A), (B), or (D).

Hot List Problem: PS 9
Beginning of Question: Which of the following...
Page in OG: 153
Page in This Book: 54

Comments:
Roots inside roots are simply frightening. On top of that, how do you take a square root or a third root of a decimal? Try converting the decimal to a power of ten. This should make the calculations easier. You might also learn what roots do to the number of decimal places: for instance, square roots cut the number of decimal places in half. The process shown in the OG is fine. It's worth studying.

Hot List Problem: PS 35
Beginning of Question: $\sqrt{(16)(20)...}$
Page in OG: 156
Page in This Book: 66

Comments:
Notice the plus sign under the square root. That complicates matters. You have to either pull out a common factor (say, 16) or add up the two terms.

The OG explanation doesn't explain why or how you get a 16 out of the second term. To save time, you pull out the largest square you can (16), and you borrow a 2 from the 32 to turn the 8 into a 16.

Hot List Problem: PS 51
Beginning of Question: If y is an integer...
Page in OG: 159
Page in This Book: 73

Comments:
This problem has a lot of great traps. Read it carefully. You need to find the least possible value of $|23 - 5y|$ itself. To do that, you need to test a bunch of y's. But notice that you are NOT asked for the value of y that produces the least possible value. Always double-check what the problem is asking you for. Or you might think, because of the absolute value sign, that you are restricted to positive values *inside* the absolute value. That's not true. Inside an absolute value expression, you can usually put either positive or negative values. The absolute value *turns* those values positive, but they don't have to be positive to begin with.

The OG explanation is needlessly confusing. Feel free to ignore it.

Hot List Problem: PS 87
Beginning of Question: If *n* is an integer...
Page in OG: 164
Page in This Book: 90

Comments:
This is a forbidding problem. Here's the key idea: when you multiply a group of numbers together, you only get a multiple of 3 if at least one of the numbers in the group is a multiple of 3. For instance, $4 \times 5 \times 7$ is not a multiple of 3, but $4 \times 5 \times 6$ is. So, how can we guarantee that one of the numbers will be a multiple of 3? In this problem, a number line is an effective visual tool.

The first method shown in the OG (picking numbers) isn't bad, but the second explanation is very tough to follow.

Hot List Problem: PS 100
Beginning of Question: On a scale that measures...
Page in OG: 166
Page in This Book: 97

Comments:
The wording of this question is quite confusing. You must keep straight the difference between the *reading* and the *intensity*. When you *add* to the reading, you *multiply* the intensity by a factor. Specifically, when you add 1 to the reading, you multiply the intensity by 10. The Richter scale of earthquake intensity works this way, incidentally.

The explanation in the OG is almost criminally brief.

Hot List Problem: PS 115
Beginning of Question: A pharmaceutical company...
Page in OG: 168
Page in This Book: 105

Comments:
Make sure to read this question very carefully. A percent change always involves an original value and a new value. The most common wrong answer on this question is (A). 9 is 8% of 108, but that's not the value the question is asking for.

Also, remember that the GMAT almost never tells you more than you need to know on Problem Solving. If you arrive at an answer without using all the information given in the question, chances are you're walking into a trap.

Hot List Problem: PS 136
Beginning of Question: In Town X, 64 percent...
Page in OG: 171
Page in This Book: 116

Comments:
This is a great example of a problem that is difficult because of a very tempting wrong answer. About 40% of people in our database who do this problem pick (A), most likely because they subtract 48 from 64.

The answer to any question on the GMAT will practically never be the result of a single addition, subtraction, multiplication, or division of two given numbers. If an answer seems too good to be true, it probably is.

Hot List Problem: PS 143
Beginning of Question: Which of the following inequalities...
Page in OG: 172
Page in This Book: 120

Comments:
Inequalities give people the willies. Regardless of your approach, you should notice the *endpoints* in any question that involves ranges. Here, the endpoints are useful because they represent the extreme values. If you plug either extreme into the correct inequality, you should get the maximum possible absolute value: in this case, 4.

The process described in the OG is correct, of course. However, since the reasons for various moves are unclear, you can easily feel as if the OG is pulling a rabbit out of a hat.

Hot List Problem: PS 162
Beginning of Question: During a trip, Francine traveled...
Page in OG: 175
Page in This Book: 129

Comments:
On difficult problems, using Smart Numbers is a viable strategy, but more care needs to be taken with the numbers used. Set up the problem first, then decide what numbers would make the calculations easier.

Also, remember that the average rate is never the simple average of the individual rates. The most common wrong answer, choice (C), is tempting if you assume that the simple average rate is the average of 40 and 60 (that is, 50).

Hot List Problem: PS 166
Beginning of Question: A border of uniform width...
Page in OG: 175
Page in This Book: 131

Comments:
When a Geometry problem doesn't provide a picture, draw it. In this problem, a picture might make it easier to see that, if you create a variable for the width of the frame, you can write expressions to describe the area of the border.

Hot List Problem: PS 170
Beginning of Question: If $d = \ldots$
Page in OG: 176
Page in This Book: 133

Comments:
While brute force can get you to the answer, you have a couple key opportunities to save time. First, recognize that $2^3 \times 5^3 = 10^3$, which you can effectively ignore because the question asks for nonzero digits. Second, while long division will work, rewriting $1/5^4$ as $(0.2)^4$ will save even more time.

Hot List Problem: PS 172
Beginning of Question: For any positive integer *n*...
Page in OG: 176
Page in This Book: 134

Comments:
This question is unusually evil, because you do not need the given formula. In fact, you shouldn't even touch it, because there is a much easier path to the answer. (Fortunately, it seems that GMAT problems pull this sort of trick very rarely. They almost never give you pointless information.) To add up the members of an evenly spaced set, you just need to know this equation: Sum = (Average) × (Number of members).

The OG explanation is extraordinarily complicated and annoying. For instance, it contains unexplained notation (Σ), which is not used anywhere else in the OG or on the GMAT itself. If you haven't yet read the OG explanation, completely avoid doing so.

Hot List Problem: PS 177
Beginning of Question: Last year the price per share...
Page in OG:
Page in This Book: 136

Comments:
Although picking Smart Numbers can be useful, picking them too soon is likely to make the problem harder, not easier. Make sure that you have a good sense of the calculations you'll need to make before deciding what smart numbers to use.

On a super-hard problem such as this, if you're not even sure how to set it up in the first place, guess and move on. It's better to get a question wrong in 30 seconds than it is to get it right in 3 or 4 minutes.

Hot List Problem: PS 178
Beginning of Question: Of the 300 subjects...
Page in OG: 177
Page in This Book: 137

Comments:
Overlapping Sets problems that divide a group into 3 categories are quite a bit more complicated than those that only divide a group into 2 categories. The key to these problems is the fact that members of the group that fall into 2 categories are double-counted, and members of the group that fall into all 3 categories are triple-counted.

Hot List Problem: PS 181
Beginning of Question: If $m > 0$...
Page in OG: 177
Page in This Book: 139

Comments:
Translating "y is what percent of x" into an equation is hard for many folks, but you can learn the process. The word "IS" becomes the equals sign (=), "percent" becomes "/100," and "of" becomes "times." The most important step is to

name a new variable to stand for the "what." Then you can solve for that variable. Alternatively, you can pick numbers, as long as you're organized and quick with calculation.

The OG explanation is fine until the last step (multiplying by 100 to convert a fraction into an equivalent percent). This is mystifying as written. What the OG means is that a fraction such as 1/2, or its equivalent decimal 0.50, can also be written as 50%. To get the number 50 that you write in front of the % sign, you multiply the 1/2 or the 0.50 by 100. Likewise, 1/4 or 0.25 is 25%, where $25 = 1/4 \times 100$. But doing this multiplication to a variable expression, while technically correct, seems to come totally out of the blue.

Hot List Problem: PS 182
Beginning of Question: A photography dealer...
Page in OG: 178
Page in This Book: 139

Comments:
On average, people in our database spend more than 4 minutes answering this question. Any question that involves as many steps as PS 182 does to solve is almost certainly not worth your time.

If you do decide to answer this question, the word *approximately* is code for "look for ways to estimate to make calculation easier."

Hot List Problem: PS 198
Beginning of Question: Last Sunday a certain store...
Page in OG: 180
Page in This Book: 147

Comments:
The numbers in the question make it very difficult to pick Smart Numbers right away. In general, using smart numbers works most efficiently when you have a good grasp of the underlying math in the problem.

Here, you need to be able to create expressions for the revenue from sales of A and from sales of B using the variables r and p. Only then will it become apparent that you can pick a number for the total number of newspapers sold to make your calculations easier.

Hot List Problem: PS 199
Beginning of Question: (0.99999999)/(1.0001)...
Page in OG: 180
Page in This Book: 149

Comments:
This problem is tough, no matter how you look at it. Sometimes the best clue you have for an approach is the answer choices. In this question, every answer choice involves powers of 10 (either 10^{-4} or 10^{-8}). That may not be much to go on, but it does give a clue that every numerator and denominator should be rewritten so that they contain powers of 10.

Hot List Problem: PS 200
Beginning of Question: The ratio, by volume...
Page in OG: 180
Page in This Book: 149

Comments:
Three-part "multiple" ratios (such as 2 : 50 : 100) can be tricky, since they contain more than one normal two-part ratio (e.g., 2 : 50). You start by adjusting one number (doubling the amount of soap), but that throws off the ratio of soap to water, and then you're not sure what to do. The safest method is to break the multiple ratio down to normal two-part ratios, make your adjustments, and then recombine. Remember also that ratios are fundamentally fractions. A ratio of 2 : 50 is really 2/50. To double this ratio, multiply 2/50 by 2. You get 4/50.

The OG explanation relies a great deal on subscripts and is rather hard to follow.

Hot List Problem: PS 204
Beginning of Question: If $n = 4p$...
Page in OG: 181
Page in This Book: 153

Comments:
The language in the question makes it clear that the answer will be the same for *every* prime number greater than 2. Therefore, save time by picking a suitable number for p.

Also, although many divisibility questions require you to break a number into prime factors, some questions are more concerned with *all* the factors of a number. In that case, a factor pair table is a great tool.

Hot List Problem: PS 205
Beginning of Question: John and Mary were each paid...
Page in OG: 181
Page in This Book: 153

Comments:
It's trickier than it looks to find simple values of x and y fitting the condition (making the hourly wage the same for each person). Think of this problem as a variation on a work problem. The work done is the dollars earned. The hourly wage, in dollars per hour, is the rate. Dollars earned divided by hours worked is the wage rate.

The OG solution is worth studying, as it's relatively good.

Hot List Problem: PS 218
Beginning of Question: List T consists of 30 positive decimals...
Page in OG: 183
Page in This Book: 160

Comments:
First of all, if you see a problem like this on the exam, RUN! Seriously. It takes long enough to understand what this question is asking, much less to figure out how to answer it. It's better to get a question like this wrong in 30 seconds than it is to get it right in 4 minutes.

If you do decide to answer it, a key feature of this question is the phrase "possible value". Most likely, this means there is a range of possible values, so you need to think about the *minimum* and *maximum* possible values.

Hot List Problem: PS 229
Beginning of Question: How many of the integers...
Page in OG: 185
Page in This Book: 167

Comments:
The most important thing for a problem such as this is to be methodical and keep clear notes. We know that x is an integer, and it must be less than 5. Start with 4 and work your way down until you are confident that you don't need to check any more numbers.

Also make sure that you read carefully. Mistaking "≥ 0" for "> 0" will lead to the most common wrong answer: only 2 solutions instead of the correct number, 4.

Hot List Problem: DS 58
Beginning of Question: What is the tens digit...
Page in OG: 280
Page in This Book: 195

Comments:
As mentioned above, remainders (when you're dealing with variables) are frightening. Rephrase the statements from "remainder" language to "multiple" language, which is much easier to understand. Instead of "x divided by 110 has a remainder of 30," think "x is 30 more than a multiple of 110." Then come up with possible values for x in each case.

In the explanation, the OG uses "R" notation for remainders. This notation, while useful in some contexts, is overkill in this one. The explanation is a little too short overall.

Hot List Problem: DS 69
Beginning of Question: Of the four numbers represented...
Page in OG: 281
Page in This Book: 201

Comments:
No actual values are given on this number line. That's terrifying. All you know is the relative order of the variables, and you have to deal with various scenarios. Replacing variables with numbers is an excellent strategy for abstract problems such as this one. For instance, when looking at Statement 1, assign values to q and s.

To its credit, the OG explanation uses diagrams and takes up a full column, but the content is overly dense in places, relying on extended mathematical inequalities that can be expressed more simply in words and pictures.

Hot List Problem: DS 72
Beginning of Question: If m is an integer...
Page in OG: 281
Page in This Book: 203

Comments:
The phrasing in Statement 1 is cunning. You are told that $m/2$ is *not* an even integer. That does not mean that $m/2$ is an odd integer. It might not be an integer at all! Here's an analogy: if you are told that a number is *not* negative, you can't say that it's definitely positive. After all, it might be zero. Your brain can also get scrambled if you mix up what's given and what you're asked for. There are very similar terms (even/odd and integer) all over the place, and the "not" will short-circuit your wiring if you don't write anything down. Keep good track of your cases on paper.

The OG solution gives you examples but doesn't really walk you through them. If m is the odd integer 3, then it's true that $m/2$ (= 3/2) is *not* an even integer (since it's not an integer at all). But if m is the even integer 10, then it's also true that $m/2$ (= 10/2 = 5) is *not* an even integer. Both $m = 3$ and $m = 10$ fit the condition, but they answer the question differently.

Hot List Problem: DS 77
Beginning of Question: A total of $60,000 was invested...
Page in OG: 281
Page in This Book: 205

Comments:
Notice that, even though the question only mentions two variables, x and y, there are two additional unknown values. Unless you know how much of the $60,000 was invested at x percent and how much was invested at y percent, neither statement by itself is sufficient.

Hot List Problem: DS 90
Beginning of Question: Is the number of seconds required...
Page in OG: 283
Page in This Book: 212

Comments:
We don't often rewrite the $RT = D$ equation to solve for time (number of seconds). The rewritten form $T = D/R$ ("Time equals Distance over Rate") is simply not as intuitive as either $R = D/T$ ("Rate equals Distance over Time") or $RT = D$ ("Rate times Time equals Distance"). You just have to trust the algebra. This problem also involves subscripted variables and inequalities, both of which are nasty.

The OG explanation plucks various sets of 4 numbers at a time out of thin air to justify its claims about each statement. How would you ever know to pick those numbers? On problems with this many variables, it's generally a better move to do Direct Algebra.

Hot List Problem: DS 93
Beginning of Question: Is the number of members...
Page in OG: 283
Page in This Book: 214

Comments:
The setup here is typical of Overlapping Sets problems. However, you have to make a key logical inference: $0.2x$ EQUALS $0.3y$. Despite the differences in language, the two statements are actually talking about the *same* subgroup: the people who are in both clubs.

The explanation in the OG is tremendously confusing. Please don't try to figure it out; it's all pain and no gain. We would never do this problem the way the OG proposes.

Hot List Problem: DS 96
Beginning of Question: If $[x]$ denotes...
Page in OG: 283
Page in This Book: 215

Comments:
Whenever a question introduces a strange symbol, you need to read very carefully. The question does not state that x must be an integer; it states that $[x]$ will be an integer.

Hot List Problem: DS 105
Beginning of Question: Material A costs $3 per kilogram...
Page in OG: 284
Page in This Book: 219

Comments:
Most problems that combine things from two different groups can be solved using weighted averages. The clue here is that two materials with different prices are being combined into one material. Weighted averages are particularly useful on Data Sufficiency, because you don't have to actually perform the tedious calculations associated with weighted averages.

Hot List Problem: DS 106
Beginning of Question: While on a straight road...
Page in OG: 284
Page in This Book: 220

Comments:
Setting up $RT = D$ relationships for each car can make this problem very difficult. All we really care about is the rate at which the distance between the cars is changing. Thus, a relative rates approach is simpler and faster.

The OG explanation is too brief; it simply doesn't do this problem justice.

Hot List Problem: DS 109
Beginning of Question: List *M* (not shown)...
Page in OG: 284
Page in This Book: 221

Comments:
Although the GMAT will never require you to compute standard deviation, you should develop a good intuitive understanding of how standard deviation works. Standard deviation is a measure of the average distance from the mean. Removing 22 and 4 from the list lowers the average distance of every number from the mean, thus shrinking the standard deviation to some smaller value that could be calculated, in theory.

Hot List Problem: DS 114
Beginning of Question: A department manager distributed...
Page in OG: 285
Page in This Book: 224

Comments:
This problem is a classic (C) trap. Even though the statements together may look sufficient at first glance, actually take the time to try to prove them insufficient. Confirm whether there is more than one possibility for the number of employees, given each statement alone.

Hot List Problem: DS 118
Beginning of Question: For any integers x and y...
Page in OG: 285
Page in This Book: 226

Comments:
On this problem, (B) is the most common wrong answer. Statement (1) is difficult to recognize as sufficient. Remember to always keep the original question in mind. Even though z can be anything, w must be at least 20, which means that min(10, w) will always be 10.

Hot List Problem: DS 128
Beginning of Question: The hypotenuse of a right triangle...
Page in OG: 286
Page in This Book: 232

Comments:
(B) is a very common answer selected on this problem. The key to Statement (1) is the fact that we have two variables (the length and width of the right triangle) and two equations (Pythagorean theorem and area formula). Together they are enough to solve for the lengths of the sides.

Hot List Problem: DS 129
Beginning of Question: In the *xy*-plane...
Page in OG: 286
Page in This Book: 232

Comments:
Although this question is tough no matter how you handle it, drawing a coordinate plane can make it a lot easier. Whenever Geometry problems do not provide a figure, make sure that you create your own.

Hot List Problem: DS 131
Beginning of Question: Six shipments of machine parts...
Page in OG: 287
Page in This Book: 235

Comments:
The constraint that more than 1/2 of the shipment must be on the first truck is the key to this question. Take the time to prove each statement sufficient or insufficient by trying to create shipments that have S3 on either truck.

Hot List Problem: DS 132
Beginning of Question: Joanna bought only...
Page in OG: 287
Page in This Book: 235

Comments:
Be careful whenever word problems in Data Sufficiency involve unknowns that must be integers. There tend to be far fewer solutions than when unknowns are not so constrained.

On these problems, at least one of the statements is very likely to be sufficient on its own. It's easy to think you need both statements; (C) is a very common wrong answer on this problem. Even if you end up guessing, choose (A), (B), or (D).

Hot List Problem: DS 135
Beginning of Question: A school administrator will assign...
Page in OG: 287
Page in This Book: 238

Comments:
This question hides the real topic very well. Asking whether students can be assigned to rooms so that each room has the same number of students is a sneaky way of asking about divisibility. Plug in numbers temporarily for n and m to make sense of the question.

In the solution, the OG assumes that you figure out right away that the question is asking about divisibility. That may be the hardest part of the problem! In addition, the content of the explanation itself is rather dense, with 4 or 5 propositions in a single sentence. That's tough to follow.

Hot List Problem: DS 141
Beginning of Question: Last year, a certain company...
Page in OG: 288
Page in This Book: 242

Comments:
By far the sneakiest part of this problem is, "If the company made a profit on product X last year..." It's pivotal because we know that the profit must be greater than 0. Any information that allows us to write a full equation or inequality is necessary to answering the question. In this question, we can write the following inequality:

Revenue – Expenses > 0

Hot List Problem: DS 160
Beginning of Question: If n is a positive integer...
Page in OG: 290
Page in This Book: 253

Comments:
This problem requires you to manipulate an exponential expression in a way most folks dislike. You might recognize that $2 \times 2^n = 2^{n+1}$, but it's easy to miss that the logic works in reverse, too.

The OG explanation is generally okay, although the discussion of statement 1 could be clarified. What's hard about this problem is the process of manipulating exponents. Redo this problem until you can do it in your sleep.

Hot List Problem: DS 162
Beginning of Question: Is 5^k less...
Page in OG: 290
Page in This Book: 254

Comments:
This problem is very similar to DS 160. In both cases, you have to break apart an exponent such as $n + 1$ or $k + 1$.

Again, the OG explanation is pretty good. It's the problem itself that's evil. As with DS 160, practice the exponent manipulations until you have them down cold.

Chapter 6
of
The Official Guide Companion

Official Guide Problem Lists by Topic

In This Chapter...

Official Guide Problem Lists by Topic

Official Guide Problem Lists by Topic

PROBLEM SOLVING GENERAL SET—FRACTIONS, DECIMALS, & PERCENTS

Digits & Decimals
13th Edition: 17, 20, 65, 85, 111, 122, 142, 146, 156, 163, 170, 212, 218, 227, D1, D11

Fractions
13th Edition: 15, 27, 41, 46, 48, 80, 97, 108, 151, 194, 195, 209, 214, 226, D8

Percents
13th Edition: 6, 11, 19, 21, 31, 57, 58, 59, 71, 84, 94, 96, 114, 115, 123, 135, 141, 144, 152, 171, 177, 181, 182, 185, 198, 201, 224, D12, D21

Ratios
13th Edition: 22, 56, 63, 66, 82, 98, 105, 113, 125, 179, 188, 200

FDPs
13th Edition: 8

DATA SUFFICIENCY GENERAL SET—FRACTIONS, DECIMALS, & PERCENTS

Digits & Decimals
13th Edition: 31, 63, 75, 80, 104, 133, 157, 170, D25

Fractions
13th Edition: 10, 29, 92, 116, 131

Percents
13th Edition: 2, 8, 25, 40, 55, 61, 62, 76, 91, 94, 127, 150, D40

Ratios
13th Edition: 23, 26, 47, 81, 114, 161, 168

FDPs
13th Edition: 46, 51, 88, 148, 151

PROBLEM SOLVING GENERAL SET—ALGEBRA

Linear Equations
13th Edition: 14, 42, 47, 54, 55, 72, 102, 187, 220

Exponents & Roots
13th Edition: 9, 35, 52, 106, 120, 150, 164, 180, 196, 217, 230, D17

Quadratic Equations
13th Edition: 37, 45, 99, 117, 157, 169, 191, 199, 216, 223, D16

Formulas
13th Edition: 70, 100, 126, 129, 134, 149, 160, 190, D3

Inequalities
13th Edition: 50, 73, 130, 138, 143, 176, 192

DATA SUFFICIENCY GENERAL SET—ALGEBRA

Linear Equations
13th Edition: 1, 17, 36, 60, 86, 98, 136, 156, 171, D35, D37

Exponents & Roots
13th Edition: 15, 41, 53, 160, 162, 169, 172, D44

Quadratic Equations
13th Edition: 67, 99, 163

Formulas
13th Edition: 24, 96, 118

Inequalities
13th Edition: 13, 33, 43, 48, 50, 52, 82, 85, 101, 159, 167, D30, D33, D38

PROBLEM SOLVING GENERAL SET—WORD PROBLEMS

Algebraic Translations
13th Edition: 1, 4, 29, 60, 64, 76, 83, 88, 89, 93, 131, 137, 140, 153, 154, 167, 184, 203, 205
Rates & Work
13th Edition: 23, 34, 38, 49, 79, 81, 86, 103, 139, 162, 168, 207, D24
Statistics
13th Edition: 12, 16, 30, 53, 91, 101, 109, 112, 119, 132, 145, 183, 208, D9
Consecutive Integers
13th Edition: 67, 90, 124, 158, 172, 221, 225, D2
Overlapping Sets
13th Edition: 25, 136, 178, 186, 189, 222, D4, D6, D14
Extra Problem Types
13th Edition: 33, 39

DATA SUFFICIENCY GENERAL SET—WORD PROBLEMS

Algebraic Translations
13th Edition: 9, 28, 44, 54, 57, 59, 65, 71, 78, 124, 126, 132, 141, 142, 147, 153, 158, 174, D27
Rates & Work
13th Edition: 12, 16, 22, 68, 90, 106, 107, 108, 115
Statistics
13th Edition: 20, 37, 38, 70, 77, 84, 87, 95, 105, 109, 110, 120, 121, 123, 139, 143, 144, 146, 154, D31, D32, D43, D46
Consecutive Integers
13th Edition: 18, 64, 112
Overlapping Sets
13th Edition: 5, 21, 34, 49, 66, 93, 134, 137, 138, D29, D34, D47
Extra Problem Types
13th Edition: 6, 45, 89, 103, 140, D45

PROBLEM SOLVING GENERAL SET—GEOMETRY

Polygons
13th Edition: 3, 13, 18, 78, 104, 121, 147, 166
Triangles & Diagonals
13th Edition: 75, 92, 159, 161, 165, 197, 206, D19
Circles & Cylinders
13th Edition: 36, 69, 175, 213, D5, D20, D22
Lines & Angles
13th Edition: 62, 210, D10
Coordinate Plane
13th Edition: 7, 28, 43, 61, 202, 211, 228

DATA SUFFICIENCY GENERAL SET—GEOMETRY

Polygons
13th Edition: 4, 42, 130, 145, D48
Triangles & Diagonals
13th Edition: 19, 56, 73, 79, 113, 119, 128, 149, 152, D28
Circles & Cylinders
13th Edition: 30, 35, 100, 102, 117, 122, 165, D36
Lines & Angles
13th Edition: 166
Coordinate Plane
13th Edition: 11, 74, 129, 155, D39

PROBLEM SOLVING GENERAL SET—NUMBER PROPERTIES

Divisibility & Primes
13th Edition: 2, 5, 26, 40, 74, 77, 87, 95, 110, 116, 118, 127, 155, 174, 204, 219, D13, D15, D18, D23
Odds & Evens
13th Edition: 44
Positives & Negatives
13th Edition: 24, 32, 51, 229
Combinatorics
13th Edition: 128, 133, 148
Probability
13th Edition: 10, 68, 107, 173, 193, 215, D7

DATA SUFFICIENCY GENERAL SET—NUMBER PROPERTIES

Divisibility & Primes
13th Edition: 58, 83, 135, D26, D42
Odds & Evens
13th Edition: 7, 14, 27, 32, 72, 111, 173
Positives & Negatives
13th Edition: 69, 97, 164, D41
Probability
13th Edition: 3, 39, 125

ALL TEST PREP IS NOT THE SAME

MANHATTAN GMAT

MANHATTAN GRE®

MANHATTAN LSAT

Elite test preparation from 99th percentile instructors.
Find out how we're different.

www.manhattanprep.com

mbaMission

EVERY CANDIDATE HAS A STORY TO TELL.

We have the creative experience to help you tell yours.

We are mbaMission, a professional MBA admissions consulting firm, specializing in helping business school applicants identify and showcase the strongest aspects of their candidacy in their applications. Our dedicated senior consultants—all published authors with elite MBA experience—will work one-on-one with you to help you discover, select and articulate your unique stories and force the admissions committees to take notice.

Every Manhattan GMAT student receives

- Free 30-minute consultation with an mbaMission senior consultant – Sign up at www.mbamission.com/consult.php
- Free copy of our 250-page book, *The Complete Start-to-Finish MBA Admissions Guide,* loaded with application advice as well as sample essays, recommendations, resumes and more
- One free Insider's Guide on one of 16 top business schools (available in the Manhattan GMAT Student Center)

mbaMission Services

- **Complete Start-to-Finish Package** offers unlimited service for a flat fee and guides you through the entire MBA application process, from brainstorming and outlining to interviews and beyond
- **A la Carte Hourly Services** focus on specific application needs, such as perfecting a single essay, reviewing your resume or analyzing a recommendation
- **Mock Interview Sessions** simulate a real MBA interview with feedback
- **MBA Application Boot Camp** demonstrates how to create a standout application in a live, classroom "workshop" environment

www.mbamission.com/manhattangmat | info@mbamission.com | (646) 485-8844

Did you know you CANNOT use any paper on the actual GMAT?

When taking the GMAT, you can only use a laminated booklet with a felt-tip pen to take notes and work out problems.

Don't be caught off-guard on test day!

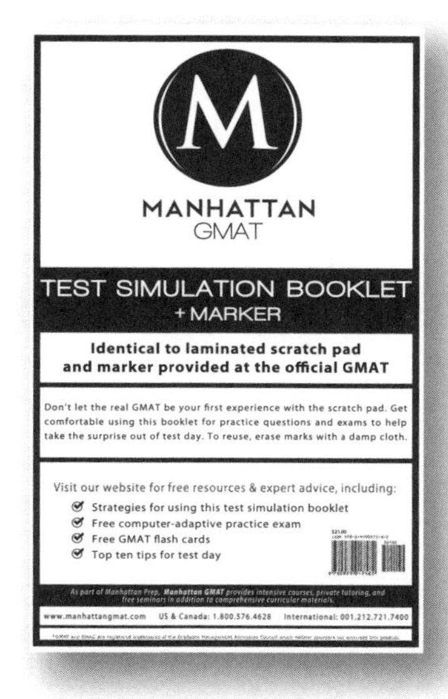

Practice with a Test Simulation Booklet

Offered Exclusively By

MANHATTAN GMAT

A GMAT Prep Essential!

Only $21.00 USD, and it includes the felt-tip pen

FREE with any Complete Prep Set purchase or any ManhattanGMAT Course

Now Available

Get one today at www.manhattangmat.com

* GMAT and GMAC are registered trademarks of the Graduate Management Admission Council which neither sponsors nor endorses this product.